Designing Evolvable Web APIs with ASP.NET

*Glenn Block, Pablo Cibraro, Pedro Felix,
Howard Dierking, and Darrel Miller*

Beijing · Cambridge · Farnham · Köln · Sebastopol · Tokyo

Designing Evolvable Web APIs with ASP.NET

by Glenn Block, Pablo Cibraro, Pedro Felix, Howard Dierking, and Darrel Miller

Printed in the United States of America.

Published by O'Reilly Media, Inc., 1005 Gravenstein Highway North, Sebastopol, CA 95472.

O'Reilly books may be purchased for educational, business, or sales promotional use. Online editions are also available for most titles (*http://my.safaribooksonline.com*). For more information, contact our corporate/institutional sales department: 800-998-9938 or *corporate@oreilly.com*.

Editors: Rachel Roumeliotis and Amy Jollymore	**Indexer:** Judy McConville
Production Editor: Nicole Shelby	**Cover Designer:** Randy Comer
Copyeditor: Rachel Monaghan	**Interior Designer:** David Futato
Proofreader: Rachel Head	**Illustrator:** Kara Ebrahim

March 2014:   First Edition

Revision History for the First Edition:

2014-03-11:   First release

See *http://oreilly.com/catalog/errata.csp?isbn=9781449337711* for release details.

ISBN: 978-1-449-33771-1

[LSI]

Table of Contents

Foreword. xiii

Preface. xvii

1. The Internet, the World Wide Web, and HTTP. 1

Web Architecture   2
    Resource   3
    URI   4
    Cool URIs   5
    Representation   5
    Media Type   5
HTTP   8
    Moving Beyond HTTP 1.1   8
    HTTP Message Exchange   8
    Intermediaries   10
    Types of Intermediaries   11
    HTTP Methods   12
    Headers   15
    HTTP Status Codes   16
    Content Negotiation   17
    Caching   17
    Authentication   20
    Authentication Schemes   21
    Additional Authentication Schemes   22
Conclusion   22

2. Web APIs. 23

What Is a Web API?   23
What About SOAP Web Services?   23
Origins of Web APIs   24

The Web API Revolution Begins   24
Paying Attention to the Web   24
Guidelines for Web APIs   25
Domain-Specific Media Types   25
Media Type Profiles   26
Multiple Representations   27
API Styles   29
  The Richardson Maturity Model   29
  RPC (RMM Level 0)   30
  Resources (RMM Level 1)   31
  HTTP VERBS (RMM Level 2)   33
  Crossing the Chasm Toward Resource-Centric APIs   36
  Hypermedia (RMM Level 3)   36
  REST   41
  REST Constraints   41
Conclusion   43

3. ASP.NET Web API 101.. 45
Core Scenarios   45
  First-Class HTTP Programming   46
  Symmetric Client and Server Programming Experience   48
  Flexible Support for Different Formats   48
  No More "Coding with Angle Brackets"   48
  Unit Testability   49
  Multiple Hosting Options   50
Getting Started with ASP.NET Web API   50
Exploring a New Web API Project   54
  WebApiConfig   54
  ValuesController   56
"Hello Web API!"   58
  Creating the Service   58
  The Client   65
  The Host   65
Conclusion   66

4. Processing Architecture.. 67
The Hosting Layer   70
Message Handler Pipeline   71
  Route Dispatching   73
Controller Handling   75
  The ApiController Base Class   75

    Conclusion   82

5. The Application.. **83**
    Why Evolvable?   84
        Barriers to Evolution   85
        What Is the Cost?   86
        Why Not Just Version?   88
        Walking the Walk   91
    Application Objectives   91
        Goals   92
        Opportunity   92
    Information Model   93
        Subdomains   93
        Related Resources   94
        Attribute Groups   95
        Collections of Attribute Groups   96
        Information Model Versus Media Type   96
        Collections of Issues   98
    Resource Models   98
        Root Resource   98
        Search Resources   98
        Collection Resources   99
        Item Resources   99
    Conclusion   102

6. Media Type Selection and Design..................... **103**
    Self-Description   103
    Types of Contracts   104
    Media Types   104
        Primitive Formats   105
        Popular Formats   107
        New Formats   108
        Hypermedia Types   110
        Media Type Explosion   110
        Generic Media Types and Profiles   110
        Other Hypermedia Types   115
    Link Relation Types   116
        Semantics   116
        Replacing Embedded Resources   118
        Indirection Layer   119
        Reference Data   119
        Workflow   120

Syntax   121
A Perfect Combination   124
Designing a New Media Type Contract   124
Selecting a Format   125
Enabling Hypermedia   126
Optional, Mandatory, Omitted, Applicable   126
Embedded Versus External Metadata   127
Extensibility   128
Registering the Media Type   129
Designing New Link Relations   130
Standard Link Relations   130
Extension Link Relations   131
Embedded Link Relations   132
Registering the Link Relation   132
Media Types in the Issue Tracking Domain   132
List Resources   133
Item Resources   135
Discovery Resource   136
Search Resource   137
Conclusion   137

7. **Building the API**. **139**
The Design   139
Getting the Source   140
Building the Implementation Using BDD   140
Navigating the Solution   141
Packages and Libraries   141
Self-Host   142
Models and Services   143
Issue and Issue Store   143
IssueState   144
IssuesState   145
Link   146
IssueStateFactory   147
LinkFactory   148
IssueLinkFactory   149
Acceptance Criteria   151
Feature: Retrieving Issues   154
Retrieving an Issue   156
Retrieving Open and Closed Issues   159
Retrieving an Issue That Does Not Exist   161
Retrieving All Issues   162

Retrieving All Issues as Collection+Json	165
Searching Issues	167
Feature: Creating Issues	169
Feature: Updating Issues	172
Updating an Issue	172
Updating an Issue That Does Not Exist	174
Feature: Deleting Issues	175
Deleting an Issue	175
Deleting an Issue That Does Not Exist	177
Feature: Processing Issues	177
The Tests	177
The Implementation	178
Conclusion	179

8. Improving the API. 181

Acceptance Criteria for the New Features	181
Implementing the Output Caching Support	183
Adding the Tests for Output Caching	184
Implementing Cache Revalidation	187
Implementing Conditional GETs for Cache Revalidation	188
Conflict Detection	191
Implementing Conflict Detection	191
Change Auditing	194
Implementing Change Auditing with Hawk Authentication	195
Tracing	199
Implementing Tracing	200
Conclusion	203

9. Building the Client. 205

Client Libraries	206
Wrapper Libraries	206
Links as Functions	210
Application Workflow	216
Need to Know	216
Clients with Missions	220
Client State	223
Conclusion	224

10. The HTTP Programming Model. 227

Messages	228
Headers	233
Message Content	239

Consuming Message Content	240
Creating Message Content	243
Conclusion	251

11. Hosting... 253

Web Hosting	254
The ASP.NET Infrastructure	254
ASP.NET Routing	257
Web API Routing	259
Global Configuration	261
The Web API ASP.NET Handler	263
Self-Hosting	266
WCF Architecture	267
The HttpSelfHostServer Class	269
The HttpSelfHostConfiguration Class	270
URL Reservation and Access Control	272
Hosting Web API with OWIN and Katana	273
OWIN	273
The Katana Project	275
Web API Configuration	277
Web API Middleware	278
The OWIN Ecosystem	281
In-Memory Hosting	282
Azure Service Bus Host	283
Conclusion	288

12. Controllers and Routing.. 289

HTTP Message Flow Overview	289
The Message Handler Pipeline	290
Dispatcher	294
HttpControllerDispatcher	295
Controller Selection	296
Controller Activation	300
The Controller Pipeline	301
ApiController	301
ApiController Processing Model	302
Conclusion	314

13. Formatters and Model Binding.................................... 317

The Importance of Models in ASP.NET Web API	317
How Model Binding Works	319
Built-In Model Binders	322

The ModelBindingParameterBinder Implementation   322
Value Providers   323
Model Binders   326
Model Binding Against URIs Only   329
The FormatterParameterBinder Implementation   329
Default HttpParameterBinding Selection   335
Model Validation   335
Applying Data Annotation Attributes to a Model   335
Querying the Validation Results   336
Conclusion   338

14. HttpClient. **341**
HttpClient Class   341
Lifecycle   341
Wrapper   342
Multiple Instances   343
Thread Safety   343
Helper Methods   343
Peeling Off the Layers   344
Completed Requests Don't Throw   344
Content Is Everything   344
Cancelling the Request   346
SendAsync   347
Client Message Handlers   347
Proxying Handlers   349
Fake Response Handlers   350
Creating Resuable Response Handlers   352
Conclusion   353

15. Security. **355**
Transport Security   355
Using TLS in ASP.NET Web API   357
Using TLS with IIS Hosting   357
Using TLS with Self-Hosting   359
Authentication   360
The Claims Model   360
Retrieving and Assigning the Current Principal   365
Transport-Based Authentication   366
Server Authentication   367
Client Authentication   370
The HTTP Authentication Framework   377
Implementing HTTP-Based Authentication   379

Katana Authentication Middleware   380
Active and Passive Authentication Middleware   385
Web API Authentication Filters   386
Token-Based Authentication   389
The Hawk Authentication Scheme   396
Authorization   398
Authorization Enforcement   400
Cross-Origin Resource Sharing   403
CORS Support on ASP.NET Web API   406
Conclusion   409

16. **The OAuth 2.0 Authorization Framework.** **411**
Client Applications   414
Accessing Protected Resources   416
Obtaining Access Tokens   417
Authorization Code Grant   419
Scope   422
Front Channel Versus Back Channel   423
Refresh Tokens   425
Resource Server and Authorization Server   426
Processing Access Tokens in ASP.NET Web API   428
OAuth 2.0 and Authentication   430
Scope-Based Authorization   433
Conclusion   434

17. **Testability.** **437**
Unit Tests   437
Unit Testing Frameworks   438
Getting Started with Unit Testing in Visual Studio   438
xUnit.NET   440
The Role of Unit Testing in Test-Driven Development   441
Unit Testing an ASP.NET Web API Implementation   445
Unit Testing an ApiController   446
Unit Testing a MediaTypeFormatter   452
Unit Testing an HttpMessageHandler   456
Unit Testing an ActionFilterAttribute   456
Unit Testing Routes   460
Integration Tests in ASP.NET Web API   462
Conclusion   464

A. **Media Types.** **465**

B. HTTP Headers. 467

C. Content Negotiation. 471

D. Caching in Action. 475

E. Authentication Workflows. 481

F. Media Type Specification for application/issue+json. 485

G. Public-Key Cryptography and Certificates. 487

Index. 497

Foreword

When Tim Berners-Lee first proposed the Web (*http://bit.ly/www-proposal*) in March 1989 at CERN (*http://info.cern.ch*), he set in motion a social revolution of creativity and opportunity that has since swept the world, changing how our society works, how we interact, and how we perceive our role as individuals within our society.

But he also set in motion an equally impressive technological revolution in how engineers think about and build software and hardware systems for the Web. The notion of a web server has changed from a standalone computer sitting in a box to a completely virtualized part of a global cloud infrastructure in which computation moves where it is needed at a moment's notice. Similarly, web clients have changed from the traditional desktop PC with a browser to a myriad of devices that sense and interact with the physical world and connect with other devices through web servers sitting in the cloud.

If we think about the changes that the Web has undergone, what makes them so breathtaking is not merely that they've happened at a dizzying pace, but also that they've happened without central control or coordination. In a word, it is *evolution* in action. New ideas and solutions are constantly introduced to accommodate new demands. These ideas compete with old ideas; sometimes they win and take hold, and other times they lose and fall by the wayside.

Evolution is as integral a piece of the Web as it is of nature. And just as in nature, individual components that are better suited to accommodate change have a greater chance of staying relevant and thriving over time.

In addition to the changes in what constitutes web servers and web clients, a sea change is taking place in how they interact with each other. Web servers used to serve HTML that was rendered by clients as web pages. Similarly, web clients would submit HTML forms to the server for processing, be it to process a pizza order, insert a blog entry, or update an issue in a bug tracking system.

This model really only exercised a fraction of what HTTP allows you to do by focusing on the use of HTTP GET and POST methods. However, from day one HTTP has defined a much broader application model for interacting with and manipulating data in general. For example, in addition to the classic GET and POST methods, it defines methods such as PUT, DELETE, and PATCH that allow for programmatic manipulation of and interaction with resources.

This is where web APIs come in: they enable web servers to expose the full HTTP application model, allowing programmatic access to resources so that clients can interact with and manipulate data in a uniform manner across a wide variety of scenarios.

There are two key drivers for the shift toward web APIs: HTML5 and mobile applications. Both leverage the computational powers of the client platform to provide engaging and fluid experiences while retrieving and manipulating data through backend web APIs. In short, web servers are changing from serving only static HTML to also providing web APIs that allow clients to interact programmatically using the full power of the HTTP application model. How to actually build such web APIs is where this book comes in. In short, it is for anyone who is building web APIs targeting HTML5 applications as well as mobile applications. It provides not only a great introduction to web APIs but also a practical set of guidelines for how to build them using ASP.NET Web API. In addition, it goes into great detail describing how ASP.NET Web API works and also serves as a reference for how it can be extended via HTTP message handlers, formatters, and more.

But the book goes beyond just showing the code or explaining the framework. It also introduces you to powerful techniques such as test-driven development (TDD) and behavior-driven development (BDD) for writing applications that can be tested and verified to function as expected.

What makes this book stand out, however, is that it doesn't just provide a "point in time" set of guidelines for how to build a web API. It takes you on a journey through how to design a web API that can evolve with changing demands and constraints. This idea of addressing evolvability goes to the very heart of how the Web works.

Building web APIs that can function effectively in this environment is not a straightforward proposition. One thing that *is* clear is the importance of accepting from day one that any web API will have to change, and that no one is in control of all parts at any given time. In other words, you can't just design a new version of your system and scrap the old one without losing existing users or causing friction—you have to move the system forward bit by bit while at the same time allowing both older clients to continue to function and newer clients to take advantage of the new features.

However, building software that is flexible and able to evolve remains a challenge. This book provides a great overview of how to build modern web applications that can change and evolve as demands do. It does so by mixing web APIs with hypermedia, which is a new and exciting direction for web applications.

The notion of hypermedia is both new and old. We are all used to browsing web pages, looking for information and diving into an aspect by clicking a link that takes us to a new page with more information and yet more links. As the information changes or evolves, new links can get added or existing ones modified to reflect that. The new links can prompt you to explore new information and dive into additional areas.

When you start merging web APIs with hypermedia, you get a powerful model for enabling applications to change and adapt in a similar way, how they interact with the server. Instead of having a fixed flow of actions baked into clients, they can now modify their actions based on the links made available in order to evolve—in short, they are able to adapt to change.

What makes this book relevant is that it provides a comprehensive overview of the state-of-the-art methods for designing web APIs that can adapt to the changing demands of providers and consumers. By introducing concepts such as hypermedia-driven web APIs with TDD, it provides an excellent starting point for anybody building web APIs.

As part of the team that built ASP.NET Web API, I have had the pleasure to work with the authors of this book. The group stands out, not just because of their collective experience in building frameworks, but also thanks to their vast real-world experience in building practical systems based on HTTP concepts. They have all provided many valuable inputs and suggestions that have contributed to ASP.NET Web API becoming a popular framework for building modern web applications.

In particular, I have enjoyed working with Glenn Block, who joined the project early on and really drove the emphasis on community engagement as well as the importance of dependency injection, TDD, and hypermedia. Without his contributions, ASP.NET Web API would not be where it is today.

If you are building or thinking about building web APIs, you will enjoy this book not only as a learning tool but also as a practical guide for how to build modern web applications based on ASP.NET Web API. It offers a wealth of information and guidelines for how to design with evolvability in mind by looking at complex issues in new and innovative ways. I, for one, am looking forward to seeing how this will evolve in the future!

—Henrick Frystyk Nielsen

Preface

Why Should You Read This Book?

Web API development is exploding. Companies are investing in droves to build systems that can be consumed by a range of clients over the Web. Think of your favorite website, and most likely there's an API to talk to it. Creating an API that can talk over HTTP is very easy. The challenge comes after you deploy the first version. It turns out that the creators of HTTP thought a lot about this and how to design for evolvability. Both media types and hypermedia were central to the design for this reason. But many API authors don't think or take advantage of this, deploying APIs that introduce a lot of coupling in the client and that don't utilize HTTP as they should. This makes it very difficult to evolve the API without breaking the client. Why does this happen? Often because this is the easiest and most intuitive path from an engineering standpoint to get things done. However, it is counterintuitive in the long term and against the fundamental principles with which the Web itself was designed.

This is a book for people who want to design APIs that can adapt to change over time. Change is inevitable: the API you build today *will* evolve. Thus, the question is not if, it is how. The decisions (or nondecisions) you make early on can drastically influence the answer:

- Will adding a new feature break your existing clients, forcing them to be upgraded and redeployed, or can your existing clients continue to operate?
- How will you secure your API? Will you be able to leverage newer security protocols?
- Will your API be able to scale to meet the demands of your users, or will you have to re-architect?
- Will you be able to support newer clients and devices as they appear?

These are the kinds of questions that you can design around. At first glance you might think this sounds like Big Design Up Front or a waterfall approach, but that is not at all the case. This is not about designing the entire system before it is built; it is not a recipe for analysis paralysis. There are definitely decisions that you must make up front, but they are higher level and relate to the overall design. They do not require you to understand or predict every aspect of the system. Rather, these decisions lay a foundation that can evolve in an iterative fashion. As you then build the system out, there are various approaches you can take that build on top of that foundation in order to continually reinforce your goal.

This is a book of application more than theory. Our desire is for you to walk away with the tools to be able to build a real, evolvable system. To get you there, we'll start by covering some essentials of the Web and web API development. Then we'll take you through the creation of a new API using ASP.NET Web API, from its design through implementation. The implementation will cover important topics like how to implement hypermedia with ASP.NET Web API and how to perform content negotiation. We'll show you how to actually evolve it once it is deployed. We'll also show how you can incorporate established practices like acceptance testing and test-driven development and techniques such as inversion of control to achieve a more maintainable code base. Finally, we'll take you through the internals of Web API to give you a deep understanding that will help you better leverage it for building evolvable systems.

What Do You Need to Know to Follow Along?

To get the most out of this book in its entirety, you should be a developer who is experienced with developing C# applications with .NET version 3.5 or greater. You should ideally also have some experience building web APIs. Which framework you have used to develop those APIs is not important; what is important is having familiarity with the concepts. It is not necessary to have any prior experience with ASP.NET Web API or ASP.NET, though familiarity with ASP.NET MVC will definitely help.

If you are not a .NET developer, then there is something here for you. One specific goal in authoring this book was for a significant portion of the content to be centered on API design and development in general and not tied to ASP.NET Web API. For that reason, we think you'll find that regardless of your development stack (Java, Ruby, PHP, Node, etc.), much of the content in the first two sections of the book will be valuable to you in learning API development.

The Hitchhiker's Guide to Navigating This Book

Before you begin your journey, here is a guide to help you navigate the book's contents:

- Part I is focused on helping you get oriented around web API development. It covers the foundations of the Web/HTTP and API development, and introduces you to ASP.NET Web API. If you are new to web API development/ASP.NET Web API, this is a great place to start. If you've been using ASP.NET Web API (or another Web API stack) but would like to learn more about how to take advantage of HTTP, this is also a good starting point.

- Part II centers on web API development in the real world. It takes you through a real-world app from design through implementation, covering the client and server. If you are comfortable with web API development and in a hurry to start building an app, jump right to the second section.

- Part III is a fairly comprehensive reference on exactly how the different parts of ASP.NET Web API work under the hood. It also covers more advanced topics like security and testability. If you are already building an app with ASP.NET Web API and trying to figure out how to best utilize Web API itself, start here.

Next we'll give a quick overview of what you'll find in each chapter.

Part I, Fundamentals

Chapter 1, The Internet, the World Wide Web, and HTTP
This chapter starts with a bit of history about the World Wide Web and HTTP. It then gives you a 5,000-foot view of HTTP. You can think of it as a "Dummies' Guide" to HTTP, giving you the essentials you need to know, without your having to read the entire spec.

Chapter 2, Web APIs
This chapter begins by giving a historical context on web API development in general. The remainder of the chapter discusses essentials of API development, starting with core concepts and then diving into different styles and approaches for designing APIs.

Chapter 3, ASP.NET Web API 101
This chapter discusses the fundamental drivers behind ASP.NET Web API as a framework. It will then introduce you to the basics of ASP.NET Web API as well as the .NET HTTP programming model and client.

Chapter 4, Processing Architecture

This chapter will describe at a high level the lifecycle of a request as it travels through ASP.NET Web API. You'll learn about each of the different actors who have a part in processing different aspects of the HTTP request and response.

Part II, Real-World API Development

Chapter 5, The Application and Chapter 6, Media Type Selection and Design

These chapters discuss the overall design for the Issue Tracker application. They cover several important design-related topics including media type selection and design, as well as hypermedia.

Chapter 7, Building the API and Chapter 8, Improving the API

These chapters will show how to actually implement and enhance the hypermedia-driven Issue Tracker API using ASP.NET Web API. They introduce you to how to develop the API using a behavior-driven development style.

Chapter 9, Building the Client

This chapter focuses entirely on how to build out a hypermedia client, which can consume the Issue Tracker API.

Part III, Web API Nuts and Bolts

Chapter 10, The HTTP Programming Model

This chapter will cover in depth the new .NET HTTP programming model on which ASP.NET Web API rests entirely.

Chapter 11, Hosting

This chapter covers all the different hosting models that exist for ASP.NET Web API, including self-host, IIS, and the new OWIN model.

Chapter 12, Controllers and Routing

In this chapter you'll take a deep dive into how Web API routing works and how controllers operate.

Chapter 13, Formatters and Model Binding and Chapter 14, HttpClient

These chapters cover everything you need to know about model binding and about using the new HTTP client.

Chapter 15, Security and Chapter 16, The OAuth 2.0 Authorization Framework

These chapters cover the overall security model in ASP.NET Web API and then talk in detail about how to implement OAuth in your API.

Chapter 17, Testability

This chapter will cover how to develop in ASP.NET Web API in a test-driven manner.

Conventions Used in This Book

The following typographical conventions are used in this book:

Italic

> Indicates new terms, URLs, email addresses, filenames, and file extensions.

`Constant width`

> Used for program listings, as well as within paragraphs to refer to program elements such as variable or function names, databases, data types, environment variables, statements, and keywords.

`Constant width bold`

> Shows commands or other text that should be typed literally by the user.

`Constant width italic`

> Shows text that should be replaced with user-supplied values or by values determined by context.

 This element signifies a tip or suggestion.

 This element signifies a general note.

 This element indicates a warning or caution.

Using Code Examples

Supplemental material (code examples, exercises, etc.) is available for download at *https://github.com/webapibook*. A forum for discussion of the book is located at *http://bit.ly/web-api-forum*.

This book is here to help you get your job done. In general, if example code is offered with this book, you may use it in your programs and documentation. You do not need to contact us for permission unless you're reproducing a significant portion of the code.

For example, writing a program that uses several chunks of code from this book does not require permission. Selling or distributing a CD-ROM of examples from O'Reilly books does require permission. Answering a question by citing this book and quoting example code does not require permission. Incorporating a significant amount of example code from this book into your product's documentation does require permission.

We appreciate, but do not require, attribution. An attribution usually includes the title, author, publisher, and ISBN. For example: *"Designing Evolvable Web APIs with ASP.NET* by Glenn Block, Pablo Cibraro, Pedro Felix, Howard Dierking, and Darrel Miller (O'Reilly). Copyright 2012 Glenn Block, Pablo Cibraro, Pedro Felix, Howard Dierking, and Darrel Miller, 978-1-449-33771-1."

If you feel your use of code examples falls outside fair use or the permission given above, feel free to contact us at *permissions@oreilly.com*.

Safari® Books Online

 Safari Books Online is an on-demand digital library that delivers expert content in both book and video form from the world's leading authors in technology and business.

Technology professionals, software developers, web designers, and business and creative professionals use Safari Books Online as their primary resource for research, problem solving, learning, and certification training.

Safari Books Online offers a range of product mixes and pricing programs for organizations, government agencies, and individuals. Subscribers have access to thousands of books, training videos, and prepublication manuscripts in one fully searchable database from publishers like O'Reilly Media, Prentice Hall Professional, Addison-Wesley Professional, Microsoft Press, Sams, Que, Peachpit Press, Focal Press, Cisco Press, John Wiley & Sons, Syngress, Morgan Kaufmann, IBM Redbooks, Packt, Adobe Press, FT Press, Apress, Manning, New Riders, McGraw-Hill, Jones & Bartlett, Course Technology, and dozens more. For more information about Safari Books Online, please visit us online.

How to Contact Us

Please address comments and questions concerning this book to the publisher:

O'Reilly Media, Inc.
1005 Gravenstein Highway North
Sebastopol, CA 95472
800-998-9938 (in the United States or Canada)
707-829-0515 (international or local)
707-829-0104 (fax)

We have a web page for this book, where we list errata, examples, and any additional information. You can access this page at *http://oreil.ly/designing-api*.

To comment or ask technical questions about this book, send email to *bookques tions@oreilly.com*.

For more information about our books, courses, conferences, and news, see our website at *http://www.oreilly.com*.

Find us on Facebook: *http://facebook.com/oreilly*

Follow us on Twitter: *http://twitter.com/oreillymedia*

Watch us on YouTube: *http://www.youtube.com/oreillymedia*

Acknowledgments

This book turned out to require much greater effort than any of us thought possible. First, thanks go to our wives and children, who had to be patient and basically leave us alone for long periods while we worked on the book!

The book would also not have been possible without the review and guidance of the following individuals: Mike Amundsen, Grant Archibald, Dominick Baier, Alan Dean, Matt Kerr, Caitie McCaffrey, Henrik Frystyk Nielsen, Eugenio Pace, Amy Palamountain, Adam Ralph, Leonard Richardson, Ryan Riley, Kelly Sommers, Filip Wojcieszyn, and Matias Woloski.

CHAPTER 1

The Internet, the World Wide Web, and HTTP

To harness the Web, you need to understand its foundations and design.

We start our journey toward Web APIs at the beginning. In the late 1960s the Advanced Research Projects Agency Network (ARPANET) (*http://bit.ly/arpanet-mp*), a series of network-based systems connected by the TCP/IP protocol, was created by the Defense Advanced Research Projects Agenecy (DARPA). Initially, it was designed for universities and research laboratories in the US to share data. (see Figure 1-1).

ARPANET continued to evolve and ultimately led in 1982 to the creation of a global set of interconnected networks known as the *Internet*. The Internet was built on top of the *Internet protocol suite* (also known as TCP/IP), which is a collection of communication protocols. Whereas ARPANET was a fairly closed system, the Internet was designed to be a globally open system connecting private and public agencies, organizations, individuals, and insitutions.

In 1989, Tim Berners-Lee, a scientist at CERN, invented the *World Wide Web*, a new system for accessing linked documents via the Internet with a web browser. Navigating the documents of the Web (which were predominantly written in HTML) required a special application protocol, the Hypertext Transfer Protocol (HTTP). This protocol is at the center of what drives websites and Web APIs.

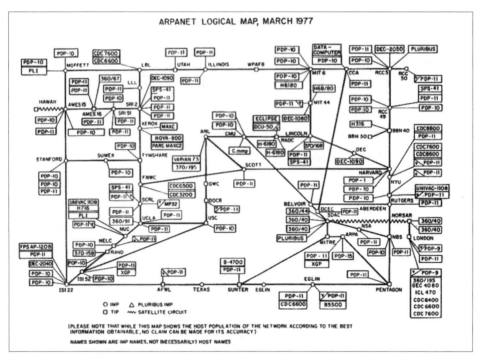

Figure 1-1. ARPANET (image from Wikimedia Commons)

In this chapter we'll dive into the fundamentals of the web architecture and explore HTTP. This will form a foundation that will assist us as we move forward into actually designing Web APIs.

Web Architecture

The Web is built around three core concepts: resources, URIs, and representations (*http://www.w3.org/TR/webarch*), as shown in Figure 1-2.

A resource has a URI that identifies it and that HTTP clients will use to find it. A *representation* is data that is returned from that resource. Also related and significant is the *media type*, which defines the format of that data.

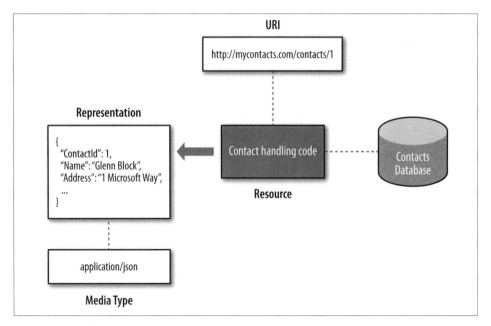

Figure 1-2. Web core concepts

Resource

A *resource* is anything that has a URI. The resource itself is a conceptual mapping (*http://bit.ly/rfc-2396*) to one or more entities. In the early years of the Web it was very common for this entity to be a file such as a document or web page. However, a resource is not limited to being file oriented. A resource can be a service that interfaces with anything such as a catalog, a device (e.g., a printer), a wireless garage door opener, or an internal system like a CRM or a procurement system. A resource can also be a streaming medium such as a video or an audio stream.

Is a Resource Bound to an Entity or a Database?

A common misnomer today with Web APIs is that each resource must map to an entity or business object backed by a database. Often, this will come up in a design conversation where someone might say, "We can't have that resource because it will require us to create a table in the database and we have no real need for a table." The previous definition described a mapping to one or more entities; this is an entity in the general sense of the word (i.e., it could be anything), *not* a business object. An application may be designed such that the resources exposed always map to business entities or tables, and in such a system the previous statement would be true. However, that is a constraint imposed by an application or framework, not the Web.

When you are building Web APIs, there are many cases where the entity/resource constraint is problematic. For example, an order processing resource actually orchestrates different systems to process an order. In this case, the resource implementation invokes various parts of the system that may themselves store state in a database. It may even store some of its own state, or not. The point is there is not a direct database correspondence for that resource. Also, there is no requirement that the orchestrated components use a database either (though in this case they do).

Keep this distinction in mind as you go forward in your Web API design. It will help you to really harness the power of the Web within you systems.

URI

As was mentioned earlier, each resource is addressable through a unique URI (*http://bit.ly/rfc-3986*). You can think of a URI as a primary key for a resource. Examples of URIs are *http://fabrikam.com/orders/100*, *http://ftp.fabrikam.com*, *mailto:John.Doe@example.com*, *telnet://192.168.1.100*, and *urn:isbn:978-1-449-33771-1*. A URI can correspond only to a single resource, though multiple URIs can point to the same resource. Each URI is of the form *scheme:hierarchical part[?query][#fragment]* with the query string and fragment being optional. The hierachical part further consists of an optional authority and hierachical path.

URIs are divided into two categories, *URLs* and *URNs*. A URL (Universal Resource Locator) is an identifier that also refers to the means of accessing the resource, while a URN (Universal Resource Name) is simply a unique identifier for a resource. Each of the preceding example URIs is also a URL except the last one, which is a URN for this book. It contains no information on how to access the resource but does identify it. In practice, however, the majority of URIs you will likely see will be URLs, and for this reason the two are often used synonymously.

Cool URIs

A *cool URI* (*http://bit.ly/cool-uris*) is a URI that is simple, easy to remember (like *http://www.example.com/people/alice*), and doesn't change. The reason for the URI not to change is so it does not break existing systems that have linked to the URI. So, if your resources are designed with the idea that clients maintain bookmarks to them, you should consider using a cool URI. Cool URIs work really well in particular for web pages to which other sites commonly link, or that users often store in their browser favorites. It is not required that URIs be cool. As you'll see throughout the book, there are benefits to designing APIs without exposing many cool URIs.

Representation

A *representation* is a snapshot of a resource's state at a point in time. Whenever an HTTP client requests a resource, it is the representation that is returned, not the resource itself. From one request to the next, the resource state can change dramatically, thus the representation that is returned can be very different. For example, imagine an API for developer articles that exposes the top article via the URI *http://devarticles.com/articles/top*. Instead of returning a link to the content, the API returns a redirect to the actual article. Over time, as the top article changes, the representation (via the redirect) changes accordingly. The resource, however, is not the article in this case; it's the logic running on the server that retrieves the top article from the database and returns the redirect. It is important to note that each resource can have one or more representations, as you'll learn about in "Content Negotiation" on page 17.

Media Type

Each representation has a specific format known as a *media type*. A media type is a format for passing information across the Internet between clients and servers. It is indicated with a two-part identifier like `text/html`. Media types serve different purposes. Some are extremely general purpose, like `application/json` (which is a collection of values or key values) or `text/html` (which is primarily for documents rendered in a browser). Other media types have more constrained semantics like `application/atom+xml` and `application/collection+json`, which are designed specifically for managing feeds and lists. Then there is `image/png`, which is for PNG images. Media types can also be highly domain specific, like `text/vcard`, which is used for electronically sharing business card and contact information. For a list of some common media types you may encounter, see Appendix A.

The media type itself actually comprises two parts. The first part (before the slash) is the *top-level media type*. It describes general type information and common handling rules. Common top-level types are `application`, `image`, `text`, `video`, and `multipart`. The second part is the *subtype*, which describes a very specific data format. For example, in `image/png` and `image/gif`, the top-level type tells a client this is an image, while the subtypes `png` and `gif` specify what type of image it is and how it should be handled. It is also common for the subtype to have different variants that share common semantics but are different formats. As an example, HAL (Hypertext Application Language) (*http://bit.ly/hal-spec*) has JSON (`application/hal+json`) and XML (`application/hal+xml`) variants. `hal+json` means it's HAL using a JSON wire format, while `hal+xml` means the XML wire format.

The Origin of Media Types

The earliest roots of media types are with ARPANET. Initially, ARPANET was a network of machines that communicated via simple text messages. As the system grew, the need for richer communication arose. Thus, a standard format (*http://bit.ly/rfc-822*) was codified for those messages to allow them to contain metadata that related to processing. Over time and with the rise of email, this standard evolved into MIME (the Multipurpose Internet Mail Extensions) (*http://bit.ly/rfc-2045*). One of the goals of MIME was to support nontextual payloads, thus the media type (*http://bit.ly/rfc-2046*) was born as a means to describe the body of a MIME entity. As the Internet flourished, it became necessary to pass similar rich bodies of information across the Web without being tied to email. Thus, media types started being used to also describe the body of HTTP requests and responses, which is how they became relevant for Web APIs.

Media type registration

Media types are conventionally registered in a central registry (*http://bit.ly/iana-registry*) managed by IANA, the Internet Assigned Numbers Authority. The registry itself contains a list of media types and links to their associated specifications. The registry is categorized by top-level media types with each top-level section containing a list of specific media types.

Application developers who want to design clients or servers that understand standard media types refer to the registry for the specifications. For example, if you want to build a client that understands image/png, you can navigate to the "image" section of the IANA media types pages (*http://bit.ly/iana-types*) and find "png" to get the image/png spec, as shown in Figure 1-3.

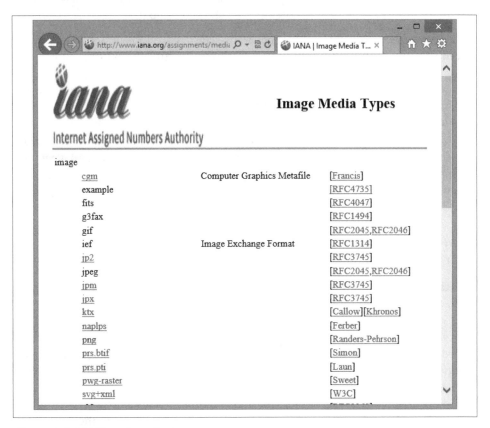

Figure 1-3. IANA registry for image

Why do we need all these different media types? The reason is because each type has either specific benefits or clients to which it is tailored. HTML is great for laying out documents such as a web page, but not necessarily the best for transferring data. JSON is great for transferring data, but it is a horribly inefficient medium for representing images. PNG is a great image format, but not ideal for scalable vector graphics; for that, we have SVG. ATOM, HAL, and Collection+JSON express richer application semantics than raw XML or JSON, but they are more constrained.

Up until this point, you've seen the key components of the web architecture. In the next section we will dive into HTTP—the glue that brings everything together.

HTTP

Now that we have covered the high-level web architecture, our next stop is HTTP. As HTTP is very comprehensive, we will not attempt to cover everything. Rather, we will focus on the major concepts—in particular, those that relate to building Web APIs. If you are new to HTTP, it should give you a good lay of the land. If you are not, you might pick up some things you didn't know, but it's also OK to skip it.

HTTP (*http://bit.ly/rfc-http*) is the application-level protocol for information systems that powers the Web. HTTP was originally authored by three computer scientists: Tim Berners-Lee, Roy Fielding, and Henrik Frystyk Nielsen. It defines a uniform interface for clients and servers to transfer information across a network in a manner that is agnostic to implementation details. HTTP is designed for dynamically changing systems that can tolerate some degree of latency and some degree of staleness. This design allows intermediaries like proxy servers to intercede in communication, providing various benefits like caching, compression, and routing. These qualities of HTTP make it ideal for the World Wide Web, as it is a massive and dynamically changing and evolving network topology with inherent latency. It has also stood the test of time, powering the World Wide Web since its introduction in 1996.

Moving Beyond HTTP 1.1

HTTP is not standing still: it is actively evolving both in how we understand it and how we use it. There have been many misconceptions around the HTTP spec RFC 2616 due to ambiguities, or in some cases due to things deemed incorrect. The IETF (Internet Engineering Task Force) formed a working body known as httpbis (*http://bit.ly/httpbis-charter*) that has created a set of drafts (*http://bit.ly/httpbis-drafts*) whose sole purpose is to clarify these misconceptions by completely replacing RFC 2616. Additionally, the group has been charged with creating the HTTP 2.0 spec (*http://bit.ly/httpbis-2*). HTTP 2.0 also does not affect any of the public HTTP surface area; rather, it is a set of optimizations to the underlying transport, including adoption of the new *SPDY* protocol (*http://bit.ly/httpbis-spdy*). Because httpbis exists as a replacement for the HTTP spec and provides an evolved understanding of HTTP, we'll use that as the basis for the remainder of this section.

HTTP Message Exchange

HTTP-based systems exchange messages in a stateless manner using a request/response pattern. We'll give you a simplified overview of the exchange. First, an HTTP *client* generates an HTTP *request*, as shown in Figure 1-4.

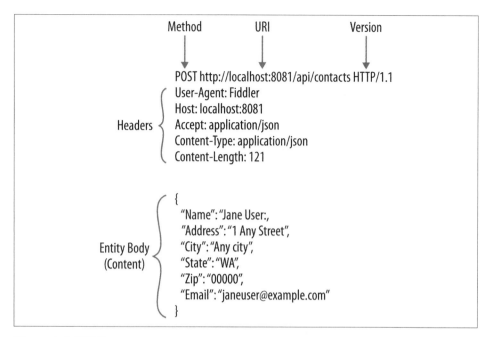

Method URI Version

POST http://localhost:8081/api/contacts HTTP/1.1
User-Agent: Fiddler
Host: localhost:8081
Headers Accept: application/json
Content-Type: application/json
Content-Length: 121

{
    "Name":"Jane User:,
    "Address":"1 Any Street",
Entity Body "City":"Any city",
(Content) "State":"WA",
    "Zip":"00000",
    "Email":"janeuser@example.com"
}

Figure 1-4. HTTP request

That request is a message that includes an HTTP version, a URI of a resource that will be accessed, request *headers*, an HTTP *method* (like GET), and an optional *entity body* (content). The request is then sent to an *origin* server where the resource presides. The server looks at the URI and HTTP method to decide if it can handle the message. If it can, it looks at the request headers that contain control information such as describing the content. The server then processes the message based on that information.

After the server has processed the message, an HTTP *response*, generally containing a *representation* of the resource (as shown in Figure 1-5), is generated.

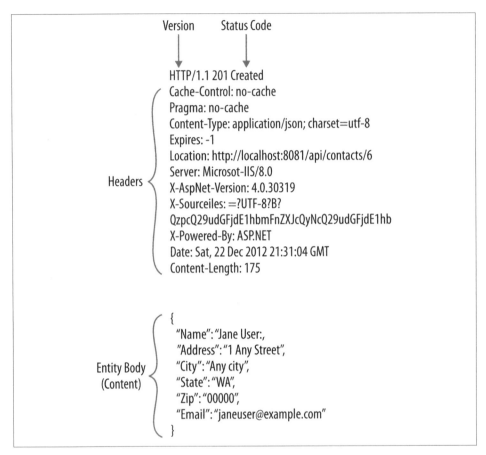

Figure 1-5. HTTP response

The response contains the HTTP version, response headers, an optional entity body (containing the representation), a *status code*, and a description. Similar to the server that received the message, the client will inspect the response headers using its control information to process the message and its content.

Intermediaries

Though accurate, the preceding description of HTTP message exchange leaves out an important piece: *intermediaries* (*http://bit.ly/rfc-inter*)). HTTP is a layered architecture in which each component/server has separation of concerns from others in the sytem; it is not required for an HTTP client to "see" the origin server. As the request travels along toward the origin server, it will encounter intermediaries, as shown in Figure 1-6, which are agents or components that inspect an HTTP request or response and may modify or replace it. An intermediary can immediately return a response, invoke some sort of process like logging the details, or just let it flow through. Intermediaries are beneficial in that they can improve or enhance communication. For example, a cache can reduce the response time by returning a cached result received from an origin server.

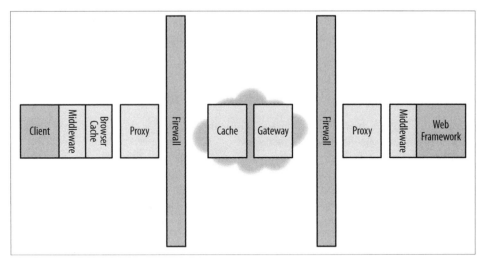

Figure 1-6. HTTP intermediaries

Notice that intermediaries can exist anywhere the request travels between the client and origin server; location does *not* matter. They can be running on the same machine as the client or origin server or be a dedicated public server on the Internet. They can be built in, such as the browser cache on Windows, or add-ons commonly known as *middleware*. ASP.NET Web API supports several pieces of middleware that can be used on the client or server, such as handlers and filters, which you will learn about in Chapters 4 and 10.

Types of Intermediaries

There are three types of intermediaries that participate in the HTTP message exchange and are visible to clients.

- A *proxy* is an agent that handles making HTTP requests and receiving responses on behalf of the client. The client's use of the proxy is deliberate, and it will be configured to use it. It is common, for example, for many organizations to have an internal proxy that users must go through in order to make requests to the Internet. A proxy that modifies requests or responses in a meaningful way is known as a *transforming proxy*. A proxy that does not modify messages is known as a *non-transforming proxy*.

- A *gateway* receives inbound HTTP messages and translates them to the server's underlying protocol, which may or may not be HTTP. The gateway also takes outbound messages and translates them to HTTP. A gateway can act on behalf of the origin server.

- A *tunnel* creates a private channel between two connections without modifying any of the messages. An example of a tunnel is when two clients communicate via HTTPS through a firewall.

Is a CDN an Intermediary?

Another common mechanism for caching on the Internet is a *content delivery network* (CDN), a distributed set of machines that cache and return static content. There are many popular CDN offerings, such as Akamai (*http://www.akamai.com*), that companies use to cache their content. So is a CDN an intermediary? The answer is that it depends on how the request is passing to the CDN. If the client makes a direct request to it, then it is acting as an origin server. Some CDNs, however, can also act as a gateway, where the client does not see the CDN, but it actually acts on behalf of the origin server as a cache and returns the content.

HTTP Methods

HTTP provides a standard set of methods (*http://bit.ly/method-def*) that form the interface for a resource. Since the original HTTP spec was published, the PATCH method (*http://bit.ly/rfc-5789*) has also been approved. As shown earlier in Figure 1-4, the method appears as part of the request itself. Next is a description of the common methods API authors implement.

GET
> Retrieves information from a resource. If the resource is returned, the server should return a status code 200 (OK).

HEAD
> Identical to a GET, except it returns headers and not the body.

POST
> Requests that the server accept the enclosed entity to be processed by the target resource. As part of the processing, the server may create a new resource, though it is not obliged to. If it does create a resource, it should return a 201 (Created) or 202 (Accepted) code and return a location header telling the client where it can find the new resource. If it does not create a resource, it should return a 200 (OK) or a 204 (No Content) code. In practice, POST can handle just about any kind of processing and is not constrained.

PUT

Requests that the server replace the state of the target resource at the specified URI with the enclosed entity. If a resource exists for the current representation, it should return a 200 (OK) or a 204 (No Content) code. However, if the resource does not exist, the server *can* create it. If it does, it should return a 201 (Created) code. The main difference between POST and PUT is that POST expects the data that is sent to be processed, while PUT expects the data to be replaced or stored.

DELETE

Requests that the server remove the entity located at the specified URI. If the resource is immediately removed, the server should return a 200 code. If it is pending, it should return a 202 (Accepted) or a 204 (No Content)..

OPTIONS

Requests that the server return information about its capabilities. Most commonly, it returns an Allow header specifying which HTTP methods are supported, though the spec leaves it completely open-ended. For example, it is entirely feasible to list which media types the server supports. OPTIONS can also return a body, supplying further information that cannot be represented in the headers.

PATCH

Requests that the server do a partial update of the entity at the specified URI. The content of the patch should have enough information that the server can use to apply the update. If the resource exists, the server can be updated and should return a 200 (OK) or a 204 (No Content) code. As with PUT, if the resource does not exist, the server *can* create it. If it does, it should return a code of 201 (Created). A resource that supports PATCH can advertise it in the Allow header of an OPTIONS response. The Accept-Patch header also allows the server to indicate an acceptable list of media types the client can use for sending a PATCH. The spec implies that the media type should carry the semantics to communicate to the server the partial update information. json-patch (*http://bit.ly/json-patch*) is a proposed media type in draft that provides a structure for expressing operations within a patch.

TRACE

Requests that the server return the request it received. The server will return the entire request message in the body with a content-type of message/http. This is useful for diagnostics, as clients can see which proxies the request passed through and how the request may have been modified by intermediaries.

Conditional requests

One of the additional features of HTTP is that it allows clients to make conditional requests. This type of request requires the client to send special headers that provide the server with information it needs to process the request. The headers include If-

Match, If-NoneMatch, and If-ModifiedSince. Each of these headers will be described in further detail in Table B-2 in Appendix B.

- A conditional GET is when a client sends headers that the server can use to determine if the client's cached representation is still valid. If it is, the server returns a 304 (Not Modified) code rather than the representation. A conditional GET reduces the network traffic (as the response is much smaller), and also reduces the server workload.

- A conditional PUT is when a client sends headers that the server can use to determine if the client's cached representation is still valid. If it is, the server returns a 409 (Preconditions Failed). A conditional PUT is used for concurrency. It allows a client to determine at the time of doing the PUT whether another user changed the data.

Method properties

HTTP methods can have the following additional properties:

- A *safe* method is a method that does not cause any side effects from the user when the request is made. This does not mean that there are no side effects at all, but it means that the user can safely make requests using the method without worrying about changing the state of the system.

- An *idempotent* method is a method in which making one request to the resource has the same effect as requesting it multiple times. All safe methods are by definition idempotent; however, there are methods that are not safe and are still idempotent. As with a *safe* method, there is no guarantee that a request with an idempotent method won't result in any side effects on the server, but the user does not have to be concerned.

- A *cachable* method is a method that can possibly receive a cached response for a previous request from an intermediary cache.

Table 1-1 lists the HTTP methods and whether they are safe or idempotent.

Table 1-1. HTTP methods

Method	Safe	Idempotent	Cachable
GET	Yes	Yes	Yes
HEAD	Yes	Yes	Yes
POST	No	No	No
PUT	No	Yes	No
DELETE	No	Yes	No
OPTIONS	Yes	Yes	No

Method	Safe	Idempotent	Cachable
PATCH	No	Yes	No
TRACE	Yes	Yes	No

Of the methods listed, the most common set used by API builders today are GET, PUT, POST, DELETE, and HEAD. PATCH, though new, is also becoming very common.

There are several benefits to having a standard set of HTTP methods:

- Any HTTP client can interact with an HTTP resource that is following the rules. Methods like OPTIONS provide discoverability for the client so it can learn how those interactions will take place.

- Servers can optimize. Proxy servers and web servers can provide optimizations based on the chosen method. For example, cache proxies know that GET requests can be cached; thus, if you do a GET, the proxy may be able to return a cached representation rather than having the request travel all the way to the server.

Headers

HTTP messages contain header fields that provide information to clients and servers, which they should use to process the request. There are four types of headers: message, request, response, and representation.

Message headers

Apply to both request and response messages and relate to the message itself rather than the entity body. They include:

- Headers related to intermediaries, including Cache-Control, Pragma, and Via

- Headers related to the message, including Transfer-Encoding and Trailer

- Headers related to the request, including Connection, Upgrade, and Date

Request headers

Apply generally to the request message and not to the entity body, with the exception of the Range header. They include:

- Headers about the request, including Host, Expect, and Range

- Headers for authentication credentials, including User-Agent and From

- Headers for content negotiation, including Accept, Accept-Language, and Accept-Encoding

- Headers for conditional requests, including If-Match, If-None-Match, and If-Modified-Since

Response headers

Apply to the response message and not the entity body. They include:

- Headers for providing information about the target resource, including `Al low` and `Server`

- Headers providing additional control data, such as `Age` and `Location`

- Headers related to the selected representation, including `ETag`, `Last-Modified`, and `Vary`

- Headers related to authentication challenges, including `Proxy-Authenticate` and `WWW-Authenticate`

Representation headers

Apply generally to the request or response entity body (content). They include:

- Headers about the entity body itself including `Content-Type`, `Content-Length`, `Content-Location`, and `Content-Encoding`

- Headers related to caching of the entity body, including `Expires`

For a comprehensive list and description of the standard headers in the HTTP specification, see Appendix B.

The HTTP specification continues to be extended. New headers can be proposed and approved by organizations like the IETF (Internet Engineering Task Force) or the W3C (World Wide Web Consortium) as extensions of the HTTP protocol. Two such examples, which are covered in later chapters of the book, are RFC 5861 (*http://bit.ly/rfc-5861*), which introduces new caching headers, and the CORS specification (*http://bit.ly/cors-spec*), which introduces new headers for cross origin access.

HTTP Status Codes

HTTP responses always return *status codes* and a description of whether the request succeeded; it is the responsibility of an origin server to always return both pieces of information. Both inform the client whether or not the request was accepted or failed and suggest possible next actions. The description is human-readable text describing the status code. Status codes range from 4xx to 5xx. Table 1-2 indicates the different categories of status codes and the associated references in httpbis.

Table 1-2. HTTP status codes

Range	Description	Reference
1xx	The request has been received and processing is continuing.	*http://tools.ietf.org/html/draft-ietf-httpbis-p2-semantics-21#section-7.2*
2xx	The request has been accepted, received, and understood.	*http://tools.ietf.org/html/draft-ietf-httpbis-p2-semantics-21#section-7.3*

Range	Description	Reference
3xx	Further action is required to complete the request.	*http://tools.ietf.org/html/draft-ietf-httpbis-p2-semantics-21#section-7.4*
4xx	The request is invalid and cannot be completed.	*http://tools.ietf.org/html/draft-ietf-httpbis-p2-semantics-21#section-7.5*
5xx	The server has failed trying to complete the request.	*http://tools.ietf.org/html/draft-ietf-httpbis-p2-semantics-21#section-7.6*

Status codes can be directly associated with other headers. In the following snippet, the server has returned a 201, indicating that a new resource was created. The Location header indicates to the client the URI of the created resources. Thus, HTTP Clients should automatically check for the Location in the case of a 201.

```
HTTP/1.1 201 Created
Cache-Control: no-cache
Pragma: no-cache
Content-Type: application/json; charset=utf-8
Location: http://localhost:8081/api/contacts/6
```

Content Negotiation

HTTP servers often have multiple ways to represent the same resources. The representations can be based on a variety of factors, including different capabilities of the client or optimizations based on the payload. For example, you saw how the Contact resource returns a vCard representation tailored to clients such as mail programs. HTTP allows the client to participate in the selection of the media type by informing the server of its preferences. This dance of selection between client and server is what is known as *content negotiation* (*http://bit.ly/conneg-spec*), or conneg.

Caching

As we learned in "Method properties" on page 14, some responses are cachable—in particular, the responses for GET and HEAD requests. The main benefit of caching is to improve general performance and scale on the Internet. Caching helps clients and origin servers in the following ways:

- Clients are helped because the number of roundtrips to the server is reduced, and because the response payload is reduced for many of those roundtrips.

- Servers are helped because intermediaries can return cached representations, thus reducing the load on the origin server.

An *HTTP cache* is a storage mechanism that manages adding, retrieving, and removing responses from the origin server to the cache. Caches will try to handle only requests that use a cachable method; all other requests (with noncachable methods) will be automatically forwarded to the origin server. The cache will also forward to the origin server requests that are cacheable, but that are either not present in the cache or expired.

httpbis defines (*http://bit.ly/fresh-cache*) a pretty sophisticated mechanism for caching. Though there are many finer details, HTTP caching is fundamentally based on two concepts: expiration and validation.

Expiration

A response has expired or becomes *stale* if its age in the cache is greater than the maximum age, which is specified via a `max-age CacheControl` directive in the response. It will also expire if the current date on the cache server exceeds the expiration date, which is specified via the response `Expires` header. If the response has not expired, it is eligible for the cache to serve it; however, there are other pieces of control data (see "Caching and negotiated responses" on page 19) coming from the request and the cached response that may prevent it from being served.

Validation

When a response has expired, the cache must revalidate it. Validation means the cache will send a conditional `GET` request (see "Conditional requests" on page 13) to the server asking if the cached response is still valid. The conditional request will contain a cache validator—for example, an `If-Modified-Since` header with the `Last-Modified` value of the response and/or an `If-None-Match` header with the response's `ETag` value. If the origin server determines it is still valid, it will return a body-less response with a status code of `304 Not Modified`, along with an updated expiration date. If the response has changed, the origin server will return a new response, which will ultimately get served by the cache and replace the current cached representation.

Serving Stale Responses

HTTP does provide for caches to serve stale responses under certain conditions, such as if the origin server is unreachable. In these conditions, a cache may still serve stale responses as long as a `Warning` header is included in the response to inform the client. "HTTP Cache-Control Extensions for Stale Content," (*http://bit.ly/rfc-5861*) by Mark Nottingham, proposes new `Cache-Control` directives (see "Cache behaviors" on page 20) to address these conditions.

The `stale-while-revalidate` directive allows a cache to serve up stale content while it is in the process of validating it in order to hide the latency of the validation. The `stale-if-error` directive allows the cache to serve up content whenever there is an error that could be due to the network or the origin server being unavailable. Both directives inform caches that it is OK to serve stale content if these headers are present,

---

while the aforementioned `Warning` header informs clients that the content they have is actually stale.

Note that RFC 5861 is marked as *informational*, meaning it has not been standardized; thus, all caches may not support these additional directives.

Invalidation

Once a response has been cached, it can also be invalidated. Generally, this will happen because the cache observes a request with an unsafe method to a resource that it has previously cached. Because a request was made that modifies the state of the resource, the cache knows that its representation is invalid. Additionally, the cache should invalidate the `Location` and `Content-Location` responses for the same unsafe request if the response was not an error.

ETags

An *entity-tag*, or ETag (*http://bit.ly/e-tag*), is a validator for the currently selected representation at a point in time. It is represented as a quoted opaque identifier and should not be parsed by clients. The server can return an ETag (which it also caches) in the response via the `ETag` header. A client can save that ETag to use as a validator for a future conditional request, passing the ETag as the value for an `If-Match` or `If-None-Match` header. Note that the client in this case may be an intermediary cache. The server matches up the ETag in the request against the existing ETag it has for the requested resource. If the resource has been modified in the time since the ETag was generated, then the resource's ETag on the server will have changed and there will not be a match.

There are two types of ETags (*http://bit.ly/etag-types*):

- A *strong ETag* is guaranteed to change whenever the server representation changes. A strong ETag must be unique across all other representations of the same resource (e.g., 123456789).
- A *weak ETag* is not guaranteed to be up to date with the resource state. It also does not have the constraints of being unique across other representations of the same resource. A weak ETag must be proceeded with `W/` (e.g., `W/123456789`).

Strong ETags are the default and should be preferred for conditional requests.

Caching and negotiated responses

Caches support the ability to serve negotiated responses through the usage of the `Vary` header (*http://bit.ly/vary-header*). The `Vary` header allows the origin server to specify one or more header fields that it used as part of performing content negotiation. Whenever a request comes in that matches a representation in the cache that has a `Vary` header, the values for those fields must match in the request in order for that representation to be eligible to be served.

The following is an example of a response using the `Vary` header to specify that the `Accept` header was used:

```
HTTP/1.1 200 OK
Content-Type: application/json; charset=utf-8
Content-Length: 183
Vary: Accept
```

Cache behaviors

The `Cache-Control` header (*http://bit.ly/cache-control*) gives instructions to caching mechanisms through which that request/response passes related to its cachability. The instructions can be provided by either the origin server as part of the response, or the client as part of the request. The header value is a list of caching directives that specifies things like whether or not the content is cachable, where it may be stored, what its expiration policy is, and when it should be revalidated or reloaded from the origin server. For example, the `no-cache` directive tells caches they must always revalidate the cached response before serving it.

The `Pragma` header (*http://bit.ly/pragma-header*) can specify a `no-cache` value that is equivalent to the `no-cache` `Cache-Control` directive.

Following is an example of a response using the `Cache-Control` header. In this case, it is specifying the max age for caches as 3,600 seconds (1 hour) from the `Last-Modified` date. It also specifies that cache servers must revalidate with the origin server once the cached representation has expired before returning it again:

```
HTTP/1.1 200 OK
Cache-Control: must-revalidate, max-age=3600
Content-Type: application/json; charset=utf-8
Last-Modified: Wed, 26 Dec 2012 22:05:15 GMT
Date: Thu, 27 Dec 2012 01:05:15 GMT
Content-Length: 183
```

For a detailed walkthrough of caching in action, see Appendix D. For more on HTTP caching in general, see "Things Caches Do," (*http://bit.ly/thingscachesdo*) by Ryan Tomayko, and "How Web Caches Work," (*http://bit.ly/cache-tutorial*) by Mark Nottingham.

Authentication

HTTP provides an extensible framework for servers that allows them to protect their resources and allows clients to access them through authentication. Servers can protect one or more of their resources, with each resource being assigned to a logical partition known as a *realm*. Each realm can have its own *authentication scheme*, or method of authorization it supports.

Upon receiving a request for accessing a protected resource, the server will return a response with a status 401 Unauthorized or a status 403 Forbidden. The response will also contain a WWW-Authenticate header containing a *challenge*, indicating that the client must authenticate to access the resource. The challenge is an extensible token that describes the authentication scheme and additional authentication parameters. For example, the challenge for accessing a protected contacts resource that specifies the use of the HTTP basic authentication scheme is Basic realm="contacts".

To explore how this challenge/response mechanism works in more detail, see Appendix E.

Authentication Schemes

In the previous section we learned about the framework for authentication. RFC 2617 (*http://bit.ly/rfc-2617*) then defines two concrete authentication mechanisms.

Basic

In this scheme, credentials are sent as a Base64-encoded username and password separated by a colon in clear text. Basic Auth (*http://bit.ly/basic-auth*) is conventionally combined with TLS (HTTPS) due to its inherent unsecure nature; thus, its advantage is that it is extremely easy to implement and access (including from browser clients), which makes it an attractive choice for many API authors.

Digest

In Digest (*http://bit.ly/digest-access*), the user's credentials are sent in clear text. Digest addresses this problem by using a checksum (MAC) that the client sends, which the server can use to validate the credentials. However, this scheme has several security and performance disadvantages and is not often used.

The following is an example of an HTTP Basic challenge response after an attempt to access a protected resource:

```
HTTP/1.1 401 Unauthorized
...
WWW-Authenticate: Basic realm="Web API Book"
...
```

As you can see, the server has returned a 401, including a WWW-Authenticate header indicating that the client must authenticate using HTTP Basic:

```
GET /resource HTTP/1.1
...
Authorization: Basic QWxpY2U6VGhlIE1hZ2ljIFdvcmRzIGFyZSBTcXVlYW1pc2ggT3NzaWZyYWdl
```

The client then sends back the original request, including the Authorization header, in order to access the protected resource.

Additional Authentication Schemes

There are additional authentication schemes that have appeared since RFC 2617, including vendor-specific mechanisms:

AWS Authentication
> This scheme, used for authenticating to Amazon Web Services S3 (*http://amzn.to/rest-services*), involves the client concatenating several parts of the request to form a string. The user then uses his AWS shared secret access key to calculate an HMAC (hash message authentication code), which is used to sign the request.

Azure Storage
> Windows Azure offers several different schemes to access Windows Azure Storage services (*http://bit.ly/azure-storage*), each of which involves using a shared key to sign the request.

Hawk
> This new scheme (*http://bit.ly/hawk-hub*), authored by Eran Hammer, provides a general-purpose shared key auth mechanism similar to AWS and Azure. The key is also never used directly in the requests; rather, it is used to calculate a MAC value that is included in the request. This prevents the key from being intercepted such as in a man-in-the-middle (MITM) attack.

OAuth 2.0
> Using this framework (*http://bit.ly/rfc-6749*) allows a *resource owner* (the user) to delegate permission to a client to access a protected resource from a *resource server* on her behalf. An authentication server grants the client a limited use access token, which the client can then use to access the resource. The clear advantage here is that the user's credentials are never directly exchanged with the client application attempting to access the resource.

You'll learn more about HTTP authentication mechanisms and implementing them (including OAuth) in Chapters 15 and 16.

Conclusion

In this chapter we've taken a broad-brush approach at surveying the HTTP landscape. The concepts covered were not meant for completeness but rather to help you wade into the pool of HTTP and give you a basic foundation for your ASP.NET Web API development. You'll notice we've included further references for each of the items discussed. These references will prove invaluable as you actually move forward with your Web API development, so keep them in your back pocket! On to APIs!

CHAPTER 2

Web APIs

In the preceding chapter, we learned about the essential aspects of the Web and HTTP, the application layer protocol that drives it. In this chapter, we'll talk about the evolution of Web APIs, cover various Web API–related concepts, and discuss different styles and approaches for designing Web APIs.

There's more to Web APIs than just returning a JSON payload.

In the preceding chapter, we learned about the essential aspects of the Web and HTTP, the application layer protocol that drives it. In this chapter, we'll talk about the evolution of Web APIs, cover various Web API–related concepts, and discuss different styles and approaches for designing Web APIs.

What Is a Web API?

A Web API is a *programmatic* interface to a system that is accessed via standard HTTP methods and headers. A Web API can be accessed by a variety of HTTP clients, including browsers and mobile devices. Web APIs can also benefit from the web infrastructure for concerns like caching and concurrency.

What About SOAP Web Services?

SOAP services are not web-friendly. They are not easily consumable from HTTP clients, such as browsers or tools like curl (*http://curl.haxx.se/*). A SOAP request has to be properly encoded in a SOAP message format. The client has to have access to a Web Service Description Language (WSDL) file, which describes the actions available on the service, and also has to know how to construct the message. This means the semantics of how to interact with the system are tunneled over HTTP rather than being first class. Additionally, SOAP web services generally require all interactions to be via HTTP POST; thus, the responses are also noncachable. Finally, SOAP services do not allow one to access HTTP headers, which severely limits clients from benefitting from features of HTTP like optimistic concurrency and content negotiation.

Origins of Web APIs

In February 2000, Salesforce.com launched a new API (*http://history.apievangel ist.com/*) that allowed customers to harness Salesforce capabilities directly within their applications.

Later that same year in November, eBay launched a new API (*http://bit.ly/ebay-api*) that allowed developers to build ecommerce applications leveraging eBay's infrastructure.

What differentiated these APIs from SOAP APIs (the other emerging trend)? These Web APIs were targeting third-party consumers and designed in an HTTP-friendly way. The traditional APIs of the time had been mostly designed for system integration and were SOAP-based. These APIs utilized plain old XML as the message exchange format and plain old HTTP as the protocol. This allowed them to be used from a very broad set of clients, including simple web browsers. These were the first of many such Web APIs to come.

For the next few years after Salesforce and eBay took these first steps, similar APIs started to appear on the scene. In 2002, Amazon officially introduced Amazon Web Services, followed by Flickr launching its Flickr API in 2004.

The Web API Revolution Begins

In the summer of 2005, ProgrammableWeb.com launched. Its goal was to be a one-stop shop for everything API related. It included a directory of public APIs (both SOAP and non-SOAP) containing 32 APIs, which was considerable growth from 2002. Over the next few years, however, that number would explode. APIs would run the gamut from major players such as Facebook, Twitter, Google, LinkedIn, Microsoft, and Amazon to then-small startups like YouTube and Foursquare. In November 2008, Programmable-Web's directory was tracking 1,000 APIs. Four years later, at the time of this writing, that number exceeds 7,000. API growth *is* accelerating, as just about a year ago the number was 4,000 (*http://bit.ly/4k-api*).

In other words, it is clear that Web APIs are here to stay.

Paying Attention to the Web

The earliest Web APIs weren't necessarily concerned with the underlying web architecture and its design constraints. This had ramifications such as the infamous Google Web Accelerator incident (*http://bit.ly/google-accel*), which resulted in a loss of customer data and content.

In recent years, however, with an exponential rise in third-party API consumers and in devices, this has changed. Organizations are finding they can no longer afford to ignore the web architecture in their API design, because doing so has negatively impacted their ability to scale, to support a growing set of clients, and to evolve their APIs without breaking existing consumers.

The remainder of this chapter is a primer on web architecture and HTTP as they relate to building Web APIs. It will give you a foundation that will allow you to leverage the power of the Web as you begin to develop your own Web APIs using ASP.NET Web API.

Guidelines for Web APIs

This section lists some guidelines for differentiating Web APIs from other forms of APIs. In general, a key differentiator for Web APIs is that they are browser-friendly. In addition, Web APIs:

- Can be accessed from a range of clients (including browsers at minimum).
- Support standard HTTP methods such as those mentioned in Table 1-1. It is not required for an API to use all of the methods, but at minimum it should support GET for retrieval of resources and POST for unsafe operations.
- Support browser-friendly formats. This means that they support formats that are easy for browsers and any other HTTP client to consume. A browser client can technically consume a SOAP message using its XML stack, but the format requires a large amount of SOAP-specific code to do it. Formats like XHTML, JSON, and Form URL encoding are very easy to consume in a browser.
- Support browser-friendly authentication. This means that a browser client can authenticate with the server without requiring any special plugins or extensions.

Domain-Specific Media Types

In the previous chapter, we learned about the concept of media types. In addition to the general-purpose types we discussed, there are also domain-specific media types. These types carry rich application-specific semantics and are useful in particular for Web API development where there are rich system interactions rather than simple document transfer.

vCard (*http://tools.ietf.org/search/rfc6350*) is a domain-specific media type that provides a standard way to electronically describe contact information. It is supported in many popular address book and email applications like Microsoft Outlook, Gmail, and Apple Mail.

In Figure 2-1, you can see the same contact represented as a vCard.

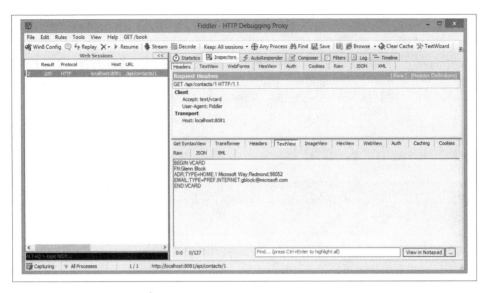

Figure 2-1. Contact vCard representation

When an email application sees a vCard it knows right away that this is contact information and how to process it. If the same application were to get raw JSON, it has no way of knowing what it received until it parses the JSON. This is because the JSON media type does not define a standard way to say "I am a contact." The format would have to be communicated out-of-band through documentation. Assuming that information was communicated, it would be application specific and not likely supported by other email applications. In the case of the vCard, however, it is a standard that is supported by many applications across different operating systems and form factors.

We can mint new media types as applications evolve and new needs emerge by following the IANA registration process (*http://bit.ly/iana-reg*). This provides a distinct advantage because we can introduce new types and clients to consume them without affecting existing clients. As we saw in the previous chapter, clients express their media type preferences through *content negotiation*.

Media Type Profiles

It makes a lot of sense for media types that are used by many different clients and servers to be registered with IANA, but what if a media type is not ubiquitous and specific to an application? Should it be registered with IANA? Some say yes, but others are exploring lighter-weight mechanisms, in particular for Web APIs. Media type profiles allow servers to leverage existing media types (like XML, JSON, etc.) and provide additional information that has the application-specific semantics.

The profile link relation (*http://bit.ly/rfc-6906*) allows servers to return a profile link in an HTTP response. A *link* is an element that contains a minimum of two pieces of information: a rel (or relation) that describes the link, and a URI. In the case of a profile, the rel will be profile. It is not necessary for the URI to actually be dereferencable (meaning you can access the resource), though in many cases it will point to a document.

The challenge with using profiles today is that many media types do not currently support a way to express links, so clients would not be expected to recognize the profile even if it were in the content. For example, JSON is a very popular format used by Web APIs, but it does not support links.

Fortunately, there is a preestablished *link header* (*http://bit.ly/rfc-5988*) that can be used in any HTTP response to pass a profile.

Using the earlier contact example, we can return this header to tell the client this is not just any old JSON, it's JSON for working with example.com's contact management system. If the client opens their browser to the URI of the link, they can get a document that describes the payload. This document can be in any format, such as the emerging *Application-Level Profile Semantics* (ALPS) data format (*http://alps.io/spec/*), which is designed specifically for this purpose.:

```
HTTP/1.1 200 OK
Content-Type: application/json; charset=utf-8
Link: <http://example.com/contactmanagement/profile>; rel="profile"
Date: Fri, 21 Dec 2012 06:47:25 GMT
Content-Length: 183

{
  "contactId":1,
  "name":"Glenn Block",
  "address":"1 Microsoft Way",
  "city":"Redmond","State":"WA",
  "zip":"98052",
  "email":"gblock@microsoft.com",
  "twitter":"gblock",
  "self":"/contacts/1"
}
```

Multiple Representations

A single resource can have multiple representations, each with a different media type. To illustrate, let's look at two different representations of the same contact resource. The first, in Figure 2-2, is a JSON representation and contains information about the contact. The second, Figure 2-3, is the avatar for the contact. Both are valid representations of state, but they have different uses.

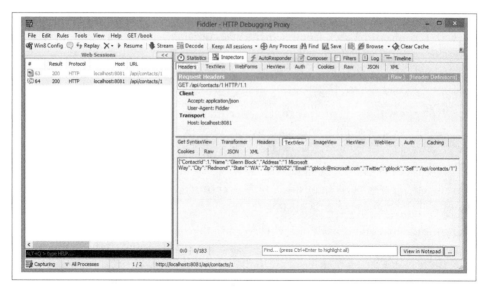

Figure 2-2. Contact JSON representation

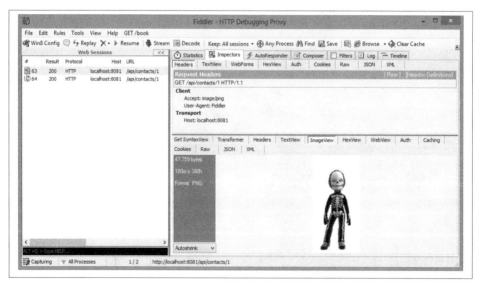

Figure 2-3. Contact PNG representation

The JSON representation will be parsed and data (such as the contact name, email address, etc.) will be extracted from the JSON and displayed to the user. The PNG representation, however, will just display as is; because it is an image, it could also easily be passed as the URL for an HTML `<img>` tag or consumed directly by an image viewer.

As the previous example shows, the advantage of supporting multiple representations is to allow many different clients with different capabilities to interact with your API.

API Styles

There are many different architectural styles for building Web APIs. By *style* we mean an approach for implementing an API over HTTP. A style is a set of common characteristics and constraints that permeate the design. Each style has trade-offs and benefits associated with it. The important thing to recognize is that the style is an *application* of HTTP; it is *not* HTTP.

For example, Gothic is a style applied to architecture. You can look at various buildings and determine which are Gothic because they possess certain qualities, such as ogival arches, ribbed vaults, and flying buttresses. In the same way, API styles share a set of qualities that manifest in different APIs. Today we see a number of styles, but they land in a spectrum with RPC on one side and REST on the other.

The Richardson Maturity Model

The Richardson Maturity Model (RMM) (*http://bit.ly/rich-sec-mod*) by Leonard Richardson introduces a framework for classifying APIs into different levels based on how well they take advantage of web technologies.

Level 0, RPC oriented
  A single URI and one HTTP method.

Level 1, Resource oriented
  Many URIs, one HTTP method.

Level 2, HTTP verbs
  Many URIs, each supporting multiple HTTP methods.

Level 3, Hypermedia
  Resources describe their own capabilities and interactions.

The model was designed to classify the existing APIs of the time. It became wildly popular and is used by many folks in the API community for classifying their APIs today.

It was not without issue, though. The model was not created to establish a rating scale to evaluate how RESTful an API is. Unfortunately, many took it for just that and began to use it as a stick to beat others for not being RESTful enough. This appears to be one of the reasons why Leonard Richardson himself has stopped promoting it.

Throughout this chapter, you'll dive more deeply into the different levels of RMM and see real-world examples. We'll use the levels to discuss the benefits and trade-offs associated with how you design your API.

RPC (RMM Level 0)

At Level 0, an API uses an RPC (remote procedure call) style. It basically treats HTTP as a transport protocol for invoking functions running on a remote server. In an RPC API, the API tunnels its own semantics into the payload, with different message types generally corresponding to different methods on the remote object and using a single HTTP method, POST. The SOAP Services, XML-RPC, and POX (plain old XML) APIs are examples of Level 0.

Consider the example of an order processsing system using POX. The system exposes a single-order processing service at the URL *orderService*. Each client POSTs different types of messages to that service in order to interact with it.

To create an order, a client sends the following:

```
POST /orderService HTTP 1.1
Content-Type: application/xml
Content-Length: xx

<createOrderRequest orderNumber = "1000">
</createOrderRequest>
```

The server then responds, telling the client the order has been created:

```
HTTP/1.1 200 OK
Content-Type: application/xml
Content-Length: xx

<createOrderResponse>
Order created
</createOrderResponse>
```

Notice the status is in the body itself, not via the status code. This is because HTTP is being used as a transport for a method invocation where all the data is sent in the payload.

To check on the list of active orders, the client sends a getOrders request:

```
POST /orderService HTTP 1.1
Content-Type: application/xml
Content-Length: xx

<getOrdersRequest status="active"/>
</getOrderRequest>
```

The server reply contains the list of orders:

```
HTTP/1.1 200 OK
Content-Type: application/xml
Content-Length: xx

<getOrdersResponse>
  <orders>
    <order orderNumber = "1000" status="active"/>
```

```
      <order orderNumber = "1200" status="active"/>
    </order>
  </getOrdersResponse>
```

To approve an order, the client sends an approval request:

```
POST /orderService HTTP 1.1
Content-Type: application/xml
Content-Length: xx

<approveOrderRequest orderNumber = "1000">
</approveOrderRequest>
```

The server responds, indicating the status of the approval:

```
HTTP/1.1 200 OK
Content-Type: application/xml
Content-Length: xx

<approveOrderResponse>
  <error code="100">Order approval failed</error>
  <reason>Missing information</reason>
</approveOrderResponse>
```

Similar to the status mentioned ealier, here the error code is part of the payload.

As you can see from the preceding examples, in this style the payload describes a set of operations to be performed and their results. Clients have explicit knowledge of each of the different message types associated with each "service," which they use to interact with it.

You might be asking, why not use another method like PUT? The reason is because in this approach all requests are sent to a single endpoint (*/orderService*) regardless of the operation. POST is the least constrained in its definition, as it is both unsafe and nonidempotent. Each of the other methods, however, has additional constraints, making it insufficient for all operations.

One benefit of this approach is that it is very easy and simple to implement and aligns well with the existing development mental model.

Resources (RMM Level 1)

At Level 1, the API is broken out into several resources, with each resource being accessed via a single HTTP method, though the method can vary. Unlike Level 0, in this case the URI represents the operation.

Returning to the preceding order processing example, here is how the requests look for a Level 0 API. To create an order, the client sends a request to the createOrder API, passing the order in the payload:

```
POST /createOrder HTTP 1.1
Content-Type: application/json
Content-Length: xx

{
  "orderNumber" : "1000"
}
```

The server then responds with an order that has an active status:

```
HTTP/1.1 200 OK
Content-Type: application/json
Content-Length: xx

{
  "orderNumber" : "1000",
  "status" : "active"
}
```

To retrieve the orders, the client makes a request to listOrders and specifies the filter in the query string. Notice that for retrieval the client is actually performing a GET request rather than a POST:

```
GET /listOrders?status=active
```

The server then responds with the list of orders:

```
HTTP/1.1 200 OK
Content-Type: application/json
Content-Length: xx

{
  [
    {
      "orderNumber : "1000",
      "status" : "active"
    },
    {
      "orderNumber" : "1200",
      "status" : "active"
    }
  ]
}
```

To approve the order, the client makes a POST request to the approveOrder resource:

```
POST /approveOrder?orderNumber=1000
...
```

A common example of an API using this style is Yahoo's Flickr API (*http://www.flickr.com/services/api/*). Looking at the documentation, we see "API Methods." Looking under galleries, we see the methods listed in Figure 2-4.

Figure 2-4. Yahoo Flickr API

There are several different URIs for working with photos. To add a photo, you'd request the addPhoto API, while to retrieve a photo you can use getPhotos. To update a photo, you can request the editPhoto or editPhoto APIs.

Notice this style is still very RPC-ish in the sense that each resource corresponds to a method on a server-side object. However, because it can use additional HTTP methods, some resources can be accessed via GET, allowing their responses to be cached as in the earlier listOrders example. This style provides additional evolvability benefits in that we can easily add new functionality to the system as resources, without having to modify existing resources, which could break current clients.

HTTP VERBS (RMM Level 2)

In the previous examples, each resource corresponded heavily to the implementation on the server, relating to one or more methods on server-side objects; thus, those examples were very functionality oriented (getOrder). A Level 2 system uses a resource-oriented approach. The API exposes one or more resources (order), which each support one or more HTTP methods. These types of APIs offer richer interactions over HTTP, supporting capabilities like caching and content negotiaion.

In these APIs, it is common to have a delineation between collection resources and item resources:

- A *collection resource* corresponds to the collection of child resources (e.g., *http://example.com/orders*). To retrieve the collection, a client issues a GET request to this resource. To add a new item to the collection a client POSTs an item to this resource.

- An *item resource* corresponds to an individual child resource within a collection (e.g., *http://example.com/orders/1* corresponds to order 1). To update the item resource, a client sends a PUT or PATCH request. To delete, it uses a DELETE method. It is also common to allow PUT to create the resource if it does not exist. An item resource is generally referred to as a *subresource*, because its URI implies a hierarchy (i.e., in */orders/1*, the 1 is a child).

- Both collection and item resources can have one or more collection and item resources as children.

Applying the order example to level style, the client now sends the following request to create an order:

```
POST /orders
Content-Type: application/json
Content-Length: xx

{
  "orderNumber" : "1000"
}
```

The server than responsds with a 201 Created status code and a location header indicating the URI of the newly created resource. The response also includes an ETag header to enable caching:

```
HTTP/1.1 201 CREATED
Location: /orders/1000
Content-Type: application/json
Content-Length: xx
ETag: "12345"

{
  "orderNumber" : "1000",
  "status" : "active"
}
```

To list active orders, the client sends a GET request to the */active* subresource under */orders:*

```
GET /orders/active
Content-Type: application/json
Content-Length: xx

{
  [
    {
      "orderNumber : "1000",
      "status" : "active"
    },
    {
      "orderNumber" : "1200",
      "status" : "active"
    }
```

```
    ]
}
```

To approve the order, the client sends a PUT request to *order/1000/approval*:

```
PUT /orders/1000/approval
```

The client then responds, indicating in this case that the order approval has been rejected:

```
HTTP/1.1 403 Forbidden
Content-Type: application/json
Content-Length: xx

{
  "error": {
    "code" : "100",
      "message" : "Missing information"
  }
}
```

Looking at the preceding examples, you can see the difference in the way the client interacts with such an API. It sends requests to one or more resources using the HTTP methods to convey the intent.

A real-world example of a resource-oriented API is the GitHub API (*http://bit.ly/gh-dev-api*). It exposes root collection resources for each of the major areas in GitHub, including Orgs, Repositories, Pull Requests, Issues, and much more. Each collection resource has its own child item and collection resources. To interact with each resource, you use standard HTTP methods.

For example, to list repositories for the current authenticated user, we can send the following request to the *repos* resource:

```
GET http://api.github.com/users/repos/ HTTP/1.1
```

To create a new repository for the current authenticated user, we issue a POST to the same URI with a JSON payload specifying the repo information:

```
POST http://api.github.com/users/repos/ HTTP/1.1
Content-Type: application/json
Content-Length:xx

{
  "name": "New-Repo",
  "description": "This is a new repo",
  "homepage": "https://github.com",
  "private": false,
  "has_issues": true,
  "has_wiki": true,
  "has_downloads": true
}
```

Crossing the Chasm Toward Resource-Centric APIs

Designing resource-oriented APIs can be challenging, as the noun-centric/non-object-oriented style is a big paradigm shift from the way developers traditionally design procedural or object-oriented APIs in 4GL programming languages. The process involves analyzing the key elements of the system that clients need to interact with and exposing those as resources.

One challenge API designers face when doing this is how to handle situations where the existing set of HTTP methods seems insufficient. For example, given an `Order` resource, how do you handle an approval? Should you create an `Approval` HTTP method? Not if you want to be a good HTTP citizen, as clients or servers would never expect to deal with an `APPROVAL` method. There are a couple of different ways to address this scenario.

- Have the client do a PUT/PATCH against the resource and have `Approved=True` included as part of the payload. It could be either in JSON or even a form URL encoded value passed in the query string:

    ```
    PATCH http://example.com/orders/1?approved=true HTTP/1.1
    ```

- Factor out APPROVAL as a separate resource and have the client POST or PUT to it:

    ```
    POST http://example.com/orders/1/approval HTTP/1.1
    ```

Hypermedia (RMM Level 3)

The last level in Richardson's scale is hypermedia. *Hypermedia* are controls or *affordances* (*http://bit.ly/mca-hyper*) present in the response that clients use for interacting with related resources for transitioning the application to different states. Although RMM defines it as a strict level, that is a bit misleading. Hypermedia can be present in an API, even in an RPC-oriented one.

The Origins of Hypermedia on the Web

Hypermedia and hypertext are concepts that are part of the very foundations of the Web and HTTP. In Tim Berners-Lee's original proposal for the World Wide Web (*http://bit.ly/w3c-prop*), he spoke about hypertext:

> *HyperText is a way to link and access information of various kinds as a web of nodes in which the user can browse at will. Potentially, HyperText provides a single user-interface to many large classes of stored information such as reports, notes, data-bases, computer documentation and on-line systems help.*

He then went on to propose the creation of a new system of servers based on this concept, which has evolved to become the World Wide Web:

> *We propose the implementation of a simple scheme to incorporate several different servers of machine-stored information already available at CERN, including an analysis of the requirements for information access needs by experiments.*

Hypermedia is derived from hypertext and expands to more than just simple documents to include content such as graphics, audio, and video. Roy Fielding used the term in Chapter 5 of his dissertation on network architecture (*http://bit.ly/REST-fielding*), where he discusses Representational State Transfer (REST). He defines right off the bat that hypermedia is a key component of REST:

> *This chapter introduces and elaborates the Representational State Transfer (REST) architectural style for distributed hypermedia systems.*

There are two primary categories of hypermedia affordances: *links* and *forms*. To see the role each plays, let's look at HTML.

HTML has many different hypermedia affordances, including `<A href>`, `<FORM>`, and `<IMG>` tags. When viewing an HTML page in a browser, a user is presented with a set of different links from the server that are rendered in the browser. Those links are identified by the user via either the link description or an image. The user then clicks the links of interest. The page can also include forms. If a form is present, such as for creating an order, the user can fill out the form fields and click Submit. In either case, the user is able to navigate the system without any knowledge of the underlying URI.

In the same way, a hypermedia API can be consumed by a nonbrowser client. Similar to the HTML example, the links and forms are present but can be rendered in different formats, including XML and JSON. For more on forms, see "Hypermedia and Forms" (*http://bit.ly/hype-forms*) on CodeBetter.

A link in a hypermedia API includes a minimum of two components:

- A URI to the related resource
- A `rel` that identifies the relationship between the linked resource and the current resource

The `rel` (and possibly other metadata) is the identifier that the user agent cares about. The `rel` indicates how the resource to which the link points relates to the current resource.

Measuring Hypermedia Affordances with H-Factors

Mike Amundsen (*http://amundsen.com/*) has created a measurement called an H-factor designed to measure the level of hypermedia syupport within a media type. H-factors are divided into two groups with their own factors:

- Link support
  — [LE]Embedding links
  — [LO]Outbound links
  — [LT]Templated queries
  — [LN]Nonidempotent updates
  — [LI]Idempotent updates
- Control data support
  — [CR]Control data for read requests
  — [CU]Control data for update requests
  — [CM]Control data for interface methods
  — [CL]Control data for links

H-factors are a useful way to compare and contrast the different types of hypermedia APIs that exist.

Returning to the order example, we can now see how hypermedia will play in. In each of the aforementioned scenarios, the client has complete knowledge of the URI space. In the hypermedia case, however, the client knows only about one root URI, which it goes to in order to discover the available resources in the system. This URI acts almost like a home page—in fact, it is a home resource:

```
GET /home
Accept: application/json; profile="http://example.com/profile/orders"
```

In this case, the client sends an `Accept` header with an `orders` profile:

```
HTTP/1.1 200 OK
Content-Type: application/json; profile="http://example.com/profile/orders"
Content-Length: xx

{
  "links" : [
    {"rel":"orders", "href": "/orders"},
    {"rel":"shipping", "href": "/shipping"}
    {"rel":"returns", "href": "/returns"}
  ]
}
```

The home resource contains pointers to the other parts of the system—in this case, orders, shipping, and returns. To find out how to interact with the resources that the links point to, the developer building the client can reference the profile documentation at the profile URL just indicated. The document states that if a client sees a link with a rel of orders, it can POST an order to that resource to create a new one. The content type can just be JSON, as the server will try to determine the correct elements:

```
POST /orders
Content-Type: application/json
Content-Length: xx

{
  "orderNumber" : "1000"
}
```

Here is the response:

```
HTTP/1.1 201 CREATED
Location: /orders/1000
Content-Type: application/json; profile="http://example.com/profile/orders"
Content-Length: xx
ETag: "12345"

{
  "orderNumber" : "1000",
  "status" : "active"
  "links" : [
    {"rel":"self", "href": "/orders/1000"},
    {"rel":"approve", "href": "/orders/1000/approval"}
    {"rel":"cancel", "href": "/orders/1000/cancellation"}
    {"rel":"hold", "href": "/orders/1000/hold"}
  ]
}
```

Notice that in addition to the order details, the server has included several links that are applicable specifically for the current order:

- "self" identifies the URL for the order itself. This is useful as a bookmark to the order resource.

- "approve" identifies a resource for approving the order.

- "cancel" identifies a resource for placing a cancellation.

- "hold" identifies a resource for putting the order on hold.

Now that the client has the order, it can follow the approval link. The profile spec indicates that the client should do a PUT against the URL associated with a rel of approve in order to approve the order:

```
PUT /orders/1000/approval
Content-Type: application/json
```

The response will be identical to the Level 2 response:

```
HTTP/1.1 403 Forbidden
Content-Type: application/json; profile="http://example.com/profile/orders"
Content-Length: xx

{
  "error": {
    "code" : "100",
    "message" : "Missing information"
  }
}
```

Paypal recently introduced a new payments API (*http://bit.ly/paypal-api*) that incorporates hypermedia in its responses.

The following is an extract of a response for a payment issued using the new API:

```
"links": [
  {
    "href": "https://api.sandbox.paypal.com/v1/payments/sale/1KE480",
    "rel": "self",
    "method": "GET"
  },
  {
    "href": "https://api.sandbox.paypal.com/v1/payments/sale/1KE480/refund",
    "rel": "refund",
    "method": "POST"
  },
  {
    "href": "https://api.sandbox.paypal.com/v1/payments/payment/PAY-34629814W",
    "rel": "parent_payment",
    "method": "GET"
  }
```

As you can see, it contains the self link mentioned previously, as well as links for submitting for a refund and accessing the parent payment. Notice that, in addition to the standard href and rel members, each link contains a method member that advises the client on which HTTP method it should use. In this case, the media type Paypal returns is application/json. This means the client cannot simply tell by the response headers that the payload is in fact a Paypal payload. However, the Paypal documentation explains the `rel`, and that it is possible to navigate the system without hardcoding against URLs.

In each of the previous examples, hypermedia provides the benefit that the client has to know only a single root URL to access the API and get the initial response. From that point on, it follows its nose by navigating to whatever URLs the server serves up. The server is free to change those URLs and offer the client specifically targeted links without affecting other clients. As with all things, there are trade-offs.

Implementing a hypermedia system is significantly more difficult, and is a mind shift. More moving parts are introduced into the system as part of the implementation. In addition, using hypermedia-based approaches for APIs is a young and evolving "science," so you do have some of your work cut out for you. In many cases the trade-off is worth it, in particular if you are building an open system that needs to support many third-party clients.

REST

REST, or Representational State Transfer, is probably one of the most misunderstood terms in Web API development today. Most people equate REST with anything that is easy to access over HTTP and forget about its constraints completely.

The term's roots are from Roy Fielding's previously mentioned dissertation on network-based architecture. In it, Roy describes REST as an architectural style for distributed hypermedia systems. In other words, REST is not a technology, it is not a framework, and it is not a design pattern. *It is a style.* There is no "one true way" to do REST, and as a result, there are many flavors of RESTful systems. However, what is most important is that all RESTful systems manifest themselves in a set of constraints, which will be mentioned in more depth in the following section.

The other common misunderstanding is that you *must* build a RESTful system. This is not the case. The RESTful constraints are designed to create a system that achieves a certain set of goals—in particular, a system that can evolve over a long period of time and can tolerate many different clients and many different changes without breaking those clients.

REST Constraints

REST defines the following six constraints (including one optional) as part of the style:

Client-server
> A RESTful system is designed to separate out the UI concerns from the backend. Clients are decoupled from the server, thus allowing both to evolve independently.

Stateless

For each request in a RESTful system, all of the application state is kept on the client and transferred in the request. This allows the server to receive all the information it needs to process the request without having to track each individual client. Removing statefulness from the server allows the application to easily scale.

Cache

Data within a request must be able to be identified as cachable. This allows client and server caches to act on behalf of the origin server and to return cached representations. Cachability greatly reduces latency, increases user-perceived performance, and improves overall system scale, as it decreases the load on the server.

Uniform interface

RESTful systems use a standardized interface for system interaction.

Identification of resources

This means that the point of interaction in a RESTful system is a *resource*. This is the same resource that we discussed earlier.

Self-descriptive messages

This means that each message contains all the information necessary for clients and servers to interact. This includes the URI, HTTP method, headers, media type, and more.

Manipulation of resources through representations

As we covered previously, a resource can have one or more representations. In a RESTful system, it is through these representations that resource state is communicated.

Hypermedia as the engine of application state

Previously we discussed hypermedia and the role it plays in driving the flow of the application. That model is a core component of a RESTful system.

Layered system

Components within a RESTful system are layered and composed with each component having a limited view of the system. This allows layers to be introduced to adapt between legacy clients and servers and enables intermediaries to provide additional services like caching, enforcing security policies, compression, and more.

Code on demand

This allows clients to dynamically download code that executes on the client in order to help it interact with the system. One very popular example of this is the way client-side JavaScript executes in the browser, as it is downloaded on demand. Being able to introduce new application code improves the the system's capacity to evolve and be extended. Because it reduces visibility, however, this constraint is considered optional.

As you can see, building a RESTful system is not free and not necessarily easy. There have been many books written in depth on the topics just mentioned. Although making a system RESTful is not trivial, it can be worth the investment depending on the system's needs. For this reason, this book does not focus on REST but rather focuses on evolvability and techniques to achieve that when building your Web APIs. Each of these techniques is a pathway toward a fully RESTful system but provides a benefit in its own right.

Put another way, focus on the needs of your system and not whether you can stamp it with a "REST" badge or not.

For more clarification on REST as a term, Kelly Sommers has a well-written post (*http:// bit.ly/kellabyte*) that covers this topic in more detail.

To learn more about building RESTful and hypermedia-based systems, check out *REST in Practice* (O'Reilly) and *Building Hypermedia APIs with HTML5 and Node* (O'Reilly).

Conclusion

In this chapter, we learned about the origin of APIs, explored the growth of APIs in the industry, and dove into APIs themselves. Now it's time to meet ASP.NET Web API, Microsoft's answer to building APIs. In the next chapter, you'll learn about the framework, its design goals, and how to get started with it for API development.

CHAPTER 3

ASP.NET Web API 101

It's easier to plot a course once you've seen the map.

Now that we've established the context around why Web APIs are important for modern networked applications, in this chapter we'll take a first look at ASP.NET Web API. ASP.NET Web API and the new HTTP programming model offer different capabilities for both building and consuming Web APIs. First we'll explore some of the core Web API goals and the capabilities that support them. We'll then see how those capabilities are exposed to your code in ASP.NET Web API by looking at its programming model. What better way to examine that than by looking at the code provided by the Visual Studio Web API project template? Finally, we'll go beyond the default template code and construct our first "Hello World" Web API.

Core Scenarios

Unlike many technologies, ASP.NET Web API has a very well-documented and accessible history (some is recorded on CodePlex (*http://wcf.codeplex.com/*)). From the beginning, the development team made the decision to be as transparent as possible so that the product could be influenced by the community of experts who would ultimately use it to build real systems. I've distilled all that history down to the core goals that ASP.NET was created to address:

- First-class HTTP programming
- Symmetric client and server programming experience
- Flexible support for different formats
- No more "coding with angle brackets"
- Unit testability

- Multiple hosting options

Now, while these are key goals, they by no means represent an exhaustive list of all that the framework enables. ASP.NET Web API brings together the best of Windows Communication Foundation (WCF), with its infinitely extensible architecture, client support, and flexible hosting model, and ASP.NET MVC, with its support for convention over configuration, improved testability, and advanced features such as model binding and validation. As we'll begin to explore in this chapter, the result is a framework that is approachable for getting started, and easily customizable as your needs evolve.

First-Class HTTP Programming

When you are building modern Web APIs—especially for simpler clients such as mobile devices—the success of that API is often related to its expressiveness. And the expressiveness of a Web API depends on how well it uses HTTP as an application protocol. Using HTTP as an application protocol goes far beyond simply handling HTTP requests and producing HTTP responses. It means that the behavior of both the application and the underlying framework is controlled by HTTP control flow and data elements rather than by some additional data that is merely (and incidentally) transmitted via HTTP. For example, consider the following SOAP request used to communicate with a WCF service:

```
POST http://localhost/GreetingService.svc HTTP/1.1
Content-Type: text/xml; charset=utf-8
SOAPAction: "HelloWorld"
Content-Length: 154

<s:Envelope xmlns:s="http://schemas.xmlsoap.org/soap/envelope/">
  <s:Body>
        <HelloWorld xmlns="http://localhost/wcf/greeting"/>
  </s:Body>
</s:Envelope>
```

In this example, the client issues a request to the server to obtain a friendly greeting message. As you can see, the request is being sent via HTTP. However, this is really where the association with HTTP stops. Rather than using HTTP methods (sometimes called *verbs*) to communicate the nature of the action requested of the service, the approach shown here sends all requests using the same HTTP method—POST—and wraps the application-specific details in both the HTTP request body and the custom SOAPAc tion header. As you might expect, we see the same pattern repeated on the response produced by the service:

```
HTTP/1.1 200 OK
Content-Length: 984
Content-Type: text/xml; charset=utf-8
Date: Tue, 26 Apr 2011 01:22:53 GMT
```

```
<s:Envelope xmlns:s="http://schemas.xmlsoap.org/soap/envelope/">
  <s:Body>
    <HelloWorldResponse xmlns="http://localhost/wcf/greeting">
      ...
    </HelloWorldResponse>
  </s:Body>
</s:Envelope>
```

As in the case of the request message, the protocol elements used to control the application—that is, the way that the client and server applications understand one another—have been pulled out of the HTTP elements and placed inside the XML bodies of the request and response, respectively.

In this approach, HTTP is not being used to express the application protocol, but rather as a simple transport for a different application protocol—SOAP, in this case. And while this can be a good thing for scenarios where a single service needs to communicate with similar clients across lots of different protocols, it can be problematic when the need is to communicate with lots of very different clients across a single protocol. These kinds of problems are illustrated perfectly in the case of Web APIs, where the diversity of not only clients, but also of the communication infrastructure between clients and services (e.g., the Internet), is large and constantly changing. In this world, clients and services should be optimized not for protocol independence but rather for creating a first-class experience around a common application protocol. In the case of applications that communicate via the Web, that protocol is HTTP.

At its core, ASP.NET Web API is built around a small set of HTTP primitive objects. The two most notable of these are `HttpRequestMessage` and `HttpResponseMessage`. The purpose of these objects is to provide a strongly typed view of an actual HTTP message. For example, consider the following HTTP request message:

```
GET http://localhost:50650/api/greeting HTTP/1.1
Host: localhost:50650
accept: application/json
if-none-match: "1"
```

Assuming that this request was received by an ASP.NET Web API service, we can access and manipulate the various elements of this request using code similar to the following in a Web API controller class:

```
var request = this.Request;
var requestedUri = request.RequestUri;
var requestedHost = request.Headers.Host;
var acceptHeaders = request.Headers.Accept;
var conditionalValue = request.Headers.IfNoneMatch;
```

This strongly typed model provides the correct level of abstraction over HTTP, empowering the developer to work directly with an HTTP request or response while freeing her from having to deal with lower-level issues such as raw message parsing or generation.

Symmetric Client and Server Programming Experience

One of the most appealing aspects of ASP.NET Web APIs being built around this HTTP-focused object library is that the library can be used not only on the server but also in client applications that are built using the .NET Framework. This means that the HTTP request shown here can be created with the same HTTP programming model classes that are ultimately used to work with the request inside of a Web API, as shown later in this chapter.

As you'll see in Chapter 10, there's a lot more to the HTTP programming model than simply manipulating the various data elements of requests and responses. Features like message handlers and content negotiation are built directly into the HTTP programming model so that you can take advantage of them on both the client and the server to deliver sophisticated client-server interactions while simultaneously reusing as much of your code as possible.

Flexible Support for Different Formats

Content negotiation will be talked about in much more depth in Chapter 13, but at a high level, it is the process whereby a client and server work together to determine the right format to use when exchanging representations over HTTP. There are several different approaches and techniques for performing content negotiation, and by default, ASP.NET Web API supports the server-driven approach using the HTTP Accept header to let clients choose between XML and JSON. If no Accept header is specified, ASP.NET Web API will return JSON by default (though, like most aspects of the framework, this default behavior can be changed).

For example, consider the following request to an ASP.NET Web API service:

```
GET http://localhost:50650/api/greeting HTTP/1.1
```

Because this request contains no Accept header to provide the server with a desired format, the server will return JSON. We can change this behavior by adding an Accept header to our request and specifying the correct media type identifier for XML:[1]

```
GET http://localhost:50650/api/greeting HTTP/1.1
accept: application/xml
```

No More "Coding with Angle Brackets"

As the .NET Framework has matured, one of the ever-growing complaints from developers has been related to the amount of XML configuration required to enable seemingly basic or even default scenarios. Even worse, because configuration controlled things such as which types should be loaded at runtime, configuration changes could introduce

---

1. The catalog of public media types is maintained by the IANA (*http://bit.ly/iana-types*).

errors into a system that would not be caught by the compiler, but only at runtime. One of the biggest examples of this complaint can be found in ASP.NET Web API's predecessor, WCF. And while WCF itself has improved in the amount of configuration it requires, the ASP.NET Web API team went a totally different direction by introducing an entirely code-based configuration mode. ASP.NET Web API configuration will be discussed at length in Chapter 11.

Unit Testability

As techniques such as test-driven development (TDD) and behavior-driven development (BDD) have become more popular, there has been a proportional increase in frustration with many of the popular service and web frameworks over their use of static context objects, sealed types, and deep inheritance trees. These techniques make unit testing challenging in that objects become difficult to create and initialize in isolation from the underlying runtime; they also are very hard to substitute with a "fake" instance for better testing isolation.

For example, ASP.NET relies heavily on the `HttpContext` object, while WCF similarly relies on `OperationContext` (or `WebOperationContext` depending on the type of service). The fundamental problem with static context objects like these is that they are set up by and rely on their respective framework's runtimes. As a result, testing a service that was developed using these context objects requires actually starting a service host and running the service. And while this technique is generally acceptable for integration-style tests, it is unsuitable for a development style such as TDD, which relies on being able to run smaller unit tests very quickly.

One of the goals in ASP.NET Web API is to provide much-improved support for these kinds of development styles, and there are two characteristics of the framework that accomplish this goal. First, ASP.NET Web API has the same programming model as the MVC framework. This enables it to take advantage of the testability work that was done a few years ago, including abstractions to avoid having to use static context objects and wrappers so that "fake" instances can be supplied to unit tests.

Second, remember that ASP.NET Web API is built around the HTTP programming model. The objects in this model are effectively simple data structures that can be created, configured, passed to an action method as a parameter, and analyzed when returned. This enables unit tests to be authored in a very clean, focused manner. As ASP.NET Web API has evolved, testing has remained a focus area for the team, as evidenced by the `HttpRequestContext` class in Web API 2. Testability will be discussed at greater length in Chapter 17.

Multiple Hosting Options

Despite some of its lesser qualities, one of the greatest attributes of WCF was its ability to "self-host"--that is, its ability to run in any process, for example a Windows service, a console application, or Internet Information Services (IIS). In fact, this kind of hosting flexibility made its limitations in unit testing almost bearable…almost.

When consolidating WCF Web API with ASP.NET to form ASP.NET Web API, the team wanted to keep this self-hosting ability, and so ASP.NET Web API services, like WCF services, can run in whatever process you choose. We'll look at hosting in much greater depth in Chapter 11.

Getting Started with ASP.NET Web API

Now that we've reviewed some of the goals behind the development of ASP.NET Web API, let's dive in and take a look at some of the various elements that you will be working with as you create your own Web APIs. One of the simplest ways to accomplish this is by creating a brand new ASP.NET Web API project and looking at the artifacts that the project template creates. To create a new ASP.NET Web API project, navigate to the Web node in the New Project dialog and select ASP.NET Web Application (Figure 3-1).

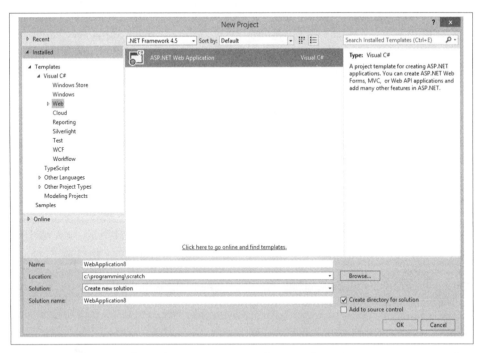

Figure 3-1. MVC 4 Web Application project in the Visual Studio 2012 New Project dialog

Once you choose to create an ASP.NET Web application, you will be presented with an additional dialog that gives you the ability to choose various project configurations. From this dialog, you will see the option to create a Web API project (Figure 3-2).

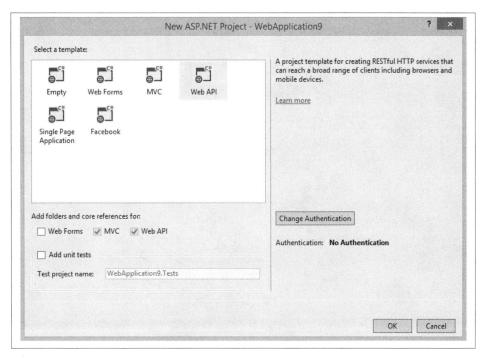

Figure 3-2. Web API project type in the MVC 4 New Project dialog

The key thing to note through this process is that Web API is simply a different project template within the family of ASP.NET projects. This means that Web API projects share all of the same core components as the other web project types, and differ only by the files that the template creates for you as a starting point. It also means that it's both valid and desired to include Web APIs in any of the other templates shown in Figure 3-2.

In fact, at the end of the day, ASP.NET Web API is simply a set of classes built on top of the Web API framework components and hosted by a process, whether it's the ASP.NET runtime as the default template sets up or your own custom host (as we will describe in more detail later in this chapter). This means that a Web API can go into any type of project, whether it's an MVC project, a console application, or a class library that you reference from multiple host projects.

The ASP.NET Framework components are made available to your Web API projects via the NuGet package management application (*http://docs.nuget.org/*). The NuGet packages listed in Table 3-1 are installed by the default project template. To create a Web API in your own project, you simply need to ensure that you've installed the same packages based on the level of functionality that you require.

Table 3-1. NuGet packages for ASP.NET Web API

Package name	Package ID[a]	Description	Package dependencies[b]
Microsoft .NET Framework 4 HTTP Client Libraries	Microsoft.Net.Http	Provides the core HTTP programming model, including `HttpRequestMessage` and `HttpResponsemessage`	(none)
Microsoft ASP.NET Web API	Microsoft.AspNet.WebApi	NuGet meta-package[c] providing a single reference for installing everything needed to create and host a Web API in ASP.NET	Microsoft.AspNet.WebApi.WebHost
Microsoft ASP.NET Web API Client Libraries	Microsoft.AspNet.WebApi.Client	Contains extensions to the core .NET Framework 4 HTTP client libraries to enable features such as XML and JSON formatting as well as the ability to perform content negotiation	Microsoft.Net.Http Newtonsoft.Json[d]
Microsoft ASP.NET Web API Core Libraries	Microsoft.AspNet.WebApi.Core	Contains the core Web API programming model and runtime components including the key `ApiController` class	Microsoft.AspNet.WebApi.Client
Microsoft ASP.NET Web API Web Host	Microsoft.AspNet.WebApi.WebHost	Contains all of the runtime components needed to host a Web API in the ASP.NET runtime	Microsoft.Web.Infrastructure Microsoft.AspNet.WebApi.Core

[a] You can use the package ID to learn more about the package by appending it to the URL ID}.

[b] A NuGet package dependency means that when you install a package, NuGet will first attempt to install all of the packages on which that the package depends.

[c] A NuGet meta-package is a package that contains no actual content of its own, but only dependencies to other NuGet packages.

[d] While used by ASP.NET Web API, Newtonsoft.Json is an external component available for free download (*http://bit.ly/nuget-json*).

In addition to the NuGet packages that are installed as a part of the default project templates, the NuGet packages shown in Table 3-2 are also available.

Table 3-2. Additional NuGet packages available for ASP.NET Web API

Package name	Package ID	Description	Package dependencies
Microsoft ASP.NET Web API Self Host	Microsoft.AspNet.WebApi.SelfHost	Contains all of the runtime components needed to host a Web API in a custom process (e.g., console application)	Microsoft.AspNet.WebApi.Core
Microsoft ASP.NET Web API OWIN	Microsoft.AspNet.WebApi.Owin	Allows you to host ASP.NET Web API within an OWIN server and provides access to additional OWIN features	Microsoft.AspNet.WebApi.Core, Microsoft.Owin, Owin

Looking at the set of NuGet packages as a graph may give you a better understanding of which package or packages to install in your project based on what you are trying to accomplish. For example, consider Figure 3-3.

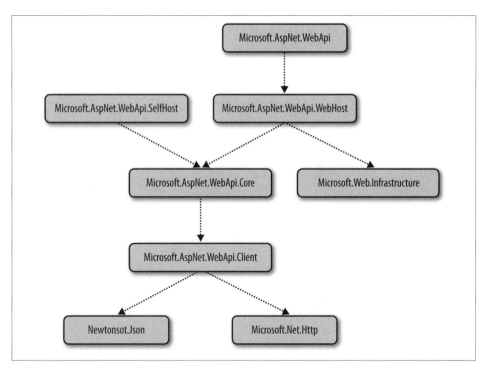

Figure 3-3. NuGet package hierarchy for Web API

As you can see from the dependency graph, installing any one of these NuGet packages will automatically install all of the NuGet packages that are connected, directly or indirectly, to it. For example, installing `Microsoft.AspNet.WebApi` will install `Micro soft.AspNet.WebApi.WebHost`, `Microsoft.AspNet.WebApi.Core`, `Microsoft.Web.In`

frastructure, Microsoft.AspNet.WebApi.Client, Newtonsoft.Json, and Micro
soft.Net.Http.

Exploring a New Web API Project

Now that we've created a new web-hosted ASP.NET Web API project, we'll explore some of the key elements created by the project template, which we will customize in order to create our own Web APIs. We will focus on two key files: *WebApiConfig.cs* and *ValuesController.cs* (Figure 3-4).

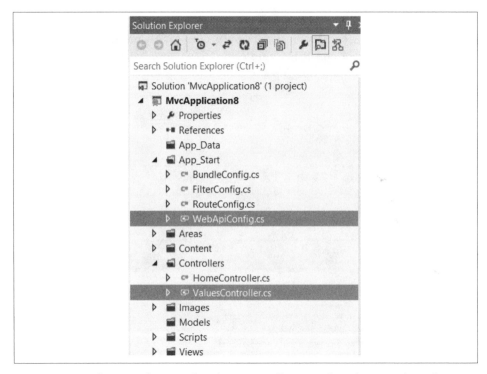

Figure 3-4. WebApiConfig.cs and ValuesController.cs within the Visual Studio 2013 Solution Explorer

WebApiConfig

This C# or Visual Basic.NET file is located in the *App_Start* top-level folder and declares the class WebApiConfig. This class contains a single method called Register and is called by code in the Application_Start method inside of *global.asax*. As its name indicates, the purpose of the class is to register various aspects of Web API's configuration. By default, the primary configuration code generated by the project template registers a default Web API route. This route is used to map inbound HTTP requests onto controller classes as well as parse out data elements that may be sent as a part of the URL and make those available to other classes in the processing pipeline. The default WebApiConfig class is shown in Example 3-1.

Example 3-1. Default WebApiConfig class

```
public static class WebApiConfig
{
    public static void Register(HttpConfiguration config)
    {
        // Web API configuration and services

        // Web API routes
        config.MapHttpAttributeRoutes();

        config.Routes.MapHttpRoute(
            name: "DefaultApi",
            routeTemplate: "api/{controller}/{id}",
            defaults: new { id = RouteParameter.Optional }
        );
    }
}
```

If you are familiar with MVC development, then you may have observed that ASP.NET Web API provides a different set of extension methods to register its routes than the default MVC routes. For example, the very same new project containing the WebApiConfig class also contains the following:

```
public class RouteConfig
{
    public static void RegisterRoutes(RouteCollection routes)
    {
        routes.IgnoreRoute("{resource}.axd/{*pathInfo}");

        routes.MapRoute(
            name: "Default",
            url: "{controller}/{action}/{id}",
            defaults: new { controller = "Home", action = "Index",
                id = UrlParameter.Optional }
        );
    }
}
```

Having two route configuration methods can be confusing on first inspection, so it's worth explaining the high-level differences between them. The point to keep in mind here is that these "Map" methods are simply extension methods that create an instance of a route and add it to the route collection associated with the host. The difference between them, and the subsequent reason behind the two different methods, is in the fact that ASP.NET MVC and ASP.NET Web API use completely different route classes and even route collection types. The details of these types will be discussed in greater detail in Chapter 11, but the reason for breaking away from the routing types used by ASP.NET MVC was to enable ASP.NET Web API to split from much of the legacy that resided alongside the `Route` and `RouteCollection` classes in the `System.Web` assembly, thereby providing a great deal more flexibility in terms of hosting options. An immediate benefit of this design decision is ASP.NET Web API's self-host capability.

Configuring ASP.NET Web API routing requires declaring and adding `HttpRoute` instances to the route collection. Even though `HttpRoute` instances are created with a different extension method than that used for ASP.NET MVC, the semantics are nearly identical, including elements such as route name, route template, parameter defaults, and even route constraints. As you can see in Example 3-1, the project template's route configuration code sets up a default API route that includes a URI prefix of "api" followed by the controller name and an optional ID parameter. Without any modification, this route declaration is typically sufficient for getting started creating APIs that allow for fetching, updating, and deleting data. This is possible because of the way in which ASP.NET Web API's controller class maps HTTP methods onto controller action methods. We'll cover HTTP method mapping in more detail later in this chapter, as well as in much greater detail in Chapter 12.

ValuesController

The `ApiController` class, which is the parent class of `ValuesController`, is at the heart of ASP.NET Web API. While we can create a valid ASP.NET Web API controller by simply implementing the various members of the `IHttpController` interface, in practice we'll create most ASP.NET Web API controllers by deriving from the `ApiController` class. This class plays the role of coordinating with various other classes in the ASP.NET Web API object model to perform a few key tasks in processing an HTTP request:

- Select and run an action method on the controller class.
- Convert elements of an HTTP request message into parameters on a controller action method and convert the return value of an action method into a valid HTTP response body.
- Run various types of filters that have been configured for the action method, the controller, or globally.
- Expose appropriate context state to the action methods of the controller class.

By deriving from `ApiController` and taking advantage of the key processing tasks that it performs, the `ValuesController` class that is included as a part of the Web API template shows the higher-level abstraction that can be built on top of `ApiController`. Example 3-2 shows the `ValuesController` code.

Example 3-2. Default ValuesController class

```
public class ValuesController : ApiController
{
    // GET api/values
    public IEnumerable<string> Get()
    {
        return new string[] { "value1", "value2" };
    }

    // GET api/values/5
    public string Get(int id)
    {
        return "value";
    }

    // POST api/values
    public void Post([FromBody]string value)
    {
    }

    // PUT api/values/5
    public void Put(int id, [FromBody]string value)
    {
    }

    // DELETE api/values/5
    public void Delete(int id)
    {
    }
}
```

The ValuesController class, while simple, provides a helpful first look at the controller programming model.

First, notice the names of the controller's action methods. By default, ASP.NET Web API follows the convention of selecting an action method, in part, by comparing the HTTP method to the action name. More precisely, ApiController looks for a controller action method whose name starts with the appropriate HTTP method. Therefore, in Example 3-2, an HTTP GET request to /api/values will be served by the parameterless Get() method. The framework offers different ways to tailor this default name-matching logic and provides extensibility points, enabling you to replace it entirely if desired. More details on controller and action selection can be found in Chapter 12.

In addition to selecting an action method based on the HTTP method, ASP.NET Web API can select the action based on additional elements of the request, such as query string parameters. More importantly, the framework supports binding these request elements to parameters of the action method. By default, the framework uses a combination of approaches to accomplish parameter binding, and the algorithm supports both simple and complex .NET types. For HTTP responses, the ASP.NET Web API programming model enables action methods to return .NET types and it converts those values into the appropriate HTTP response message body using content negotiation. You can find much more detail on parameter binding and content negotiation in Chapter 13.

At this point, we've discussed some of ASP.NET Web API's design, and we've scratched the surface of the programming model in looking at the code provided as a part of the project template. We'll now go a bit deeper and create our first "Hello World" Web API.

"Hello Web API!"

For our first ASP.NET Web API, we're going to build a simple greeting service. And what greeting is more ubiquitous in programming literature than "Hello World!"? Therefore, we'll start out with this simple read-only greeting API and then add several improvements throughout the remainder of this chapter to illustrate other aspects of ASP.NET Web API's programming model.

Creating the Service

To create the service, simply create a new ASP.NET Web Application from Visual Studio's New Project dialog. From the Web Application Refinement dialog, select Web API. This action will create a new ASP.NET Web API project from the default template.

A read-only greeting service

Starting from the default Web API project template, add a new controller. You can do this by either adding a new class or leveraging the controller item template provided by Visual Studio. To add the controller using the item template, right-click on the *controllers* folder and select the Add → Controller option from the context menu (Figure 3-5).

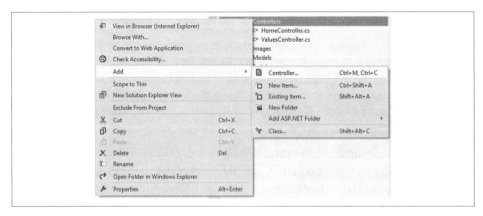

Figure 3-5. Visual Studio context menu for adding a new controller

This will display another dialog from which you'll provide additional configuration details about the controller being created. We are going to create a controller called GreetingController and will use the Empty API controller item template (Figure 3-6).

Figure 3-6. Web API controller scaffolding

Completing the item template dialog will produce a new GreetingController class, which derives from the ApiController class. To have our new API return a simple greeting, we need to add a method capable of responding to an HTTP GET request for the controller. Remember that because of our default routing rule, GreetingControl ler will be selected for an HTTP request, api/greeting. Therefore, let's add a simple method to handle GET requests as follows:

```
public class GreetingController : ApiController
{
    public string GetGreeting() {
        return "Hello World!";
    }
}
```

We can now test our Web API to see that it is in fact returning our simple greeting. For this, we'll use the HTTP debugging proxy tool called Fiddler (*http://www.fiddler2.com/*). One particularly helpful feature of Fiddler when it comes to testing Web APIs is its ability to compose HTTP messages and execute them. We can use this feature to test our greeting API as shown in Figure 3-7.

Figure 3-7. Using Fiddler to compose a new HTTP request

When we execute the request, we can then explore both the request and response using Fiddler's session inspector as shown in Figure 3-8.

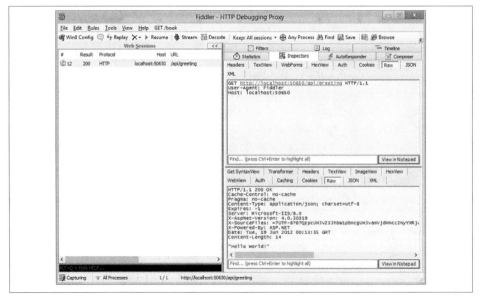

Figure 3-8. Examining HTTP requests and responses using Fiddler

As expected, this basic HTTP GET request to the greeting service returns the simple string "Hello World!"

Content negotiation

Returning to Figure 3-8, take a closer look at the HTTP Content-Type response header. By default, ASP.NET Web API will transform return values from action methods into the JSON format using the popular Json.NET library first referenced in Figure 3-3. However, as described earlier in this chapter, ASP.NET Web API supports server-driven content negotiation, and by default supports content negotiation between JSON and

XML. To see this in action, go back to Fiddler's request composer and add the following line to the request headers text box:

```
accept: application/xml
```

Then execute the request again and notice that the response now contains the header Content-Type: application/xml and the response body is now formatted as XML (Figure 3-9).

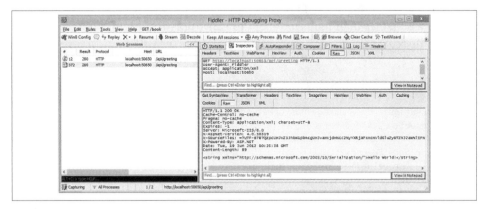

Figure 3-9. The content-negotiated request and response for our basic greeting

Add a greeting

While it's interesting to be able to get a greeting in different formats, any nontrivial API needs the ability to manipulate the state, or the data, of the system. Therefore, we'll extend the greeting service and give clients the ability to add new greetings. The idea is that a client can specify a greeting name and message, add it to the service, and then GET it again later via a URL that includes the greeting name. In addition, we need to handle cases where a client misspells or otherwise incorrectly specifies the greeting name in the URL by returning an HTTP 404 status code indicating that the resource could not be found.

To allow the client to create new greetings on the server, we need to create a model class to hold the greeting message's name and message properties. We accomplish this by adding the following class to the project's *Models* folder:

```
public class Greeting
{
    public string Name    {
        get;
        set;
    }

    public string Message    {
        get;
```

```
      set;
   }
}
```

We then create an action method on the GreetingController, which handles the HTTP POST request and is capable of accepting a Greeting instance as a parameter.

The action adds the greeting to a static list of greetings and returns an HTTP 201 status code along with a Location header pointing to the URL of the newly created greeting resource. The additional location header makes it possible for clients to simply follow the link value rather than requiring them to construct the URL for the new greeting resource, thereby making them more resilient since server URL structures can change over time:

```
public static List<Greeting> _greetings = new List<Greeting>();

public HttpResponseMessage PostGreeting(Greeting greeting) {
    _greetings.Add(greeting);

    var greetingLocation = new Uri(this.Request.RequestUri,
        "greeting/" + greeting.Name);
    var response = this.Request.CreateResponse(HttpStatusCode.Created);
    response.Headers.Location = greetingLocation;

    return response;
}
```

After adding the new greeting to the static collection, we create a URI instance representing the location where the new greeting can be found in subsequent requests. We then create a new HttpResponseMessage using the CreateResponse factory method of the HttpRequestMessage instance provided by the ApiController base class. The ability to work with HTTP object model instances from within action methods is a key feature of ASP.NET Web API; it provides fine-grained control over the HTTP message elements, such as the location header, in a way that does not rely on static context objects like HttpContext or WebOperationContext. This proves particularly beneficial when it comes to writing unit tests for Web API controllers, as we'll discuss next.

Finally, we need to add an overload for the GetGreeting method that is capable of fetching and returning a client-supplied, custom greeting:

```
public string GetGreeting(string id) {
    var greeting = _greetings.FirstOrDefault(g => g.Name == id);
    return greeting.Message;
}
```

This method simply looks up the first greeting where the Name property matches the supplied id parameter and then returns the Message property. It is worth noting that there is currently not any sort of input validation on the id parameter. This will be discussed in the next section.

By default, an HTTP POST body will be handled by a MediaTypeFormatter object that is chosen based on the Content-Type request header. Accordingly, the following HTTP request will be handled by the default JSON formatter, which will use Json.NET to deserialize the JSON string into an instance of the Greeting class:

```
POST http://localhost:50650/api/greeting HTTP/1.1
Host: localhost:50650
Content-Type: application/json
Content-Length: 43

{"Name": "TestGreeting","Message":"Hello!"}
```

This resulting instance can then be passed to the PostGreeting method, where it is added to the collection of greetings. After PostGreeting has processed the request, the client will see the following HTTP response:

```
HTTP/1.1 201 Created
Location: http://localhost:50650/api/greeting/TestGreeting
```

From the location header, the client can then issue a request for the new greeting:

```
GET http://localhost:50650/api/greeting/TestGreeting HTTP/1.1
Host: localhost:50650
```

And, as in the case of our initial read-only greeting service, the client can expect the following response:

```
HTTP/1.1 200 OK
Content-Type: application/json; charset=utf-8
Content-Length: 8

"Hello!"
```

Handling errors

The previous HTTP exchange works wonderfully so long as the server never has any errors and all clients follow the same rules and conventions. However, what happens in the event of a server error or an invalid request? This is another area where the ability to create and work with instances of the HTTP object model proves quite helpful. In Example 3-3, we want the action method to return a greeting's string given its name. However, if the requested greeting name is not found, we want to return a response with the HTTP 404 status code. For this task, ASP.NET Web API provides the HttpRespon seException.

Example 3-3. Returning a 404 status code when a greeting cannot be found

```
public string GetGreeting(string id) {
    var greeting = _greetings.FirstOrDefault(g => g.Name == id);
    if (greeting == null)
        throw new HttpResponseException(HttpStatusCode.NotFound);
```

```
    return greeting.Message;
}
```

While it would have been reasonable to simply return a new `HttpResponseMessage` that included the 404 status code, this would have required always returning an `HttpRes ponseMessage` from the `GetGreeting` action method—unneccessarily overcomplicating the nonexception code path. Additionally, the response message would have needed to flow back through the entire Web API pipeline, which would likely be unnecessary in the case of an exception. For these reasons, we will throw an `HttpResponseExcep tion` rather than return an `HttpResponseMessage` from the action method. In the event that an exception contains a response body that supports content negotiation, you can use the `Request.CreateErrorResponse` method from the base controller class and pass the resulting `HttpResponseMessage` to the `HttpResponseException` constructor.

Testing the API

One additional benefit of working directly with HTTP object model instances rather than static context objects is that it enables you to write meaningful unit tests against your Web API controllers. Testing will be covered in greater depth in Chapter 17, but as an introductory example, let's write a quick unit test for the `GreetingController`'s `PostGreeting` action method:

```
[Fact]
public void TestNewGreetingAdd()
{
    //arrange
    var greetingName = "newgreeting";
    var greetingMessage = "Hello Test!";
    var fakeRequest = new HttpRequestMessage(HttpMethod.Post,
        "http://localhost:9000/api/greeting");
    var greeting = new Greeting { Name =
        greetingName, Message = greetingMessage };

    var service = new GreetingController();
    service.Request = fakeRequest;

    //act
    var response = service.PostGreeting(greeting);

    //assert
    Assert.NotNull(response);
    Assert.Equal(HttpStatusCode.Created, response.StatusCode);
    Assert.Equal(new Uri("http://localhost:9000/api/greeting/newgreeting"),
        response.Headers.Location);
}
```

This test follows the standard *arrange, act, assert* pattern of writing unit tests. We create some control state, including a new `HttpRequestMessage` instance, to represent the entire HTTP request. We then call the method under test using the context and finally process a few assertions about the response. In this case, the response is an instance of HttpResponseMessage, and as a result, we are able to process assertions on data elements of the response itself.

The Client

As mentioned at the beginning of this chapter, one of the other key benefits to building ASP.NET Web API around a core HTTP programming model is the fact that the same programming model can be used to build great HTTP applications for both the server and the client. For example, we can use the following code to construct a request that will be handled by our first GetGreeting action method:

```
class Program
{
    static void Main(string[] args)
    {
        var greetingServiceAddress =
            new Uri("http://localhost:50650/api/greeting");

        var client = new HttpClient();
        var result = client.GetAsync(greetingServiceAddress).Result;
        var greeting = result.Content.ReadAsStringAsync().Result;

        Console.WriteLine(greeting);
    }
}
```

Just like on the server, the client code here creates and processes instances of HttpRequestMessage and HttpResponseMessage. Additionally, ASP.NET Web API extension components, such as media type formatters and message handlers, work for clients as well as servers.

The Host

Developing an ASP.NET Web API for hosting in a traditional ASP.NET application feels very much the same as developing any other ASP.NET MVC application. One of the great characteristics of ASP.NET Web API, however, is that it can be hosted in any process that you designate with hardly any additional work. Example 3-4 shows the code required for hosting our GreetingController in a custom host process (a console application, in this case).

Example 3-4. A simple Web API console host

```
class Program
{
    static void Main(string[] args)
    {
```

```
        var config = new HttpSelfHostConfiguration(
        new Uri("http://localhost:50651"));

        config.Routes.MapHttpRoute(
            name: "DefaultApi",
            routeTemplate: "api/{controller}/{id}",
            defaults: new { id = RouteParameter.Optional });

        var host = new HttpSelfHostServer(config);

        host.OpenAsync().Wait();

        Console.WriteLine("Press any key to exit");
        Console.ReadKey();

        host.CloseAsync().Wait();
    }
}
```

In order to host our Web API in a custom process, we did not modify the controller and we didn't have to add any magical XML in the *app.config* file. Rather, we simply created an instance of `HttpSelfHostConfiguration`, configured it with address and routing information, and then opened the host. Once the host is open and listening for requests, we block the main console thread in order to avoid closing the server. When the user chooses to close the host (by pressing any key), we close the Web API host and exit the console application. Hosting is discussed in greater detail in Chapter 11.

Conclusion

In this chapter, we described some of the key design goals behind ASP.NET Web API. We then used the Web API project template to see how the different components that compose the framework are organized and distributed via NuGet, and also to begin to explore the framework's programming model by looking at the default template code. Finally, we wrote our own "Hello World!" Web API and took advantage of ASP.NET Web API's self-hosting abilities.

The chapters that follow will drill into each of the topics introduced here and provide a great deal more depth, starting with Chapter 4, which explores the underlying mechanics that make the ASP.NET Web API work.

Processing Architecture

And now for something completely different.

The previous chapter presented the core ASP.NET Web API *programming model*, introducing the set of fundamental concepts, interfaces, and classes exposed by this framework. Before we address the book's core subject of designing evolvable Web APIs, this chapter takes a short detour to look under the hood and present the underlying ASP.NET Web API *processing architecture*, detailing what happens between the reception of an HTTP request and the return of the corresponding HTTP response message. It also serves as a road map for the more advanced ASP.NET Web API features that we will be addressing in the third part of this book.

During this chapter we will be using the HTTP request presented in Example 4-1, associated with the controller defined in Example 4-2, as a concrete example to illustrate the runtime behavior of this architecture. The `ProcessesController` contains a `Get` action that returns a representation of all the machine's processes with a given image name. The exemplifying HTTP request is a `GET` on the resource identified by `http://localhost:50650/api/processes?name=explorer`, which represents all the explorer processes currently executing.

Example 4-1. Sample HTTP request message

```
GET http://localhost:50650/api/processes?name=explorer HTTP/1.1
User-Agent: Fiddler
Host: localhost:50650
Accept: application/json
```

Example 4-2. Sample controller

```
public class ProcessesController : ApiController
{
    public ProcessCollectionState Get(string name)
    {
```

```
        if (string.IsNullOrEmpty(name))
        {
            throw new HttpResponseException(HttpStatusCode.NotFound);
        }
        return new ProcessCollectionState
        {
            Processes = Process
                .GetProcessesByName(name)
                .Select(p => new ProcessState(p))
        };
    }
}

public class ProcessState
{
    public int Id { get; set; }
    public string Name { get; set; }
    public double TotalProcessorTimeInMillis { get; set; }
    ...

    public ProcessState() { }
    public ProcessState(Process proc)
    {
        Id = proc.Id;
        Name = proc.ProcessName;
        TotalProcessorTimeInMillis = proc.TotalProcessorTime.TotalMilliseconds;
        ...
    }
}

public class ProcessCollectionState
{
    public IEnumerable<ProcessState> Processes { get; set; }
}
```

The ASP.NET web processing architecture, represented in Figure 4-1, is composed of three layers:

- The *hosting* layer is the interface between Web API and the underlying HTTP stacks.

- The *message handler pipeline* layer can be used for implementing cross-cutting concerns such as logging and caching. However, the introduction of OWIN (*http://owin.org*) (discussed in Chapter 11) moves some of these responsibilties down the stack into OWIN middleware.

- The *controller handling* layer is where controllers and actions are called, parameters are bound and validated, and the HTTP response message is created. Additionally, this layer contains and executes a *filter pipeline*.

Let's delve a bit deeper into each layer.

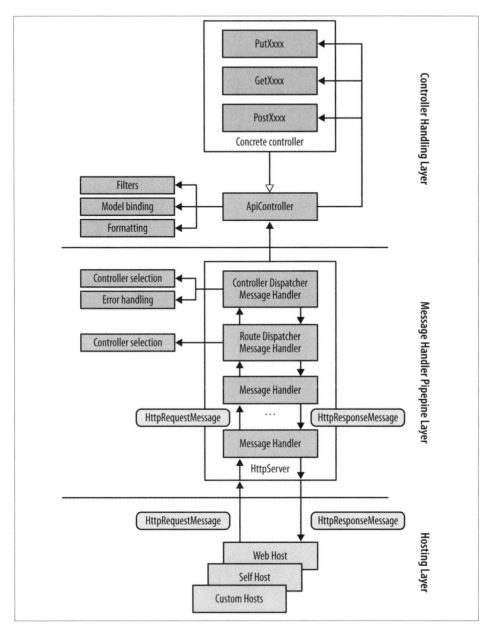

Figure 4-1. Simplified .ASP.NET Web API processing model

The Hosting Layer

The bottom layer in the Web API processing architecture is responsible for the hosting and acts as the interface between Web API and an underlying HTTP infrastructure, such as the classic ASP.NET pipeline, the HttpListener class found in the .NET Framework's System.Net assembly, or an OWIN host. The hosting layer is responsible for creating HttpRequestMessage instances, representing HTTP requests, and then pushing them into the upper message handler pipeline. As part of processing a response, the hosting layer is also responsible for taking an HttpResponseMessage instance returned from the message handler pipeline and transforming it into a response that can be processed by the underlying network stack.

Remember that HttpRequestMessage and HttpResponseMessage are the new classes for representing HTTP messages, introduced in version 4.5 of the .NET Framework. The Web API processing architecture is built around these new classes, and the primary task of the hosting layer is to bridge them and the native message representations used by the underlying HTTP stacks.

At the time of writing, ASP.NET Web API includes several hosting layer alternatives, namely:

- *Self-hosting* in any Windows process (e.g., console application or Windows service)
- *Web hosting* (using the ASP.NET pipeline on top of Internet Information Services (IIS))
- *OWIN hosting* (using an OWIN-compliant server, such as Katana)[1]

The first hosting alternative is implemented on top of WCF's self-hosting capabilities and will be described in Chapter 10 in greater detail.

The second alternative—web hosting—uses the ASP.NET pipeline and its routing capabilities to forward HTTP requests to a new ASP.NET handler, HttpControllerHandler. This handler bridges the classical ASP.NET pipeline and the new ASP.NET Web API architecture by translating the incoming HttpRequest instances into HttpRequestMessage instances and then pushing them into the Web API pipeline. This handler is also responsible for taking the returned HttpResponseMessage instance and copying it into the HttpResponse instance before returning to the underlying ASP.NET pipeline.

Finally, the third hosting option layers Web API on top of an OWIN-compliant server. In this case, the hosting layer translates from the OWIN context objects into a new HttpRequestMessage object sent to Web API. Inversely, it takes the HttpResponseMessage returned by Web API and writes it into the OWIN context.

---

1. OWIN hosting support was introduced in ASP.NET Web API, version 2.

There is a fourth option, which removes the hosting layer entirely: requests are sent directly by `HttpClient`, which uses the same class model, into the Web API runtime without any adaptation. Chapter 11 presents a deeper exploration of the hosting layer.

Message Handler Pipeline

The middle layer of the processing architecture is the *message handler pipeline*. This layer provides an extensibility point for interceptors that addresses cross-cutting concerns such as logging and caching. It is similar in purpose to the middleware concept found in Ruby's Rack (*http://bit.ly/ruby-rack*), Python's WSGI (Web Server Gateway Interface) (*http://bit.ly/pep-3333*), and the Node.js Connect framework (*http:// www.senchalabs.org/connect/*).

A *message handler* is simply an abstraction for an operation that receives an HTTP request message (`HttpRequestMessage` instance) and returns an HTTP response message (`HttpResponseMessage` instance). The ASP.NET Web API message handler pipeline is a composition of these handlers, where each one (except the last) has a reference to the next, called the *inner handler*. This pipeline organization provides a great deal of flexibility in the type of operations that can be performed, as depicted in Figure 4-2.

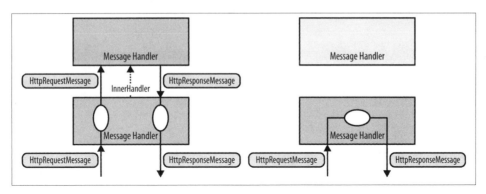

Figure 4-2. Message handler processing examples

The diagram on the left illustrates the usage of a handler to perform some pre- and postprocessing over request and response messages, respectively. Processing flows from handler to handler via the `InnerHandler` relationship—in one direction for request processing and in the reverse direction for response processing. Examples of pre- and postprocessing are:

- Changing the request HTTP method, based on the presence of a header such as `X-HTTP-Method-Override`, before it arrives to the controller's action
- Adding a response header such as `Server`

- Capturing and logging diagnostic or business metric data

You can use handlers to short-circuit the pipeline by directly producing an HTTP response, as shown on the right side of Figure 4-2. A typical use case for this behavior is the immediate return of an HTTP response with a 401 (Unauthorized) status if the request isn't properly authenticated.

In the .NET Framework, message handlers are classes that derive from the new HttpMessageHandler abstract class, as shown in Figure 4-3.

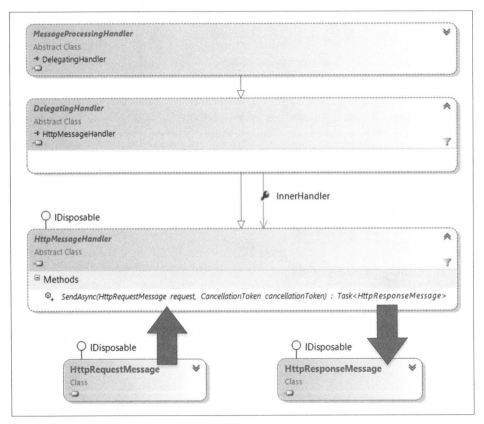

Figure 4-3. Message handler class hierarchy

The abstract SendAsync method receives an HttpRequestMessage and asynchronously produces an HttpResponseMessage by returning Task<HttpResponseMessage>. This method also receives a CancellationToken, following the TAP (Task Asynchronous Pattern) (*http://bit.ly/micro-TAP*) guidelines for cancellable operations.

The message handler pipeline organization just described requires a data member to hold a reference to an inner handler as well as data flow logic to delegate requests and response messages from a handler to its inner handler. These additions are implemented by the `DelegatingHandler` class, which defines the `InnerHandler` property to connect a handler with its inner handler.

The sequence of delegating message handlers that constitute the pipeline is defined in ASP.NET Web API's configuration object model on the `HttpConfiguration.Message Handlers` collection property (e.g., `config.MessageHandlers.Add(new TraceMessage Handler());`). The message handlers are ordered in the pipeline according to the `con fig.MessageHandlers` collection order.

ASP.NET Web API 2.0 introduces support for the OWIN model, providing the OWIN middleware as an alternative to message handlers as a way to implement cross-cutting concerns. The main advantage of OWIN middleware is that it can be used with other web frameworks (e.g., ASP.NET MVC or SignalR), since it isn't tied specifically to Web API. As an example, the new security features introduced in Web API 2.0 and presented in Chapter 15 are mostly implemented as OWIN middleware and reusable outside of Web API. On the other hand, message handlers have the advantage of also being usable on the client side, as described in Chapter 14.

Route Dispatching

At the end of the message handler pipeline, there are always two special handlers:

- The *routing dispatcher* implemented by the `HttpRoutingDispatcher` class
- The *controller dispatcher* implemented by the `HttpControllerDispatcher` class

The *routing dispatcher* handler performs the following:

- Obtains the routing data from the message (e.g., when web hosting is used) or performs the route resolution if it wasn't performed previously (e.g., when self-hosting is used). If no route was matched, it produces a response message with the `404 Not Found` HTTP status code.
- Uses the route data to select the next handler to which to forward the request, based on the matched `IHttpRoute`.

The *controller dispatcher* handler is responsible for:

- Using the route data and a *controller selector* to obtain a *controller description*. If no controller description is found, a response message with the `404 Not Found` status code is returned.

- Obtaining the controller instance and calling its `ExecuteAsync` method, passing the request message.
- Handling exceptions returned by the controller and converting them into response messages with a `500 Internal Error` status code.

For instance, using the HTTP request of Example 4-1 and the default route configuration, the route data will contain only one entry with the `controller` key and `process es` value. This single route data entry is the result of matching the *http://localhost:50650/api/processes?name=explorer* request URI with the `/api/{controller}/{id}` route template.

By default, the *routing dispatcher* forwards the request message to the *controller dispatcher*, which then calls the controller. However, it is possible to explicitly define a per-route handler, as shown in Figure 4-4.

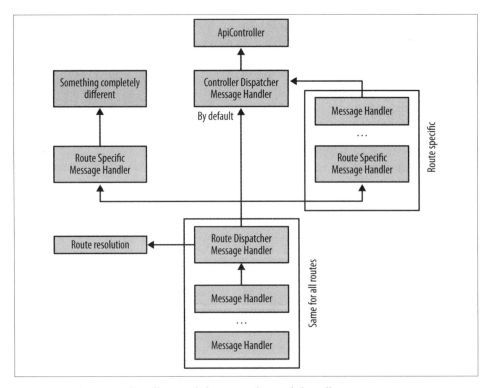

Figure 4-4. Per-route handlers and the route dispatch handler

In this case, the request is forwarded to the handler defined by the route, not to the default controller dispatcher. Reasons for using per-route dispatching include flowing the request message through a route-specific handler pipeline. A concrete example is the use of distinct authentication methods, implemented in message handlers, for different routes. Another reason for using per-route dispatching is the substitution of an alternative framework for the Web API top layer (controller handling).

Controller Handling

The final and uppermost layer in the processing architecture is the controller handling. This layer is responsible for receiving a request message from the underlying pipeline and transforming it into a call to a controller's action method, passing the required method parameters. It also is responsibile for converting the method's return value into a response message and passing it back to the message handler pipeline.

Bridging the message handler pipeline and the controller handling is performed by the *controller dispatcher*, which is still a message handler. Its main task is to select, create, and call the correct controller to handle a request. This process is detailed in Chapter 12, which presents all the relevant classes and shows how you can change the default behavior using the available extensibility points.

The ApiController Base Class

The concrete controller that ultimately handles the request can directly implement the IHttpController interface. However, the common scenario, as presented in the previous chapter, is for the concrete controller to derive from the abstract ApiController class, as shown in Figure 4-5.

It is the job of ApiController.ExecuteAsync to select the appropriate action, given the HTTP request method (e.g., GET or POST), and call the associated method on the derived concrete controller. For instance, the GET request in Example 4-1 will be dispatched to the ProcessesController.Get(string name) method.

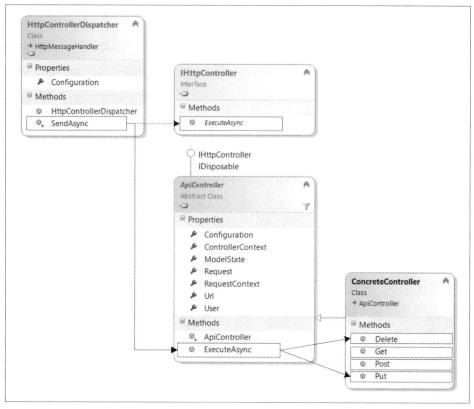

Figure 4-5. Concrete controller deriving from the abstract ApiController class

After the action is selected but before the method is invoked, the `ApiController` class executes a *filter pipeline*, as shown in Figure 4-6. Each action has its own pipeline composed of the following functionalities:

- Parameter binding
- Conversion from the action's return into an `HttpResponseMessage`
- Authentication, authorization, and action filters
- Exception filters

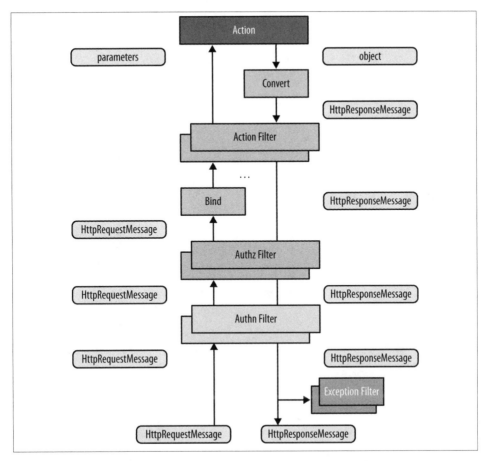

Figure 4-6. Per-action filter pipeline, parameter binding, and result conversions

Parameter binding

Parameter binding is the computation of the action's parameter values, used when calling the action's method. This process is illustrated in Figure 4-7 and uses information from several sources, namely:

- The route data (e.g., route parameters)
- The request URI query string
- The request body
- The request headers

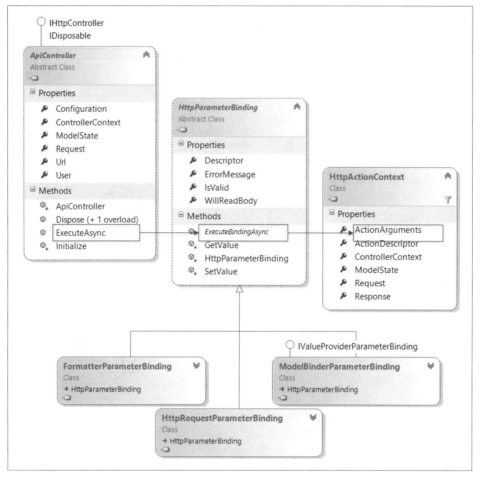

Figure 4-7. Parameter binding

When executing the action's pipeline, the `ApiController.ExecuteAsync` method calls a sequence of `HttpParameterBinding` instances, where each one is associated with one of the action's method parameters. Each `HttpParameterBinding` instance computes the value of one parameter and adds it to the `ActionArguments` dictionary in the `HttpAc tionContext` instance.

`HttpParameterBinding` is an abstract class with multiple derived concrete classes, one for each type of parameter binding. For instance, the `FormatterParameterBinding` class uses the request body content and a *formatter* to obtain the parameter value.

Formatters are classes that extend the abstract `MediaTypeFormatter` class and perform bidirectional conversions between CLR (Common Language Runtime) types and byte stream representations, as defined by *Internet media types* (*http://bit.ly/iana-types*). Figure 4-8 illustrates the functionality of these formatters.

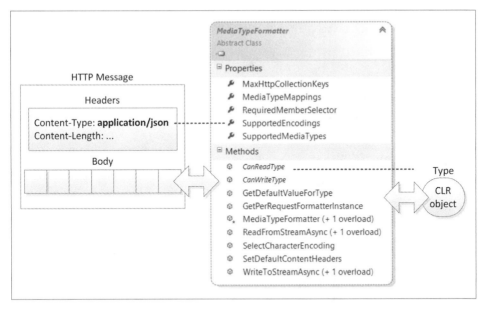

Figure 4-8. Formatters and conversions between message bodies and CLR objects

A different kind of parameter binding is the `ModelBinderParameterBinding` class, which instead uses the concept of model binders to fetch information from the route data, in a manner similar to ASP.NET MVC. For instance, consider the action in Example 4-2 and the HTTP request in Example 4-1: the `name` parameter in the `GET` method will be bound to the value `explorer`—that is, the value for the query string entry with `name` key. We'll provide more detail on formatters, model binding, and validation in Chapter 13.

Conversion into an HttpResponseMessage

After the action method ends and before the result is returned to the filter pipeline, the action result, which can be *any* object, must be converted into an `HttpResponseMes sage`. If the return type is assignable to the `IHttpActionResult` interface[2] (presented in Example 4-3), then the result's `ExecuteAsync` method is called to convert it into a response message. There are several implementations of this interface, such as `OkRe sult` and `RedirectResult`, that can be used in the action's code. The `ApiController` base class also includes several protected methods (not shown in Figure 4-5) that can

---

2. The `IHttpActionResult` interface was introduced in version 2.0 of Web API.

be used by derived classes to construct `IHttpActionResult` implementations (e.g., `protected internal virtual OkResult Ok()`).

Example 4-3. The IHttpActionResult interface

```
public interface IHttpActionResult
{
    Task<HttpResponseMessage> ExecuteAsync(CancellationToken cancellationToken);
}
```

If the return isn't a `IHttpActionResult`, then an external *result converter*, implementing the `IActionResultConverter` interface as defined in Example 4-4, is selected and used to produce the response message.

Example 4-4. Result converters: Converting the action's return into response messages

```
public interface IActionResultConverter
{
    HttpResponseMessage Convert(
        HttpControllerContext controllerContext,
        object actionResult);
}
```

For the HTTP request in Example 4-1, the selected result converter will try to locate a formatter that can read a `ProcessCollectionState` (i.e., the type returned by the action's method), and produce a byte stream representation of it in `application/json` (i.e., the value of the request's `Accept` header). In the end, the resulting response is the one presented in Example 4-5.

Example 4-5. HTTP response

```
HTTP/1.1 200 OK
Cache-Control: no-cache
Pragma: no-cache
Content-Type: application/json; charset=utf-8
Expires: -1
Server: Microsoft-IIS/8.0
Date: Thu, 25 Apr 2013 11:50:12 GMT
Content-Length: (...)

{"Processes":[{"Id":2824,"Name":"explorer",
"TotalProcessorTimeInMillis":831656.9311}]}
```

Formatters and content negotiation are addressed in more detail in Chapter 13.

Filters

Authentication, authorizations, and action filters are defined by the interfaces listed in Example 4-6, and have a role similar to message handlers—namely, to implement cross-cutting concerns (e.g., authentication, authorization, and validation).

Example 4-6. Filter interfaces

```
public interface IFilter
{
    bool AllowMultiple { get; }
}

public interface IAuthenticationFilter : IFilter
{
    Task AuthenticateAsync(
        HttpAuthenticationContext context,
        CancellationToken cancellationToken);

    Task ChallengeAsync(
        HttpAuthenticationChallengeContext context,
        CancellationToken cancellationToken);
}

public interface IAuthorizationFilter : IFilter
{
    Task<HttpResponseMessage> ExecuteAuthorizationFilterAsync(
        HttpActionContext actionContext,
        CancellationToken cancellationToken,
        Func<Task<HttpResponseMessage>> continuation);
}

public interface IActionFilter : IFilter
{
    Task<HttpResponseMessage> ExecuteActionFilterAsync(
        HttpActionContext actionContext,
        CancellationToken cancellationToken,
        Func<Task<HttpResponseMessage>> continuation);
}

public interface IExceptionFilter : IFilter
{
    Task ExecuteExceptionFilterAsync(
        HttpActionExecutedContext actionExecutedContext,
        CancellationToken cancellationToken);
}
```

For authorization and action filters, the pipeline is organized similarly to the message handler pipeline: each filter receives a reference to the next one in the pipeline and has the ability to perform pre- and postprocessing over the request and the response. Alternatively, the filter can produce a new response and end the request immediately, thereby short-circuiting any further processing (namely, the action's invocation). Authentication filters operate under a slightly different model, as we will see in Chapter 15.

The main difference between authorization and action filters is that the former are located before parameter binding takes place, whereas the latter are located after this binding. As a result, authorization filters are an adequate extension point to insert operations that should be performed as early in the pipeline as possible. The typical example is verifying if the request is authorized and immediately producing a 401 (Not authorized) HTTP response message if it is not. On the other hand, action filters are appropriate when access to the bound parameters is required.

A fourth filter type, exception filters, is used only if the Task<HttpResponseMessage> returned by the filter pipeline is in the faulted state; that is, there was an exception. Each exception filter is called in sequence and has the chance to handle the exception by creating an HttpResponseMessage. Recall that if the controller dispatcher handler receives an unhandled exception, an HTTP response message with a status code of 500 (Internal Server Error) is returned.

We can associate filters to controllers or actions in multiple ways:

- Via attributes, similarly to what is supported by ASP.NET MVC
- By explicitly registering filter instances in the configuration object, using the HttpConfiguration.Filters collection
- By registering IFilterProvider implementation in the configuration service's container

After the HttpResponseMessage instance has left the action pipeline, it is returned by ApiController to the controller dispatcher handler. Then it descends through the message handler pipeline until it is converted into a native HTTP response by the hosting layer.

Conclusion

This chapter concludes the first part of the book, the aim of which was to introduce ASP.NET Web API, the motivation behind its existence, its basic programming model, and its core processing architecture. Using this knowledge, we will shift focus in the next part to the design, implementation, and consumption of evolvable Web APIs, using ASP.NET Web API as the supporting platform.

CHAPTER 5

The Application

Evolve or die.

Up to this point we have discussed the tools that you can use to build Web APIs. We have discussed the fundamentals of the HTTP protocol, the basics of using ASP.NET Web API, and how the architectural pieces fit together. This is essential knowledge, but not the only objective of this book. This book is also about how to build *evolvable* Web APIs. This chapter is where we begin to talk about how to create a Web API that can evolve over a period of years—a long enough span of time that business concerns and technology will change.

Rather than discuss the issues in abstract scenarios, we will walk the walk and build an API that demonstrates the concepts we wish to convey. This API will concern a domain that should be familiar to every developer and is sufficiently realistic that it could be adopted in real-world scenarios.

Before delving into the details of the domain, we must ensure that evolvability is something we are truly prepared to pay for. It does not come for free. In order to achieve evolvability, where appropriate, we will apply the constraints of the REST architectural style. It is critical to recognize that we are not attempting to create a "RESTful API." REST is not the objective, but rather a means to an end. It is quite possible that we will choose to violate some of the REST constraints in certain scenarios. Once you understand the value and costs of an architectural constraint, you can make an informed decision about whether that constraint should be applied to achieve your goal. Evolvability is *our* goal.

Before we can begin designing our Web API, we need to define the building blocks for our application domain. This is part of the process that is so often ignored when people attempt to build distributed systems today. When you are building a classic browser-based application, the solution architecture is largely already defined. HTTP, HTML pages, CSS, and JavaScript all form the components of the solution. However, with a

Web API, you are no longer constrained by the choices of the web browser. A web browser may be only one of many different client components in the distributed system.

With the building blocks defined, Chapter 7 will provide a sample API that assembles these components into a Web API. These component pieces will be essential knowledge for building a client application in Chapter 8. By defining the reusable components independently of the API, we can build the client with the capability to interact with these components without needing to know the precise shape of the Web API. Hypermedia will allow the client to discover the shape of the API and adapt to changes as it evolves.

Why Evolvable?

What exactly do we mean by an *evolvable* API? To an extent, *evolve* is just a fancy word for change. However, evolution implies a continuous set of small changes that can, over many iterations, cause the end solution to look unrecognizable to the starting point.

There are a variety of ways that a Web API may need to evolve over the course of its life:

- Individual resources may need to hold more or less information.
- The way individual pieces of information are represented may change. A name or a data type may be changed.
- Relationships between resources can be added, can be removed, or can have their cardinality changed.
- Completely new resources may be added to represent new information in the API.
- Resources may need new representations to support different types of clients.
- New resources may be created to provide access to information with a finer or coarser granularity.
- The flow of processes supported by the API may change.

For many years, the software development industry attempted to follow the lead of more traditional engineering practices when it came to managing change. Conventional wisdom stated that change early in a product's development was many times less expensive than a change that occurred at later stages in its development. The solution was often to strictly manage change and attempt to limit it by performing extensive up-front planning and design work. In recent years, the rise of agile software development practices has taken us on a different path, where change is accepted as part of the process. Embracing change in small iterations allows a software system to evolve to meet the needs of its users. It is not uncommon to hear of websites that release new versions of their software many times a day.

However, with Web APIs, where the plan is to allow external teams to develop their own software to consume the API, our industry has regressed to its old habits. Very often the mindset is that we need to plan and design the API so we can get it right, because if we make changes to the API that break the software, our customers will be unhappy. There are many examples of well-known API developers who have introduced a v2 API that required client applications to do lots of rework to migrate to the new version.

SOAP is Honest at Least

For all of the problems that people have had with SOAP-based solutions, it was at least honest in trying to control and manage change. SOAP was explicit in defining a precise contract between the consumer and provider of the API. It is the *waterfall* approach to integration. Do the work up front so that you can avoid change. This is in contrast to the many examples today of people developing systems under the banner of REST, hoping that it has some magical properties that make managing change easy. Unfortunately, they are just deferring the pain.

Barriers to Evolution

There are a few factors that impact the difficulty of dealing with change. One of the biggest factors is who is impacted by the change. It is very common for the consumers of the API to be a different team than the producers of the API. In addition, the consuming team often belongs to a different company than the producing team. In fact, it is likely that there are many consumers from many different companies. Implementing a breaking change can make lots of customers unhappy.

Even when consumer and producer applications are managed by the same team, there can be constraints that prevent the client and server from being deployed simultaneously. When client code is deployed onto a large number of clients, it can be tricky to synchronize the updates of clients and servers. When clients are installed on locked-down machines, there can be additional complications. Sometimes forcing client updates just creates a bad user experience. If a user wishes to use a client application but before he can he must apply an update, he might get frustrated. Most popular auto-updating client software applications download new versions in the background while they are running and apply on the next restart. This requires the server software to be able to continue to support the old version of the client for at least a short period of time.

One of the challenging things about changing software is that some changes are really easy and have a very low impact, whereas other changes can affect many parts of the system significantly. Identifying what kind of change you are trying to perform is critical. Ideally, we should be able to compartmentalize our software so that we can separate the pieces that can be changed with minimal impact from those that have the potential for significant impact. As a simple example, consider making a change to the HTML specification versus adding a new page to a website. Changing HTML might require everyone to update their web browser, which is a mammoth endeavor, while adding a new web page to a site will not have any impact on web browsers. The web architecture has intentionally made this division to allow the world of websites (servers) to evolve without users having to continually update the web browser (clients).

Change needs to be managed. It requires control and coordination. Any steps we can take to facilitate change over the long term will easily pay for themselves many times over. However, building evolvable systems is not free. There are definitely costs involved.

What Is the Cost?

In order to achieve evolvability, the REST constraints prevent our client applications from making certain assumptions. We cannot allow the client to know in advance about the resources that are available on the server. They must be discovered at runtime based on a single entry point URL.

Once the client has discovered the URL for a resource, it cannot make any assumptions about what types of representations might be returned. The client must use metadata returned in the response to identify the type of information that is being returned.

These limitations require building clients that are far more dynamic than a traditional client/server client. Clients must do a form of "feature detection" to determine what is possible, and they must be reactive to the responses that are returned.

A simple example of this is a server API that returns an invoice. Assuming a client knows how to render plain-text, HTML, and PDF documents, it is not necessary for the server to define in advance what format it will return. Maybe in the first version of the software a simple plain-text invoice is returned. Newer versions of the server might implement the ability to return the invoice as HTML. As long as a mechanism exists to allow the client to parse the response and identify the returned type, the client can continue working unchanged. This notion of messages that contain metadata that identifies the content of the message is called *self-descriptive messaging*.

Additionally, when defining API specifications you should specify the minimum detail necessary, not every detail. Apply Einstein's wisdom of "Everything should be as simple as possible, but not simpler." Overconstraining an API will increase the chances of change impacting larger parts of the system.

Examples of overspecifying include:

- Requiring pieces of data to be provided in a certain order, when the order is not important to the semantics of the message
- Considering data as required when it is needed only under certain contexts

- Constraining interactions to specific serializations of platform-defined types

The following two sidebars describe real-life scenarios that demonstrate how being overly prescriptive can have a negative impact on the outcome.

The Wedding Photographer

In this real-world scenario, you'll see how contracts can be written to adapt to change. Compare the following two sets of instructions from contracts provided by a bride to her wedding photographer:

1. We would like to have the following photos:

   - Bride in and outside church

   - Bride and groom on church steps

   - Bride and groom by large oak tree in front of church

   - Bride with bridesmaids in front of duck pond

   - Groom and best man by the limo

2. We would like some photos that can be given to family members with us and their relatives. We also would like other, more personal photos for us to decorate our house. We would like some photos to be black and white to fit the decor of our living room. We prefer more outdoor photos than indoor.

The contracts differ in that the first is very prescriptive but provides no explanation of intent. The second is more flexible but still ensures that the customer's needs are met. It allows the photographer more creative freedom, which will help him adapt when the wedding day comes and he finds the large oak tree has been chopped down, or the limo is parked on a busy street where background traffic cannot be avoided.

In the following example, instead of simply stifling creativity and producing an inferior product, the result completely fails to satisfy the original requirements.

The Will with Intent

Change is inevitable, and making precise decisions today may invalidate them in the future when circumstances change. Consider the mother of four who is writing her will. She loves her children dearly and wishes to help provide for them when she passes, as none of them are particularly comfortable financially. Unfortunately, Johnny has a gambling problem and she does not want to throw money away. She chooses to write Johnny out of the will and distribute her wealth evenly among the other three. Sadly, she has a stroke and falls into a coma for several years before passing away. In that time, Johnny quits gambling and starts to clean up his act. Billy wins $10 million in the lottery and becomes estranged from his family. Jimmy loses his job and is struggling to make ends meet. The will specified by the mother no longer satisfies her intent. Her intent was to use her money to help her children as best as possible. Billy doesn't need the money, but Johnny could really use it to help him get back on his feet. But the will is very precise on how the money should be shared. By choosing wording that would provide more flexibility to the executor of the will to meet her intent, the mother could have made a significantly different impact.

We often see similar results in software project management, where customers and business analysts try to use requirements to precisely define their envisioned solution, instead of capturing their true intent and letting the software professionals do what they do best. The contracts we use when building distributed systems must capture the intent of our business partners if they are going to survive over the long term.

The combination of runtime discovery, self-descriptive messaging, and reactive clients is not the easiest concept to grasp or implement, but it is a critical component of evolvable systems and brings flexibility that far outweighs the costs.

Why Not Just Version?

The traditional approach to dealing with breaking changes in APIs is to use the notion of versioning.

From the perspective of developing evolvable systems, it is useful to consider versioning as a last resort, an admission of failure. Assigning a v1 to your initial API is a proclamation that you already know it cannot evolve and you will need to make breaking changes in your v2. However, sometimes we do get it wrong. Versioning is what we do when we have exhausted all other options.

The techniques discussed in this book are to help you avoid the need to create versions of your API. However, if and when you do need to version some piece of your API, try to limit the scope of that declaration of failure.

Do not interpret this guidance as saying you must do "big design up front" and get everything right the first time. The intent is to encourage an attitude of minimalism. Don't specify what you don't need to; don't create resources you don't need. Evolvable APIs are designed to change so that when you identify new things that must be added you can do it with minimum effort.

Versioning involves associating an identifier to a snapshot of an API, or some part of an API. If changes occur to the API, then a new identifier is assigned. Version numbers enable coordination between client and server so that a client can identify whether it can communicate with the server. Ideas like semantic versioning have created ways to distinguish between changes that are breaking and those that are nonbreaking. There are several ways to use versioning within evolvable systems with varying degrees of impact severity.

Versioning can be done:

- Within the payload (e.g., XML, HTML)
- With the payload type (e.g., `application/vnd.acme.foo.v2+xml`)
- At the beginning of the URL (e.g., */v2/api/foo/bar*)
- At the end of the URL (e.g., */api/foo/bar.v2*)

What Changes Are Considered Breaking?

It would make life really easy if we could classify API changes into *breaking* and *nonbreaking* buckets. Unfortunately, context plays a large role in the process. A breaking change is one that impacts the *contract*, but without any hard and fast rules of what API contracts look like, we are no further ahead. In the REST architectural style, contracts are defined by media type and link relations, so changes that don't affect either of these should be considered nonbreaking, and changes that do affect these specifications may or may not be breaking.

Payload-based versioning

One of the most important characteristics of the web architecture is that it promotes the concept of payload format into a first-class architectural concept. In the world of RPC, parameters are simply an artifact of the procedural signature and do not stand alone. An example of this is HTML. HTML is a largely self-contained specification that describes the structure of a document. The specification has evolved hugely over the years. The HTML-based Web does not use URI-based versioning or media type versioning. However, the HTML document does contain metadata to assist the parser in interpreting the meaning of the document. This type of versioning helps to limit the impact of version changes to the media type parser codebase. Parsers can be created to support different versions of wire formats, making support for older document formats fairly easy. It remains a challenge to ensure that new document formats don't break old parsers.

Versioning the media type

In recent years, the idea of versioning the media type identifier has become popular. One advantage of this approach is that a user agent can use the `Accept` header to declare which versions of the media type it supports. With well-behaving clients you can introduce breaking changes into a media type without breaking existing clients. The existing clients continue asking for the old version of the media type, and new clients can ask for the new version.

Opaque Identifier

From the perspective of HTTP, what is being done is not really versioning at all—it is simply creating a brand new media type. As far as HTTP is concerned, media type identifiers are opaque strings, so no meaning should be inferred from the characters in the string. So, in effect, `application/vnd.acme.foo` is no more related to `application/vnd.acme.foo.v2` as it is to `text/plain`. The identifiers are different; therefore, the media types are different. The fact that the parsing library for the two versions might be 99% similar is an implementation detail.

A downside to using media types to version is that it exacerbates one of the existing problems with server-driven negotiation. It is not unlikely that a service may use many different media types to expose a wide variety of content. Requiring that a client declare, on every request, all of the media types that it is capable of rendering adds a significant amount of overhead to each request. Adding versions into the mix compounds that problem. If a client supports v1,v2, and v3 of a particular media type, should all of them be included in an `Accept` header in case the server is only capable of rendering an old version? Some user agents have started to take the approach where they only send a subset of media types in the `Accept` header, depending on the link relation being accessed. This does help reduce the size of the `Accept` header, but it introduces an additional complexity where the user agent must be able to correlate link relations to appropriate media types.

Versioning in the URL

Versioning in the URL is probably the most commonly seen approach in public APIs. To be more precise, it is very common to put a version number in the first segment of a URL (e.g., *http://example.org/v2/customers/34*). It is also the approach most heavily criticized by REST practitioners. The objection is usually related to the fact that by adding URLs with a new version number, you are implicitly creating a duplicate set of resources with the new version number while many of those resources may not have changed at all. If URLs have previously been shared, then those URLs will point to the old version of the resource rather than the new version. The challenge is that sometimes this is the desired behavior and other times it is not. If a client is capable of consuming the new version, it would prefer the new one instead of the old version that it bookmarked. If the resource with the new version is actually identical to old version, then it introduces a new problem where there are two distinct URLs for the same resource. This has numerous downsides when you are trying to take advantage of HTTP caching.

Caches end up storing multiple copies of the same resource, and cache invalidation becomes ineffective.

An alternative approach to URL versioning is appending the version number near the end of the URL (e.g., *http://example.org/customer/v2/34*). This allows individual resources to be versioned independently within an API and eliminates the problem of creating duplicate URLs for identical resources. Clients that construct URLs have a much more difficult time consuming this type of versioned URL, because it is not as simple as just changing the first path segment in all request URLs. Hypermedia-driven clients can't even take advantage of this type of versioning because URIs are opaque to them. New resource versions must be identified via a versioned link relation to be accessible to this type of client.

Versioning of APIs is a difficult topic that has many pitfalls. Making the effort to avoid versioning as much as possible will likely provide many long-term benefits.

Walking the Walk

So far in this chapter, we have discussed in general the pros and cons to developing evolvable applications. At many points in the development of an evolvable distributed application, you'll have choices to make and the right answer is frequently "it depends." There is no way, in any reasonable number of pages, to consider every possibility and every outcome; however, there is value in demonstrating a particular set of choices to a particular set of circumstances. In the remainder of the chapter, we will focus on a specific application that presents common challenges, and we will consider the options and make a decision. In no way are we suggesting the choices we will make in the following chapters are the best for every scenario, but they should be illustrative of the types of decisions and choices that you will need to make while building an evolvable API.

Application Objectives

It is always challenging to pick a domain for a sample application for demonstration purposes. It should be realistic but not to the point of getting bogged down in domain details. It should be complex enough to provide a wide range of scenarios but not so large that the architectural guidance gets lost in the implementation details. To eliminate the need for you to learn domain specifics, we chose a domain that software developers are already familiar with: issue tracking. It is an area in which we have all seen a variety of implementations of both client and server. It is naturally distributed because its primary focus is communicating and sharing information among different team members. There are many use cases that surround the lifecycle of an issue. There are many different types of issues that have their own set of distinct states. Issues have a wide variety of metadata associated with them.

Goals

We want to define the types of information that we believe fall within the domain of issue tracking. We wish to:

- Define the minimal set of information required to represent an issue.
- Define a core set of information that is commonly associated with issues.
- Identify relationships between the information in our system.
- Examine the lifecycle of an issue.
- Identify the behavior associated with an issue.
- Classify the types of aggregations, filtering, and statistics that are done on issues.

This is not an attempt to exhaustively define the ultimate, all-encompassing issue schema. Our objective is not to define functionality for every possible scenario in the domain of issue tracking, but to identify a common set of information and terminology that delivers value to people who wish to build some form of issue tracking application, without limiting the scope of those applications. What we are defining will evolve.

When you look at different applications that attempt to address the same domain, you will often find they have taken slightly different approaches to the same problem. We are looking to identify those differences where it doesn't matter which option is chosen; let's just pick one, or enable both. When we eventually distill this domain down into media type specifications, link relations, and semantic profiles, we should be left with a common ground that enables a degree of interoperability without limiting individual applications from providing unique features.

Opportunity

The domain of issue tracking is ripe for improvement. There are dozens of commercial and open source applications that address this domain, and yet they all use proprietary formats for interacting between server and client components. Issue data is locked in proprietary data stores that are tied to the application that created that data. We are limited to using client tools that were designed specifically for a particular issue data store. Why can't I use my favorite issue management client to manage both the work items defined in my Bitbucket repositories and in my GitHub repositories? Why do I even need multiple stores? No one ever considered writing a web browser that is specific to Apache or IIS, so why do we insist on coupling client and server applications in other domains that are focused on distributed data?

Unfortunately, the type of sharing and reuse that the web architecture enables through the reuse of standard media types does not appear to be in the best interests of commercial organizations. Usually, it requires open source efforts to get the initial momentum going before commercial organizations take notice and realize that integration and interoperability can actually be major benefits to commercial software.

Information Model

Before we can begin to develop web artifacts like media types, link relations, or semantic profiles, we must have a clearer understanding of the semantics that we need to communicate across the Web.

At its most basic, an issue could be described in just a short string of text. For example, "The application fails when clicking on button X in screen Y." Additionally, it is often desirable to include a more detailed description of the issue.

Consider the following extremely simple definition:

```
Issue
  Title
  Description (Optional)
```

This definition is potentially sufficient for someone to take this issue and resolve it. Although the issue contains no information about who created it or when, it is possible to capture that information from available ambient information when the request to create the issue is made. Having this extremely minimalist representation of an issue provides a very low barrier of entry that can later be evolved. It is good for getting a working application for demo purposes, and it is also useful for low-power clients like phones. There is nothing to stop someone from later using a more powerful client to fill in additional data.

Subdomains

Before charging ahead and implementing this minimal representation, let's get a better understanding of the larger set of data that can be associated with an issue. For organizational purposes I have broken down the information into four subdomains: descriptive, categorization, current state, and historical.

Descriptive

The descriptive subdomain includes the information we already discussed such as title and description, but also environmental information, such as software version, host operating system, hardware specifications, steps to reproduce, and screen captures. Any information used to provide precision about the situation that produced the issue will fall into this subdomain. One important characteristic of this information is that it is primarily just human readable. It does not tend to affect the issue workflow or impact any kind of algorithms.

Categorization

These pieces of information are used to help deal with sets of issues in meaningful groups. Attributes that belong to a certain predefined domain of values can be attached to an issue for the purpose of classifying issues for processing. Examples of this type of information include priority, severity, software module, application area, and issue type (defect, feature, etc). This information is used for searching, filtering, and grouping and is often used to dictate application workflow. Generally, this information is specified early on in the issue lifecycle and does not change unless information was specified erroneously.

Current state

An issue will generally have a set of attributes that define its current state. This includes information such as the current workflow state, the person actively assigned to the issue, hours remaining, and percent complete. This information will change numerous times over the life of an issue. It can also be used as classification attributes. The current state of an issue may also be annotated with textual comments.

Historical

Historical information is usually a record of an issue's current state at a prior point in time. This information is generally not important for the processing of the issue, but may be useful for analytics of past issues, or investigating the history of an individual issue.

Related Resources

All of these information attributes that we mentioned will likely be represented in one of two ways—either by a simple serialization of the native data type (e.g., strings, dates, Boolean), or via an identifier that represents another resource. For example, for identifying the people who are involved, we might have `IssueFoundBy` and `IssueResolvedby`.

We could simply include a string value, but it would be much more valuable to have a resource identifier, as it is likely that the users of the issue tracking system would be exposed as resources. The natural choice for a resource identifier is a URL. By using a URL, we give the client software the opportunity to discover additional information about the person involved by dereferencing the URL. This separation of issue attributes and person attributes into two distinct resources is useful also because the information contained in those two resources has very different lifetimes. The volatility of the data is different and therefore will likely have a different caching strategy.

It is likely that we will not want to display a URL to a human who is viewing the issue representation. We address this by way of a link. Usually, we do not embed URLs directly into representations, as there is often other metadata that is associated with the URL. A

Link is a URL with its associated metadata, and one standardized piece of metadata is a Title attribute. The Title attribute is intended to provide a human-readable version of the URL. This gives us the best of both worlds: an embedded, human-readable description and a URL that points to a distinct resource that contains additional information about the related person.

Here is an example of a related resource:

```
<resource>
    <Title>App blows up</Title>
    <Description>Pressing three buttons at once causes crash</Description>
        <links>
                <Link    rel="IssueFoundBy"
                            title="Found by"
                            href="http://example.org/api/user/bob"/>
        </links>
</resource>
```

Attribute Groups

Sometimes it is useful to group attributes together. This can help to make a representation easier to read. The groups can sometimes be used to simplify client code when a set of attributes can be processed as a whole. Perhaps a user agent does not want to deal with environmental attributes and therefore an entire group can be ignored. It is also possible to use attribute groups to introduce a conditional requirement for mandatory information. For example, if you include group X, then you must include attribute Y in the group. This allows us to support a very minimal representation but still ensure that key information is provided if a particular aspect of the issue is to be included. One specific example of this might be that when you include a history record that specifies the state of an issue at an earlier point in time, you must also provide the date and time attribute.

There is, however, a danger to having groups and using those groups within a media type. Deciding that an attribute has been put in a wrong group and moving it to a new group may end up being a breaking change, so it is important to be cautious with the use of groups.

Here is an example of an attribute group:

```
<resource>
    <Title>App blows up</Title>
    <Environment>
        <OperatingSystem>Windows ME</OperatingSystem>
        <AvailableRAM>284MB</AvailableRAM>
        <AvailableDiskSpace>1.2GB</AvailableDiskSpace>
    </Environment>
</resource>
```

Collections of Attribute Groups

Attribute groups can be used when you want to represent a multiplicity in parts of a representation. Issues may have documents attached to them. Those documents would most likely be represented as links, but there may be additional attributes associated with the documents that can be grouped together. This allows multiple groups of these document attributes to be included in a single representation while maintaining the relationship between the document and its related attributes.

The following is an example of an attribute group collection:

```
<resource>
    <Title>App blows up</Title>
    <Documents>
        <Document>
                <Name>ScreenShot.jpg</Name>
                <LastUpdated>2013-11-03 10:15AM</LastUpdated>
                <Location>/documentrepository/123233</Location>
        </Document>
        <Document>
                <Name>StepsToReproduce.txt</Name>
                <LastUpdated>2013-11-03 10:22AM</LastUpdated>
                <Location>/documentrepository/123234</Location>
        </Document>
    </Documents>
</resource>
```

Information Model Versus Media Type

So far, we have talked about the information model that surrounds the domain of issue tracking. We have discussed, in abstract, how these pieces of information can be represented, grouped, and related (Figure 5-1). I have avoided the discussion of specific formats like XML and JSON because it is important to understand that the definition of the information model is independent of specific representation syntax. In the next chapter, when we talk about media types we will address the physical mapping of our conceptual model to the syntax of real media types and their particular formats.

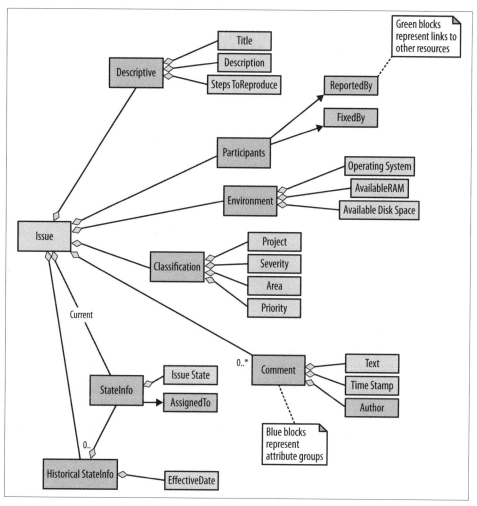

Figure 5-1. Information model

There are several things to consider in relation to the reusability of this information model. Although it is quite extensive in its listed capabilities, the majority of this information is optional. This allows us to use the same model in both the simplest scenarios and the most sophisticated. However, in order to achieve any kind of interoperability we must draw a line in the sand and give specific names to attributes. Fortunately, what we are defining is purely an interface specification. There is no requirement for applications to use these same names when they persist data to their data stores, nor is it necessary for them to use those names in the client application's user interface. As long as the semantic meaning of that data is accurately portrayed to the user, all is good.

When defining the media types we must consider what happens when an application wishes to include semantics that our information model currently does not support. Extensibility is an important goal; however, for this application, building interoperable extensibility is out of scope and so will not be part of the information model. That doesn't mean we can't allow media types to define their own extensibility options that will allow specific clients and servers to deal with extended data.

Collections of Issues

In addition to the representation of an `issue`, our applications will probably need to be able to represent sets of issues. These are most likely to be representations returned from some kind of query request. In the next chapter, we will discuss the relative merits of building new media types to represent a set of issues versus reusing the list capabilities of existing media types and the variety of hybrid approaches that exist.

Resource Models

Another major piece of application architecture to consider when building Web APIs are the resources exposed. It is not my intent to predefine a set of resources that must exist with an issue tracking API. One of the major differences between an evolvable API and and RPC/SOAP API is that the available resources are not part of the contract. It is expected that the client will discover resources, and the capabilities of the client will be limited to the resources that it can discover.

I do want to discuss the types of resources that an API might expose so that we have some ideas to work with when exploring the types of media types that our client needs to support. It is always good to start with a minimal set of resources. Resources should be quick and easy to create in a system, so as we gain real experience with consumers using the service we can easily add new resources to meet additional requirements.

Root Resource

Every evolvable Web API needs a root resource. Without it, clients just cannot begin the discovery process. The URL of the root resource is the one URL that cannot change. This resource will mainly contain a set of links to other resources within the application. Some of those links may point to search resources.

Search Resources

The canonical example of a search resource is an HTML form that has an input box and does a `GET` using the input value as a query string value. Search resources can be significantly more sophisticated than this, and sometimes can be completely replaced by the use of a URI template. Search resources will usually contain a link that returns some kind of collection resource.

Collection Resources

A collection resource normally returns a representation that contains a list of attribute groups. Often each attribute group will contain a link to a resource that is being represented by the information in the attribute group.

An issue tracking application is likely to predefine a large number of collection resources, such as:

- Active issues
- Closed issues
- List of users
- List of projects

Often a very large number of collection resources can be defined for a Web API by using search parameters to produce filtered collections. It is important that when we use the term *resource* we understand the distinction between the concept and the underlying implementation that generates the representation. If I create an `IssuesController` that allows a client application to search on subsets of issues, the URLs */issues?foundBy='Bob'* and */issues?foundBy='Bill'* are two different resources even though it is likely that the exact same code generated the two representations. To my knowledge, there is no term in common usage that describes the shared characteristics of a set of resources that represent different instances of the same concept. From this point on, I will use the term *resource class* to identify this scenario.

Item Resources

The bulk of the information retrieved via the API will be communicated via *item* resources. An item resource provides a representation that contains some or all of the information belonging to a single instance of some information model concept. It is likely that we will need to support multiple different levels of details. Considering the example of an `issue`, some clients may only want the descriptive attributes. Other clients may want all the details that could be edited.

There is a wide variety of subsets of information that a client may need for a particular use case. This is one reason why it is important that, for any `issue`-related media type that we might define, we remain very flexible regarding what information may or may not be included. Just because a representation of an issue resource does not contain the details of the issue history does not mean the information does not exist. This is where the idea of generating resource representations based on domain object serialization falls apart. An object has just one class definition; you cannot pick and choose which parts of the object you wish to serialize based on context with a generic object serializer.

When you are determining the appropriate subsets of attributes to include in a resource, it is important to consider several factors. Large representations have the advantage of requiring fewer roundtrips. However, when only a small amount of data is required, there will be some wasted bandwidth and processing time. Also, large representations have a higher chance of containing attributes with different levels of volatility. Including *descriptive* attributes in the same resource as *current state* attributes, we may find that the we cannot cache the resource representation for as long as we might like because the *current state* information changes frequently. Using data volatility as a guide for segregating data into distinct resources can be a very useful technique. The downside to breaking a single concept into multiple resources is that it can make doing atomic updates using a PUT more difficult, and it introduces more complexity during cache invalidation.

Having more, smaller resources means more links and more representations to manage, but it means there is more opportunity for reuse.

There is no formulaic approach for determining the best granularity for resources. It is essential to consider the specific use cases and the various factors we have just discussed and choose the most appropriate resource sizes for the situation.

Figure 5-2 shows one particular resource model that an issue tracking service might implement. Each of these resource or resource classes will be exposed at a particular URL by the service. We have chosen not to show what those URLs will be because they are not relevant to our design, nor should they be relevant to the client.

All too often, developers try to do "design by URL" when building an API. There are a number of problems with this approach. Designing by URL steers people to try to define their application as a hierarchial data structure rather than the application workflow/ state machine that should be being modeled. Limitations of the chosen implementation framework's ability to parse, process, and route URLs will tend to constrain the system design even further. Designing by URL also encourages developers to try to create a consistency in their URI structure that is completely unnecessary and potentially constraining to the design. Identifying resources and the relations between them can be completely independent of URI structure, and later on a URI space can be mapped to the resources. This is a unique benefit of systems where clients are hypermedia driven. When clients construct URIs based on knowledge of the server's URI space, the need for a uniform URI space with a significant structure becomes pressing.

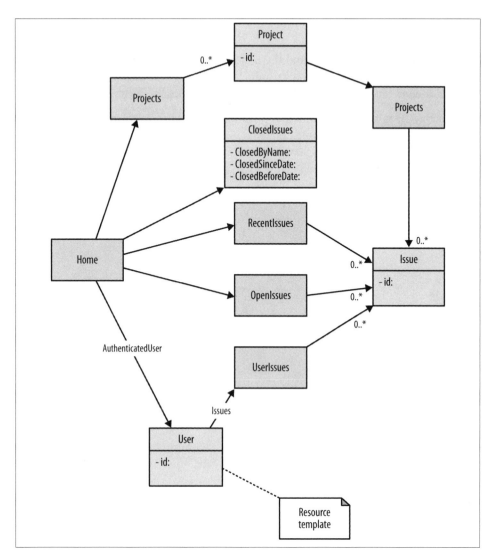

Figure 5-2. Resource model

Any client who understands the media types and link relations that we will be discussing in the next chapter will be able to consume this service without any prior knowledge of any of these resources other than the root."

Conclusion

In this chapter, we have considered the conceptual design of our application. We reviewed why we would want to build a system that can evolve and the costs of that choice. We identified the building blocks of our design and reviewed the application domain.

Fundamentally, this is a distributed application and will require communication between different systems. To implement this in a manner that will successfully evolve, we need to define the contracts that will be used to convey application semantics between the system components. This will be the focus of the next chapter.

CHAPTER 6

Media Type Selection and Design

A good contract lets friends stay friends.

It is common to hear developers explain how REST-based systems are better than alternatives for building Web APIs because they are simpler. The lack of contracts, such as WSDL (Web Service Description Language), is often cited as one of the reasons for the simplicity.

However, when building distributed systems, you cannot avoid coming to some kind of prearranged agreement between components. Without some form of shared knowledge, those components cannot interact in a meaningful way.

This chapter is about the types of contracts used in web architecture, the process of selecting the best contracts to meet our needs, and identifying where it's necessary to create new contracts.

Self-Description

One of the key concepts around designing contracts is self-description. Ideally, a message should contain all the information the recipient needs to understand the intent of the sender, or at least provide references to where the necessary information can be found.

Imagine you receive a letter in the mail that has the numbers 43.03384,−71.07338 written on it. That letter provides you with all the data that you need to achieve a very specific goal, but you are missing all of the context required to do anything useful with it. If I were to tell you that the pair of numbers were latitude and longitude coordinates, then you would have some understanding of their meaning. Obviously, I am assuming that you either already understand that coordinate system or are capable of searching for information on how to use it. Self-descriptive does not mean that the message needs to actually include a description of the longitude/latitude system. It simply needs to reference it in some way.

Knowing that the information included in the letter is coordinates is only half the story. What are you supposed to do with those coordinates? More context is needed for you to know what you should do with that information. If you see that the letter's return address is "Great Places To Drink, PO Box 2000, Nevada," you have a hint that maybe the coordinates are the location of a recommended pub.

Types of Contracts

In the web world, media types are used to convey *what* a resource represents, and a link relation suggests *why* you should care about that resource. These are the contracts that we can use when building evolvable systems. These pieces of the architecture represent the shared knowledge. These are the parts of the system that we have to be careful to design well, because when they change, they could break components that depend on them.

Media Types

Media types are platform-independent types designed for communication between distributed systems. Media types carry information. How that information is represented is defined in a written specification.

Unfortunately, the potential for media types is woefully underused in the world of Web APIs. The vast majority of Web APIs limit their support to `application/xml` and `application/json`. These two media types have very little capability to carry meaningful semantics and often lead people to use *out-of-band* knowledge to interpret them. Out-of-band knowledge is the opposite of self-descriptive. To return to our letter example, if the "Great Places To Drink" company were to tell you ahead of your receiving the letter that the numbers written on your letter would be geographic coordinates, that would be considered out-of-band knowledge. The information needed to interpret the data is communicated in some way separate from the message itself. In the case of generic types like `application/xml` and `application/json`, it requires us to communicate the semantics of the message in some other way. Depending on how we do that, it can make evolving a system much more difficult because it requires communicating changes to the system in that out-of-band manner. When out-of-band knowledge is used, clients assume that the server will send certain content and therefore they are unable to automatically adapt if a server returns something different. The result is that server behavior becomes locked down by the existence of clients. This can become a major inhibitor of change.

Primitive Formats

This section includes examples that show how the same set of data is communicated through different media types.

The media type `application/octet-stream`, shown in Example 6-1, is about as basic a media type as you can get. It is simply a stream of bytes. User agents who receive this media type usually cannot do anything with the payload other than allow the user to save the bytes in a file. There are no application semantics defined at all.

Example 6-1. A stream of bytes

```
GET /some-mystery-resource
200 OK
Content-Type: application/octet-stream
Content-Length: 20

00 3b 00 00 00 0d 00 01 00 11 00 1e 00 08 01 6d 00 03 FF FF
```

In Example 6-2, media type `text/plain` tells us that the content can be safely rendered directly to a end user, who will be able to read the data. In its current form, the example body does not provide any hints as to what the data is for; however, there is nothing to stop a server from including a paragraph of prose in the body with an explanation of the information.

Example 6-2. Human readable

```
GET /some-mystery-resource
200 OK
Content-Type: text/plain
Content-Length: 29

59,0,13,1,17,30,8,365,3,65535
```

Who Knows My Business?

In the last 50 years of computing, we have played distributed ping-pong with the semantics of our business applications. In the days of the mainframe, the server knew everything about your data and the client was a terminal that knew nothing more than how to display characters and detect keypresses.

In the 80s and early 90s, with the rise of personal computers and local area networks, the clients became king. Shared data was still stored on a file server, but as far as the server was concerned it was just dealing with files, rows, columns, and indexes. All the intelligence was on the client.

Toward the end of the 90s client/server databases gained popularity due to the fact that PC-based networked applications were being stretched to the limits of their extremely

---

chatty architecture, and client/server databases promised huge scalability improvements.

Client/server databases had limited success in driving rich client applications—not because of any technical problem but because many developers had insufficient training and tried to apply the techniques used for ISAM (indexed sequential access method) databases on client/server databases. This problem was exacerbated by vendors pushing client/server databases as a "drop-in replacement" to achieve scalability.

The new millennium saw the rise of the web application. Web applications worked well because they moved the application workflow and business logic onto a server that lives close to the data. This addressed the problem of chatty PC-based networks and avoided some of the concurrency problems that were tricky to handle using client/server databases.

In recent years, JavaScript has gone from augmenting HTML-based web experiences to creating and controlling web experiences. We are seeing a trend of moving application workflow and logic back onto the client but within the runtime environment of a web browser.

If we are to move logic back to the client, it is important we understand why this has failed in the past, so as to avoid repeating the mistakes of our predecessors.

Hypermedia-enabled media types are a very important part of this critical architectural decision because they are able to carry both workflow and application semantics across the wire and allow a more intelligent distribution of workload between client and server.

In Example 6-3, the media type text/csv provides some structure to the information being returned. The data model is defined as a set of comma-separated values that are then broken down into lines of (usually) structurally similar data. We still have no idea what the data is, but we could at least format the data for presentation to a user, assuming the user knows what she is looking at.

Example 6-3. Simply structured data

```
GET /some-mystery-resource
200 OK
Content-Type: text/csv
Content-Length: 29

59,0
13,1
17,30
8,365
3,65535
```

Popular Formats

Consider Example 6-4.

Example 6-4. Markup

```
GET /some-mystery-resource
 200 OK
 Content-Type: application/xml
 Content-Length: 29

 <root>
        <element attribute1="59" attribute2="0"/>
        <element attribute1="13" attribute2="1"/>
        <element attribute1="17" attribute2="30"/>
        <element attribute1="8" attribute2="365"/>
        <element attribute1="3" attribute2="65535"/>
 </root>
```

In this particular case, returning the content as XML did not add any more semantics than the text/csv format did. We still just have five pairs of digits, but it does provide a place to name the pieces of data. However, the meaning of those names is not being defined in the specification for application/xml, so any client that tries to assign meaning to those names is depending on out-of-band knowledge and therefore introducing hidden coupling. Later in this chapter, we will discuss other ways to layer semantics on top of generic media types without creating hidden coupling.

For more complex scenarios, application/xml can be useful to represent hierarchies of data and allow blocks of text to be marked up with additional data. However, we still have the problem that application/xml provides limited ways to assign semantics.

As far as communicating semantics, application/json (shown in Example 6-5) has even less capability than application/xml. The advantage of consuming JSON within a web browser environment is that we can download JavaScript code that can apply semantics to the document. This allows clients and servers to evolve simultaneously, but it has the disadvantage of limiting clients to those that can support a JavaScript runtime. This also impacts the ability for intermediary components to interact with the message, thereby limiting the benefits of the HTTP layered architecture.

Example 6-5. Object serialization

```
GET /some-mystery-resource
 200 OK
 Content-Type: application/json
 Content-Length: 29

 { "objects" : [
        {"property1"="59", "property2"="0"},
        {"property1"="13", "property2"="1"},
        {"property1"="17", "property2"="30"},
```

```
        {"property1"="8", "property2"="365"},
        {"property1"="3", "property2"="65535"}
    ]
}
```

If generic media types are at one end of a continuum of media types, then the next example is at the opposite end. In this case, we have defined a new media type that is specific to our particular application and has exactly the semantics that the server understands. To deliver this content, we need to write a specification for the media type, make it publicly available on the Internet, and preferably register the media type with IANA, so that it can easily be found by a developer who wishes to understand the meaning of the representation he just received.

New Formats

Now let's consider Example 6-6.

Example 6-6. Service-specific format

```
GET /some-mystery-resource
200 OK
Content-Type: application/vnd.acme.cache-stats+xml
Content-Length: ??

<cacheStats>
      <cacheMaxAge percent="59" daysLowerLimit="0" daysUpperLimit="0">
      <cacheMaxAge percent="13" daysLowerLimit="0" daysUpperLimit="1">
      <cacheMaxAge percent="17" daysLowerLimit="1" daysUpperLimit="30">
      <cacheMaxAge percent="8" daysLowerLimit="30" daysUpperLimit="365">
      <cacheMaxAge percent="3" daysLowerLimit="365" daysUpperLimit="65535">
</cacheStats>
```

This media type finally conveys that the data we have been dealing with is the series of data points for a graph that shows the frequency distribution of the length of the max-age cache control header of requests on the Internet. This media type provides all the information a client needs for rendering a graph of this information. However, the applicability of this media type is fairly specific. How often is someone going to write an application that needs to render a graph of caching statistics? The idea of writing a specification and submitting that specification to IANA for registration seems like overkill. The vast majority of today's Web APIs create these narrowly focused payloads but just don't bother with the specification and registration part of the process. There are alternatives, though, that provide all the information needed by the client, and yet can be applicable to far more scenarios.

Consider the scenario in Example 6-7.

Example 6-7. Domain-specific format

```
GET /some-mystery-resource
200 OK
Content-Type: application/data-series+xml
Content-Length: ??

<series        xAxisType="range"
                      yAxisType="percent"
                      title="% of requests with their max-age value in days">
      <dataPoint yValue="59" xLowerValue="0" xUpperValue="0">
      <dataPoint yValue="13" xLowerValue="0" xUpperValue="1">
      <dataPoint yValue="17" xLowerValue="1" xUpperValue="30">
      <dataPoint yValue="8" xLowerValue="30" xUpperValue="365">
      <dataPoint yValue="3" xLowerValue="365" xUpperValue="65535">
</series>
```

In this case, we have created a media type whose purpose is to deliver a series of data points that can be used to plot a graph. It could be a line graph, a pie chart, a histogram, or even just a table of data. The client can understand the semantics of the data points from the perspective of drawing a graph. It doesn't know what the graph is about; that is left for the human consumer to appreciate. However, the additional semantics allow the client to do things like overlay graphs, switch axes, and zoom to portions of the graph.

The reusability of this media type is vastly higher than that of the application/ vnd.acme.cachestats+xml. Any application scenario where there is some data to be graphed could make use of this media type. The time and effort put into writing a specification to completely describe this format could quickly pay off.

It is my opinion that this kind of domain-specific, but not service-specific, media type is the optimal balance of semantics that media types should convey. There are a few examples of this sort of media type that have proven quite successful:

- HTML was conceived as a way of communicating hyperlinked textual documents.
- Atom (*http://bit.ly/rfc-4287*) was designed as a way to enable syndication of web-based blogs.
- ActivityStream (*http://activitystrea.ms/*) is a way of representing streams of events.
- Json-home (*http://bit.ly/json-home*) is designed to enable discovery of resources made available in an API.
- Json-problem (*http://bit.ly/json-problem*) is a media type designed to provide details on errors returned from an API.

All of these media type examples have several things in common. They have semantics that are intended to solve a specific problem, but they are not specific to any particular application. Every API needs to return error information; most applications have areas where there is some stream of events. These media types are defined in a completely platform- and language-agnostic way, which means that they can be used by every developer in any type of application. There remain many opportunities for defining new media types that would be reusable across many applications.

Hypermedia Types

Hypermedia types are a class of media types that are usually text based and contain links to other resources. By providing links within representations, user agents are able to navigate from one representation to another based on their understanding of the meaning of the link.

Hypermedia types play a huge role in decoupling clients from servers. Through hypermedia, clients no longer need to have preexisting knowledge of resources exposed on the Web. Resources can be discovered at runtime.

Despite the obvious benefits of hypermedia in HTML for web applications, hypermedia has so far played a very minor role in the development of Web APIs. Web application developers have tended to avoid hypermedia due to lack of tooling, a perception that links create unnecessary bloat in the size of representations, and a general lack of appreciation of its benefits.

There are scenarios where the cost of hypermedia cannot be justified—for example, when performance is absolutely critical. For performance-critical systems, the HTTP protocol is probably not the best choice either. When evolvability is a key goal in an HTTP-based system, hypermedia cannot be ignored.

Media Type Explosion

So far we have seen how generic media types require out-of-band knowledge to provide semantics, and we have seen examples of more specific media types that carry domain semantics. Some members of the web development community are reluctant to encourage the creation of new media types. There is a fear of an "explosion of media types" —that the creation of a large number of new media types would produce badly designed specifications, duplicated efforts, and service-specific types, and any possibility of serendipitous reuse would be severely hindered. It is not an unfounded fear, but it's likely that, just as with evolution, the strong would survive and the weak would have little impact.

Generic Media Types and Profiles

There is another approach to media types that is favored by some. Its basic premise is to use a more generic media type and use a secondary mechanism to layer semantics onto the representation.

One example of this is a media type called Resource Description Framework (RDF) (*http://www.w3.org/RDF/*). To dramatically oversimplify, RDF is a media type that allows you to make statements about things using triples, where a triple consists of a subject, an object, and a predicate that describes the relationship between the subject and object. The significant portion of the semantics of an RDF representation are provided by standardized vocabularies of predicates that have documented meanings. The RDF specification provides the way to relate pieces of data together but does not actually define any domain semantics itself.

In Example 6-8, taken from the RDF Wikipedia entry (*http://bit.ly/wiki-rdf*), the URI *http://purl.org./dc/elements/1.1* refers to a vocabulary defined by the Dublin Core Metadata Initiative.

Example 6-8. RDF Example

```
<rdf:RDF
  xmlns:rdf="http://www.w3.org/1999/02/22-rdf-syntax-ns#"
  xmlns:dc="http://purl.org/dc/elements/1.1/">
        <rdf:Description rdf:about="http://en.wikipedia.org/wiki/Tony_Benn">
                <dc:title>Tony Benn</dc:title>
                <dc:publisher>Wikipedia</dc:publisher>
        </rdf:Description>
</rdf:RDF>
```

Another example of layering semantics is the use of application-level profile semantics (ALPS) (*http://bit.ly/alps-docs*). ALPS is a method of specifying domain semantics that can then be applied to a base media type like XHTML, as shown in Example 6-9. The recently ratified link relation `profile` is a way of attaching these kinds of additional semantic specifications to existing media types.

Example 6-9. ALPS over XHTML

```
GET /some-mystery-resource
200 OK
Content-Type: application/xhtml
Content-Length: 29

<html>
      <head>
      <link rel="profile" href="http://example.org/profiles/stats" />
   </head>
      <title>% of requests with their cache-control: max-age value in days </title>
      <body>
              <table class="data-series">
                      <thead>
                              <td>from</td>
                              <td>to (days)</td>
                              <td>percent</td>
                      </thead>
                      <tr class="data-point">
```

```
                                    <td class="xLowerValue"></td>
                                    <td class="xUpperValue">0</td>
                                    <td class="yValue">59</td>
                            </tr>
                            <tr class="data-point">
                                    <td class="xLowerValue">0</td>
                                    <td class="xUpperValue">1</td>
                                    <td class="yValue">13</td>
                            </tr>
                            <tr class="data-point">
                                    <td class="xLowerValue">1</td>
                                    <td class="xUpperValue">30</td>
                                    <td class="yValue">17</td>
                            </tr>
                            <tr class="data-point">
                                    <td class="xLowerValue">30</td>
                                    <td class="xUpperValue">365</td>
                                    <td class="yValue">8</td>
                            </tr>
                            <tr class="data-point">
                                    <td class="xLowerValue">365</td>
                                    <td class="xUpperValue"></td>
                                    <td class="yValue">3</td>
                            </tr>
                    </table>
            </body>
    </html>


GET http://example.org/profiles/stats
200 OK
Content-Type: application/alps+xml

<alps version="1.0">
    <doc format="text">
        Types to support the domain of statistical data
    </doc>

    <descriptor id="data-series" type="semantic">
        <descriptor id="data-point" type="semantic">
         <doc>A data point</doc>
                <descriptor id="xValue" type="semantic"">
                        <doc>X value on graph</doc>
                </descriptor>
                <descriptor id="xLowerValue" type="semantic">
                        <doc>Lower bound on X range of values</doc>
                </descriptor>
                <descriptor id="xUpperValue" type="semantic">
                        <doc>Upper bound on X range of values</doc>
                </descriptor>
                <descriptor id="yValue" type="semantic" >
                        <doc>Y value on graph</doc>
```

```
                    </descriptor>
                    <descriptor id="yLowerValue" type="semantic">
                            <doc>Lower bound on Y range of values</doc>
                    </descriptor>
                    <descriptor id="yUpperValue" type="semantic">
                            <doc>Upper bound on Y range of values</doc>
                    </descriptor>
                    </descriptor>
        </descriptor>


</alps>
```

The Hypermedia Application Language (HAL) (*http://bit.ly/hal-spec*), demonstrated in Example 6-10, is a generic media type that uses link relations as a way to apply domain semantics.

Example 6-10. HAL in both application/hal+xml and application/hal+json

```
<resource       xAxisType="range"
                        yAxisType="percent"
                        title="% of requests with their max-age value in days">
        <resource       rel="http://example.org/stats/data-point"
                                yValue="59"
                                xLowerValue="0"
                                xUpperValue="0">
        <resource       rel="http://example.org/stats/data-point"
                                yValue="13"
                                xLowerValue="0"
                                xUpperValue="1">
        <resource       rel="http://example.org/stats/data-point"
                                yValue="17"
                                xLowerValue="1"
                                xUpperValue="30">
        <resource       rel="http://example.org/stats/data-point"
                                yValue="8"
                                xLowerValue="30"
                                xUpperValue="365">
        <resource       rel="http://example.org/stats/data-point"
                                yValue="3"
                                xLowerValue="365"
                                xUpperValue="65535">
</resource>

{
        "xAxisType" : "range",
        "yAxisType" : "percent",
        "title" : "% of requests with their max-age value in days",
        "_embedded" : {
                "http://example.org/stats/data-point" :
                { "yValue" : "59", "xLowerValue" : "0", "xUpperValue" : "0"},
                "http://example.org/stats/data-point" :
```

```
                    { "yValue" : "13", "xLowerValue" : "0", "xUpperValue" : "1"},
                    "http://example.org/stats/data-point" :
                    { "yValue" : "17", "xLowerValue" : "1", "xUpperValue" : "30"},
                    "http://example.org/stats/data-point" :
                    { "yValue" : "8", "xLowerValue" : "30", "xUpperValue" : "365"},
                    "http://example.org/stats/data-point" :
                    { "yValue" : "3", "xLowerValue" : "365", "xUpperValue" : "65535"}

            }

    }
```

HAL relies on link relations to provide the semantics needed to interpret the non-HAL parts of the representation. This means that in the documentation for the link relation type http://example.org/stats/data-point, the meaning of yValue, xLowerValue, and xUpperValue needs to be defined. HAL doesn't care whether these values are specified as attributes or elements; it is up to the consumer of the HAL document to discover where the information is stored.

One challenge with using the link relation to communicate semantics is that entry point URIs often do not have link relations. When you type a link into a browser address bar, there is no link relation. There are a couple of workarounds for this. You can keep the root resource limited to just embedded resources and links, or you can use a link with the link relation type to associate semantics to the root resource.

The advantage of using a generic media type is that tooling to generate, parse, and render those formats likely already exists and can be reused. It also means that you can define semantic profiles that have mappings to multiple different base media types. This can be advantageous when one particular media type is more suitable for a particular platform. When defining domain-specific media types, if it is desirable to support both XML and JSON variants, you must write two specifications because the format and semantics are both defined by the media type.

Efforts are under way to try to formalize the process of describing a semantic profile (*http://alps.io/spec/index.html*), and it is likely that there will be multiple viable approaches.

The disadvantage of using the generic media type combined with a secondary semantic profile is that the semantics of the message are less visible to intermediary components. Media types specified in the Content-Type header can easily be processed by any layer in the HTTP architecture. Using techniques like link relations and profiles to attach semantics makes it more difficult for intermediaries to discover that information and make processing decisions based on it. As is commonly the case in web architecture, there is not only one way to do things. There are advantages and disadvantages, and systems must be engineered to meet the requirements.

The use of a secondary semantic profile is definitely an interesting space to watch, and I look forward to a future where there are more prescriptive solutions to defining the semantics of a message.

From these examples, you can see there are many ways you can communicate the same data between the client and server. Some media types carry more semantics, some less. How much application-specific semantics you use to drive your client depends on the availability of existing standard media types that suit your needs and your tolerance for coupling.

Other Hypermedia Types

The last few years have seen a number of new hypermedia types introduced. The following sections summarize a few examples.

Collection+Json

The Collection+Json media type addresses the domain of lists of things. It is interesting in that it is generic and specific at the same time. It specifically supports only lists of things, but it does not care what the list of things is. It also has interesting semantic affordances that can describe how to query the list and add new items to it. Although it has minimal semantics for the items in the list, it does support the notion of profiles for describing the list items.

Siren

Siren (*http://bit.ly/gh-siren*) is another fairly new hypermedia type that is similar to HAL in that it is effective in representing nested data structures and embedded resources. It differs from HAL in the way it attaches semantics to data elements. Siren borrows the notion of a `class` from HTML as a way to identify semantic information. It also makes a distinction between links that are for navigating between resources and those that represent behaviors. The `action` links also have their own style of link hints that describe to the client how to invoke the `action`.

Although some people argue that we should all just standardize on a single format, I would rather let natural selection take its course than try to force-fit a single hypermedia format into every scenario. HTTP makes it easy for APIs to support multiple representations of a resource, and clients can pick the one they prefer, so having multiple formats in use is not a major hindrance to progress.

Up to this point, we have talked primarily about media types as a way of communicating semantics, but as we hinted when discussing HAL, semantics can also be communicated via link relations. The next section will discuss this further.

Link Relation Types

In the introduction to this section on contract types, I noted that link relation types suggest *why* you might be interested in a particular resource.

Link relation types were first introduced in HTML. The most common link relation type is probably the `rel="stylesheet"` value, which connects an HTML page to the stylesheet used to help render it:

```
<link href="..." media="all" rel="stylesheet" type="text/css" />
```

More recently, there has been an effort to fully specify what a link relation type really is. This results of this effort can be found in RFC 5988 (*http://bit.ly/rfc-5988*).

Semantics

In the same way that media types can be very generic about the semantics they communicate, so can link relations. There are some standardized link relation types—like `next`, `previous`, `current`, `item`, `collection`, `first`, and `last`—that are very generic. However, they do provide important contextual information about the related resource. On the other hand, there are some standardized link relations that have very specific usages. Examples of these are `help`, `monitor`, `payment`, `license`, `copyright`, and `terms-of-service`.

Reviewing the standard registry of link relations (*http://bit.ly/link-relation*) only hints at the power of link relations. Most of the standard link relations do not define any behavior or constraints; they simply identify the target resource or describe the relationship between the context resource and the target resource.

Politics

If you spend any amount of time reading about the world of web and Internet specifications, you will quickly learn there are lots of politics involved in the process. I will warn you that I am biased in favor of the Internet Engineering Task Force (IETF) as the keeper of Internet-related specifications. The IETF defers to IANA for registries, which is why I refer to the IANA media type registry and IANA link relation registry. However, there are other organizations that are unhappy with the IETF/IANA registration procedures and have chosen to use an alternate registry (*http://bit.ly/exist-rel-values*) for link relations.

A few link relations have begun to suggest we can do more with them than just identify a relation. Consider `noreferrer` and `prefetch`. `noreferrer` tells the user agent that if it follows the link, it should not specify the `referer` header. `prefetch` tells the user agent that it should retrieve the target resource prior to the user requesting to follow the link so that the representation will already be in the cache. In these cases, the link relation is actually instructing the user agent about how the server would like it to interact with the link. These instructions can go much further. A link relation type specification could indicate that only the POST method should be used with a particular link, or that when the link is followed, the returned representation will always be application/json.

Instead of defining interaction mechanisms in a specification, some people prefer to embed metadata into links to describe to the client how to interact with the link. For example, an HTML <FORM> tag has a method property that indicates to the browser whether to use a GET or POST method. A variation on this is the use of link hints, which allow a server to embed metadata that suggests how a link might be used. It does not preclude there being other valid ways of using the link.

All these approaches are valid ways to communicate link mechanics to a client. Using embedded metadata with a fairly general link relation is the most reusable approach but requires the most bytes over the wire. It also potentially reduces the number of link relations of which a client needs to be aware. Using a precise link relation with all the details of the interaction specified in the documentation is more bandwidth-friendly but puts more requirements on the client application.

If we take this idea of a precise link relation to an extreme, a link relation address could require the use of the GET method and return application/json with properties street, city, state, country, and zipcode. The more constrained the link relation the less reusable it becomes, and it is highly unlikely that such a link relation would be accepted by the subject matter experts who manage the registry. However, there is the notion of *extended link relation types*, where you use a URI as an identifier to uniquely identify the relation. When using an extended link relation type, you are not required to register the link relation with IANA, and you are free to do what makes sense to you.

The interesting effect of using a link relation to precisely describe the expected response is that it allows the use of generic types like application/xml and application/json to convey data without depending on out-of-band knowledge.

However, my personal experience has been that dividing the semantics between link relations and media types more evenly produces more reusable contract types.

Link relations and media types work together in a manner similar to how adjectives and nouns work in language. The adjective *happy* can be used in combination with many nouns. By combining the independent adjective and noun, we can avoid the need for an explosion of nouns such as *happydog*, *happycow*, *happyfish*, and so on.

```
{ "collection" :
  {
    "version" : "1.0",
    "href" : "http://example.org/journal/?fromDate=20130921&toDate=20130922"
    "items" : [
      {
```

```
    "href" : "http://example.org/transaction/794",
    "data" : [
      {"amount" : "14576", "currency" : "USD", "date" : "20130921"}
    ],
    "links" : [
      {"rel" : "origin", "href" : "http://examples.org/account/bank1000"},
      {"rel" : "destination",
        "href" : "http://examples.org/account/payables/HawaiiTravel"}
    ]
  },
  "items" : [
    {
      "href" : "http://example.org/transaction/794",
      "data" : [
        {"amount" : "150000", "currency" : "USD", "date" : "20130922"}
      ],
      "links" : [
        {"rel" : "origin",
          "href" : "http://examples.org/account/receivables/acme"},
        {"rel" : "destination",
          "href" : "http://examples.org/account/bank1000"}
      ]
    }
  }
}
```

As an example, imagine that we are to register two link relation types, origin and
destination. There are many scenarios in which we need to represent where something
has come from and where it is going—whether it is a file copy, a bank transfer, or a route
on a map. The same link relations can be reused in many different scenarios. Sometimes
the semantics of these reusable relations are sufficient to implement generic functionality on the client regardless of what the links may be pointing to. This is very similar
to the way polymorphism works in object-oriented development.

Usually when people think of links in hypermedia documents, they think about defining
relationships between domain concepts. This is the primary use of links in the field of
linked data. However, it is possible to use links for much more than making declarations
about the relationships in our domain.

Replacing Embedded Resources

In the world of HTML, we are used to creating links to images, scripts, and stylesheets;
however, in APIs it is uncommon to see these kinds of static resources exposed. With
careful use of client-side private caching, an API can efficiently expose static resources
for all kinds of information that would normally be embedded into a client application.

Indirection Layer

Links are used as a way of providing a layer of indirection. By creating discovery documents at API entry points, we can enable clients to dynamically identify the location of certain resources without having to hardcode URIs into the client application (see Example 6-11).

Example 6-11. A GitHub discovery resource

```
GET https://api.github.com/
{
        "current_user_url":"https://api.github.com/user",
        "authorizations_url":"https://api.github.com/authorizations",
        "emails_url":"https://api.github.com/user/emails",
        "emojis_url":"https://api.github.com/emojis",
        "events_url":"https://api.github.com/events",

        ...
        "user_search_url":"https://api.github.com/legacy/user/search/{keyword}"
}
```

This layer of indirection allows a server to reorganize its URI structure without clients needing to make changes. Imagine that GitHub wanted to allow searching for users by location. It could make the following change:

```
"user_search_url":"https://api.github.com/legacy/user/search{?keyword,country}"
```

Assuming the client was following the rules of URI Template (RFC 6570) token replacement, there would be no client changes necessary to adopt this new URI format.

We can also use indirection to provide a type of intelligent load balancing. If certain resources are putting a disproportionate amount of load on a server, the URIs could be changed to point to alternative servers with additional capacity. This can be useful when different types of requests create very different types of workloads.

Indirection can also be useful for finding geolocated resources. Using client location based on IP address, response representations can contain links to servers that are geographically close. This can be very important because network latency can be a significant factor over long distances. Accessing a server on the East Coast of the US from a client on the West Coast will likely be on the order of 80 milliseconds. When there are numerous resources to be retrieved to render a user interface, this can quickly be very noticeable to an end user.

Reference Data

It is common in data entry user interfaces to provide the user a list of options to select from. These lists don't need to be predefined in a client application, and in fact a client doesn't even need to know in advance what list needs to be associated with a particular input field. By annotating an input field with a link to a list of options, a client application can generically identify the valid list of items without any knowledge of the input domain.

For example:

```
<InputForm>
  <Street>/<Street>
  <City></City>
  <Province domainUrl="http://api.example.org/lists/provinces&country=CAN"/>
  <Country>Canada</Country>
</InputForm>
```

HTML forms achieve a similar goal by embedding the entire list into the input element, but that is not a particularly efficient approach. Links can be used as a way to reduce payload size. Sometimes certain pieces of information are required less often and can be moved off into a distinct resource. You can often offset the extra cost of the second roundtrip with the savings from not retrieving the additional information when it is not needed.

A second reason for splitting resources is when the volatility of the data is very different. Retrieving a representation of sensor readings from a device that includes all the device configuration details is wasteful because the sensor readings would likely change far more often than the device configuration. Adding a link to the device configuration enables us to retrieve device configuration information only when needed.

The third reason for splitting resources is to enable reuse. This is the case in our address/province list example. The list of provinces is the same for any Canadian address. If a user is entering many addresses, then being able to use a client cached copy of the list can be very effective.

Workflow

Probably one of the most unique features of REST-based systems is the way that application workflow is defined and communicated. In RPC-based systems, the client must understand the application interaction protocol. For example, it must know that it has to call open before it calls send and close when it has finished. These rules have to be baked into the clients and any dynamic detection of state must be built ad hoc.

Links, embedded into representations, can be used to instruct clients of the valid interactions based on state. A client must still be aware of the types of interactions that exist in order to use them, but it no longer has the burden of knowing when it is allowed to make a certain type of request.

Consider Example 6-12, a version of the same scenario using hypermedia.

Example 6-12. Using hypermedia to define workflow

```
GET /deviceApi
200 OK
```

```
Content-Type:  application/hal+xml

<resource>
        <link rel="http://example.org/rels/open" href="/deviceApi/sessions"/>
</resource>

POST /deviceApi/sessions
Content-Length: 0

201 Created Session
Content-Type:  application/hal+xml
Location: http://example.org/deviceApi/session/1435

<resource>
  <link rel="http://example.org/rels/send" href="/deviceApi/session/1435{?message}"/>
  <link rel="http://example.org/rels/close" href="/deviceApi/session/1435"/>
</resource>

DELETE /deviceApi/session/1435
200 OK
```

The client still needs to understand the open/send/close link relations, but the server can guide the client through the process. The client must know that to activate the open link, it should send a POST with no body, and to activate the close link it must use the DELETE method. In this example the responses use HAL, but there is no reason the server could not return more than one hypermedia type. The link relations do not need to constrain the returned media type. It is necessary, however, that the client understand at least one of the media types returned by the server.

If a client is designed to understand that links may be dynamic, then it can adapt to changes in the workflow. For example, if it used an algorithm where it first looks for the send link, if it does not find one it looks for an open link, follows it, and looks once again for a send link. With this approach, if a later version of the API does not require the open/close dance, then the initial /deviceApi representation can be changed to immediately include the send. The client would automatically adapt to the new protocol and continue working without change.

This is an extremely simple example. More complex applications have more complex interaction protocols and more opportunities to take advantage of this dynamic workflow capability.

Syntax

RFC 5988 also specifies the format for embedding links into HTTP headers so that even with binary content like images and video, you can still include hypermedia with the returned representation. What is not specified, however, is how links should be embedded into other media types. The way links are serialized must be specified by the media type specification itself. This is another reason why using media types like `application/json` and `application/xml` can be problematic, as they don't define how links should be represented. There have been a number of different conventions used, but without a hard spec it is difficult to write reusable code to parse links. It would seem like a trivial thing to define, but I've seen people debate for hours over whether a JSON object should be called `links` or `_links`.

Here are some examples of link syntax:

application/hal+json

```
"_links": {
    "self": { "href": "/orders" },
    "next": { "href": "/orders?page=2" },
    "find": {
        "href": "/orders{?id}",
        "templated": true
    },
    "admin": [{
        "href": "/admins/2",
        "title": "Fred"
    }]
},
```

application/collection+json
```
"links" : [
    {"rel" : "blog", "href" : "http://examples.org/blogs/jdoe",
        "prompt" : "Blog"},
    {"rel" : "avatar", "href" : "http://examples.org/images/jdoe",
        "prompt" : "Avatar", "render" : "image"}
]
```

application/vnd.github.v3+json

```
"assignee": {
    "login": "octocat",
    "id": 1,
    "avatar_url": "https://github.com/images/error/octocat_happy.gif",
    "gravatar_id": "somehexcode",
    "url": "https://api.github.com/users/octocat"
}
```

application/hal+xml
```
<link rel="admin" href="/admins/5" title="Kate" />
```

application/atom+xml
```
<link href="http://www.example.org/data/q1w2e3r4" rel="related" hreflang="en" />
<collection href="http://example.org/blog/main" />
<content src="http://www.example.org/blog-posts/123" />
<icon>http://www.example.org/images/icon</icon>
```

```
text/html
 <link  rel="stylesheet" type="text/css"
        href="http://cdn2.sstatic.net/stackoverflow/all.css?v=c9b143e6d693">

 <a href="/faq">faq</a>

<form id="search" action="/search" method="get" autocomplete="off">
        <div>
            <input      autocomplete="off" name="q" class="textbox"
                        placeholder="search" tabindex="1" type="text"
                        maxlength="240" size="28" value="">
        </div>
</form>
```

As you can see from these examples, links can take on many shapes in hypermedia representations. In the coming years, I hope we will see some more convergence on styles to remove some of the cosmetic differences. It is worth noting that although many of these examples do not have a rel attribute, they have the notion of a link relation type. In the case of HTML, an <a> tag could just as easily been represented as:

```
<link rel="a" href="/faq"/>
```

The same argument can be made for representing a <FORM> tag as:

```
<link rel="form" id="search" action="/search" method="get" autocomplete="off">
        <div>
            <input      autocomplete="off" name="q" class="textbox"
                        placeholder="search" tabindex="1" type="text"
                        maxlength="240" size="28" value="">
        </div>
</link>
```

The two styles simply demonstrate two different ways of identifying the link relation semantics. They also introduce an interesting workaround to one problem some people have with link relations as defined by RFC 5988. In order to use a simple token like rel="destination", you must register this relationship with IANA, which means there will be a review by domain experts. The intent of this registry is to encourage the development of link relations that are suitable for use across many different media types. As mentioned earlier, you can use the notion of extended media types and create a link relation that uses a URI. However, URIs can be long and noisy in representations. If you want to create a link relation that is specific to your particular media type, then you can choose to use a serialization such as:

```
<family>
  <mother href="/people/bob"/>
  <father href="/people/mary"/>
</family>
```

By making the link relation type an integral part of the media type syntax, you are explicitly stating that the link relation is defined only within this media type and you can avoid the URI naming requirement of extended link relation types.

There is another interesting property of link relations. Links can have multiple relations assigned to them. For example:

```
<link rel="first previous" href="/foo" />
<link rel="nofollow noreferrer" href="/bar" />
```

Be aware that this capability is simply a serialization optimization; it does allow the behavior of the links to be combined. RFC 5988 says:

> Relation types SHOULD NOT infer any additional semantics based upon the presence or absence of another link relation type, or its own cardinality of occurrence.

Semantically, there is no difference between the previous example and the following:

```
<link rel="first" href="/foo" />
<link rel="previous" href="/foo" />

<link rel="nofollow" href="/bar" />
<link rel="noreferrer" href="/bar" />
```

RFC 5988 also defines a number of other metadata properties of a link that can provide information to the user agent on how links should be processed. Instead of being specified in a written document, the instructions can be embedded in the representation of the link:

```
<link href="..." rel="related" title="More info...." hreflang="en"
    type="text/plain" >
```

These attributes are simply hints to the user agent; they do not guarantee the server will provide compliant representations.

A Perfect Combination

Link relation types and media types are the peanut butter and jelly of the distributed application world. Link relation types bind together resource representations to create a complete application that allows users to achieve their goals. These contract types work best when your semantics are evenly spread between them to encourage serendipitous reuse.

Designing a New Media Type Contract

When trying to identify the best media type to use for a particular resource, you should always first look for standard media types. Creating media can be challenging and sometimes standard media types may not be an exact fit, but they may be capable of carrying enough semantics to allow the client to achieve the users' goals.

In the case where you determine that there is no existing media type or link relation that carries the needed semantics, then it may be worth considering creating one. When creating a media type, aim for the following characteristics:

- The captured semantics could be used by more than one application.

- The required syntax is minimal and makes an open world assumption. In other words, the absence of information does not make any statement about that information.

- Unrecognized information should be ignored unless it specifically violates other rules.

Selecting a Format

Most of the time when developers think of selecting a format for their media type, they think of using XML or JSON as the base format. The advantage is that there is so much tooling available that can process these formats, and they provide a flexible structure on which to define additional semantics. Both formats have varying strengths and weaknesses, and in many cases it is simply a matter of preference. However, the types of clients that you wish to support do have an influence on the decision. If you expect that JavaScript clients will be the primary consumers of your media type, then JSON is the obvious choice. For systems that are integrating with large enterprise applications, XML may be more appropriate. Either way, as web developers we need to become comfortable with both formats and use whichever one makes the most sense.

However, I would caution against doing both. XML and JSON are quite different in their approach to data representation, and you risk creating a lowest-common-denominator format that doesn't really take advantage of either format. If you really do feel you need to support both, then recognize that managing two different spec formats is double the work and the community using the media type will end up being fragmented. For generic formats like HAL, it may make sense to support both variants, but it is a decision that you should not take lightly: having two variants that work slightly differently may end up causing more confusion than it is worth to attract the larger audience that refuses to adopt the single chosen format.

Sometimes, neither XML nor JSON may be the right choice. I've seen numerous occasions where people have been using a JSON document for the purposes of updating a single property value. In some cases, a plain-text format representation is the simplest choice. All languages have libraries that allow converting from simple text into native data types. If all you want to do is transfer a simple value, then consider `text/plain` or some derivative of it as an option.

The use of `text/plain` format is a good example of why it is smart to keep metadata out of the body of your HTTP representation. Many APIs have taken this approach, including status codes and other metadata in the body of their responses. However, if you do this, you are limiting the media types that you can use and duplicating the intent of the HTTP headers. If you are forced to support clients that cannot access HTTP headers, then define special media types just for those clients. Try not to constrain your API for other, more capable clients.

Creative use of media types does not need to be limited to text-based types. In a blog post (*http://bit.ly/paper-tigers*), Roy Fielding shows how to use a monochrome image format as a sparse array to identify resources that have changed in a single representation to avoid polling large numbers of them.

Enabling Hypermedia

As covered in Chapter 1, for media types that are not text based, the best option for hypermedia is to use link headers as defined in RFC 5988. For text-based formats, we discussed the variety of link syntaxes that are currently in use when covering link relations. However, there are a few other concerns that we need to address at the media type level. Should the media type allow two links with the same relation? If so, how can a user agent distinguish between those two links? In HAL, a link can have a `name` attribute associated with the link to identify it. HTML allows tags to have an id attribute associated for the purposes of identification.

Is there a need for hyperlinks to reference a particular element within an instance of the media type? Should a syntax be defined for identifying fragments?

What are the rules for resolving relative URIs?

Optional, Mandatory, Omitted, Applicable

When designing media types, especially ones used to represent writeable resources, I have found it necessary to convey semantics about the presence or absence of a particular piece of information. The most obvious scenario is that of a `mandatory` element. In the case of our `Issue item` media type, the `title` attribute is the one property that is mandatory.

For properties that are not mandatory, there are a number of reasons why a property may not be present in a representation. A resource may have chosen to include only a subset of properties in a representation for performance reasons, and therefore certain properties may be omitted. Another possibility is that the property is considered non-applicable.

Applicability refers to when the relevance of one property is dependent on the value of another property of the resource. For example, in an employee record, there may be a `TerminatedDate` field. If the employee status is `Current`, then it is likely that the `TerminatedDate` field is not applicable. Database tables and classes don't have the flexibility to change their shape dynamically per entity instance, so we often end up using null values to indicate that a property does not have any meaningful value. Unfortunately, a null value is also used to indicate that a property has not yet been supplied a value. This is not the same as a property being not applicable.

With media type representations, we can completely omit any syntax relating to the nonapplicable property and include the property syntax, but set the value as `null` or `empty` for those where a value has not yet been defined.

The policy of removing nonapplicable properties from representations can simplify client code and reduce coupling. There is often business logic that correlates the controlling property and the dependent properties. If the client assumes that the presence of a property infers applicability, then the client never needs to be aware of that business logic and can evolve without impacting the client.

> The ability to distinguish between mandatory, applicable, and omitted properties is one example of how explicitly defined media types are more expressive than object serialization formats, as those formats are limited to the semantics that can be expressed by a class.

When defining representations that contain only a subset of the resource properties, you need to avoid ambiguity between information that is being omitted and information that's nonapplicable. Attribute groups can sometimes help in these cases in the same way they allow partitioning of mandatory fields.

Embedded Versus External Metadata

Annotating representations is one way to include metadata such as a `mandatory` flag, type definitions, and range conditions. For example:

```
<foo>
    <fooDate required="true" type="Date" minValue="2001/01/01"
             maxValue="2020/12/31">2010/04/12</fooDate>
</foo>
```

This approach makes it easy for the client to access the metadata because it will be parsed at the same time as the actual data. However, as the amount of metadata increases it can significantly increase the size of the representation, and usually the metadata changes far less frequently than the data does. Also, the same metadata can usually be reused for many resources that belong to a single resource class.

When a resource contains two distinct sets of data that have different lifetimes, often the best option is to break it into two resources and link the resource with the shorter lifetime to the resource with the longer lifetime. This allows caching layers to reduce the data transmitted across the network.

One challenging aspect of using external metadata is that we must correlate which pieces of metadata apply to which pieces of representation data. Some media types define a selection syntax that allows us to point to a specific fragment of data within a document. For example, CSS stylesheets use `selectors` (*http://bit.ly/w3c-selectors*), and XML-based representations can use XPath queries to identify nodes within a document.

Extensibility

Media types are the point of coupling between the client and the server. A breaking change to a media type specification will potentially break clients. Ensuring that media types are designed to be extensible will help to minimize breaking changes while accommodating changing requirements. Writing client code to handle extensible formats can be trickier, as you can't make as many assumptions about the format. However, the up-front cost of writing more tolerant parsing code will quickly pay off.

One common tactic is to achieve extensibility to ignore unknown content. This may seem like counterintuitive advice to someone with lots of experience with schemas like XSD. However, this enables existing parsers to continue to process new versions of the media type that contain additional information. Returning to our minimal information model of an `Issue`, it could be represented in XML by:

```
<Issue>
    <Title>This is a bug</Title>
    <Description>Here are the details of the bug.</Description>
</Issue>
```

Assuming we wrote a parser that looked for the elements using the XPath queries `/Issue/Title` and `/Issue/Description`, then if the media type were enhanced to allow:

```
<Issue>
    <Title>This is a bug</Title>
    <FoundBy href='http://issueapi.example.org/user/342'/>
    <Description>Here are the details of the bug.</Description>
</Issue>
```

the existing parser would still be able to process this document even if there were missing information. What happens to that extra information is very much dependent on the use case. In some scenarios, it can be safely ignored. In others, the user should be warned about the fact that some information cannot be processed. Some services may choose to refuse to accept additional information that is not understood. All these are valid options, but there is no need to constrain the media type to support only one of the scenarios.

Another constraint that is often applied by XSD schemas is the ordering of elements. Unless the order of properties has some semantic significance, there is no need for a media type specification to enforce the order. I can imagine there are some simplicity and performance benefits for the parsing logic when properties appear in a specific order; however, once you allow unknown properties, those benefits are minimal. Facilitating extensibility is as much about avoiding unnecessary constraints as it is about applying constraints.

A media type specification should try to limit itself to constraints defined by the domain and not be limited by the implementation constraints of the service. For example, when a service is backed by a database, it is common to define field lengths. Field lengths are a constraint of the database used by the service; other implementations that use the media type will likely have different physical constraints. Arbitrarily enforcing a lowest-common-denominator constraint due to current implementation limitations is both unnecessary and unwise.

JSON Numeric Values

There is an interesting ongoing debate about JSON as a standard. Most JSON implementations limit the range of a numeric value in a JSON document to the same limit as those defined by JavaScript (64-bit floating-point value). However, Douglas Crockford, the author of JSON, has argued that JSON should exist independent of JavaScript (*http://bit.ly/json-limits*) and that there should be no constraint on the numeric value that can be represented in a JSON document. This is a forward-looking perspective that acknowledges the fact that JSON will most likely outlast the current JavaScript implementations. Admittedly, this decision makes life more difficult for the parser implementors, but I believe it is a worthwhile price to pay.

As a general rule of thumb, when it comes to defining a constraint in a media type, I ask myself if it is possible to parse the representation without the constraint and still convey the same meaning. If so, then I drop the constraint. The fewer the rules, the more likely it is for any extension to the media type to be harmless to existing code.

Registering the Media Type

In order for this "distributed type system" of media types to work, there needs to be a way for people to discover what valid types exist. The IANA registry is that central location. However, we have to be honest and say the current state of the IANA media type registry is pretty dismal. Currently, it consists of a few web pages with a bunch of links. Many of those links point to little more than an email message from 20 years ago (*http://bit.ly/atomicmail*). However, the fact that these entries still exist highlights the permanence of deploying types on the Internet. Once a new type has been let out onto the Internet, there is no guaranteed way of removing it. This is another reason why versioning media types can be problematic. There is no easy way to say "don't use that version anymore."

Many of the IANA registries have been updated to a newer XML/XSLT/XHTML format that makes them easier to consume by crawlers. However, the media type registry has not yet had this makeover and remains a pain to harvest (*http://bit.ly/getting-mtypes*).

The registration process is also fairly barbaric. It suggests you read six different RFCs and then asks you to submit an HTML form (*http://bit.ly/mt-apply*). It is recommended that before you submit the application form, you publish the proposed specification on the Internet and send an announcement of intent to submit to the IETF Types mailing list (*http://bit.ly/ietf-types*). The experts who moderate this list will likely provide feedback to assist in any perceived problems with the proposal. Be aware that these experts provide this guidance for free and are not there to educate people on media type design. When participating in these lists, try not to misinterpret bluntness and brevity for hostility!

There definitely is a need for some community pressure on IANA to improve the media type registry and its registration process. This is a critical piece of Internet infrastructure, and yet many visitors get the impression it is obsolete and abandoned because of its unkempt appearance.

Designing New Link Relations

After searching the link relation registry (*http://bit.ly/link-rel-reg*) and failing to find a link relation that describes the type of resource that you want to link to, you have the option to create your own link relation type. There are three distinct paths that you could take for this:

- Define the specifications for a new standard link relation type and submit that for approval.
- Create an "extended" link relation type for your own purposes.
- Integrate the link specification into your media type specification if you are already creating one.

Standard Link Relations

Creating a standard link relation has the benefit of your being able to use a short name for the `rel` value. The effort required to specify and register a link relation type does not have to be significant. The specification for the `license` link relation (*http://bit.ly/rfc-4946*) is a good example to review.

It is interesting to note that the RFC 4946 specification discusses only the use of the license relation within the context of Atom documents. In the IANA link relation registry, there is also a pointer that refers to a discussion in the HTML specification of its use within HTML documents. Another similar example comes from reading the specification on the monitor link relation, which implies it is for use only with the SIP protocol. It is unfortunate that these specifications are suggesting that their use is tied to particular media types. I'm quite sure that we need to be able to assign licenses to more than just HTML and Atom feeds, and I know that SIP is not the only way to monitor the status of resources.

One challenge of working in any complex discipline is knowing when you must follow the rules and knowing when you can break them. In these scenarios, I believe that these link relations have value beyond the context within which they have been defined and I am prepared to use them in other scenarios. I hope that as more people adopt the use of link relations in new scenarios, more awareness will follow about their reusability and new specifications will avoid tying them to specific media types.

The guidance for creating new link relations is very similar to that for media types. You want the relation to be as generic as possible while still providing sufficient semantics to address a particular domain issue. Some examples that are currently not standardized link relations but would be good candidates are:

Owner
  A link to a resource that is responsible for the current resource.

Home
  A link to an API entry point or root resource.

Like
  An unsafe link to indicate a user's appreciation of a resource.

Favorite
  An unsafe link to request that the resource be stored as a favorite of a user.

The Microformats website (*http://bit.ly/exist-rel-values*) documents many other proposed link relations and ones discovered in use in the wild. One interesting example is sitemap (*http://bit.ly/rel-sitemap*), which is widely used on the Web. In its specification, it prescribes the exact formats of the responses that are expected. This is an example of putting all the semantics in the link relation and none in the media type.

Extension Link Relations

Extension link relations are defined in RFC 5988 and allow you to create link relations that are not registered with IANA. To avoid naming conflicts, you must make the relation name a URI. This enables the use of the domain naming system to ensure uniqueness. Unfortunately, using URIs for link relations can become large and ugly within a representation. You can use CURIEs (*http://bit.ly/curie-syntax*) to abbreviate link relations, but some people don't like them because they look like XML namespaces but don't behave in the same way.

Having this capability is extremely useful, but it does lead to the possibility of link relation abuse. Once developers realize the power of link relations, they tend to go overboard and start creating service-specific link relations. Although this will work in the short term, it is not the best choice for the system's evolution or the overall web ecosystem due to the service-specific coupling that it introduces.

Embedded Link Relations

If the link relation is closely related to the semantics of a media type, it may make sense to make the link relation part of the media type specification and valid only within the media type itself. The HTML <FORM> tag is an example of a link relation that is defined within the media type itself. However, it is unfortunate that it was defined this way because there are currently efforts to duplicate very similar functionality in all the other hypermedia media types. If <FORM> had been defined as an independent link relation, it would make it easier to reuse in other media types.

Registering the Link Relation

The process for registering link relations is fairly straightforward and is documented fully in RFC 5988 (*http://bit.ly/rfc-5988*).

Media Types in the Issue Tracking Domain

In Chapter 4, we identified several different categories of resources: list resources, item resources, discovery resources, and search resources. For each of these resource categories, we need to identify which media types we believe are the most appropriate to carry the required semantics.

Homogeneous APIs

Some developers tend to try and pick a single media type and reuse it across an entire API. There is a perception that delivering just one media type will reduce the effort of the client developer. In many cases, it does exactly the opposite; trying to package all the semantics of a nontrivial API into a single media type means either that the specification is going to be complex, or some semantics are going to be communicated out of band. Limiting the client to processing only a single media type becomes problematic when the API starts to integrate links with external systems. If the client is designed to process only the dedicated API media type, then it may be difficult to build in support for other media types from other APIs.

> Building clients that can easily process many different media types encourages seren-
> dipitous reuse and facilitates system evolution and integration.

List Resources

For resources that return a list of items, we will be using the media type called `collec`
`tion+json` (*http://bit.ly/mt-collect*). This is a hypermedia-enabled type designed explicitly to support lists of items. This media type supports associating an arbitrary set
of data with each item in the list. It includes queries to enable searching for various
subsets of items as well as a template property to facilitate creating a new item in the
list.

We could have used HAL or even XHTML, as both are capable of representing a list of
items; however, as `collection+json` is specifically designed for the purpose of representing lists, it seems a more natural fit. Example 6-13 demonstrates how `collection`
`+json` can be used to represent a list of issues.

Example 6-13. Sample issue list

```
{
  "collection": {
    "href": "http://localhost:8080/Issue",
    "links": [],
    "items": [
      {
        "href": "http://localhost:8080/issue/1",
        "data": [
          {
            "name": "Description",
            "value": "This is an issue"
          },
          {
            "name": "Status",
            "value": "Open"
          },
          {
            "name": "Title",
            "value": "An issue"
          }
        ],
        "links": [
          {
            "rel": "http://webapibook.net/rels#issue-processor",
            "href": "http://localhost:8080/issueprocessor/1?action=transition"
          },
          {
            "rel": "http://webapibook.net/rels#issue-processor",
            "href": "http://localhost:8080/issueprocessor/1?action=close"
          }
        }
```

```
        ]
      },
      {
        "href": "http://localhost:8080/issue/2",
        "data": [
          {
            "name": "Description",
            "value": "This is a another issue"
          },
          {
            "name": "Status",
            "value": "Closed"
          },
          {
            "name": "Title",
            "value": "Another Issue"
          }
        ],
        "links": [
          {
            "rel": "http://webapibook.net/rels#issue-processor",
            "href": "http://localhost:8080/issueprocessor/2?action=transition"
          },
          {
            "rel": "http://webapibook.net/rels#issue-processor",
            "href": "http://localhost:8080/issueprocessor/2?action=open"
          }
        ]
      }
    ],
    "queries": [
      {
        "rel": "http://webapibook.net/rels#search",
        "href": "/issue",
        "prompt": "Issue search",
        "data": [
          {
            "name": "SearchText",
            "prompt": "Text to match against Title and Description"
          }
        ]
      }
    ],
    "template": {
      "data": []
    }
  }
}
```

Item Resources

We have several options for representing each individual issue. We could use HAL and define a link relation issue that specifies the content. We could use XHTML and define a semantic profile that annotates the HTML with semantics from the issue tracking domain. Or we could define a new media type to represent an issue.

The notion of an *issue* is sufficiently generic that it could easily be reused by many services, and therefore it justifies the creation of a new media type. This is not a niche domain; it is one used by every software developer and many customer support call centers. Having an interoperable format, even if implementation variations prevent a full-fidelity communication, has the potential to be extremely valuable.

A sample representation of this media type is shown in Example 6-14. For the moment, this media type will be defined as JSON. Early adopters of web technology are more likely to be comfortable with JSON, and if the media type gains traction, then an XML variant will be defined to enable wider adoption.

The full specification for this media type can be found in Appendix E.

Supporting Multiple Formats

One interesting approach to avoid creating two distinct specifications for the XML and JSON variant is demonstrated in the api-problem documentation (*http://bit.ly/api-problem*). In this case, the core specification assumes JSON as the format but includes an appendix for mapping the media type onto XML.

Example 6-14. Sample issue

```
{
  "id": "1",
  "title": "An issue",
  "description": "This is an issue",
  "status": "Open",
  "Links": [
    {
      "rel": "self",
      "href": "http://localhost:8080/issue/1"
    },
    {
      "rel": "http://webapibook.net/rels#issue-processor",
      "href": "http://localhost:8080/issueprocessor/1?action=transition",
      "action": "transition"
    },
    {
      "rel": "http://webapibook.net/rels#issue-processor",
      "href": "http://localhost:8080/issueprocessor/1?action=close",
```

```
        "action": "close"
      }
    ]
}
```

Discovery Resource

The discovery resource is an entry point resource that points to other resources that are available in the system. For this resource, we will be using a recently proposed media type called json-home (*http://bit.ly/json-home*). This media type is designed specifically to provide a representation for an entry point resource that allows dynamic discovery of resources. It is similar to the Atom Service Document (*http://bit.ly/rfc-5023*) but not limited to pointing to Atom feeds. The json-home document can have links to any arbitrary resource and can contain additional metadata that can be used to discover how to activate those links. Example 6-15 shows a possible json-home document for the Issue Tracker API.

Example 6-15. Sample root resource

```
{
  "resources": {
    "http://webapibook.net/rels#issue": {
      "href": "/issue/{id}",
      "hints": {
        "allow": [
          "GET"
        ],
        "formats": {
          "application/json": {},
          "application/vnd.issue+json": {}
        }
      }
    },
    "http://webapibook.net/rels#issues": {
      "href": "/issue",
      "hints": {
        "allow": [
          "GET"
        ],
        "formats": {
          "application/json": {},
          "application/vnd.collection+json": {}
        }
      }
    },
    "http://webapibook.net/rels#issue-processor": {
      "href": "/issueprocessor/{id}{?action}",
      "hints": {
        "allow": [
          "POST"
```

```
        ]
      }
    }
  }
}
```

Search Resource

For searching we will likely be able to rely on the query capability of `collection +json`. Where this proves insufficient, we will try to use the link relation `search` and the protocol defined by OpenSearch (*http://www.opensearch.org*).

Conclusion

Media types and link relations are the tools used to manage the coupling between the components in your distributed application. This chapter has covered the different ways to use that coupling to communicate application semantics. Being aware of existing specifications, and how and when to create new ones, provides a solid foundation on which to actually start building an API. In the next chapter, we begin to write a sample API based on the knowledge we have gained.

CHAPTER 7

Building the API

The proof of the pudding is in the eating, so let's eat.

In the previous two chapters, you learned about the design of the issue tracker system, and the media types that it will support for its interactions. Throughout this chapter, you'll see how to build the basic implementation of the Web API that supports that design. The goal for this exercise is not that the API should be fully functional or implement the entire design. It is to get the essential pieces in place that will enable us to address other concerns and to evolve the system.

This chapter is also not going to delve into too much detail on any of the individual parts, as the focus here is to put the pieces together. Later chapters will cover each of the different aspects of ASP.NET Web API in more detail.

The Design

At a high level, the design of the system is the following:

1. There is a backend system (such as GitHub) that manages issues.

2. The `Issue collection` resource retrieves items from the backend. It returns a response in either the `Issue+Json` or `Collection+Json` formats. This resource can also be used for creating new issues via an HTTP `POST`.

3. The `Issue item` resources contain representations of a single issue from the backend system. Issues can be updated via `PATCH` or deleted via a `DELETE` request.

4. Each issue contains links with the following `rel` values:

   self
   > Contains the URI for the issue itself

open
: Requests that the issue status be changed to `Closed`

close
: Requests that the issue status be be changed to `Open`

transition
: Requests to move the issue to the next appropriate status (e.g., from `Open` to `Closed`)

5. A set of `Issue processor` resources handles the actions related to transitioning the state of the issue.

Getting the Source

The implementation and unit tests for the API are available in the *WebApiBook* (*http://bit.ly/web-api-implement*) repo, or by cloning the issuetracker repo (*http://bit.ly/api-issuetracker*) and checking out the dev *BuildingTheApi* branch.

Building the Implementation Using BDD

The API was built in a test-driven manner using BDD-style (*http://bit.ly/bdd-style*) acceptance tests to drive out the implementation. The main difference between this and traditional TDD style is its focus on the end-to-end scenarios rather than the implementation. With acceptance-style tests, you'll get to see the full end-to-end process starting with the initial request.

BDD Primer

Behavior-driven development (BDD) is a style of test-driven development (TDD) that focuses on verifying the behavior of the system, whereas traditional TDD focuses on the implementation of different components. In BDD, requirements are generally written by a business expert in a form that can then be executed by the developer.

There are various forms of BDD, but the most common uses the Gherkin syntax (*http://bit.ly/gherkin-lang*) or Given, When, Then syntax. This syntax breaks up tests into features and scenarios. A feature is a single component that is being tested. Each feature has one or more scenarios that cover different parts of the feature. Each scenario is then broken down by steps, where each step is a Given, When, and Then, And, or But statement.

The Given clause sets the initial state of the system, When specifies something performed on the system, and Then is an assertion of the expected behavior. Each clause can have multiple parts joined together with And for inclusion or But for exclusion.

Navigating the Solution

Open up the *WebApiBook.IssueTrackerApi.sln*, located in the *src* folder. You'll notice the following projects:

WebApiBook.IssueTrackerApi
    Contains the API implementation.

WebApiBook.IssueTrackerApi.AcceptanceTests
    Contains BDD acceptance tests that verify the behavior of the system. Within the project file, you will see a *Features* folder with test files per feature, each of which contains one or more tests for that feature.

WebApiBook.IssueTrackerApi.SelfHost
    Contains a self-host for the API.

Packages and Libraries

Throughout the code, you'll notice the following packages and tools:

Microsoft.AspNet.WebApi.Core
    ASP.NET Web API is used for authoring and hosting our API. The Core package provides the minimum set of functionality needed.

Microsoft.AspNet.WebAp.SelfHost
    This package provides the ability to host an API outside of IIS.

Autofac.WebApi
    Autofac is used for dependency and lifetime management.

xunit
    XUnit is used as the test framework/runner.

Moq
    Moq is used for mocking objects within tests.

Should
    The Should library is used for "Should" assertion syntax.

XBehave
    The XBehave library is used for Gherkin-style syntax in the tests.

`CollectionJson`

This adds support for the `Collection+Json` media type.

Self-Host

Included in the source is a self-host for the Issue Tracker API. This will allow you to fire up the API and send it HTTP requests using a browser or a tool such as Fiddler. This is one of the nice features of ASP.NET Web API that make it really easy to develop with. Open the application (make sure to use admin privileges) and run it. Immediately you will see you have a host up and running, as shown in Figure 7-1.

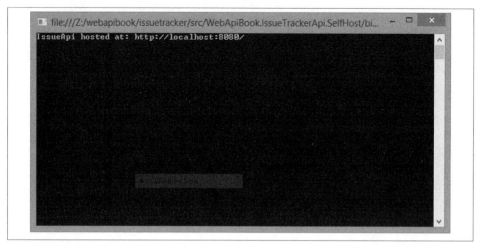

Figure 7-1. Self-host

One thing to keep in mind is that running self-hosted projects in Visual Studio requires either running as an administrator or reserving a port using the `netsh` command.

Sending a request to *http://localhost:8080* using an `Accept` header of `application/vnd.image+json` will give you the collection of issues shown in Figure 7-2.

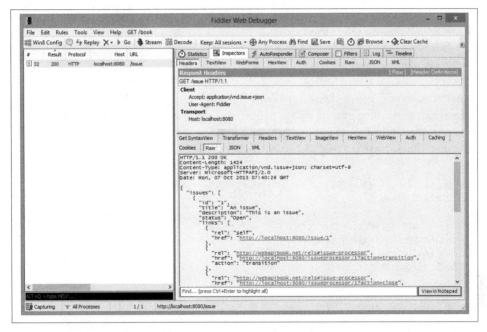

Figure 7-2. Sending a request for issues to the self-hosted API

If at any time throughout this chapter, you want to try out the API directly, using the self-host is the key! You can then put breakpoints in the API and step through to see exactly what is going on.

Now, on to the API!

Models and Services

The Issue Tracker API relies on a set of core services and models in its implementation.

Issue and Issue Store

As this is an issue tracker project, there needs to be a place to store and retrieve issues. The `IIssueStore` interface (*WebApiBook.IssueTrackerApi\Infrastructure\IIssueStore.cs*) defines methods for the creation, retrieval, and persistence of issues as shown in Example 7-1. Notice all the methods are async, as they will likely be network I/O-bound and should not block the application threads.

Example 7-1. IIssueStore interface

```
public interface IIssueStore
{
    Task<IEnumerable<Issue>> FindAsync();
    Task<Issue> FindAsync(string issueId);
```

```
    Task<IEnumerable<Issue>> FindAsyncQuery(string searchText);
    Task UpdateAsync(Issue issue);
    Task DeleteAsync(string issueId);
    Task CreateAsync(Issue issue);
}
```

The Issue class (*WebApiBook.IssueTrackerApi\Models\Issue.cs*) in Example 7-2 is a *data model* and contains data that is persisted for an issue in the store. It carries only the *resource state* and does not contain any links. Links are *application state* and do not belong in the domain, as they are an API-level concern.

Example 7-2. Issue class

```
public class Issue
{
    public string Id { get; set; }
    public string Title { get; set; }
    public string Description { get; set; }
    public IssueStatus Status { get; set; }
}

public enum IssueStatus {Open, Closed}
```

IssueState

The IssueState class (*WebApiBook.IssueTrackerApi\Models\IssueState.cs*) in Example 7-3 is a *state model* designed to carry both resource and application state. It can then be represented in one or more media types as part of an HTTP response.

Example 7-3. IssueState class

```
public class IssueState
{
    public IssueState()
    {
        Links = new List<Link>();
    }

    public string Id { get; set; }
    public string Title { get; set; }
    public string Description { get; set; }
    public IssueStatus Status { get; set; }
    public IList<Link> Links { get; private set; }
}
```

Notice the IssueState class has the same members as the Issue class with the addition of a collection of links. You might wonder why the IssueState class doesn't inherit from Issue. The answer is to have better separation of concerns. If IssueState inherits from Issue, then it is tightly coupled, meaning any changes to Issue will affect it. Evolvability is one of the qualities we want for the system; having good separation contributes to this, as parts can be modified independently of one another.

IssuesState

The IssuesState class (*WebApiBook.IssueTrackerApi\Models\IssuesState.cs*) in Example 7-4 is used for returning a collection of issues. The collection contains a set of top-level links. Notice the collection also explicitly implements the CollectionJson library's IReadDocument interface. This interface, as you will see, is used by the Collec tionJsonFormatter to write out the Collection+Json format if the client sends an Accept of application/vnd.collection+json. The standard formatters, however, will use the public surface.

Example 7-4. IssuesState class

```
using CJLink = WebApiContrib.CollectionJson.Link;

public class IssuesState : IReadDocument
{
    public IssuesState()
    {
        Links = new List<Link>();
    }

    public IEnumerable<IssueState> Issues { get; set; }
    public IList<Link> Links { get; private set; }

    Collection IReadDocument.Collection
    {
        get
        {
            var collection = new Collection(); // <1>
            collection.Href = Links.SingleOrDefault(l => l.Rel ==
                IssueLinkFactory.Rels.Self).Href; // <2>
            collection.Links.Add(new CJLink {Rel="profile",
                Href = new Uri("http://webapibook.net/profile")}); // <3>
            foreach (var issue in Issues) // <4>
            {
                var item = new Item(); // <5>
                item.Data.Add(new Data {Name="Description",
                    Value=issue.Description}); // <6>
                item.Data.Add(new Data {Name = "Status",
                    Value = issue.Status});
                item.Data.Add(new Data {Name="Title",
                    Value = issue.Title});
                foreach (var link in issue.Links) // <7>
                {
                    if (link.Rel == IssueLinkFactory.Rels.Self)
                        item.Href = link.Href;
                    else
```

```
            {
                item.Links.Add(new CJLink{Href = link.Href,
                    Rel = link.Rel});
            }
        }
        collection.Items.Add(item);

    }
    var query = new Query {
        Rel=IssueLinkFactory.Rels.SearchQuery,
        Href = new Uri("/issue", UriKind.Relative),
            Prompt="Issue search" }; // <8>

    query.Data.Add(
        new Data() { Name = "SearchText",
            Prompt = "Text to match against Title and Description" });
    collection.Queries.Add(query);
    return collection; // <9>
        }
    }
}
```

The most interesting logic is the Collection, which manufactures a Collection +Json document:

- A new Collection+Json Collection is instantiated. *<1>*
- The collection's href is set. *<2>*
- A profile link is added to link to a description of the collection *<3>*.
- The issues state collection is iterated through *<4>*, creating corresponding Collec tion+Json Item instances *<5>* and setting the Data *<6>* and Links *<7>*.
- An "Issue search" query is created and added to the document's query collection. *<8>*
- The collection is returned. *<9>*

Link

The Link class (*WebApiBook.IssueTrackerApi\Models\Link.cs*) in Example 7-5 carries the standard Rel and Href shown earlier and includes additional metadata for describing an optional action associated with that link.

Example 7-5. Link class

```
public class Link
{
    public string Rel { get; set; }
    public Uri Href { get; set; }
```

```
    public string Action { get; set; }
}
```

IssueStateFactory

Now that the system has an `Issue` and an `IssueState`, there needs to be a way to get from the `Issue` to the `State`. The `IssueStateFactory` (*WebApiBook.IssueTrackerApi \Infrastructure\IssueStateFactory.cs*) in Example 7-6 takes an `Issue` instance and manufactures a corresponding `IssueState` instance including its links.

Example 7-6. IssueStateFactory class

```
public class IssueStateFactory : IStateFactory<Issue, IssueState> // <1>
{
    private readonly IssueLinkFactory _links;

    public IssueStateFactory(IssueLinkFactory links)
    {
        _links = links;
    }

    public IssueState Create(Issue issue)
    {
        var model = new IssueState // <2>
            {
                Id = issue.Id,
                Title = issue.Title,
                Description = issue.Description,
                Status = Enum.GetName(typeof(IssueStatus),
                    issue.Status)
            };

        //add hypermedia
        model.Links.Add(_links.Self(issue.Id)); // <2>
        model.Links.Add(_links.Transition(issue.Id));

        switch (issue.Status) { // <3>
            case IssueStatus.Closed:
                model.Links.Add(_links.Open(issue.Id));
                break;
            case IssueStatus.Open:
                model.Links.Add(_links.Close(issue.Id));
                break;
        }

        return model;
    }
}
```

Here is how the code works:

- The factory implements IStateFactory<Issue, IssueState>. This interface is implemented so that callers can depend on it rather than the concrete class, thereby making it easier to mock in a unit test.

- The create method initializes an IssueState instance and copies over the data from the Issue *<1>*.

- Next, it contains business logic for applying standard links, like Self and Transition *<2>*, as well as context-specific links, like Open and Close *<3>*.

LinkFactory

Whereas the StateFactory contains the logic for adding links, the IssueLinkFacto ry creates the link objects themselves. It provides strongly typed accessors for each link in order to make the consuming code easier to read and maintain.

First comes the LinkFactory class (*WebApiBook.IssueTrackerApi\Infrastructure\Link-Factory.cs*) in Example 7-7, which other factories derive from.

Example 7-7. LinkFactory class

```
public abstract class LinkFactory
{
    private readonly UrlHelper _urlHelper;
    private readonly string _controllerName;
    private const string DefaultApi = "DefaultApi";

    protected LinkFactory(HttpRequestMessage request, Type controllerType) // <1>
    {
        _urlHelper = new UrlHelper(request); // <2>
        _controllerName = GetControllerName(controllerType);
    }

    protected Link GetLink<TController>(string rel, object id, string action,
        string route = DefaultApi) // <3>
    {
        var uri = GetUri(new { controller=GetControllerName(
            typeof(TController)), id, action}, route);
        return new Link {Action = action, Href = uri, Rel = rel};
    }

    private string GetControllerName(Type controllerType) // <4>
    {
        var name = controllerType.Name;
        return name.Substring(0, name.Length - "controller".Length).ToLower();
    }

    protected Uri GetUri(object routeValues, string route = DefaultApi) // <5>
    {
        return new Uri(_urlHelper.Link(route, routeValues));
```

```
    }

    public Link Self(string id, string route = DefaultApi) // <6>
    {
        return new Link { Rel = Rels.Self, Href = GetUri(
            new { controller = _controllerName, id = id }, route) };
    }

    public class Rels
    {
        public const string Self = "self";
    }
}

public abstract class LinkFactory<TController> : LinkFactory // <7>
{
    public LinkFactory(HttpRequestMessage request) :
        base(request, typeof(TController)) { }
}
```

This factory generates URIs given route values and a default route name:

- It takes the `HttpRequestMessage` as a constructor parameter *<1>*, which it uses to construct a `UrlHelper` instance *<2>*. It also takes a controller type which it will use for generating a "self" link.

- The `GetLink` generic method manufactures a link based on a rel, a controller to link to, and additional parameters. *<3>*

- The `GetControllerName` method extracts the controller name given a type. It is used by the `GetLink` method. *<4>*

- The `GetUri` method uses the `UrlHelper` method to generate the actual URI. *<5>*

- The base factory returns a `Self` link *<6>* for the specified controller. Derived factories can add additional links, as you will see shortly.

- The `LinkFactory<TController>` convenience class *<7>* is provided to offer a more strongly typed experience that does not rely on magic strings.

IssueLinkFactory

The `IssueLinkFactory` (*WebApiBook.IssueTrackerApi\Infrastructure\IssueLinkFactory.cs*) in Example 7-8 generates all the links specific to the Issue resource. It does not contain the logic for whether or not the link should be present in the response, as that is handled in the `IssueStateFactory`.

Example 7-8. IssueLinkFactory class

```
public class IssueLinkFactory : LinkFactory<IssueController> // <1>
{
    private const string Prefix = "http://webapibook.net/rels#"; // <5>

    public new class Rels : LinkFactory.Rels { // <3>
        public const string IssueProcessor = Prefix + "issue-processor";
        public const string SearchQuery = Prefix + "search";
    }

    public class Actions { // <4>
        public const string Open="open";
        public const string Close="close";
        public const string Transition="transition";
    }

    public IssueLinkFactory(HttpRequestMessage request) // <2>
    {
    }

    public Link Transition(string id) // <6>
    {
        return GetLink<IssueProcessorController>(
            Rels.IssueProcessor, id, Actions.Transition);
    }

    public Link Open(string id) { // <7>
        return GetLink<IssueProcessorController>(
            Rels.IssueProcessor, id, Actions.Open);
    }

    public Link Close(string id) { // <8>
        return GetLink<IssueProcessorController>(
            Rels.IssueProcessor, id, Actions.Close);
    }
}
```

Here's how the class works:

- This factory derives from `LinkFactory<IssueController>` as the self link it generates is for the `IssueController` *<1>*.

- In the constructor it takes an `HttpRequestMessage` instance, which it passes to the base. It also passes the controller name, which the base factory uses for route generation *<2>*.

- The factory also contains inner classes for `Rels` *<3>* and `Actions` *<4>*, removing the need for magic strings in the calling code.

- Notice the base `Rel` *<5>* is a URI pointing to documentation on our website with a # to get to the specific `Rel`.

- The factory includes `Transition` *<6>*, `Open` *<7>*, and `Close` *<8>* methods to generate links for transitioning the state of the system.

Acceptance Criteria

Before getting started, let's identify at a high level acceptance criteria for the code using the BDD Gherkin syntax.

Following are the tests for the Issue Tracker API, which covers CRUD (create-read-update-delete) access to issues as well as issue processing:

```
Feature: Retrieving issues
  Scenario: Retrieving an existing issue
    Given an existing issue
    When it is retrieved
    Then a '200 OK' status is returned
    Then it is returned
    Then it should have an id
    Then it should have a title
    Then it should have a description
    Then it should have a state
    Then it should have a 'self' link
    Then it should have a 'transition' link

  Scenario: Retrieving an open issue
    Given an existing open issue
    When it is retrieved
    Then it should have a 'close' link

  Scenario: Retrieving a closed issue
    Given an existing closed issue
    When it is retrieved
    Then it should have an 'open' link

  Scenario: Retrieving an issue that does not exist
    Given an issue does not exist
    When it is retrieved
    Then a '404 Not Found' status is returned

  Scenario: Retrieving all issues
    Given existing issues
    When all issues are retrieved
    Then a '200 OK' status is returned
    Then all issues are returned
    Then the collection should have a 'self' link

  Scenario: Retrieving all issues as Collection+Json
    Given existing issues
    When all issues are retrieved as Collection+Json
    Then a '200 OK' status is returned
```

```
      Then Collection+Json is returned
      Then the href should be set
      Then all issues are returned
      Then the search query is returned

   Scenario: Searching issues
      Given existing issues
         When issues are searched
         Then a '200 OK' status is returned
         Then the collection should have a 'self' link
         Then the matching issues are returned

Feature: Creating issues
   Scenario: Creating a new issue
      Given a new issue
      When a POST request is made
      Then a '201 Created' status is returned
      Then the issue should be added
      Then the response location header will be set to the resource location

Feature: Updating issues
   Scenario: Updating an issue
      Given an existing issue
      When a PATCH request is made
      Then a '200 OK' is returned
      Then the issue should be updated

   Scenario: Updating an issue that does not exist
      Given an issue does not exist
      When a PATCH request is made
      Then a '404 Not Found' status is returned

Feature: Deleting issues
   Scenario: Deleting an issue
      Give an existing issue
      When a DELETE request is made
      Then a '200 OK' status is returned
      Then the issue should be removed

   Scenario: Deleting an issue that does not exist
      Given an issue does not exist
      When a DELETE request is made
      Then a '404 Not Found' status is returned

Feature: Processing issues
   Scenario: Closing an open issue
      Given an existing open issue
      When a POST request is made to the issue processor
      And the action is 'close'
      Then a '200 OK' status is returned
      Then the issue is closed
```

```
Scenario: Transitioning an open issue
  Given an existing open issue
  When a POST request is made to the issue processor
  And the action is 'transition'
  Then a '200 OK' status is returned
  The issue is closed

Scenario: Closing a closed issue
  Given an existing closed issue
  When a POST request is made to the issue processor
  And the action is 'close'
  Then a '400 Bad Request' status is returned

Scenario: Opening a closed issue
  Given an existing closed issue
  When a POST request is made to the issue processor
  And the action is 'open'
  Then a '200 OK' status is returned
  Then it is opened

Scenario: Transitioning a closed issue
  Given an existing closed issue
  When a POST request is made to the issue processor
  And the action is 'transition'
  Then a '200 OK' status is returned
  Then it is opened

Scenario: Opening an open issue
  Given an existing open issue
  When a POST request is made to the issue processor
  And the action is 'open'
  Then a '400 Bad Request' status is returned

Scenario: Performing an invalid action
  Given an existing issue
  When a POST request is made to the issue processor
  And the action is not valid
  Then a '400 Bad Request' status is returned

Scenario: Opening an issue that does not exist
  Given an issue does not exist
  When a POST request is made to the issue processor
  And the action is 'open'
  Then a '404 Not Found' status is returned

Scenario: Closing an issue that does not exist
  Given an issue does not exist
  When a POST request is made to the issue processor
  And the action is 'close'
  Then a '404 Not Found' status is returned

Scenario: Transitioning an issue that does not exist
```

```
Given an issue does not exist
When a POST request is made to the issue processor
And the action is 'transition'
Then a '404 Not Found' status is returned
```

Throughout the remainder of the chapter, you will delve into all the tests and implementation for retrieval, creation, updating, and deletion. There are additional tests for issue processing, which will not be covered. The `IssueProcessor` controller, however, will be covered, and all the code and implementation is available in the GitHub repo.

Feature: Retrieving Issues

This feature covers retrieving one or more issues from the API using an HTTP GET method. The tests for this feature are comprehensive in particular because the responses contain hypermedia, which is dynamically generated based on the state of the issues.

Open the *RetrievingIssues.cs* tests (*WebApiBook.IssueTrackerApi.AcceptanceTests/Features/RetrievingIssues.cs*). Notice the class derives from `IssuesFeature`, demonstrated in Example 7-9 (*IssuesFeature.cs*). This class is a common base for all the tests. It sets up an *in-memory* host for our API, which the tests can use to issue HTTP requests against.

Example 7-9. IssuesFeature class

```
public abstract class IssuesFeature
{
    public Mock<IIssueStore> MockIssueStore;
    public HttpResponseMessage Response;
    public IssueLinkFactory IssueLinks;
    public IssueStateFactory StateFactory;
    public IEnumerable<Issue> FakeIssues;
    public HttpRequestMessage Request { get; private set; }
    public HttpClient Client;

    public IssuesFeature()
    {
        MockIssueStore = new Mock<IIssueStore>(); // <1>
        Request = new HttpRequestMessage();
        Request.Headers.Accept.Add(
            new MediaTypeWithQualityHeaderValue("application/vnd.issue+json"));
        IssueLinks = new IssueLinkFactory(Request);
        StateFactory = new IssueStateFactory(IssueLinks);
        FakeIssues = GetFakeIssues(); // <2>
        var config = new HttpConfiguration();
        WebApiConfiguration.Configure(
            config, MockIssueStore.Object);
        var server = new HttpServer(config); // <3>
        Client = new HttpClient(server); // <4>
    }
```

```
private IEnumerable<Issue> GetFakeIssues()
{
    var fakeIssues = new List<Issue>();
    fakeIssues.Add(new Issue { Id = "1", Title = "An issue",
        Description = "This is an issue",
        Status = IssueStatus.Open });
    fakeIssues.Add(new Issue { Id = "2", Title = "Another issue",
        Description = "This is another issue",
        Status = IssueStatus.Closed });
    return fakeIssues;
}
}
```

The `IssuesFeature` constructor initializes instances/mocks of the services previously mentioned, which are common to all the tests:

- Creates an `HttpRequest` *<1>* and sets up test data *<2>*.

- Initializes an `HttpServer`, passing in the configuration object configured via the `Configure` method *<3>*.

- Sets the `Client` property to a new `HttpClient` instance, passing the `HttpServer` in the constructor *<4>*.

Example 7-10 demonstrates the `WebApiConfiguration` class.

Example 7-10. WebApiConfiguration class

```
public static class WebApiConfiguration
{

    public static void Configure(HttpConfiguration config,
    IIssueStore issueStore = null)
    {
        config.Routes.MapHttpRoute("DefaultApi", // <1>
            "{controller}/{id}", new { id = RouteParameter.Optional });
        ConfigureFormatters(config);
        ConfigureAutofac(config, issueStore);
    }

    private static void ConfigureFormatters(HttpConfiguration config)
    {
        config.Formatters.Add(new CollectionJsonFormatter()); // <2>
        JsonSerializerSettings settings = config.Formatters.JsonFormatter.
            SerializerSettings; // <3>
        settings.NullValueHandling = NullValueHandling.Ignore;
        settings.Formatting = Formatting.Indented;
        settings.ContractResolver =
            new CamelCasePropertyNamesContractResolver();
        config.Formatters.JsonFormatter.SupportedMediaTypes.Add(
            new MediaTypeHeaderValue("application/vnd.issue+json"));
    }
```

```
        private static void ConfigureAutofac(HttpConfiguration config,
                IIssueStore issueStore)
        {
            var builder = new ContainerBuilder(); // <4>
            builder.RegisterApiControllers(typeof(IssueController).Assembly);

            if (issueStore == null) // <5>
                builder.RegisterType<InMemoryIssueStore>().As<IIssueStore>().
                            InstancePerLifetimeScope();
            else
                builder.RegisterInstance(issueStore);

            builder.RegisterType<IssueStateFactory>(). // <6>
                As<IStateFactory<Issue, IssueState>>().InstancePerLifetimeScope();
            builder.RegisterType<IssueLinkFactory>().InstancePerLifetimeScope();
            builder.RegisterHttpRequestMessage(config); // <7>
            var container = builder.Build(); // <8>
            config.DependencyResolver = new AutofacWebApiDependencyResolver(container);
        }
    }
}
```

The `WebApiConfiguration.Configure` method in Example 7-10 does the following:

- Registers the default route *<1>*.

- Adds the `Collection+Json` formatter *<2>*.

- Configures the default JSON formatter to ignore nulls, force camel casing for properties, and support the `Issue` media type *<3>*.

- Creates an Autofac `ContainerBuilder` and registers all controllers *<4>*.

- Registers the store using the passed-in store instance if provided (used for passing in a mock instance) *<5>* and otherwise defaults to the `InMemoryStore`.

- Registers the remaining services *<6>*.

- Wires up Autofac to inject the current `HttpRequestMessage` as a dependency *<7>*. This enables services such as the `IssueLinkFactory` to get the request.

- Creates the container and passes it to the Autofac dependency resolver *<8>*.

Retrieving an Issue

The first set of tests verifies retrieval of an individual issue and that all the necessary data is present:

```
Scenario: Retrieving an existing issue
    Given an existing issue
    When it is retrieved
    Then a '200 OK' status is returned
```

```
    Then it is returned
    Then it should have an id
    Then it should have a title
    Then it should have a description
    Then it should have a state
    Then it should have a 'self' link
    Then it should have a 'transition' link
```

The associated tests are in Example 7-11.

Example 7-11. Retrieving an issue

```
[Scenario]
public void RetrievingAnIssue(IssueState issue, Issue fakeIssue)
{
    "Given an existing issue".
        f(() =>
            {
                fakeIssue = FakeIssues.FirstOrDefault();
                MockIssueStore.Setup(i => i.FindAsync("1")).
                    Returns(Task.FromResult(fakeIssue)); // <1>
            });
    "When it is retrieved".
        f(() =>
            {
                Request.RequestUri = _uriIssue1; // <2>
                Response = Client.SendAsync(Request).Result; // <3>
                issue = Response.Content.ReadAsAsync<IssueState>().Result; // <4>
            });
    "Then a '200 OK' status is returned".
        f(() => Response.StatusCode.ShouldEqual(HttpStatusCode.OK)); // <5>
    "Then it is returned".
        f(() => issue.ShouldNotBeNull()); // <6>
    "Then it should have an id".
        f(() => issue.Id.ShouldEqual(fakeIssue.Id)); // <7>
    "Then it should have a title".
        f(() => issue.Title.ShouldEqual(fakeIssue.Title)); // <8>
    "Then it should have a description".
        f(() => issue.Description.ShouldEqual(fakeIssue.Description)); // <9>
    "Then it should have a state".
        f(() => issue.Status.ShouldEqual(fakeIssue.Status)); // <10>
    "Then it should have a 'self' link".
        f(() =>
            {
                var link = issue.Links.FirstOrDefault(l => l.Rel ==
                                IssueLinkFactory.Rels.Self);
                link.ShouldNotBeNull(); // <11>
                link.Href.AbsoluteUri.ShouldEqual(
                    "http://localhost/issue/1"); // <12>
            });
    "Then it should have a transition link".
        f(() =>
            {
```

```
                    var link = issue.Links.FirstOrDefault(l =>
                        l.Rel == IssueLinkFactory.Rels.IssueProcessor &&
                        l.Action == IssueLinkFactory.Actions.Transition);
                    link.ShouldNotBeNull(); // <13>
                    link.Href.AbsoluteUri.ShouldEqual(
                        "http://localhost/issueprocessor/1?action=transition"); // <14>
                });
        }
```

Understanding the tests

For those who are not familiar with XBehave.NET, the test syntax used here might look confusing. In XBehave, tests for a specific scenario are grouped together in a single class method, which is annotated with a [Scenario] attribute. Each method can have one or more parameters (e.g., issue and fakeIssue), which XBehave will set to their default values rather than defining variables inline.

Within each method there is one more test that will be executed. XBehave allows a "free from string" syntax that allows for describing the test in plain English. The f() function is an extension method of System.String, which takes a lambda. The string provided is only documentation for the user reading the test code and/or viewing the results—it has no meaning to XBehave itself. In practice, Gherkin syntax will be used within the strings, but this is not actually required. XBehave cares only about the lambdas, which it executes in the order that they are defined.

Another common pattern you will see in the tests is the usage of the Should library. This library introduces a set of extension methods that start with Should and perform assertions. The syntax it provides is more terse than Assert methods. In the retrieving issue tests, ShouldEqual and ShouldNotBeNull method calls are both examples of using this library.

Here is an overview of what the preceding tests perform:

- Sets up the mock store to return an issue *<1>*.
- Sets the request URI to the issue resource *<2>*.
- Sends the request *<3>* and extracts the issue from the response *<4>*.
- Verifies that the status code is 200 *<5>*.
- Verifies that the issue is not null *<6>*.
- Verifies that the id *<7>*, title *<8>*, description *<9>*, and status *<10>* match the issue that was passed to the mock store.
- Verifies that a Self link was added, pointing to the issue resource.
- Verifies that a Transition link was added, pointing to the issue processor resource.

Requests for an individual issue are handled by the `Get` overload on the `IssueControl ler`, as shown in Example 7-12.

Example 7-12. IssueController Get overload method

```
public async Task<HttpResponseMessage> Get(string id)
{
    var result = await _store.FindAsync(id); // <1>
    if (result == null)
        return Request.CreateResponse(HttpStatusCode.NotFound); // <2>

    return Request.CreateResponse(HttpStatusCode.OK,
    _stateFactory.Create(result)); // <3>
}
```

This method queries for a single issue *<1>*, returns a `404 Not Found` status code if the resource cannot be found *<2>*, and returns only a single item rather then a higher-level document *<3>*.

As you'll see, most of these tests are actually not testing the controller itself but rather the `IssueStateFactory.Create` method shown earlier in Example 7-6.

Retrieving Open and Closed Issues

```
Scenario: Retrieving an open issue
  Given an existing open issue
  When it is retrieved
  Then it should have a 'close' link

Scenario: Retrieving a closed issue
  Given an existing closed issue
  When it is retrieved
  Then it should have an 'open' link
```

The scenario tests can be seen in Examples 7-13 and 7-14.

The next set of tests are very similar, checking for a *close* link on an open issue (Example 7-13) and an *open* link on a closed issue (Example 7-14).

Example 7-13. Retrieving an open issue

```
[Scenario]
public void RetrievingAnOpenIssue(Issue fakeIssue, IssueState issue)
{
    "Given an existing open issue".
        f(() =>
            {
                fakeIssue = FakeIssues.Single(i =>
                    i.Status == IssueStatus.Open);
                MockIssueStore.Setup(i => i.FindAsync("1")).Returns(
                    Task.FromResult(fakeIssue)); // <1>
            });
```

```
"When it is retrieved".
    f(() =>
        {
            Request.RequestUri = _uriIssue1; // <2>
            issue = Client.SendAsync(Request).Result.Content.
                ReadAsAsync<IssueState>().Result; // <3>
        });
"Then it should have a 'close' action link".
    f(() =>
        {
            var link = issue.Links.FirstOrDefault(
                l => l.Rel == IssueLinkFactory.Rels.IssueProcessor &&
                l.Action == IssueLinkFactory.Actions.Close); // <4>
            link.ShouldNotBeNull();
            link.Href.AbsoluteUri.ShouldEqual(
                "http://localhost/issueprocessor/1?action=close");
        });
}
```

Example 7-14. Retrieving a closed issue

```
public void RetrievingAClosedIssue(Issue fakeIssue, IssueState issue)
{
    "Given an existing closed issue".
        f(() =>
            {
                fakeIssue = FakeIssues.Single(i =>
                    i.Status == IssueStatus.Closed);
                MockIssueStore.Setup(i => i.FindAsync("2")).Returns(
                    Task.FromResult(fakeIssue)); // <1>
            });
    "When it is retrieved".
        f(() =>
            {
                Request.RequestUri = _uriIssue2; // <2>
                issue = Client.SendAsync(Request).Result.Content.
                    ReadAsAsync<IssueState>().Result; // <3>
            });
    "Then it should have a 'open' action link".
        f(() =>
            {
                var link = issue.Links.FirstOrDefault(
                    l => l.Rel == IssueLinkFactory.Rels.IssueProcessor &&
                    l.Action == IssueLinkFactory.Actions.Open); // <4>
                link.ShouldNotBeNull();
                link.Href.AbsoluteUri.ShouldEqual(
                    "http://localhost/issueprocessor/2?action=open");
            });
}
```

The implementation for each test is also very similar:

- Sets up the mock store to return the open (id=1) or closed issue (id=2) appropriate for the test *<1>*.
- Sets the request URI for the resource being retrieved *<2>*.
- Sends the request and captures the issue in the result *<3>*.
- Verifies that the appropriate Open or Close link is present *<4>*.

Similar to the previous test, this test also verifies logic present in the IssueStateFactory, which is shown in Example 7-15. It adds the appropriate links depending on the status of the issue.

Example 7-15. IssueStateFactory Create method

```
public IssueState Create(Issue issue)
{
    ...
    switch (model.Status) {
        case IssueStatus.Closed:
            model.Links.Add(_links.Open(issue.Id));
            break;
        case IssueStatus.Open:
            model.Links.Add(_links.Close(issue.Id));
            break;
    }

    return model;
}
```

Retrieving an Issue That Does Not Exist

The next scenario verifies the system returns a 404 Not Found if the resource does not exist:

```
Scenario: Retrieving an issue that does not exist
    Given an issue does not exist
    When it is retrieved
    Then a '404 Not Found' status is returned
```

The scenario tests are in Example 7-16.

Example 7-16. Retrieving an issue that does not exist

```
[Scenario]
public void RetrievingAnIssueThatDoesNotExist()
{
    "Given an issue does not exist".
        f(() => MockIssueStore.Setup(i =>
            i.FindAsync("1")).Returns(Task.FromResult((Issue)null))); // <1>
    "When it is retrieved".
        f(() =>
```

```
            {
                Request.RequestUri = _uriIssue1; // <2>
                Response = Client.SendAsync(Request).Result; // <3>
            });
        "Then a '404 Not Found' status is returned".
            f(() => Response.StatusCode.ShouldEqual(HttpStatusCode.NotFound)); // <4>
}
```

How the tests work:

- Sets up the store to return a null issue *<1>*. Notice the Task.FromResult extension is used to easily create a Task that contains a null object in its result.
- Sets the request URI *<2>*.
- Issues the request and captures the response *<3>*.
- Verifies the code is verified to be HttpStatusCode.NotFound *<4>*.

In the IssueController.Get method, this scenario is handled with the code in Example 7-17.

Example 7-17. IssueController Get method returning a 404

```
if (result == null)
    return Request.CreateResponse(HttpStatusCode.NotFound);
```

Retrieving All Issues

This scenario verifies that the issue collection can be properly retrieved:

```
Scenario: Retrieving all issues
  Given existing issues
  When all issues are retrieved
  Then a '200 OK' status is returned
  Then all issues are returned
  Then the collection should have a 'self' link
```

The tests for this scenario are shown in Example 7-18.

Example 7-18. Retrieving all issues

```
private Uri _uriIssues = new Uri("http://localhost/issue");
private Uri _uriIssue1 = new Uri("http://localhost/issue/1");
private Uri _uriIssue2 = new Uri("http://localhost/issue/2");

[Scenario]
public void RetrievingAllIssues(IssuesState issuesState)
{
    "Given existing issues".
        f(() => MockIssueStore.Setup(i => i.FindAsync()).Returns(
            Task.FromResult(FakeIssues))); // <1>
    "When all issues are retrieved".
```

```
    f(() =>
        {
            Request.RequestUri = _uriIssues; // <2>
            Response = Client.SendAsync(Request).Result; // <3>
            issuesState = Response.Content.
                ReadAsAsync<IssuesState>().Result; // <4>
        });
    "Then a '200 OK' status is returned".
        f(() => Response.StatusCode.ShouldEqual(HttpStatusCode.OK)); // <5>
    "Then they are returned".
        f(() =>
        {
            issuesState.Issues.FirstOrDefault(i => i.Id == "1").
                ShouldNotBeNull(); // <6>
            issuesState.Issues.FirstOrDefault(i => i.Id == "2").
                ShouldNotBeNull();
        });
    "Then the collection should have a 'self' link".
        f(() =>
        {
            var link = issuesState.Links.FirstOrDefault(
                l => l.Rel == IssueLinkFactory.Rels.Self); // <7>
            link.ShouldNotBeNull();
            link.Href.AbsoluteUri.ShouldEqual("http://localhost/issue");
        });
}
```

These tests verify that a request sent to /issue returns all the issues:

- Sets up the mock store to return the collection of fake issues *<1>*.

- Sets the request URI to the issue resource *<2>*.

- Sends the request and captures the response *<3>*.

- Reads the response content and converts it to an IssuesState instance *<4>*. The ReadAsAsync method uses the formatter associated with the HttpContent instance to manufacture an object from the contents.

- Verifies that the returned status is OK *<5>*.

- Verifies that the correct issues are returned *<6>*.

- Verifies that the Self link is returned *<7>*.

On the server, the issue resource is handled by the *IssueController.cs* file (*WebApi-Book.IssueTrackerApi/Controllers/IssueController*). The controller takes an issues store, an issue state factory, and an issue link factory as dependencies (as shown in Example 7-19).

Example 7-19. IssueController constructor

```
public class IssueController : ApiController
{
    private readonly IIssueStore _store;
    private readonly IStateFactory<Issue, IssueState> _stateFactory;
    private readonly IssueLinkFactory _linkFactory;

    public IssueController(IIssueStore store,
        IStateFactory<Issue, IssueState> stateFactory,
        IssueLinkFactory linkFactory)
    {
        _store = store;
        _stateFactory = stateFactory;
        _linkFactory = linkFactory;
    }
    ...
}
```

The request for all issues is handled by the parameterless `Get` method (Example 7-20).

Example 7-20. IssueController Get method

```
public async Task<HttpResponseMessage> Get()
{
    var result = await _store.FindAsync(); // <1>
    var issuesState = new IssuesState(); // <2>
    issuesState.Issues = result.Select(i => _stateFactory.Create(i)); // <3>
    issuesState.Links.Add(new Link{
        Href=Request.RequestUri, Rel = LinkFactory.Rels.Self}); // <4>

    return Request.CreateResponse(HttpStatusCode.OK, issuesState); // <5>
}
```

Notice the method is marked with the `async` modifier and returns `Task<HttpRespon seMessage>`. By default, API controller operations are sync; thus, as the call is executing it will block the calling thread. In the case of operations that are making I/O calls, this is bad—it will reduce the number of threads that can handle incoming requests. In the case of the issue controller, all of the calls involve I/O, so using `async` and returning a `Task` make sense. I/O-intensive operations are then awaited via the `await` keyword.

Here is what the code is doing:

- First, an async call is made to the issue store `FindAsync` method to get the issues *<1>*.
- An `IssuesState` instance is created for carrying issue data *<2>*.
- The issues collection is set, but invokes the `Create` method on the state factory for each issue *<3>*.
- The Self link is added via the URI of the incoming request *<4>*.

- The response is created, passing the `IssuesState` instance for the content *<5>*.

In the previous snippet, the `Request.CreateResponse` method is used to return an `HttpResponseMessage`. You might ask, why not just return a model instead? Returning an `HttpResponseMessage` allows for directly manipulating the components of the `HttpResponse`, such as the status and the headers. Although currently the response headers are not modified for this specific controller action, this will likely happen in the future. You will also see that the rest of the actions do manipulate the response.

Where Is the Proper Place to Handle Hypermedia?

The following question often arises: where in the system should hypermedia controls be applied? Should they be handled in the controller, or via the pipeline with a message handler, filter, or formatter? There is no one right answer—all of these are valid places to handle hypermedia—but there are trade-offs to consider:

- If links are handled in a controller, they are more explicit/obvious and easier to step through.
- If links are handled in the pipeline, controller actions are leaner and have less logic.
- Message handlers, filters, and controllers have easy access to the request, which they can use for link generation.

In this book, we've chosen to handle the logic in the controller, either inline as in the `Get` method for retrieving multiple issues, or via an injected service as in the `Get` method for a single issue. The reasoning for this is that the link logic is more explicit/closer to the controller. The controller's job is to translate between the business domain and the HTTP world. As links are an HTTP-specific concern, handling them in a controller is perfectly reasonable.

That being said, the other approaches are workable and there is nothing fundamentally wrong with using them.

Retrieving All Issues as Collection+Json

As mentioned in the previous chapter, `Collection+Json` is a format that is well suited for managing and querying lists of data. The issue resource supports `Collection +Json` for requests on resources that return multiple items. This test verifies that it can return `Collection+Json` responses.

The next scenario verifies that the API properly handles requests for `Collection+Json`:

```
Scenario: Retrieving all issues as Collection+Json
  Given existing issues
  When all issues are retrieved as Collection+Json
```

```
Then a '200 OK' status is returned
Then Collection+Json is returned
Then the href should be set
Then all issues are returned
Then the search query is returned
```

The test in Example 7-21 issues such a request and validates that the correct format is returned.

Example 7-21. Retrieving all issues as Collection+Json

```
[Scenario]
public void RetrievingAllIssuesAsCollectionJson(IReadDocument readDocument)
{
    "Given existing issues".
        f(() => MockIssueStore.Setup(i => i.FindAsync()).
            Returns(Task.FromResult(FakeIssues)));
    "When all issues are retrieved as Collection+Json".
        f(() =>
            {
                Request.RequestUri = _uriIssues;
                Request.Headers.Accept.Clear(); // <1>
                Request.Headers.Accept.Add(
                    new MediaTypeWithQualityHeaderValue(
                        "application/vnd.collection+json"));
                Response = Client.SendAsync(Request).Result;
                readDocument = Response.Content.ReadAsAsync<ReadDocument>(
                    new[] {new CollectionJsonFormatter()}).Result; // <2>
            });
    "Then a '200 OK' status is returned".
        f(() => Response.StatusCode.ShouldEqual(HttpStatusCode.OK)); // <3>
    "Then Collection+Json is returned".
        f(() => readDocument.ShouldNotBeNull()); // <4>
    "Then the href should be set".
        f(() => readDocument.Collection.Href.AbsoluteUri.ShouldEqual(
            "http://localhost/issue")); // <5>
    "Then all issues are returned"
        f(() =>
            {
                readDocument.Collection.Items.FirstOrDefault(
                    i=>i.Href.AbsoluteUri=="http://localhost/issue/1").
                                        ShouldNotBeNull(); // <6>
                readDocument.Collection.Items.FirstOrDefault(
                    i=>i.Href.AbsoluteUri=="http://localhost/issue/2").
                                        ShouldNotBeNull();
            });
    "Then the search query is returned".
        f(() => readDocument.Collection.Queries.SingleOrDefault(
            q => q.Rel == IssueLinkFactory.Rels.SearchQuery).
            ShouldNotBeNull()); // <7>
}
```

After the standard setup, the tests do the following:

- Sets the `Accept` header to `application/vnd.collection+json` and sends the request *<1>*.

- Reads the content using the `CollectionJson` packages' `ReadDocument` *<2>*.

- Verifies that a `200 OK` status is returned *<3>*.

- Verifies that the returned document is not null (this means valid `Collection +Json` was returned) *<4>*.

- Checks that the document's `href` (`self`) URI is set *<5>*.

- Checks that the expected items are present *<6>*.

- Checks that the search query is present in the `Queries` collection *<7>*.

On the server, the same method as in the previous test is invoked—that is, `IssueCon troller.Get()`. However, because the `CollectionJsonFormatter` is used, the returned `IssuesState` object will be written via the `IReadDocument` interface that it implements, as shown previously in Example 7-4.

Searching Issues

This scenario validates that the API allows users to perform a search and that the results are returned:

```
Scenario: Searching issues
    Given existing issues
        When issues are searched
        Then a '200 OK' status is returned
        Then the collection should have a 'self' link
        Then the matching issues are returned
```

The tests for this scenario are shown in Example 7-22.

Example 7-22. Searching issues

```
[Scenario]
public void SearchingIssues(IssuesState issuesState)
{
    "Given existing issues".
        f(() => MockIssueStore.Setup(i => i.FindAsyncQuery("another"))
            .Returns(Task.FromResult(FakeIssues.Where(i=>i.Id == "2")))); // <1>
    "When issues are searched".
        f(() =>
        {
            Request.RequestUri = new Uri(_uriIssues, "?searchtext=another");
            Response = Client.SendAsync(Request).Result;
            issuesState = Response.Content.ReadAsAsync<IssuesState>().Result; // <2>
        });
    "Then a '200 OK' status is returned".
        f(() => Response.StatusCode.ShouldEqual(HttpStatusCode.OK)); // <3>
```

```
"Then the collection should have a 'self' link".
    f(() =>
    {
        var link = issuesState.Links.FirstOrDefault(
            l => l.Rel == IssueLinkFactory.Rels.Self); // <4>
        link.ShouldNotBeNull();
        link.Href.AbsoluteUri.ShouldEqual(
            "http://localhost/issue?searchtext=another");
    });
"Then the matching issues are returned".
    f(() =>
        {
            var issue = issuesState.Issues.FirstOrDefault(); // <5>
            issue.ShouldNotBeNull();
            issue.Id.ShouldEqual("2");
        });
}
```

Here's how the tests work:

- Sets the mock issue store to return issue 2 when `FindAsyncQuery` is invoked *<1>*.

- Appends the query string to the query URI, issues a request, and reads the content as an `IssuesState` instance *<2>*.

- Verifies that a `200 OK` status is returned *<3>*.

- Verifies that the Self link is set for collection *<4>*.

- Verifies that the expected issue is returned *<5>*.

The code for the search functionality is shown in Example 7-23.

Example 7-23. IssueController GetSearch method

```
public async Task<HttpResponseMessage> GetSearch(string searchText) // <1>
{
    var issues = await _store.FindAsyncQuery(searchText); // <2>
    var issuesState = new IssuesState();
    issuesState.Issues = issues.Select(i => _stateFactory.Create(i)); // <3>
    issuesState.Links.Add( new Link {
        Href = Request.RequestUri, Rel = LinkFactory.Rels.Self }); // <4>
    return Request.CreateResponse(HttpStatusCode.OK, issuesState); // <5>
}
```

- The method name is `GetSearch` *<1>*. ASP.NET Web API's selector matches the current HTTP method conventionally against methods that start with the same HTTP method name. Thus, it is reachable by an HTTP `GET`. The parameter of the method matches against the query string param `searchtext`.

- Issues matching the search are retrieved with the `FindAsyncQuery` method *<2>*.

- An `IssuesState` instance is created and its issues are populated with the result of the search *<3>*.
- A Self link is added, pointing to the original request *<4>*.
- An OK response is returned with the issues as the payload *<5>*.

 Similar to requests for all issues, this resource also supports returning a `Collection+Json` representation.

This finishes off all of the scenarios for the issue retrieval feature; now, on to creation!

Feature: Creating Issues

This feature contains a single scenario that covers when a client creates a new issue using an HTTP POST:

```
Scenario: Creating a new issue
    Given a new issue
    When a POST request is made
    Then the issue should be added
    Then a '201 Created' status is returned
    Then the response location header will be set to the new resource location
```

The test is in Example 7-24.

Example 7-24. Creating issues

```
[Scenario]
public void CreatingANewIssue(dynamic newIssue)
{
    "Given a new issue".
        f(() =>
            {
                newIssue = new JObject();
                newIssue.description = "A new issue";
                newIssue.title = "NewIssue"; // <1>
                MockIssueStore.Setup(i => i.CreateAsync(It.IsAny<Issue>())).
                    Returns<Issue>(issue=>
                        {
                            issue.Id = "1";
                            return Task.FromResult("");
                        }); // <2>
            });
    "When a POST request is made".
        f(() =>
            {
```

```
                Request.Method = HttpMethod.Post;
                Request.RequestUri = _issues;
                Request.Content = new ObjectContent<dynamic>(
                    newIssue, new JsonMediaTypeFormatter()); // <3>
                Response = Client.SendAsync(Request).Result;
        });
    "Then the issue should be added".
        f(() => MockIssueStore.Verify(i => i.CreateAsync(
        It.IsAny<Issue>())));  // <4>
    "Then a '201 Created' status is returned".
        f(() => Response.StatusCode.ShouldEqual(HttpStatusCode.Created)); // <5>
    "Then the response location header will be set to the resource location".
        f(() => Response.Headers.Location.AbsoluteUri.ShouldEqual(
            "http://localhost/issue/1"));  // <6>
}
```

Here's how the tests work:

- Creates a new issue to be sent to the server *<1>*.

- Configures the mock store to set the issue's Id *<2>*. Notice the call to `Task.FromResult`. The `CreateAsync` method expects a `Task` to be returned. This is a simple way to create a dummy task. You will see the same approach is used in other tests if the method on the store returns a `Task`.

- Configures the request to be a `POST` with the request content being set to the new issue *<3>*. Notice here that instead of using a static CLR type like `Issue`, it uses a `JObject` instance (from Json.NET) cast to `dynamic`. We can use a similar approach for staying typeless on the server, which you'll see shortly.

- Verifies that the `CreateAsync` method was called to create the issue *<4>*.

- Verifies that the status code was set to a `201` in accordance with the HTTP spec (covered in Chapter 1) *<5>*.

- Verifies that the location header is set to the location of the created resource *<6>*.

The Web Is Typeless

In Example 7-24 the client creates a dynamic type to send to the server rather than a static type. This may make a whole bunch of people in the room ask, "Where is my static type?" It is true that .NET is a (mostly) static language; the Web, however, is typeless. As we saw in Chapter 1, the foundation of the Web is message based, not type based. Clients send messages to servers in a set of known formats (media types). A media type describes the structure of a message; it is not the same as a static type in a programming stack like .NET. This typelessness is not an accident; it is by design.

Because the Web is typeless, resources are easily accessible to the largest possible set of clients and servers. Typelessness is also a big factor in allowing clients and servers to independently evolve and allowing side-by-side versioning. Servers can understand new elements in the messages they receive without requiring existing clients to upgrade. The message formats can even evolve in ways that are breaking but still don't force clients to upgrade. In a typed world, this is not possible due to the inherent constraints that a type imposes.

SOAP Services are an example of a protocol that introduced typing to the Web, and that was wrought with issues. One of the biggest pains you hear in practice from companies that implemented SOAP Services is around the clients. Communication with a SOAP Service requires a WSDL document describing the operations and the types. Whenever the services change in a significant way, they generally break all the clients. This either requires clients to upgrade, or calls for a parallel version of the service to be deployed, which newer clients can access only by getting the WSDL.

All this being said, this is not a recommendation to not use types at all as a more developer-friendly way to access API requests and responses. Those types should not, however, become a requirement for interacting with the system, and there is nothing wrong with using dynamic types (in fact, there may be cases where it is even advantageous).

The implementation within the controller is shown in Example 7-25.

Example 7-25. IssueController Post method

```
public async Task<HttpResponseMessage> Post(dynamic newIssue) // <1>
{
    var issue = new Issue {
        Title = newIssue.title, Description = newIssue.description}; // <2>
    await _store.CreateAsync(issue); // <3>
    var response = Request.CreateResponse(HttpStatusCode.Created); // <4>
    response.Headers.Location = _linkFactory.Self(issue.Id).Href; // <5>
    return response; // <6>.
}
```

The code works as follows:

- The method itself is named Post in order to match the POST HTTP method *<1>*. Similarly to the client in test, this method accepts dynamic. On the server, Json.NET will create a JObject instance automatically if it sees dynamic. Though JSON is supported by default, we could add custom formatters for supporting alternative media types like application/x-www-form-urlencoded.

- We create a new issue by passing the properties from the dynamic instance *<2>*.

- The CreateAsync method is invoked on the store to store the issue *<3>*.

- The response is created to return a 201 Created status *<4>*.
- We set the location header on the response by invoking the Self method of the _linkFactory *<5>*, and the response is returned *<6>*.

This covers creation; next, on to updating!

Feature: Updating Issues

This feature covers updating issues using HTTP PATCH. PATCH was chosen because it allows the client to send partial data that will modify the existing resource. PUT, on the other hand, completely replaces the state of the resource.

Updating an Issue

This scenario verifies that when a client sends a PATCH request, the corresponding resource is updated:

```
Scenario: Updating an issue
   Given an existing issue
   When a PATCH request is made
   Then a '200 OK' is returned
   Then the issue should be updated
```

The test for this scenario is shown in Example 7-26.

Example 7-26. IssueController PATCH method

```
[Scenario]
public void UpdatingAnIssue(Issue fakeIssue)
{
    "Given an existing issue".
        f(() =>
            {
                fakeIssue = FakeIssues.FirstOrDefault();
                MockIssueStore.Setup(i => i.FindAsync("1")).Returns(
                    Task.FromResult(fakeIssue)); // <1>
                MockIssueStore.Setup(i => i.UpdateAsync(It.IsAny<Issue>())).
                    Returns(Task.FromResult(""));
            });
    "When a PATCH request is made".
        f(() =>
            {
                dynamic issue = new JObject(); // <2>
                issue.description = "Updated description";
                Request.Method = new HttpMethod("PATCH"); // <3>
                Request.RequestUri = _uriIssue1;
                Request.Content = new ObjectContent<dynamic>(issue,
                    new JsonMediaTypeFormatter()); // <4>
                Response = Client.SendAsync(Request).Result;
            });
```

```
    "Then a '200 OK' status is returned".
        f(() => Response.StatusCode.ShouldEqual(HttpStatusCode.OK)); // <5>
    "Then the issue should be updated".
        f(() => MockIssueStore.Verify(i =>
            i.UpdateAsync(It.IsAny<Issue>()))); // <6>
    "Then the descripton should be updated".
        f(() => fakeIssue.Description.ShouldEqual("Updated description")); // <7>
    "Then the title should not change".
        f(() => fakeIssue.Title.ShouldEqual(title)); // <8>
}
```

Here's how the tests work:

- Sets up the mock store to return the expected issue that will be updated when
  FindAsync is called and to handle the call to UpdateAsync *<1>*.

- News up a JObject instance, and only the description to be changed is set *<2>*.

- Sets the request method to PATCH *<3>*. Notice here an HttpMethod instance is constructed, passing in the method name. This is the approach to use when you are
  using an HTTP method that does not have a predefined static property off the
  HttpMethod class, such as GET, PUT, POST, and DELETE.

- News up an ObjectContent<dynamic> instance with the issue and sets it to the
  request content. The request is then sent *<4>*. Notice the usage of dynamic: it works
  well for PATCH because it allows the client to just send the properties of the issue
  that it wants to update.

- Validates that the status code is 200 OK *<5>*.

- Validates that the UpdateAsync method was called, passing the issue *<6>*.

- Validates that the description of the issue was updated *<7>*.

- Validates that the title has not changed *<8>*.

The implementation is handled in the Patch method of the controller, as Example 7-27
demonstrates.

Example 7-27. IssueController Patch method

```
public async Task<HttpResponseMessage> Patch(string id, dynamic issueUpdate) // <1>
{
    var issue = await _store.FindAsync(id); // <2>
    if (issue == null) // <3>
        return Request.CreateResponse(HttpStatusCode.NotFound);

    foreach (JProperty prop in issueUpdate) // <4>
    {
        if (prop.Name == "title")
            issue.Title = prop.Value.ToObject<string>();
        else if (prop.Name == "description")
```

```
        issue.Description = prop.Value.ToObject<string>();
    }
    await _store.UpdateAsync(issue); // <5>
    return Request.CreateResponse(HttpStatusCode.OK); // <6>
}
```

Here's what the code does:

- The method accepts two parameters *<1>*. The id comes from the URI (*http://local-host/issue/1*, in this case) of the request. The issueUpdate, however, comes from the JSON content of the request.

- The issue to be updated is retrieved from the store *<2>*.

- If no issue is found, a 404 Not Found is immediately returned *<3>*.

- A loop walks through the properties of issueUpdate, updating only those properties that are present *<4>*.

- The store is invoked to update the issue *<5>*.

- A 200 OK status is returned *<6>*.

Updating an Issue That Does Not Exist

This scenario ensures that when a client sends a PATCH request for a missing or deleted issue, a 404 Not Found status is returned:

```
Scenario: Updating an issue that does not exist
    Given an issue does not exist
    When a PATCH request is made
    Then a '404 Not Found' status is returned
```

We've already seen the code for this in the controller in the previous section, but the test in Example 7-28 verifies that it actually works!

Example 7-28. Updating an issue that does not exist

```
[Scenario]
public void UpdatingAnIssueThatDoesNotExist()
{
    "Given an issue does not exist".
        f(() => MockIssueStore.Setup(i => i.FindAsync("1")).
                Returns(Task.FromResult((Issue)null))); // <1>
    "When a PATCH request is made".
        f(() =>
            {
                Request.Method = new HttpMethod("PATCH"); // <2>
                Request.RequestUri = _uriIssue1;
                Request.Content = new ObjectContent<dynamic>(new JObject(),
                    new JsonMediaTypeFormatter()); // <3>
                response = Client.SendAsync(Request).Result; // <4>
```

```
        });
    "Then a 404 Not Found status is returned".
        f(() => response.StatusCode.ShouldEqual(HttpStatusCode.NotFound)); // <5>
}
```

Here's how the tests work:

- Sets up the mock store to return a null issue when FindAsync is called.
- Sets the request method to PATCH *<2>*.
- Sets the content to an empty JObject instance. The content here really doesn't matter *<3>*.
- Sends the request *<4>*.
- Validates that the 404 Not Found status is returned.

This completes the section on updates.

Feature: Deleting Issues

This feature covers handling of HTTP DELETE requests for removing issues.

Deleting an Issue

This scenario verifies that when a client sends a DELETE request, the corresponding issue is removed:

```
Scenario: Deleting an issue
  Give an existing issue
  When a DELETE request is made
  Then a '200 OK' status is returned
  Then the issue should be removed
```

The tests (Example 7-29) for this scenario are very straightforward, using concepts already covered throughout the chapter.

Example 7-29. Deleting an issue

```
[Scenario]
public void DeletingAnIssue(Issue fakeIssue)
{
    "Given an existing issue".
        f(() =>
            {
                fakeIssue = FakeIssues.FirstOrDefault();
                MockIssueStore.Setup(i => i.FindAsync("1")).Returns(
                    Task.FromResult(fakeIssue)); // <1>
                MockIssueStore.Setup(i => i.DeleteAsync("1")).Returns(
                    Task.FromResult(""));
            });
```

```
"When a DELETE request is made".
    f(() =>
        {
            Request.RequestUri = _uriIssue;
            Request.Method = HttpMethod.Delete; // <2>
            Response = Client.SendAsync(Request).Result; // <3>
        });
"Then the issue should be removed".
    f(() => MockIssueStore.Verify(i => i.DeleteAsync("1"))); // <4>
"Then a '200 OK status' is returned".
    f(() => Response.StatusCode.ShouldEqual(HttpStatusCode.OK)); // <5>
}
```

Here's how the tests work:

- Configures the mock issue store to return the issue to be deleted when FindAsync is called, and to handle the DeleteAsync call *<1>*.

- Sets the request to use DELETE *<2>* and sends it *<3>*.

- Validates that the DeleteAsync method was called, passing in the Id *<4>*.

- Validates that the response is a 200 OK *<5>*.

The implementation can be seen in Example 7-30.

Example 7-30. IssueController Delete method

```
public async Task<HttpResponseMessage> Delete(string id) // <1>
{
    var issue = await _store.FindAsync(id); // <2>
    if (issue == null)
        return Request.CreateResponse(HttpStatusCode.NotFound); // <3>
    await _store.DeleteAsync(id); // <4>
    return Request.CreateResponse(HttpStatusCode.OK); // <5>
}
```

The code does the following:

- The method name is Delete to match against an HTTP DELETE *<1>*. It accepts the id of the issue to be deleted.

- The issue is retrieved from the store for the selected id *<2>*.

- If the issue does not exist, a 404 Not Found status is returned *<3>*.

- The DeleteAsync method is invoked on the store to remove the issue *<4>*.

- A 200 OK is returned to the client *<5>*.

Deleting an Issue That Does Not Exist

This scenario verifies that if a client sends a DELETE request for a nonexistent issue, a 404 Not Found status is returned:

```
Scenario: Deleting an issue that does not exist
  Given an issue does not exist
  When a DELETE request is made
  Then a '404 Not Found' status is returned
```

The test in Example 7-31 is very similar to the previous test for updating a missing issue.

Example 7-31. Deleting an issue that does not exist

```
[Scenario]
public void DeletingAnIssueThatDoesNotExist()
{
    "Given an issue does not exist".
        f(() => MockIssueStore.Setup(i => i.FindAsync("1")).Returns(
            Task.FromResult((Issue) null))); // <1>
    "When a DELETE request is made".
        f(() =>
            {
                Request.RequestUri = _uriIssue;
                Request.Method = HttpMethod.Delete; // <2>
                Response = Client.SendAsync(Request).Result;
            });
    "Then a '404 Not Found' status is returned".
        f(() => Response.StatusCode.ShouldEqual(HttpStatusCode.NotFound)); // <3>
}
```

Here's how the tests work:

- Sets up the mock store to return null when the issue is requested *<1>*.
- Sends the request to delete the resource *<2>*.
- Validates that a 404 Not Found is returned *<3>*.

Feature: Processing Issues

The Tests

As mentioned earlier, discussing the tests for this feature is beyond the scope of this chapter. However, you now have all the concepts necessary to understand the code, which can be found in the GitHub repo (*http://bit.ly/issuetracker-test*).

Separating out processing resources provides better separation for the API implementation, making the code more readable and easier to maintain. It also helps with evolvabililty, as you can make changes to handle processing without needing to touch the IssueController, which is also fulfilling the *Single Responsibility Principle*.

The Implementation

The issue processor resources are backed by the IssueProcessorController shown in Example 7-32.

Example 7-32. IssueProcessorController

```
public class IssueProcessorController : ApiController
{
    private readonly IIssueStore _issueStore;

    public IssueProcessorController(IIssueStore issueStore)
    {
        _issueStore = issueStore; // <1>
    }

    public async Task<HttpResponseMessage> Post(string id, string action) // <2>
    {
        bool isValid = IsValidAction(action); // <3>
        Issue issue = null;

        if (isValid)
        {
            issue = await _issueStore.FindAsync(id); // <4>

            if (issue == null)
                return Request.CreateResponse(HttpStatusCode.NotFound); // <5>

            if ((action == IssueLinkFactory.Actions.Open ||
                action == IssueLinkFactory.Actions.Transition) &&
                issue.Status == IssueStatus.Closed)
            {
                issue.Status = IssueStatus.Open; // <6>
            }
            else if ((action == IssueLinkFactory.Actions.Close ||
                action == IssueLinkFactory.Actions.Transition) &&
                issue.Status == IssueStatus.Open)
            {
                issue.Status = IssueStatus.Closed; // <7>
            }
            else
                isValid = false; // <8>
        }

        if (!isValid)
            return Request.CreateErrorResponse(HttpStatusCode.BadRequest,
                string.Format("Action '{0}' is invalid", action)); // <9>

        await _issueStore.UpdateAsync(issue); // <10>
```

```
        return Request.CreateResponse(HttpStatusCode.OK); // <11>
    }

    public bool IsValidAction(string action)
    {
        return (action == IssueLinkFactory.Actions.Close ||
            action == IssueLinkFactory.Actions.Open ||
            action == IssueLinkFactory.Actions.Transition);
    }
}
```

Here's how the code works:

- The `IssueProcessorController` accepts an `IIssueStore` in its constructor similar to the `IssueController` *<1>*.
- The method is `Post` and accepts the `id` and `action` from the request URI *<2>*.
- The `IsValidAction` method is called to check if the action is recognized *<3>*.
- The `FindAsync` method is invoked to retrive the issue *<4>*.
- If the issue is not found, then a `400 Not Found` is immediately returned *<5>*.
- If the action is `open` or `transition` and the issue is closed, the issue is opened *<6>*.
- If the action is `close` or `transition` and the issue is open, the issue is closed *<7>*.
- If neither clause matched, the action is flagged as invalid for the current state *<8>*.
- If the action is invalid, then an error is returned via `CreateErrorResponse`. This method is used because we want an error response that contains a payload *<9>*.
- We update the issue by calling `UpdateAsync` *<10>*, and a `200 OK` status is returned *<11>*.

This completes coverage of the Issue Tracker API!

Conclusion

This chapter covered a lot of ground. We went from the high-level design of the system to the detailed requirements of the API and the actual implementation. Along the way, we learned about many aspects of Web API in practice, as well as how to do integration testing with in-memory hosting. These concepts are a big part of your journey toward building evolvable APIs with ASP.NET. Now the fun stuff starts! In the next chapter, you'll see how to harden up that API and the tools that are necessary to really allow it to scale, like caching.

CHAPTER 8

Improving the API

No pain, no gain. That's what makes you a champion.

In the previous chapter we discussed the initial implementation of the issue tracker system. The idea was to have a fully functional implementation that we could use to discuss the design of the API and the media types to support it. As part of this chapter, we will try to improve that existing implementation by adding new features like caching, conflict detection, and security. All the requirements for these new features will be described in terms of BDD as we did with the initial implementation. As we add those new features, we will dive into the details of the implementation, showing real code, and also some of the introductory theory behind them. Later chapters will complement that theory in more detail.

Acceptance Criteria for the New Features

Following are the tests for our API, which cover the new requirements for the tracker system:

```
Feature: Output Caching
  Scenario: Retrieving existing issues
    Given existing issues
    When all issues are retrieved
    Then a CacheControl header is returned
    Then a '200 OK' status is returned
    Then all issues are returned

  Scenario: Retrieving an existing issue
    Given an existing issue
    When it is retrieved
    Then a LastModified header is returned
    Then a CacheControl header is returned
    Then a '200 OK' status is returned
    Then it is returned
```

Feature: Cache revalidation

    Scenario: Retrieving an existing issue that has not changed
      Given an existing issue
      When it is retrieved with an IfModifiedSince header
      Then a CacheControl header is returned
      Then a '304 NOT MODIFIED' status is returned
      Then it is returned

    Scenario: Retrieving an existing issue that has changed
      Given an existing issue
      When it is retrieved with an IfModifiedSince header
      Then a LastModified header is returned
      Then a CacheControl header is returned
      Then a '200 OK' status is returned
      Then it is returned

Feature: Conflict detection

    Scenario: Updating an issue with no conflicts
      Given an existing issue
      When a PATCH request is made with an IfModifiedSince header
      Then a '200 OK' is returned
      Then the issue should be updated

    Scenario: Updating an issue with conflicts
      Given an existing issue
      When a PATCH request is made with an IfModifiedSince header
      Then a '409 CONFLICT' is returned
      Then the issue is not updated

Feature: Change Auditing

    Scenario: Creating a new issue
      Given a new issue
      When a POST request is made with an Authorization header containing the user
          identifier
      Then a '201 Created' status is returned
      Then the issue should be added with auditing information
      Then the response location header will be set to the resource location

    Scenario: Updating an issue
      Given an existing issue
      When a PATCH request is made with an Authorization header containing the user
          identifier
      Then a '200 OK' is returned
      Then the issue should be updated with auditing information

Feature: Tracing

    Scenario: Creating, Updating, Deleting, or Retrieving an issue

```
Given an existing or new issue
When a request is made
When the diagnostics tracing is enabled
Then the diagnostics tracing information is generated
```

Implementing the Output Caching Support

Caching is one of the fundamental aspects that makes it possible to scale on the Internet, as it provides the following benefits when it is implemented correctly:

- Reduces load on the origin servers.
- Decreases network latencies. Clients can get responses much faster.
- Saves network bandwidth. Fewer network hops are required, as the content might be found in some caching intermediary before the request reaches the origin server.

Implementing caching correctly on a Web API mainly involves two steps:

1. Set the right headers to instruct intermediaries and clients (e.g., proxies, reverse proxies, local caches, browsers, etc.) to cache the responses.
2. Implement conditional GETs so the intermediaries can revalidate the cached copies of the data after they become stale.

The first step requires the use of either the Expires or Cache-Control header. The Expires HTTP header is useful for expressing absolute expiration times. It only tells caches how long the associated representation is fresh for. Most implementations use this header to express the last time that the client retrieved the representation or the last time the document changed on your server. The value for this header has to be expressed in GTM, not a local time—for example, Expires: Mon, 1 Aug 2013 10:30:50 GMT. On the other hand, the Cache-Control header provides more granular control for expressing sliding expiration dates and also who is allowed to cache the data. The following list describes well-known values for the Cache-Control header:

no-store
: Indicates that caches should not keep a copy of the data under any circumstance.

private
: Indicates that the data is intended for a single user, so it should be cached on private caches like a browser but not on shared caches like proxies.

public
: Indicates that the data can be cached anywhere.

no-cache
: Forces caches to revalidate the cached copies after they become stale.

`max-age`

Indicates a delta in seconds representing the maximum amount of time that a cached copy will be considered fresh (e.g., `max-age[300]` means the cached copy will expire 300 seconds after the request was made).

`s-maxage`

Is equivalent to `max-age` but valid for shared caches only.

Adding the Tests for Output Caching

The first thing we need to do is add a new file, *OutputCaching*, for all our tests related to output caching. Our first test involves adding output caching support in the operation for returning all the issues:

```
Scenario: Retrieving existing issues
    Given existing issues
    When all issues are retrieved
    Then a CacheControl header is returned
    Then a '200 OK' status is returned
    Then all issues are returned
```

We translate this scenario to a unit test using BDD, as shown in Example 8-1.

Example 8-1. Retrieving all issues with caching headers

```
public class OutputCaching : IssuesFeature
{
  private Uri _uriIssues = new Uri("http://localhost/issue");

  [Scenario]
  public void RetrievingAllIssues()
  {
    IssuesState issuesState = null;

    "Given existing issues".
      f(() =>
      {
        MockIssueStore.Setup(i => i.FindAsync())
          .Returns(Task.FromResult(FakeIssues))
      });
    "When all issues are retrieved".
      f(() =>
      {
        Request.RequestUri = _uriIssues;
        Response = Client.SendAsync(Request).Result;
        issuesState = Response.Content
          .ReadAsAsync<IssuesState>()
          .Result;
      });
    "Then a CacheControl header is returned".
      f(() =>
```

```
    {
      Response.Headers.CacheControl.Public
        .ShouldBeTrue(); // <1>
      Response.Headers.CacheControl.MaxAge
        .ShouldEqual(TimeSpan.FromMinutes(5)); // <2>
    });
  "Then a '200 OK' status is returned".
    f(() => Response.StatusCode.ShouldEqual(HttpStatusCode.OK));
  "Then they are returned".
    f(() =>
    {
      issuesState.Issues
        .FirstOrDefault(i => i.Id == "1")
        .ShouldNotBeNull();
      issuesState.Issues
        .FirstOrDefault(i => i.Id == "2")
        .ShouldNotBeNull();
    });
  }
}
```

The unit test is self-explanatory; the part that matters is in lines *<1>* and *<2>*, where the assertions for the CacheControl and MaxAge headers are made. To pass this test, the response message returned in the Get method of the IssuesController class is modified to include those two headers, as shown in Example 8-2.

Example 8-2. The new version of the Get method

```
public async Task<HttpResponseMessage> Get()
{
  var result = await _store.FindAsync();
  var issuesState = new IssuesState();
  issuesState.Issues = result.Select(i => _stateFactory.Create(i));

  var response = Request.CreateResponse(HttpStatusCode.OK, issuesState);

  response.Headers.CacheControl = new CacheControlHeaderValue();
  response.Headers.CacheControl.Public = true; // <1>
  response.Headers.CacheControl.MaxAge = TimeSpan.FromMinutes(5); // <2>

  return response;
}
```

The CacheControl header is set to Public *<1>*, so it can be cached anywhere, and the MaxAge header is set to a relative expiration of 5 minutes *<2>*.

The next scenario, shown in Example 8-3, involves adding output caching to the operation for retrieving a single issue:

```
    Scenario: Retrieving an existing issue
    Given an existing issue
    When it is retrieved
```

```
           Then a LastModified header is returned
           Then a CacheControl header is returned
           Then a '200 OK' status is returned
           Then it is returned
```

Example 8-3. Retrieving a single issue with caching headers

```csharp
public class OutputCaching : IssuesFeature
{
  private Uri _uriIssue1 = new Uri("http://localhost/issue/1");

  [Scenario]
  public void RetrievingAnIssue()
  {
    IssueState issue = null;

    var fakeIssue = FakeIssues.FirstOrDefault();
    "Given an existing issue".
      f(() => MockIssueStore
        .Setup(i => i.FindAsync("1"))
        .Returns(Task.FromResult(fakeIssue)));
    "When it is retrieved".
      f(() =>
      {
        Request.RequestUri = _uriIssue1;
        Response = Client.SendAsync(Request).Result;
        issue = Response.Content.ReadAsAsync<IssueState>().Result;
      });
    "Then a LastModified header is returned".
      f(() =>
      {
        Response.Content.Headers.LastModified
          .ShouldEqual(new DateTimeOffset(new DateTime(2013, 9, 4))); // <1>
      });
    "Then a CacheControl header is returned".
      f(() =>
      {
        Response.Headers.CacheControl.Public
          .ShouldBeTrue(); // <2>
        Response.Headers.CacheControl.MaxAge
          .ShouldEqual(TimeSpan.FromMinutes(5)); // <3>
      });
    "Then a '200 OK' status is returned".
      f(() => Response.StatusCode.ShouldEqual(HttpStatusCode.OK));
    "Then it is returned".
      f(() => issue.ShouldNotBeNull());
  }
}
```

The test in Example 8-3 is slightly different from the one we wrote for retrieving all the issues. In addition to retrieving a single issue, it checks for the LastModified header in the response *<1>*. This header will be used later in other scenarios for performing cache revalidation. Also, the expected values for the `CacheControl` *<2>* and `MaxAge` *<3>* headers are `Public` and 5 minutes, respectively.

Implementing Cache Revalidation

Once a cached copy of a resource representation becomes stale, a cache intermediary can revalidate that copy by sending a conditional `GET` to the origin server. A conditional `GET` involves the use of two response headers, `If-None-Match` and `If-Modified-Since`. `If-None-Match` corresponds to an `Etag` header, which represents an opaque value that only the server knows how to re-create. This `Etag` could represent anything, but it is typically a hash representing the resource version, which we can generate by hashing the whole representation content or just some parts of it like a timestamp. On the other hand, `If-Modified-Since` corresponds to the `Last-Modified` header, which represents a datetime that the server can use to determine whether the resource has changed since the last time it was served.

Example 8-4 illustrates a pair of request/response messages exchanged by the client/server with the corresponding caching headers.

Example 8-4. Pair of request and response messages with the caching headers

```
Response ->

Connection close
Date Thu, 02 Oct 2013 14:46:57 GMT
Expires Sat, 01 Nov 2013 14:46:57 GMT
Last-Modified Mon, 29 Sep 2013 15:40:27 GMT
Etag a9331828c518ac6d97f93b3cfdbcc9bc
Content-Type application/json

Request ->

Host localhost
Accept */*
If-Modified-Since Mon, 29 Sep 2013 15:40:27 GMT
If-None-Match a9331828c518ac6d97f93b3cfdbcc9bc
```

By using either of these two headers, a caching intermediary can determine whether the resource representation has changed in the origin server. If the resource has not changed according to the values in those headers (`If-Modified-Since` for `Last-Modified` and `If-None-Match` for `Etag`), the service can return an HTTP status code of `304 Not Modified`, which instructs the intermediary to keep the cached version and refresh the expiration times. Example 8-4 shows both headers, but in practice, the intermediary uses only one of them.

Implementing Conditional GETs for Cache Revalidation

Our first test, shown in Example 8-5, will revalidate the cached representation of an issue that has not changed on the server. You will find these tests in the class CacheVa lidation.

```
Scenario: Retrieving an existing issue that has not changed
    Given an existing issue
    When it is retrieved with an IfModifiedSince header
    Then a CacheControl header is returned
    Then a '304 Not Modified' status is returned
    Then it is not returned
```

Example 8-5. Unit test for validating a cached copy that has not changed

```
private Uri _uriIssue1 = new Uri("http://localhost/issue/1");

[Scenario]
public void RetrievingNonModifiedIssue()
{
  IssueState issue = null;

  var fakeIssue = FakeIssues.FirstOrDefault();
  "Given an existing issue".
    f(() => MockIssueStore.Setup(i => i.FindAsync("1"))
        .Returns(Task.FromResult(fakeIssue)));
  "When it is retrieved with an IfModifiedSince header".
    f(() =>
    {
      Request.RequestUri = _uriIssue1;
      Request.Headers.IfModifiedSince = fakeIssue.LastModified; // <1>
      Response = Client.SendAsync(Request).Result;
    });
  "Then a CacheControl header is returned".
    f(() =>
    {
      Response.Headers.CacheControl.Public.ShouldBeTrue();
      Response.Headers.CacheControl.MaxAge.ShouldEqual(TimeSpan.FromMinutes(5));
    });
  "Then a '304 NOT MODIFIED' status is returned".
    f(() => Response.StatusCode.ShouldEqual(HttpStatusCode.NotModified)); // <2>
  "Then it is not returned".
    f(() => Assert.Null(issue));
}
```

Example 8-5 shows the unit test that we created for validating the scenario in which the resource representation has not changed on the origin server since it was cached. This test emulates the behavior of a caching intermediary that sends a conditional GET to the server using the IfModifiedSince header that was previously stored *<1>*. As part of the expectations of the test, the status code in the response should be 304 NOT MODIFIED *<2>*.

The Get method in the IssuesController class has to be modified to include all the conditional GET logic (see Example 8-6). If a request message with an IfModified Since header is received, that date must be compared with the LastModified field in the requested issue to check whether the issue has changed since the last time it was served to the caching intermediary.

Example 8-6. The new version of the Get method that supports conditional GETs

```
public async Task<HttpResponseMessage> Get(string id)
{
  var result = await _store.FindAsync(id);
  if (result == null)
    return Request.CreateResponse(HttpStatusCode.NotFound);

  HttpResponseMessage response = null;

  if( Request.Headers.IfModifiedSince.HasValue &&
      Request.Headers.IfModifiedSince == result.LastModified) // <1>
  {
    response = Request
      .CreateResponse(HttpStatusCode.NotModified); // <2>
  }
  else
  {
    response = Request
      .CreateResponse(HttpStatusCode.OK, _stateFactory.Create(result));
    response.Content.Headers.LastModified = result.LastModified;
  }

  response.Headers.CacheControl = new CacheControlHeaderValue(); // <3>
  response.Headers.CacheControl.Public = true;
  response.Headers.CacheControl.MaxAge = TimeSpan.FromMinutes(5);

  return response;
}
```

Example 8-6 shows the new code that checks whether the IfModifiedSince header has been included in the request and is the same as the LastModified field in the retrieved issue *<1>*. If that condition is met, a response with the status code 304 Not Modified is returned *<2>*. Finally, the caching headers are updated and included as part of the response as well *<3>*.

Our next test, shown in Example 8-7, addresses the scenario in which the resource representation has changed on the origin server since the last time it was cached by the intermediary:

```
Scenario: Retrieving an existing issue that has changed
    Given an existing issue
    When it is retrieved with an IfModifiedSince header
    Then a LastModified header is returned
```

```
                Then a CacheControl header is returned
                Then a '200 OK' status is returned
                Then it is returned
```

Example 8-7. Unit test for validating a cached copy that has changed

```
private Uri _uriIssue1 = new Uri("http://localhost/issue/1");

[Scenario]
public void RetrievingModifiedIssue()
{
  IssueState issue = null;

  var fakeIssue = FakeIssues.FirstOrDefault();

  "Given an existing issue".
    f(() => MockIssueStore.Setup(i => i.FindAsync("1"))
        .Returns(Task.FromResult(fakeIssue)));
  "When it is retrieved with an IfModifiedSince header".
    f(() =>
  {
    Request.RequestUri = _uriIssue1;
    Request.Headers.IfModifiedSince = fakeIssue.LastModified
        .Subtract(TimeSpan.FromDays(1)); // <1>
    Response = Client.SendAsync(Request).Result;
    issue = Response.Content.ReadAsAsync<IssueState>().Result;
  });
  "Then a LastModified header is returned".
    f(() =>
    {
      Response.Content.Headers.LastModified.ShouldEqual(fakeIssue.LastModified);
    });
  "Then a CacheControl header is returned".
    f(() =>
    {
      Response.Headers.CacheControl.Public.ShouldBeTrue();
      Response.Headers.CacheControl.MaxAge.ShouldEqual(TimeSpan.FromMinutes(5));
    });
  "Then a '200 OK' status is returned".
    f(() => Response.StatusCode.ShouldEqual(HttpStatusCode.OK)); // <2>
  "Then it is returned".
    f(() => issue.ShouldNotBeNull()); // <3>
}
```

There are some minor changes compared with the previous test that we implemented for sending a conditional GET. This test changes the value of the IfModifiedSince header to send a time in the past that differs from one set in the LastModified field for the issue. In this case, the implementation of the Get method will return a status code 200 OK with a fresh copy of the resource representation *<3>*.

Conflict Detection

We have discussed how you can use a conditional GET to revalidate a cached representation, and now we'll cover the equivalent for updates: the conditional PUT or PATCH. A conditional PUT/PATCH can be used to detect possible conflicts when multiple updates are performed simultaneously over the same resource. It uses a first-write/first-win approach for conflict resolution, which means a client can commit an update operation only if the resource has not changed in the origin server since it was initially served; otherwise, it may receive a conflict error (HTTP status code 409 Conflict).

It also uses the If-None-Match and If-Modified-Since headers to represent the version or the timestamp associated with the resource representation that is going to be updated. The following steps illustrate how this approach works in detail with two clients (X1 and X2) trying to update the same resource R1:

1. Client X1 performs a GET over R1 (version 1). The HTTP response includes the resource representation and an ETag header with the resource version—V1, in this case (Last-Modified could also be used).

2. Client X2 performs a GET over the same resource R1 (version 1). It gets the same representation as client X1.

3. Client X2 performs a PUT/PATCH over R1 to update its representation. This request includes the modified version of the resource representation and a header If-None-Match with the current resource version (V1). As a result of this update, the server returns a response with status code OK and increments the resource version by one (V2).

4. Client X1 performs a PUT/PATCH over R1. This request message also includes a If-None-Match header with the resource version V1. The server detects that the resource has changed since it was obtained with version V1, so it returns a response with status code 409 Conflict.

Implementing Conflict Detection

Our first test, shown in Example 8-8, will update an issue with no conflicts, which means the value for IfModifiedSince will be the same as the one stored as part of the issue in the *LastModified() field. You will find these tests in the class ConflictDetection.

```
Scenario: Updating an issue with no conflicts
    Given an existing issue
    When a PATCH request is made with an IfModifiedSince header
    Then a '200 OK' is returned
    Then the issue should be updated
```

Example 8-8. Unit test for updating an issue with no conflicts

```
private Uri _uriIssue1 = new Uri("http://localhost/issue/1");

[Scenario]
public void UpdatingAnIssueWithNoConflict()
{
  var fakeIssue = FakeIssues.FirstOrDefault();

  "Given an existing issue".
    f(() =>
    {
      MockIssueStore.Setup(i => i.FindAsync("1"))
        .Returns(Task.FromResult(fakeIssue));
      MockIssueStore.Setup(i => i.UpdateAsync("1", It.IsAny<Object>()))
        .Returns(Task.FromResult(""));
    });
  "When a PATCH request is made with IfModifiedSince".
    f(() =>
    {
      var issue = new Issue();
      issue.Title = "Updated title";
      issue.Description = "Updated description";
      Request.Method = new HttpMethod("PATCH");
      Request.RequestUri = _uriIssue1;
      Request.Content = new ObjectContent<Issue>(issue,
          new JsonMediaTypeFormatter());
      Request.Headers.IfModifiedSince = fakeIssue.LastModified; // <1>
      Response = Client.SendAsync(Request).Result;
    });
  "Then a '200 OK' status is returned".
    f(() => Response.StatusCode.ShouldEqual(HttpStatusCode.OK)); // <2>
  "Then the issue should be updated".
    f(() => MockIssueStore.Verify(i => i.UpdateAsync("1",
        It.IsAny<JObject>()))); // <3>
}
```

Example 8-8 shows the implementation of the first test scenario in which the `IfModi fiedSince` header is set to the value of the `LastModified` property of the issue to be updated *<1>*. No conflicts should be detected on the server side, as the values for `IfMo difiedSince` and `LastModified` should match, so a status code of `200 OK` is returned *<2>*. Finally, the issue is updated in the issues store *<3>*.

The `Patch` method in the `IssuesController` class has to be modified to include all the conditional update logic, as Example 8-9 demonstrates.

Example 8-9. The new version of the Patch method that supports conditional updates

```
public async Task<HttpResponseMessage> Patch(string id, JObject issueUpdate)
{
    var issue = await _store.FindAsync(id);
    if (issue == null)
```

```
        return Request.CreateResponse(HttpStatusCode.NotFound);

    if (!Request.Headers.IfModifiedSince.HasValue) // <1>
        return Request.CreateResponse(HttpStatusCode.BadRequest,
                "Missing IfModifiedSince header");

    if (Request.Headers.IfModifiedSince != issue.LastModified) // <2>
        return Request.CreateResponse(HttpStatusCode.Conflict); // <3>

    await _store.UpdateAsync(id, issueUpdate);
    return Request.CreateResponse(HttpStatusCode.OK);

}
```

Example 8-9 shows the new changes introduced in the Patch method. When the client does not send an IfModifiedSince header, the implementation simply returns a response with status code 400 Bad Request, as the request is considered to be invalid *<1>*. Otherwise, the IfModifiedSince header received in the request message is compared with the LastModified field of the issue to be updated *<2>*. If they don't match, a response with status code 409 Conflict is returned *<3>*. In any other case, the issue is finally updated and a response with status code 200 OK is returned.

The next test, shown in Example 8-10, addresses the scenario in which a conflict is detected:

```
Scenario: Updating an issue with conflicts
    Given an existing issue
    When a PATCH request is made with an IfModifiedSince header
    Then a '409 CONFLICT' is returned
    Then the issue is not updated
```

Example 8-10. Unit test for updating an issue with conflicts

```
[Scenario]
public void UpdatingAnIssueWithConflicts()
{
  var fakeIssue = FakeIssues.FirstOrDefault();

  "Given an existing issue".
    f(() =>
    {
      MockIssueStore.Setup(i => i.FindAsync("1"))
        .Returns(Task.FromResult(fakeIssue));
    });
  "When a PATCH request is made with IfModifiedSince".
    f(() =>
    {
      var issue = new Issue();
      issue.Title = "Updated title";
      issue.Description = "Updated description";
      Request.Method = new HttpMethod("PATCH");
```

```
        Request.RequestUri = _uriIssue1;
        Request.Content = new ObjectContent<Issue>(issue,
          new JsonMediaTypeFormatter());
        Request.Headers.IfModifiedSince = fakeIssue.LastModified.AddDays(1); // <1>
        Response = Client.SendAsync(Request).Result;
    });
  "Then a '409 CONFLICT' status is returned".
    f(() => Response.StatusCode
      .ShouldEqual(HttpStatusCode.Conflict)); // <2>
  "Then the issue should be not updated".
    f(() => MockIssueStore.Verify(i =>
      i.UpdateAsync("1", It.IsAny<JObject>()), Times.Never())); // <3>
}
```

Example 8-10 shows the implementation of the scenario in which a conflict is detected.
We sent the IfModifiedSince header into the future by adding one day to the value of
LastModified property in the issue that is going to be updated *<1>*. Since the values for
IfModifiedSince and LastModified are different, the server will return a response with
status code 409 Conflict, which is what the test expects *<2>*. Finally, the test also verifies
that the issue was not updated in the issue store *<3>*.

Change Auditing

Another feature that Web API will support is the ability to identify the user or client
who created a new issue or updated an existing one. That means the implementation
has to authenticate the client using a predefined authentication scheme based on application keys, username/password, HMAC (hash-based message authentication code),
or security tokens such as OAuth.

Using application keys is probably the simplest scenario. Every client application is
identified with a simple and fixed application key. This authentication mechanism is
perhaps a bit weak, but the data that the service has to offer is not sensitive at all. The
data is available for everyone with a key, and it's pretty much used for public services
such as Google Maps or a search for public pictures (in Instagram, for example). The
only purpose of the key is to identify clients and apply different service-level agreements
such as API quotas or availability. Anyone can impersonate the client application by
knowing the application key.

HMAC is similar to the application key authentication mechanism, but uses cryptography with a secret key to avoid the impersonation issues found in the first scheme. As
opposed to basic authentication, the secret key or password is not sent on every message
in plain text. A hash or HMAC is generated from some parts of the HTTP request
message via the secret key, and that HMAC is included as part of the authorization
header. The server can authenticate the client by validating the attached HMAC in the
authorization header. This model fits well with cloud computing, where a vendor such
as AWS (Amazon Web Services) or Windows Azure uses a key for identifying the tenant

and provides the right services and private data. No matter which client application is used to consume the services and data, the main purpose of the key is to identify the tenant. Although there are several existing implementations of HMAC authentication, we will cover one called Hawk, which represents an emergent specification to standardize HMAC authentication.

The last scheme is based on security tokens, and it is probably the most complicated one. Here you can find OAuth, which was designed with the idea of delegating authorization in Web 2.0. The service that owns the data can use OAuth to share that data with other services or applications without compromising the owner credentials.

All these schemes will be discussed more in detail in Chapter 15. As part of this chapter, Hawk will be used to authenticate the client application before setting the auditing information on the issue.

Implementing Change Auditing with Hawk Authentication

The first test will create a new issue with auditing information about who created the issue. Therefore, this test will also have to authenticate the client first using HMAC authentication with Hawk. You will find the code for these tests in the `CodeAuditing` class.

```
Scenario: Creating a new issue
    Given a new issue
    When a POST request is made with an Authorization header containing the user
        identifier
    Then a '201 Created' status is returned
    Then the issue should be added with auditing information
    Then the response location header will be set to the resource location
```

To add Hawk authentication as part of the implementation, we'll use an existing open source implementation called HawkNet, which is available on GitHub (*http://bit.ly/ hawknet*). This implementation provides integration with multiple Web API frameworks in .NET, including ASP.NET Web API. It accomplishes the integration with ASP.NET Web API through HTTP message handlers, as you can see in Example 8-11. One handler is used on the client side to automatically add the Hawk authorization header in every ongoing call, and another handler on the server side validates that header and authenticates the client.

Example 8-11. Injecting the HawkClientMessageHandler in the HttpClient instance

```
Credentials = new HawkCredential
{
    Id = "TestClient",
    Algorithm = "hmacsha256",
    Key = "werxhqb98rpaxn39848xrunpaw3489ruxnpa98w4rxn",
```

```
    User = "test"
}; // <1>

var server = new HttpServer(GetConfiguration());
Client = new HttpClient(new HawkClientMessageHandler(server, Credentials)); // <2>
```

Example 8-11 shows how the HawkClientMessageHandler is injected into the HttpClient instance used by the tests. HawkCredential is the class used by HawkNet to configure different settings that specify how the Hawk header will be generated. The test configures this class to use SHA-256 as the algorithm for issuing the HMAC, the private key, the application id (TestClient), and the user associated with that key (test) *<1>*. Once the HawkCredential class is instantiated and configured, it is passed to the HawkClientMessageHandler injected in the HttpClient instance *<2>*.

In addition, the server also has to be configured with the message handler counterpart to validate the header and authenticate the client. HawkNet provides a HawkMessage Handler class for that purpose, which can be injected as part of the route configuration or as a global handler (see Example 8-12).

Example 8-12. Injecting the HawkMessageHandler in the route configuration

```
Credentials = new HawkCredential
{
    Id = "TestClient",
    Algorithm = "hmacsha256",
    Key = "werxhqb98rpaxn39848xrunpaw3489ruxnpa98w4rxn",
    User = "test"
};

var config = new HttpConfiguration();

var serverHandler = new HawkMessageHandler(new HttpControllerDispatcher(config),
(id) => Credentials);

config.Routes.MapHttpRoute("DefaultApi", "{controller}/{id}", new { id =
RouteParameter.Optional }, null, serverHandler);
```

Once the handlers for sending and authenticating the Hawk header are in place, we can finally start working on the tests for our first scenario about creating issues. Example 8-13 shows the final implementation of this test.

Example 8-13. Creating a new issue implementation

```
[Scenario]
public void CreatingANewIssue()
{
  Issue issue = null;

  "Given a new issue".
    f(() =>
```

```
{
  issue = new Issue
  {
    Description = "A new issue",
    Title = "A new issue"
  };

  var newIssue = new Issue { Id = "1" };

  MockIssueStore
    .Setup(i => i.CreateAsync(issue, "test"))
    .Returns(Task.FromResult(newIssue));
});
"When a POST request is made with an Authorization header containing the user
identifier".
  f(() =>
  {
    Request.Method = HttpMethod.Post;
    Request.RequestUri = _issues;
    Request.Content = new ObjectContent<Issue>(issue,
      new JsonMediaTypeFormatter());
    Response = Client.SendAsync(Request).Result;
  });
"Then a '201 Created' status is returned".
  f(() => Response.StatusCode.ShouldEqual(HttpStatusCode.Created));
"Then the issue should be added with auditing information".
  f(() => MockIssueStore.Verify(i => i.CreateAsync(issue, "test"))); // <1>
"Then the response location header will be set to the resource location".
  f(() => Response.Headers.Location.AbsoluteUri.ShouldEqual
    ("http://localhost/issue/1"));
}
```

The test mainly verifies that the issue is correctly persisted in the issue store along with
the authenticated user test *<1>*. The CreateAsync method in the IIssueStore interface
is modified to receive an additional argument representing the user who created the
user. It is now the responsibility of the Post method in the IssueController class to
pass that value inferred from the authenticated user (see Example 8-14).

Example 8-14. Updated version of the Post method

```
[Authorize]
public async Task<HttpResponseMessage> Post(Issue issue)
{
    var newIssue = await _store.CreateAsync(issue, User.Identity.Name); // <1>
    var response = Request.CreateResponse(HttpStatusCode.Created);
    response.Headers.Location = _linkFactory.Self(newIssue.Id).Href;
    return response;
}
```

The authenticated user becomes available in the User.Identity property, which was
set by the HawkMessageHandler after the received Authorization header was validated.

This user is passed to the CreateAsync method right after the received issue *<1>*. Also, the Post method has been decorated with the Authorize attribute to reject any anonymous call.

```
Scenario: Updating an issue
    Given an existing issue
    When a PATCH request is made with an Authorization header containing the
    user identifier
    Then a '200 OK' is returned
    Then the issue should be updated with auditing information
```

The implementation of the test for verifying this scenario also needs to check if changes are persisted in the IIssueStore along with the authenticated user, as shown in Example 8-15.

Example 8-15. Updating issue implementation

```
[Scenario]
public void UpdatingAnIssue()
{
  var fakeIssue = FakeIssues.FirstOrDefault();

  "Given an existing issue".
    f(() =>
    {
      MockIssueStore
        .Setup(i => i.FindAsync("1"))
        .Returns(Task.FromResult(fakeIssue));
      MockIssueStore
        .Setup(i => i.UpdateAsync("1", It.IsAny<Object>(), It.IsAny<string>()))
        .Returns(Task.FromResult(""));
    });
  "When a PATCH request is made with an Authorization header containing the user
  identifier".
    f(() =>
    {
      var issue = new Issue();
      issue.Title = "Updated title";
      issue.Description = "Updated description";
      Request.Method = new HttpMethod("PATCH");
      Request.Headers.IfModifiedSince = fakeIssue.LastModified;
      Request.RequestUri = _uriIssue1;
      Request.Content = new ObjectContent<Issue>(issue, new JsonMediaTypeFormatter());
      Response = Client.SendAsync(Request).Result;
    });
  "Then a '200 OK' status is returned".
    f(() => Response.StatusCode.ShouldEqual(HttpStatusCode.OK));
  "Then the issue should be updated with auditing information".
    f(() => MockIssueStore.Verify(i => i.UpdateAsync("1", It.IsAny<JObject>(),
        "test"))); // <1>
}
```

The UpdateAsync method in the IIssueStore interface was also modified to receive an additional argument representing the user who created the user *<1>*.

Example 8-16 shows the modified version of the Patch method. The UpdateAsync call to the configured IIssueStore has been modified to pass the additional argument with the authenticated user.

Example 8-16. Updated version of the Patch method

```
[Authorize]
public async Task<HttpResponseMessage> Patch(string id, JObject issueUpdate)
{
  var issue = await _store.FindAsync(id);
  if (issue == null)
      return Request.CreateResponse(HttpStatusCode.NotFound);

  if (!Request.Headers.IfModifiedSince.HasValue)
      return Request.CreateResponse(HttpStatusCode.BadRequest,
          "Missing IfModifiedSince header");

  if (Request.Headers.IfModifiedSince != issue.LastModified)
      return Request.CreateResponse(HttpStatusCode.Conflict);

  await _store.UpdateAsync(id, issueUpdate, User.Identity.Name); // <1>
  return Request.CreateResponse(HttpStatusCode.OK);
}
```

Tracing

Tracing is an irreplaceable feature for troubleshooting or debugging a Web API in environments where a developer IDE or code debugging tool is not available, or in early stages of development when the API is not yet stabilized and some random, hard-to-identify issues occur. ASP.NET Web API ships with a tracing infrastructure out of the box that you can use to trace any activity performed by the framework itself or any custom code that is part of the Web API implementation.

The core component or service in this infrastructure is represented by the interface System.Web.Http.Tracing.ITraceWriter, which contains a single method, Trace, to generate a new trace entry.

Example 8-17. ITraceWriter interface definition

```
public interface ITraceWriter
{
  void Trace(HttpRequestMessage request, string category, TraceLevel level,
  Action<TraceRecord> traceAction);
}
```

The Trace method expects the following arguments:

request

Request message instance associated to the trace.

category

The category associated with the trace entry. This might become handy to group or filter the traces.

level

Detail level associated with the entry. This is also useful to filter the entries.

traceAction

A delegate to a method where the trace entry is generated.

Although this infrastructure is not tied to any existing logging framework in .NET—such as Log4Net, NLog, or Enterprise Library Logging—a default implementation has been provided. It is called `System.Web.Http.Tracing.SystemDiagnosticsTraceWrit`er, and it uses `System.Diagnostics.Trace.TraceSource`. For the other frameworks, an implementation of the service interface `ITraceWriter` must be provided.

Example 8-18 illustrates how a custom implementation can be injected in the Web API configuration object.

Example 8-18. ITraceWriter configuration

```
HttpConfiguration config = new HttpConfiguration();
config.Services.Replace(typeof(ITraceWriter), new SystemDiagnosticsTraceWriter());
```

Implementing Tracing

There is a single scenario or test that covers tracing in general for all the methods in the `IssueController` class. That test can be found in the `Tracing` class.

```
Scenario: Creating, Updating, Deleting, or Retrieving an issue
    Given an existing or new issue
    When a request is made
    When the diagnostics tracing is enabled
    Then the diagnostics tracing information is generated
```

The first thing we'll do before writing the test for this scenario is to configure an instance of `ITraceWriter` to check that tracing is actually working. See Example 8-19.

Example 8-19. ITraceWriter configuration for the tests

```
public abstract class IssuesFeature
{
  public Mock<ITraceWriter> MockTracer;

  public IssuesFeature()
  {
  }
```

```
  private HttpConfiguration GetConfiguration()
  {
    var config = new HttpConfiguration();

    MockTracer = new Mock<ITraceWriter>(MockBehavior.Loose);

    config.Services.Replace(typeof(ITraceWriter), MockTracer.Object); // <1>

    return config;
  }
}
```

Example 8-19 shows how a mock instance is injected in the HttpConfiguration instance used by Web API *<1>*. The test will use this mock instance (shown in
Example 8-20) to verify the calls to the Trace method from the controller methods.

Example 8-20. Tracing test implementation

```
public class Tracing : IssuesFeature
{
  private Uri _uriIssue1 = new Uri("http://localhost/issue/1");

  [Scenario]
  public void RetrievingAnIssue()
  {
    IssueState issue = null;
    var fakeIssue = FakeIssues.FirstOrDefault();

    "Given an existing or new issue".
      f(() =>
      {
        MockIssueStore
          .Setup(i => i.FindAsync("1"))
          .Returns(Task.FromResult(fakeIssue)));
      }
    "When a request is made".
      f(() =>
      {
        Request.RequestUri = _uriIssue1;

        Response = Client
          .SendAsync(Request)
          .Result;

        issue = Response.Content
          .ReadAsAsync<IssueState>()
          .Result;
      });
    "When the diagnostics tracing is enabled".
      f(() =>
      {
```

```
    Configuration.Services
      .GetService(typeof(ITraceWriter)).ShouldNotBeNull(); // <1>
  });
"Then the diagnostics tracing information is generated".
  f(() =>
  {
    MockTracer.Verify(m => m.Trace(It.IsAny<HttpRequestMessage>(), // <2>
      typeof(IssueController).FullName,
      TraceLevel.Debug,
      It.IsAny<Action<TraceRecord>>()));
  });
  }
}
```

The test implementation in Example 8-20 verifies that the `ITraceWriter` service is currently configured in the `HttpConfiguration` instance, and also checks that the `Issue Controller` class (shown in Example 8-21) is sending tracing messages to the configured mock instance.

Example 8-21. Tracing in the IssueController

```
public async Task<HttpResponseMessage> Get(string id)
{
    var tracer = this.Configuration.Services.GetTraceWriter(); // <1>

    var result = await _store.FindAsync(id);
    if (result == null)
    {
        tracer.Trace(Request,
            TraceCategory, TraceLevel.Debug,
                "Issue with id {0} not found", id); // <2>

        return Request.CreateResponse(HttpStatusCode.NotFound);
    }

    .....
}
```

The `HttpConfiguration` class provides an extension method or shortcut to obtain an instance of the configured `ITraceWriter` so it can be used by custom code in the implementation. Example 8-21 shows how the `IssueController` class has been modified to get a reference to the `ITraceWriter` *<1>*, which is used to trace information about an issue not found *<2>* before the response is returned.

Conclusion

This chapter covered several important aspects of improving an existing Web API, such as caching, conflict management, auditing, and tracing. Although they might not apply in certain scenarios, it is always useful to know which benefits they bring to the table so you can use them correctly.

CHAPTER 9

Building the Client

It takes two to tango.

Throughout this book we have had a stated goal of building a system that can evolve. Most of our attention so far has been around building an API that enables clients to remain loosely coupled so as to achieve this goal. Unfortunately, the server API can only enable loose coupling; it cannot prevent tight coupling. No matter how much we employ hypermedia, standard media types, and self-descriptive messages, we cannot prevent clients from hardcoding URIs or assuming they know the content type and semantics of a response.

Part of the role of exposing a Web API is to provide guidance to consumers on how to use the service in a way that takes advantage of the Web's architecture. We need to show client developers how they can consume the API without taking hard dependencies on artifacts that may change.

Guidance to client developers can take the form of documentation, but usually that is only a partial solution. API providers want to make the experience of consuming their API as painless as possible and therefore frequently provide client libraries that attempt to get client developers up and running quickly. Sadly, there is a popular attitude toward software libraries where if it isn't obvious how to use something in five minutes, it must be poorly written. Unfortunately, this optimization toward ease of use misses the subtle difference between simple and easy (*http://bit.ly/simple-easy*).

In the process of making APIs easy to use, API providers frequently create client libraries that encapsulate the HTTP-based API, and in the process lose many benefits of web architecture and end up tightly coupling client applications to the client library, which is in turn tightly coupled to the server API. In this chapter, we will discuss more about the negative effects of this type of client library. Then, we will show an alternative approach that is just as easy to use as a wrapper API but does not suffer the same issues.

Following that, we will discuss techniques for structuring client logic and managing client state that will lead to clients that are adaptive and resilient to change.

Client Libraries

The purpose of a client library is to raise the level of abstraction so that client application developers can write code in terms that are relevant to the application domain. By enabling reuse of boilerplate code that is used for creating HTTP requests and parsing responses, developers can focus on getting their job done.

Wrapper Libraries

There are countless examples of API wrapper libraries. Searching a site like Programmable Web (*http://www.programmableweb.com/*) will lead to many sites where client libraries are offered in dozens of different programming languages. In some cases, these client libraries are from the API providers themselves; however, these days, many libraries are community contributions. API providers have discovered it is a huge amount of work trying to keep all the different versions of these libraries up to date.

Generally, a client API wrapper will look something like this, regardless of the specific provider:

```
var api = new IssueTrackingApi(apiToken);
var issue = api.GetIssue(issueId);
issue.Description = "Here is a description for my issue";
issue.Save();
```

One of the most fundamental problems with the preceding example is that the client developer no longer knows which of those four lines of code make a network request and which ones don't. There is no problem abstracting away the boilerplate code that is required to make a network request, but by completely hiding when those high-latency interactions occur, it can be very difficult for client application developers to write network-efficient applications.

Reliability

One of the challenges of network-based programming is that the network is not reliable. This is especially true in the world of wireless and cellular communication. HTTP as an application protocol has a number of features that enable an application to tolerate such an unreliable medium. Calling a method like GetIssue or Save provides two potential outcomes: success and the expected return type, or an exception. HTTP identifies requests as safe or unsafe, idempotent or nonidempotent. With this knowledge, a client application can interpret the standardized status codes and decide what remedial action to take upon a failure. There are no such conventions in the object-oriented and procedural world. I can make a guess that GetIssue is safe, and Save is unsafe and—in this particular code sample—idempotent. However, that is possible only because I am interpreting the method names and guessing at the underlying client behavior. By hiding the HTTP requests behind a procedural call, I am hiding the reliability features of HTTP and forcing the client developer to reinvent her own conventions and standards to regain that capability.

It is possible that certain reliability mechanisms, like retry, could be built into the client library, and some of the better-written libraries likely do that. However, the developers writing the library do not know the reliability requirements of the client application. A corrective action that is a good idea for one client application may be a terrible idea for another. A batch application that crawls data sources overnight may be happy to retry a request two or three times, waiting a few minutes between each request, but one with a human being waiting for a response is not likely to be so patient.

Handling temoprary service interruptions is not the only way that the outcome of HTTP requests can differ. The requested resource may be Gone (410), it may have been moved See Other (303), you may be Forbidden (403) to retrieve it, or you may have to wait for the representation to be created (202). The Content-Type of the response may have changed since the last time this resource was requested. All of these results are not a failure to execute the request. They are valid responses when requesting information from a system that we expect to evolve over time. A client needs to be built to handle any and all of these situations if it is to be reliable for many years.

I regularly see API documentation that describes what response codes may be returned from a particular API resource. Unfortunately, there is no way to constrain what response codes will be returned from an API. In every HTTP request there are many intermediaries that participate in the request: client-connectors, proxies, caches, load-balancers, reverse-proxies, and application middleware, to name a few. All of these could short-circuit a request and return some other status code. Clients need to be built to handle all of the response codes for all resources. Building a client that assumes a resource will never return a 303 is introducing hidden coupling just as if you had hard-coded the URI.

Response types

A method such as GetIssue makes an assumption that the response returned can be translated into an Issue object. With some basic content negotiation code in a client library, you can build in resilience to deal with the eventuality of JSON falling out of favor for some other wire format (just as XML is currently falling out of favor). However, there are some nice things that can be done with HTTP that are prohibited by such a tightly constrained contract. Consider this request:

```
GET /IssueSearch?priority=high&AssignedTo=Dave
```

In a procedural wrapper library, the signature would be something like:

```
public List<Issue> SearchIssues(int priority, string assignedTo);
```

The media type of the returned resource could be something like `Collection+Json`, which is ideally suited for returning lists of things. However, what happens if the server finds that there is only one issue that matches the filter criteria? A server may decide that instead of returning a `Collection+JSON` list of one `Issue`, it would prefer to return an entire `application/Issue+Json` representation. A procedural library cannot support this flexibility without resorting to returning type `object`, which somewhat defeats the purpose of the strongly typed wrapper library. There are many reasons why an API developer may not want to introduce this type of variance in responses, but there are certain circumstances where it can be invaluable. Consider the expense report with a list of items and the associated expense receipt. That receipt may be in the form of a PDF, a TIFF, a bitmap, an HTML page, or an email message. There is no way to strongly type the representation in a single method signature.

Lifetime

In our tiny client snippet, we instantiated an `Issue` object. That object was populated with state from a representation returned from the server. The representation returned from the server quite possibly had a cache control header associated with it. If that cache controller header looked like the following, then the server is making a statement that the data should be considered fresh for at least the next 60 seconds:

```
Cache-Control: private;max-age=60
```

Assuming the appropriate caching infrastructure, any attempt to request that `Issue` again within 60 seconds would not actually make a network roundtrip but would return the representation from the cache. Beyond 60 seconds, any attempt to retrieve that issue information would cause a network request and up-to-date information would be retrieved. By copying the representation data into a local object and discarding the returned representation, you tie the lifetime of that data to the lifetime of the object. The `max-age` of 60 seconds has been lost. That data will be held and reused until the object is thrown away and a new one retrieved, regardless of how stale the information is. Enabling the server to control data lifetime is very important when you are dealing with issues of concurrency. The server is the owner of the data and the one that is most capable of understanding the data's volatility. Relying on clients to dictate caching rules requires them to know more than they really need to know about the server's data.

The problem of object instances containing stale data gets far worse when client libraries build object graphs. Frequently, in wrapping APIs you will see one object being used to retrieve representations to populate other related objects. Often you do this using property-based lazy loading:

```
var issue = api.GetIssue(issueId);
var reportedByuser = issue.ReportedBy;
```

Using this type of navigation to load properties is very common in object-relational mapping (ORM) libraries when you are retrieving information from a database. Unfortunately, by doing this in an API wrapper library, you end up tying the lifetime of the User object to the lifetime of the Issue object. This means you are not only ignoring the HTTP caching lifetime directives but are also creating lifetime interdependencies between representation data. The natural result of this pattern is also often directly the opposite of what we want. It is likely that an issue resource will change more frequently than a user resource, and it is likely that a user resource may be reused by multiple issue resources. However, our object graph ties the lifetime of the User to the Issue, which is suboptimal. ORM libraries often address this by creating a new lifetime scope called a *session* or *unit of work*, and object lifetimes are managed by those containers. This creates additional complexity for the client that is unnecessary if we can take advantage of the caching directives provided by the server using the HTTP protocol. To do that, we need to stop hiding the HTTP behind a wrapper.

Everyone has his or her own style

Another way that client wrapper libraries can make API usage confusing is by maintaining their own pieces of protocol state. Through a sequence of interations with the client library, future interactions are modified based on stored state. This may be authentication information or other preferences that modify requests. When different APIs each implement their own client libraries and invent their own interaction models, it increases the developer learning curve. It becomes additionally annoying when a client library must work with multiple APIs to achieve its goal. Working with multiple client libraries that behave differently to access remote interfaces that conform to the standard uniform interface of HTTP is maddening.

Unfortunately, many of these libraries are an all-or-nothing proposition. Either you do raw HTTP, or you use the API for everything. Usually there is no way to access the HTTP request that is sent by the wrapper library to make minor modifications to the request. The same goes for the response: if the client library doesn't know about some part of the response, then there is no way to get at the information. This usually means that a minor change to the server-side API either forces you to move to a new version of the client library, or at best prevents you from taking advantage of new API features until you upgrade.

Hypermedia hostile

Hypermedia-driven APIs are dynamic in the resources that they expose. This type of API is particularly difficult to create API wrappers for. There is no way to define a class that sometimes has methods and other times does not. I believe one of the reasons that we have seen very little adoption of hypermedia-driven APIs is due to the fact that few people have found convenient ways to consume hypermedia APIs on the client.

The real difference with a hypermedia API is that the distributed function that is exposed by the API is delivered to the client as a piece of data. It is represented as a link embedded in the returned representation. The idea of manipulating functions as data is not new, but in this case we are considering a link as a piece of data that represents a remote call.

The next section will discuss an alternative approach to building client libraries where we promote a link to a first-class concept that can be used to make remote calls to an API. This approach is more compatible with hypermedia-driven APIs but also can be used very effectively to access APIs that have not adopted all of the REST constraints.

Links as Functions

The most important part of a link is the URL. However, the URL itself is simply an identifier to be interpreted by the server. The significance of the identifier is provided by the *link relation type*. Without understanding the purpose of a link, a client application will find it very difficult to do anything useful with that link.

Consider again the stylesheet link relation. The link relation specification simply says "Refers to a stylesheet." However, web browsers have explicit logic that knows to automatically dereference these types of links using a GET method, and use the returned representation to make visual changes to the context document. Clients can associate any arbitrary logic of their choosing to particular link relation types.

The vast majority of link relations have nothing to say about how a client might process a response. However, there are some relations that declare some kind of supported protocol related to how the link might be activated. Examples include search, oauth2-token, and oauth2-authorize.

By implementing a link as a class, we can incorporate the behavior necessary to create an appropriate HTTP request and in some scenarios process the response to the request:

```
var tokenLink = new OAuth2TokenLink
{
    Target = new Uri("https://login.live.com/oauth20_token.srf"),
    RedirectUri = new Uri("https://login.live.com/oauth20_desktop.srf"),
    ClientId = "000000007C0B306F",
    ClientSecret = "LsKOqUbIv5HSPHt2OM9Z4Ay219Mf-DNA",
    GrantType = "authorization_code",
    AuthorizationCode = "3eab54b1-86fa-4596-ce5e-91cb4e55bbd3"
};

var client = new HttpClient();
var response = await client.SendAsync(tokenLink.CreateRequest());
var body = await response.Content.ReadAsStringAsync();

if (response.IsSuccessStatusCode)
{
    var token = OAuth2TokenLink.ParseTokenBody(body);
```

```
        }
        else
        {
            var error = OAuth2TokenLink.ParseErrorBody(body);
        }
```

In this example, OAuth2TokenLink represents a link to an OAuth token generation resource. The link exposes all the parameters that will be needed to make the request.
These parameters can be exposed in whatever types are most natural in .NET. The details
of converting those into the required format for the HTTP request are abstracted away.

By calling CreateRequest, the OAuthTokenLink class creates an instance of HttpRe
questMessage with the method POST and the Content property contains an instance of
FormEncodedUrlContent with all the necessary parameters. The HttpRequestMes
sage object can then be used just like any other request. This allows the reuse of a
standard HttpClient with all the usual DefaultRequestHeaders and MessageHandlers.

Once an HttpResponseMessage has been retrieved, we can use the OAuthTokenLink to
parse the response body. By taking this approach, we encapsulate all of the semantics of
the link in the link class without the library class having to deal with the mechanics of
making the request.

Service antipattern

It is common for developers creating client wrapper libraries to define a service class
that exposes a set of methods that correspond to remote resources. For example, if we
were creating a wrapper library for our Issue API, it might look like:

```
public class IssueApi {

        public Issue GetIssue(int id) {...}
        public Issue CreateIssue(IssueDto issueInfo) {...}
        public List<Issue> GetOpenIssues() {...}
        public List<Issue> GetMyIssues(int userId) {...}

}

var issueApi = new IssueApi("http://example.org/issueApi");
var issue = issueApi.GetIssue(77);

List<Issues> openIssues = issueApi.GetOpenIssues();
```

One of the problems of this approach is that the entire API is now defined by the Service
API class. The available resources, the return types, and the parameters are all fixed by
a client-side library.

We can implement the same capability using an IssueLink and an IssuesLink. There
are even more generic ways of accessing these resources, but for the sake of simplicity,
let us consider these two classes.

To access an issue and lists of issues, we can do the following:

```
var httpClient = new HttpClient();

var issueLink = new IssueLink() {
        Target = new Uri("http://example.org/issueApi/Issue/{id}"),
        Id = 77
}

var issue = issueLink.ParseResponse(
            await httpClient.SendAsync(issueLink.CreateRequest()));

var issuesLink = new IssuesLink() {
        Target = new Uri("http://example.org/issueApi/OpenIssues")
}

List<Issues> issues = issuesLink.ParseResponse(
            await httpClient.SendAsync(issueLink.CreateRequest()));
```

By ensuring that our API coupling is limited to link types and not to specific resources, we can be confident that our IssuesLink will work when the API adds more resources (e.g., /ClosedIssues, /CriticalIssues, and /LateIssues):

```
var httpClient = new HttpClient();

var closedIssuesLink = new IssuesLink {
        Target = new Uri("http://acme.org/issueApi/ClosedIssues"),
};

List<Issues> closedIssues = issuesLink.ParseResponse(
            httpClient.SendAsync(closedIssuesLink.CreateRequest()));

var criticalIssuesLink = new IssuesLink {
        Target = new Uri("http://acme.org/issueApi/CriticalIssues"),
};

List<Issues> criticalIssues = issuesLink.ParseResponse(
            httpClient.SendAsync(criticalIssuesLink.CreateRequest()));

var lateIssuesLink = new IssuesLink {
        Target = new Uri("http://acme.org/issueApi/LateIssues"),
};

List<Issues> lateIssues = issuesLink.ParseResponse(
            httpClient.SendAsync(lateIssuesLink.CreateRequest()));
```

The semantics of each of these requests is identical. It is a GET request that returns a media type that contains a list of issues. The fact that each link returns different subsets of issues has no impact on the semantics of the link. In a wrapper API, it would be necessary to create new methods on the client library to expose these resources. Consumers of the API must wait for the release of a new client library and must update their client code before they can access these new resources.

To work around the inability to easily expose new resources to clients, people often attempt to build sophisticated query capabilities into their API. The problem with this approach, beyond the coupling on the query syntax, is that just a few query parameters can open up a huge number of potential resources, some of which may be expensive to generate. Numerous API providers are starting to discover the challenging economics of exposing arbitrary query capabilities to third parties. A much more managable approach is to enable a few highly optimized resources that address the majority of use cases. It is critical, however, that new resources can be added quickly to the API to address new requirements.

Deserializing links

Once you embrace the notion of embedding links into representations, deserializing representations has the added benefit of automatically generating link instances. All that is required is to retreive those links from the representation object model.

When you are consuming links with relations that are not specific to a particular media type, it is necessary for the representation deserialization code to use some form of link factory in order to create links of the correct type. You can use the link relation value as a lookup value into a dictionary of types to determine the correct type to instantiate.

Separating request and response

One of the most significant differences between making a wrapper method call and using a link to make a request is the separation of the request and response. Using a link has two distinct steps. First, the request is created and sent to the origin server; then, optionally, the response is handed over to the link for processing. There are several benefits to separating these parts. Making an HTTP request is proportionately an extremely expensive operation hence all HTTP requests using HttpClient are done asynchronously. Asynchronous operations, by their very nature, split apart the request and response code. Recent versions of C# and .NET have made it possible to syntactically hide this separation, but fundamentally it is still there. Separating the request and response processing of a link is a more natural fit for this type of asynchronous operation.

With a wrapper API, there is an assumption that the HTTP request will be handled completely within the wrapper method. This implies that every method that accesses a resource must also handle all the non-2XX responses that can be returned from an API. The wrapper library must decide what to do with 3XX redirects, 401 Unauthorized responses, and 503 Server Unavailable responses. When you are interacting with multiple APIs, there is the possibility that different wrapper APIs may handle these responses differently, adding even more complexity into the mix.

With a typed link, you can inspect the response for non-2XX statuses before passing it on to the typed link for handling. This makes it easier to have consistent, centralized handling for redirects and error statuses.

```
var httpClient = new HttpClient();

var issueLink = new IssueLink() {
        Target = new Uri("http://example.org/issueApi/Issue/{id}"),
        Id = 77
}

var response = await httpClient.SendAsync(issueLink.CreateRequest());

if (response.IsSuccessStatusCode) {
   var issue = issueLink.ParseResponse(response);
} else {
        GlobalNonSuccessResponseHandler.Handle(response)
}
```

The HttpClient class has an extensible handler pipeline that makes adding these cross-cutting handlers even easier and cleaner. In Chapter 14, we go into more depth on how you can take advantage of the separated request and response handling to build reactive clients.

The important point here is that client application developers are no longer tied to decisions made by the writers of API wrapper libraries when it comes to dealing with cross-cutting concerns. The API providers can supply strongly typed links that focus only on delivering code that is specific to their API and leave generic HTTP concerns to generic HTTP libraries.

Links as bookmarks

One nice side benefit of using links to generate HttpRequestMessage instances is that they are handy for making repeated requests. An HttpRequestMessage instance can be used only to make a single HTTP request, whereas a link object can be created and configured once and be used to make multiple requests. Or a link object can have one or more parameter values changed and create a new request.

Links can also be stored as part of the client state as a kind of temporary bookmark. One complaint that I hear often when developers first start looking at hypermedia APIs is that they are concerned about making multiple requests to traverse from the root of the API to their desired resource. By bookmarking links, a client can cache links for reuse so that additional roundtrips will be minimal.

Consider if we were to add a json-home document to the root of our Issue API. It might look something like this:

```
{
        "resources": {
```

```
      "http://example.org/rel/issue": {
      "href-template": "/example.org/issueApi/issue/{id}",
            "href-vars": {
              "id": "http://example.org/param/issueid"
            }
      },
    "http://example.org/rel/issues": {
      "href": "/issueApi/issues",
    }

    "http://eample.org/rel/issueprocessor" : {
                "href-template" : "issues/{id}/issueprocessor",
                "href-vars": {
              "id": "http://example.org/param/issueid"
                }
      }
    }
  }
}
```

An initial request to the root of the API can retrieve the home document, parse the links, create link objects, and store them in a globally accessible dictionary. For example:

```
var httpClient = new HttpClient();

var homeLink = new HomeLink() {
      Target = new Uri("http://example.org/issueApi")
}

var response = await httpClient.GetAsync(homeLink.CreateRequest());

var homedoc = homeLink.ParseHomeDocument(response, LinkFactory);

GlobalLinks = homeDoc.GetResourcesAsDictionary();


var issueLink = GlobalLinks["http://example.org/rel/issue"];
...
```

In this simplified example, we are using a single root document to populate a Global Links dictionary with all the discovered links. This code would be run just once on startup of a client application, and the overhead of supporting hypermedia becomes just one extra roundtrip per execution of the client application.

Having all the links of the application stored as a single root document is not a best practice of hypermedia APIs because you lose the benefits of being able to make links available only when the context is appropriate. However, in every API there will be some links that can be exposed at the root. Other links can be discovered at other resources in the system, and some of those will be bookmarkable.

There is no single prescriptive solution for every Web API. Some techniques will work in some scenarios, but not necessarily all. Our goal here is to explore what techniques may be possible to address challenges introduced by seeking evolvability.

Regardless of the disadvantages of creating a single root discovery document and caching all the links globally, it is a far more evolvable approach than hardcoding URIs into a client library and requires minimal effort to achieve.

Application Workflow

Using links to encapsulate interaction semantics and provide a layer of indirection allows the server to evolve its own URI space. These are significant steps toward the goal of decoupling distributed components.

However, clients and servers can still become coupled by the protocol of interactions across multiple resources. If a client has encoded logic that says it should retrieve resource A, retrieve resource B, present that information, capture some input, and then send the result to resource C, you cannot change this workflow without changing the client. It is impossible for the server to introduce an additional resource A' between A and B and have the client automatically consume it. However, if resource A were to contain a link with rel='next' and the client were instructed to follow the next links until it finds a link to resource C, then the server has the option to add and remove intermediate steps without breaking the client.

Need to Know

Moving the application workflow to the server leads to a client architecture where the client can be extremely smart about processing individual representations based on their declared media types, and can implement sophisticated interaction mechanisms based on the semantics of link relations. However, the user agent can remain completely uninformed about how its individual actions fit into the application as a whole. This ignorance both simplifies the client code and facilitates change over time. It also enables the same web browser client to let you perform banking transactions and then browse recipe websites looking for inspiration for dinner.

Often, client applications may not want to completely hand over the workflow control to the server. Maybe a client is actually interacting with multiple unrelated services, or perhaps trying to achieve goals never envisioned by the server developers. Even in these cases, there can be benefits to taking a more moderate approach to giving up workflow control.

One way to enable the server to take over some of the workflow responsibilities is to start defining client behavior in terms of goals expressed in the application domain, rather than in terms of HTTP interactions. In traditional client applications, it is common to see a 1:1 relationship between application methods and HTTP requests. However, actually satisfying the user's intent may require multiple HTTP requests. By encapsulating the interactions required to achieve that goal, we can build a unit of work that is more resilient to change.

Assuming we have a way to encapsulate the process of achieving the user's goal, we want to enable some flexibility in how that goal might be achieved. Today, it may require two HTTP requests, but in the future when the server identifies that this particular sequence is called frequently by many users, it may optimize the API to achieve the goal in a single request. Ideally, the client can take advantage of this optimization without having to change.

To enable that kind of flexibility, we need to react to HTTP responses rather than expecting them. Standard HTTP client libraries already do this to an extent. Consider a scenario where a client retrieves a representation from resource A. The server API has some resources that require authentication, and others that do not. The HttpClient has a set of credentials but does not use them when accessing resource A because it is not required. Due to external forces, the server decides it must change its behavior and require authorization for resource A. When the client attempts to retrieve resource A, it receives a 401 error and a www-authenticate header. The client understands the problem and can react by resending the request with the credentials. This set of interactions can all happen completely transparently to the client application making the HTTP request.

Some HTTP clients see the same reactive behavior when receiving redirect (3XX) status codes. The HTTP library takes care of converting the single request into multiple ones that achieve the original goal.

By taking this same idea but implementing it within the application domain, we can achieve a similar level of resiliency to many more kinds of changes that previously would be considered breaking changes.

Consider the following code snippet, which could be part of a client application:

```
public void SelectIssue(IssueLink issueLink) {

        var response = await _httpClient.SendAsync(issueLink.CreateRequest());

        var issue = issueLink.ParseResponse(response);

        var form = new IssueForm();
        form.Display(issue);

    }
```

Now consider the following:

```
public void Select(Link aLink) {

        var response = await _httpClient.SendAsync(aLink.CreateRequest());
```

```
List<Issue> issues =  new List<Issue>();

switch(response.Content.Headers.ContentType.MediaType) {

        case "application/collection+json" :
                LoadIssues(issues, response.Content)
                break;

        case "application/issue+json" :
                issues.Add(issueLink.ParseResponse(response));
                break;
}

foreach(var issues in issues) {
        var form = IssueFormFactory.CreateIssueForm();
        form.Display(issue);
    }
}
```

This is a fairly contrived example that only begins to hint at what is possible. In this example, we recognize that there may be different media types returned from the request. If the link returns just a single issue, then we display that; if it returns a collection, then we search for links to issues, load the entire set, and display each of them.

Client applications get really interesting when you can do the following:

```
public void Select(Link aLink) {

        var response = await _httpClient.SendAsync(aLink.CreateRequest());
        GlobalHandler.HandleResponse(aLink, response);
}
```

With this approach, the client application has no more context than the link used to retrieve the response, and the actual response message itself, with which to process the response message. This provides the ultimate in workflow decoupling and is much like how a web browser works.

Handle all the versions

When a server makes an optimization to its API, it is quite likely that the client does not have the necessary knowledge to take advantage of the optimization. As long as the server leaves the unoptimized interaction mechanism in place, clients will continue to operate, blissfully unaware of the fact that there is a faster way. In the next release of the client, code can be introduced to take advantage of the optimization, if it is available. The key is for the client to do the necessary feature detection to determine if the feature is available. This is less of a concern when there is only one instance of the server API, like Twitter or Facebook, for example. However, if you are developing a client library for a product like WordPress, you cannot guarantee what features of a server API will be available.

This combination of reactive behavior and feature detection is what enables clients and servers to continue to interoperate without the need for version number coordination. This capability is something that should be planned from the beginning. It is not something that would likely be easy to retrofit into an existing client.

Change is inevitable

There are a variety of scenarios where a server can make changes to which a client can adapt. We'll discuss a few that occur fairly regularly.

By regularly analyzing the paths that clients take through an API, a server may decide to introduce a shortcut link that bypasses some intermediary representations. Sometimes it does this by adding an extra parameter to a URI template. Clients can look for the shortcut link by link relation; if the link isn't there, then they can revert to the long way.

An API may introduce a new representation format that might be more efficient or carry more semantics. New media types are being created all the time. When a client implements support for this new format, it can add that type to its Accept header to let the server know that it supports that new format. In order to remain compatible with old versions of the API, the client still needs to maintain support for the old format. Assuming the client is designed with the knowledge that multiple return formats are possible, this is usually trivial to do.

When doing representation design, servers need to decide when to embed information about related resources or provide a link. Sometimes they need to change that decision. If a representation gets too large, then embedded resources may need to be replaced by links. If certain related links are always followed, then it may be more efficient to return the content embedded. Building a client that can transparently embed a linked representation if necessary allows the server to change the nature of the representation and not break the client.

Clients that are human-driven often are responsible for presenting a set of available resource links to a user. In these cases, iterating through the links in a page and displaying each link is a better approach than binding static UI elements to known links. By building UI dynamically, the server can add resource links and the client can automatically access them.

When resource links are removed, even if they are bound to fixed UI elements, those elements can be disabled to indicate that the resource is no longer available. Clients should not break just because a link no longer exists. Sometimes the removal of a link may prohibit the user from achieving a specific goal, but we can assume that other goals are still possible. The removal of a capability should not be a breaking change for clients.

Servers can move resources to a new URI, either due to some reorganization of the URI space, or perhaps due to an effort to partition server load by moving a resource to a new host. Clients should be able to handle the redirection requests transparently.

Whenever a server adds new query parameters to a link, it should provide default values for those additional parameters. If it doesn't then it would be a breaking change, in which case it should add a new link and link relation to define the new requirements. A client application should be able to safely continue to use a link without specifiying the new parameter. Future updates to the client should be able to take advantage of the new parameter.

A server that finds it no longer needs a parameter to identify the resource should update the URI template to not include the value token. Client code should not fail when trying to set a parameter that is not in the URI template. The resolved URL should not include the removed parameter, or the server could return a 404.

In some scenarios, a resource that previously accepted both GET and POST may be split and a distinct resource created to handle the POST. In these cases, a secondary link and link relation should be included and a redirect from the original POST should be implemented to handle the transition period.

A sequence of interactions may require an additional step. In this case, it may be possible to annotate a link in the extra step as a "default" link and to build a client to follow a default link if it does not know how else to process a particular representation.

The Link Hints IETF Internet draft (*http://bit.ly/ietf-draft*) introduces the ability to decorate links with deprecated attributes. This is one way to notify clients that links will no longer be supported in the future. Additionally, server developers should log the use of deprecated links and record the user agents that accessed the resource. This allows out-of-band communication to occur to encourage client developers to remove their use of deprecated links.

Undoubtedly, there are many other changes that can occur to a server API. However, these examples indicate that the web architecture has been designed in such a way that clients can adapt to these changes. By redirecting our efforts away from the drudgery of managing client and server version compliance, and toward handling potential changes in the API, we can evolve faster and keep our users happier.

Clients with Missions

In a completely human-driven experience like a web browser, it feels like a 1:1 interaction model, but it is not. Clicking on a single link causes a single HTML page to load; however, from that the browser loads linked stylesheets, images, and scripts. Only once all of these requests have been made can the goal of displaying the page be considered complete.

As much as I have tried, I am unable to find a name that better describes this encapsulation of interactions than *mission*. A *mission* is an implementation of the necessary requests and response handling to achieve a client's goal. One advantage of it being a fairly goofy-sounding name is that we avoid overloading some other software term, like *task* or *transaction*. It also highlights the fact that it is the objective that is important rather than the details of how it is achieved. It also happens to fit rather amusingly with the fact that HTTP clients are regularly referred to as *agents*.

Previously we have discussed how link relations can be used to identify the semantics of an HTTP interaction. Sometimes link relations also confer the need for multiple interactions. The link relation search is one example. A search link points to an Open SearchDescription document that contains information about how to conduct a search of resources on a website or API. At its simplest, the description document contains a URL template with a {searchTerms} token that can be replaced by the client's actual search terms.

The following class demonstrates how to create a mission that encapsulates the behavior of getting the OpenSearchDescription document, interpreting it, constructing a URL, performing the search, and returning the results of the search:

```
public class SearchMission
    {
        private readonly HttpClient _httpClient;
        private readonly SearchLink _link;

        public SearchMission(HttpClient httpClient, SearchLink link)
        {
            _httpClient = httpClient;
            _link = link;
        }

        public async Task<HttpResponseMessage> GoAsync(string param)
        {
            var openSearchDescription = await LoadOpenSearchDescription();
            var link = openSearchDescription.Url;
            link.SetParameter("searchTerms", param);
            return await _httpClient.SendAsync(link.CreateRequest());
        }

        private async Task<OpenSearchDescription> LoadOpenSearchDescription()
        {
            var response = await _httpClient.SendAsync(_link.CreateRequest());
            var desc = await response.Content.ReadAsStreamAsync();
            return new OpenSearchDescription(
                    response.Content.Headers.ContentType, desc);
        }

    }
```

The mission class itself does not include the details of how to interpret the OpenSearch Description; that is left to a media type parser library. The mission focuses just on the coordination of the interactions. A SearchMission object can be held to perform multiple searches.

Missions can be completely algorithmic-based interactions with HTTP resources. A client application initiates a mission, and execution continues until either a goal is reached or the mission fails. Missions can become a unit of reuse and can be combined to achieve larger goals.

Missions can also be interactive processes where after some set of interactions, control is returned to a human to provide further direction. To achieve this, missions need to be designed with some kind of interface to a user interface layer. This interface must allow a mission to display the current state to the user and accept further direction. The user interface layer must provide the human with a set of links to select from and then convey the selected link back to the mission.

The following example is a very simple interactive mission and a small console application that works as a hypermedia REPL (read-eval-print loop). The client application must call GoAsync with a link. The mission will follow the link and extract any links that are included in the returned representation. Those links are made available as a dictionary keyed by link relation. A simple console application uses a loop to allow a user to view the initial representation and choose to follow another link by entering the link relation name. The client then requests that the mission follows that link and reparses the links.

```
public class ExploreMission
{
    private readonly HttpClient _httpClient;

    public Link ContextLink { get; set; }
    public HttpContent CurrentRepresentation { get; set; }
    public Dictionary<string,Link> AvailableLinks { get; set; }

    public ExploreMission(HttpClient httpClient)
    {
        _httpClient = httpClient;
    }

    public async Task GoAsync(Link link)
    {
        var response = await _httpClient.SendAsync(link.CreateRequest());
        if (response.IsSuccessStatusCode)
        {
            ContextLink = link;
            CurrentRepresentation = response.Content;
            AvailableLinks = ParseLinks(CurrentRepresentation);
        }
```

```
        }

        private Dictionary<string,Link>
                ParseLinks(HttpContent currentRepresentation)
        {
            // Parse Links from representation based on the returned media type
        }
    }

    static void Main(string[] args)
    {
        var exploreMission = new ExploreMission(new HttpClient());

        var link = new Link() {Target = new Uri("http://localhost:8080/")};
        string input = null;
        while (input != "exit")
        {
            exploreMission.GoAsync(link).Wait();
            Console.WriteLine(exploreMission.CurrentRepresentation
                    .ReadAsStringAsync().Result);

            Console.Write("Enter link relation to follow link : ");
            input = Console.ReadLine();
            link = exploreMission.AvailableLinks[input];
        }
    }
```

Useful interactive client applications will obviously have to do significantly more work than the preceding example. However, the basic premise remains the same: follow a link, update the client state, present the user with available links, allow the user to select a link, and repeat.

Client State

Client state, or what is often also referred to as *client application state*, is the aggregation of all the ongoing missions that a client application is currently tracking. A web browser is made up of a set of *browsing contexts* (*http://bit.ly/browsing-context*). Each of these browsing contexts is effectively a top-level mission.

By building a client application framework that can manage a set of active missions, you can break down the problem into developing goal-oriented missions that are specified in terms of application domain concepts.

Although the set of active missions makes up the client application state, each individual mission must use caution when accumulating state during the execution of the mission.

Returning to the example of the SearchMission, it would be possible for the Search Mission object to hold a reference to the OpenSearchDescription object for the purposes of reuse. However, as soon as the client does that, it takes ownership of the lifetime of that representation, and removes control from the server. Ideally, the server will have specified caching directives that allow the OpenSearchDescription representation to be cached locally for a long period of time. This ensures that multiple uses of the SearchMission object will not cause a network roundtrip when requesting the description document. It also removes the need for the client to manage and share the Search Mission object reference, and because the local HTTP cache is persistent, the stored OpenSearchDescription document can be reused across multiple executions of the client application.

The idea of avoiding holding on to client state is counterintuitive for many people. Conventional wisdom for building client applications tells us that if we hold on to state that we have retrieved from a remote server, we may be able to avoid making network roundtrips in the future. The problem with allowing clients to manage the lifetime of the resource state is that you can end up with a wide range of ad hoc caching mechanisms. Usually, these client mechanisms are far less sophisticated than what HTTP can provide. Often clients support only two lifetime scopes, a global scope constrained by the lifetime of the application, and some kind of *unit of work* scope. There is often no notion of cache expiry, and certainly no equivalent to conditional GETs. By deferring the majority of client-side caching to HTTP caching, the client code gets simpler, there are fewer consistency problems because the server can dictate resource lifetimes, and debugging is simpler because there is less context impacting the reaction of the client to a server response.

Conclusion

Despite the Web being part of our lives for close to 20 years, our experience with building clients that embrace its architecture is still very limited. True web clients are mainly limited to web browsers, RSS feed readers, and web crawlers. There are very few developers who have experience developing any of these tools. The recent rise in popularity of single-page applications has brought a new paradigm where people are trying to build a user agent inside a user agent, which has its own unique set of challenges.

The rising popularity of native "apps" that rely on distributed services has brought a renewed interest in building web clients. This first wave of these distributed applications has tried to replicate the client/server architectures of the 1990s. However, to build apps that really take advantage of the Web like the web browser does, we need to emulate some of the architectural characteristics of the web browser.

The techniques discussed in this chapter enable developers to build clients that will last longer, break less often, perform better, and be more tolerant of network failures. Unfortunately, to date, there are very few support libraries available to make this easier. Hopefully, as more developers start to understand the benefits of building loosely coupled clients that can evolve, more tooling will become available.

As the first step down this path, when you are writing client code that makes a network request, stop, think, and ask yourself, what happens if what I am expecting to happen, doesn't? How can HTTP help me handle that?

CHAPTER 10

The HTTP Programming Model

The messages, the whole messages, and nothing but the messages.

This chapter presents the new .NET Framework HTTP programming model, which is at the core of both ASP.NET Web API and the new client-side HTTP support, specifically the `HttpClient` class. This model was introduced with .NET 4.5 but is also available for .NET 4.0 via NuGet packages (*http://bit.ly/1dGyiA1*). It defines a new assembly—`System.Net.Http.dll`—with typed programming abstractions for the main HTTP concepts (namely, request and response messages, headers, and body content).

This model is complemented by the `System.Net.Http.Formatting.dll` assembly, which introduces the media type formatter concept, described in Chapter 13, as well as some utility extension methods and custom HTTP content types. This assembly is available via the "Microsoft ASP.NET Web API Client Libraries" (*http://bit.ly/nuget-lib-511*) NuGet package, and its source code is part of the ASP.NET project (*http://bit.ly/asp-net-api*). Despite its name, this package is usable on both the client and server sides. In this chapter we will be describing features from both assemblies, without making any distinction between them.

The .NET Framework already contains more than one programming model for dealing with HTTP concepts. On the client side, the `System.Net.HttpWebRequest` class can be used to initiate HTTP requests and process the associated responses. On the server side, the `System.Web.HttpContext` and related classes (e.g., `HttpRequest` and `HttpResponse`) are used in the ASP.NET context to represent individual requests and responses. Also on the server side, the `System.Net.HttpListenerContext` is used by the self-hosted `System.Net.HttpListener` to provide access to the HTTP request and response objects.

Unfortunately, all these programming models have several problems that the new one aims to solve. Namely, the new `System.Net.Http` programming model:

- Uses the same classes on the client and server sides
- Is based on the new Task Asynchronous Pattern (TAP), not on the old Asynchronous Programming Model (APM), meaning that it can take advantage of the `async` and `await` language constructs introduced with .NET 4.5
- Is easier to use in test scenarios
- Has a more *strongly typed* representation of HTTP messages—namely, by representing HTTP header values as types, not as loose string dictionaries
- Is more faithful to the HTTP specification, namely by not layering different abstractions on top of it
- Packages the more recent versions as a portable class library, allowing its use on a wide range of platforms

In the next sections, all these properties will become clearer as we present this new model in more detail. We begin by introducing the types for representing the fundamental HTTP concepts, namely request and response messages. Afterward, we show how both message and content headers are represented and processed via a set of specific classes. Finally, we end by showing how to produce and consume the message payload content.

Before we start, note that the old HTTP programming models are still used and supported; for instance, the ASP.NET pipeline is still based on the old `System.Net.HttpWebRequest`.

Messages

As presented in Chapter 1, the HTTP protocol operates by exchanging request and response messages between clients and servers. Naturally, the message abstraction is at the center of the HTTP programming model, and is represented by two concrete classes, `HttpRequestMessage` and `HttpResponseMessage`, that belong to the new `System.Net.Http` namespace and are represented in Figure 10-1. Both messages comprise:

- A *start line*
- A sequence of *header fields*
- An optional payload body

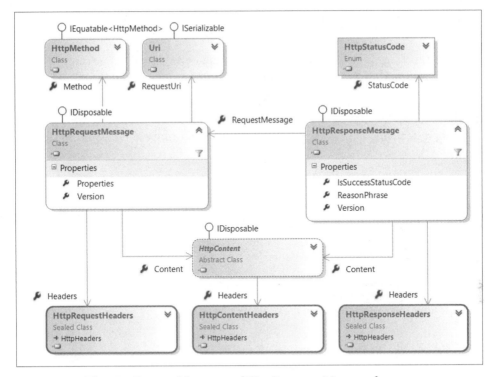

Figure 10-1. The HttpRequestMessage and HttpResponseMessage classes

For requests, the start line is represented by the following HttpRequestMessage properties:

- The request's Method (e.g., GET or POST), defining the request purpose
- The RequestUri, identifying the targeted resource
- The protocol Version (e.g., 1.1)

For responses, the start line is represented by the following HttpResponseMessage properties:

- The protocol Version (e.g. 1.1)
- The request StatusCode (a three-digit integer) and the informational Reason Phrase string

The response message also contains a reference to the associated request message, via the RequestMessage property.

Both the request and response messages can contain an optional message body, represented by the Content property. In the section "Message Content" on page 239, we will address in greater detail how the message content is represented, created, and consumed, including a description of the HttpContent-based class hierarchy.

These two message types as well as the content can be enriched with metadata, in the form of associated headers. The programming model for dealing with these headers will be addressed in the section "Headers" on page 233.

The HttpRequestMessage and HttpResponseMessage classes are nonabstract and can be easily instantiated in user code, as shown in the following examples:

```
[Fact]
public void HttpRequestMessage_is_easy_to_instantiate()
{
    var request = new HttpRequestMessage(
        HttpMethod.Get,
        new Uri("http://www.ietf.org/rfc/rfc2616.txt"));

    Assert.Equal(HttpMethod.Get, request.Method);
    Assert.Equal(
        "http://www.ietf.org/rfc/rfc2616.txt",
        request.RequestUri.ToString());
    Assert.Equal(new Version(1,1), request.Version);
}
[Fact]
public void HttpResponseMessage_is_easy_to_instantiate()
{
    var response = new HttpResponseMessage(HttpStatusCode.OK);
    Assert.Equal(HttpStatusCode.OK, response.StatusCode);
    Assert.Equal(new Version(1,1), response.Version);
}
```

This makes these message classes very easy to use in testing scenarios, which contrasts with other .NET Framework classes used to represent the same concepts:

- The System.Web.HttpRequest class, used in the ASP.NET System.Web.HttpCon
  text to represent a request, has a public constructor but is reserved for infrastructure only.

- The System.Web.HttpRequestBase class, used in ASP.NET MVC, is abstract and cannot be directly instantiated.

- The System.Net.HttpWebRequest class, used to represent HTTP requests on the client side, has public constructors, but they are obsolete. Instead, this class should be instantiated via the WebRequest.Create factory method.

The HttpRequestMessage and HttpResponseMessage classes are also usable both on the client side and on the server side, because they represent only the HTTP messages and not other contextual properties. This contrasts with other HTTP classes, such as the ASP.NET `HttpRequest` class that contains a property with the virtual application root path on the server, which obviously doesn't make sense on the client side.

The request method is represented by `HttpMethod` instances, containing the method string (e.g., `GET` or `POST`). This class also contains a set of static public properties with the methods defined in RFC 2616:

```
public class HttpMethod : IEquatable<HttpMethod>
{
        public string Method {get;}
        public HttpMethod(string method);

        public static HttpMethod Get {get;}
        public static HttpMethod Put {get;}
        public static HttpMethod Post {get;}
        public static HttpMethod Delete {get;}
        public static HttpMethod Head {get;}
        public static HttpMethod Options {get;}
        public static HttpMethod Trace {get;}
}
```

To use a new method, such as the PATCH method defined in RFC 5789, we must explicitly instantiate an `HttpMethod` with the method's string, as shown in the following example:

```
[Fact]
public async Task New_HTTP_methods_can_be_used()
{
    var request = new HttpRequestMessage(
        new HttpMethod("PATCH"),
        new Uri("http://www.ietf.org/rfc/rfc2616.txt"));
    using(var client = new HttpClient())
    {
        var resp = await client.SendAsync(request);
        Assert.Equal(HttpStatusCode.MethodNotAllowed, resp.StatusCode);
    }
}
```

The response's status code is represented by the `HttpStatusCode` enumeration, containing all the status codes defined by the HTTP specification:

```
public enum HttpStatusCode
  {
    Continue = 100,
    SwitchingProtocols = 101,
    OK = 200,
    Created = 201,
    Accepted = 202,
    ...
    MovedPermanently = 301,
    Found = 302,
    SeeOther = 303,
    NotModified = 304,
```

```
    ...
    BadRequest = 400,
    Unauthorized = 401,
    ...
    InternalServerError = 500,
    ...
}
```

We can also use new status codes by casting integers to HttpStatusCode:

```
[Fact]
public void New_status_codes_can_also_be_used()
{
    var response = new HttpResponseMessage((HttpStatusCode) 418)
                        {
                            ReasonPhrase = "I'm a teapot"
                        };
    Assert.Equal(418, (int)response.StatusCode);
}
```

The HttpRequestMessage also contains a Properties property:

```
public IDictionary<string, Object> Properties { get; }
```

This is used to hold additional message information, while it is being processed locally on the server or client side. For instance, it can hold information that is produced at the bottom layers of the processing stack (e.g., message handlers) and is consumed at the upper layers (e.g., controllers).

The Properties property doesn't reflect any standard HTTP message part and is not retained when the message is serialized for transfer. Instead, it is just a generic container for local message *properties*, such as:

- The client certificate associated with the connection on which the message was received
- The route data resulting from matching the message with the set of configured routes

These properties are stored in a dictionary and associated with string keys. The HttpPropertyKeys class defines a set of commonly used keys. Typically, these message properties are accessed via extension methods, such as the ones defined in the System.Net.Http.HttpRequestMessageExtensions class as follows:

```
public static IHttpRouteData GetRouteData(this HttpRequestMessage request)
{
  if (request == null)
    throw System.Web.Http.Error.ArgumentNull("request");
  else
    return HttpRequestMessageExtensions.GetProperty<IHttpRouteData>(
```

```
                        request, HttpPropertyKeys.HttpRouteDataKey);
}
```

The HttpRequestContext class, introduced with Web API v2, is another example of
information that is attached to the request's properties by the lower hosting layer and
then consumed by the upper layers:

```
public static HttpRequestContext
    GetRequestContext(this HttpRequestMessage request)
{
    ...
    return request.GetProperty<HttpRequestContext>(
        HttpPropertyKeys.RequestContextKey);
}

public static void
    SetRequestContext(this HttpRequestMessage request,
                      HttpRequestContext context)
{
    ...
    request.Properties[HttpPropertyKeys.RequestContextKey] = context;
}
```

Namely, this class aggregates a set of properties, such as the client certificate or the
requestor's identity, into one typed model:

```
public class HttpRequestContext
{
    public virtual X509Certificate2 ClientCertificate { get; set; }
    public virtual IPrincipal Principal { get; set; }
    // ...
}
```

Headers

In HTTP, both the request and response messages, and the message content itself, can
be augmented with information in the form of extra fields called *headers*. For instance:

- The User-Agent header field extends a *request* with information describing the
  application that produced it.

- The Server header field extends a *response* with information about the origin-
  server software.

- The Content-Type header field defines the media type used by the representation
  in the request or response payload body.

Each header is characterized by a name and a value, which can be a list. The HTTP
specification allows for multiple headers with the same name on a message. However,
this specification also states that this is equivalent to only one header occurrence with

both values combined. The set of registered HTTP headers is maintained by IANA (*http://bit.ly/message-headers*).

As demonstrated in Figure 10-1, both the request and the response message classes have a Headers property referencing a typed header container class. However, the content headers (e.g., Content-Type) are not in the request or response header collection. Instead, they are in a *content* header collection, accessible via the HttpContent.Headers property:

```
[Fact]
public async void Message_and_content_headers_are_not_in_same_coll()
{
    using(var client = new HttpClient())
    {
        var response = await client
            .GetAsync("http://tools.ietf.org/html/rfc2616");
        var request = response.RequestMessage;
        Assert.Equal("tools.ietf.org",request.Headers.Host);
        Assert.NotNull(response.Headers.Server);
        Assert.Equal("text/html",
            response.Content.Headers.ContentType.MediaType);
    }
}
```

Notice how the Server header is in the response.Headers container, but the Content Type header is in the response.Content.Headers container.

The HTTP programming model defines three header container classes, one for each of the header contexts:

- The HttpRequestHeaders class contains the request headers
- The HttpResponseHeaders class contains the response headers
- The HttpContentHeaders class contains the content headers

These three classes have a set of properties exposing the standard headers in a strongly typed way. For instance, the HttpRequestHeaders class contains an Accept property, declared as a MediaTypeWithQualityHeaderValue collection, where each item contains:

- The MediaType string property with the media type identifier (e.g., application/xml)
- The Quality property (e.g., 0.9)
- The CharSet string property
- The Parameters collection property

The following excerpt shows how easy it is to consume the `Accept` header, since the class model provides access to all the constituent parts (e.g., quality parameter, char set):

```
[Fact]
public void Classes_expose_headers_in_a_strongly_typed_way()
{
    var request = new HttpRequestMessage();
    request.Headers.Add(
        "Accept",
        "text/html,application/xhtml+xml,application/xml;q=0.9,*/*;q=0.8");

    HttpHeaderValueCollection<MediaTypeWithQualityHeaderValue> accept =
        request.Headers.Accept;
    Assert.Equal(4,accept.Count);

    MediaTypeWithQualityHeaderValue third = accept.Skip(2).First();
    Assert.Equal("application/xml", third.MediaType);
    Assert.Equal(0.9, third.Quality);
    Assert.Null(third.CharSet);
    Assert.Equal(1,third.Parameters.Count);
    Assert.Equal("q",third.Parameters.First().Name);
    Assert.Equal("0.9", third.Parameters.First().Value);
}
```

This feature greatly simplifies both the production and consumption of headers, abstracting away the sometimes cumbersome HTTP syntactical rules. These properties can also be used to easily construct header values:

```
[Fact]
public void Properties_simplify_header_construction()
{
    var response = new HttpResponseMessage();
    response.Headers.Date =
        new DateTimeOffset(2013,1,1,0,0,0, TimeSpan.FromHours(0));
    response.Headers.CacheControl = new CacheControlHeaderValue
    {
        MaxAge = TimeSpan.FromMinutes(1),
        Private = true
    };

    var dateValue = response.Headers.First(h => h.Key == "Date")
        .Value.First();
    Assert.Equal("Tue, 01 Jan 2013 00:00:00 GMT", dateValue);

    var cacheControlValue = response.Headers
        .First(h => h.Key == "Cache-Control").Value.First();
    Assert.Equal("max-age=60, private", cacheControlValue);
}
```

Notice how the `CacheControlHeaderValue` class contains a property for each HTTP cache directive (e.g., `MaxAge` and `Private`). Notice also how the `Date` header is constructed from a `DateTimeOffset` and not from a string, simplifying the construction of correctly formated header values.

Some header values are scalar (e.g., `Date`) and can be assigned directly, while others are collections represented by the `HttpHeaderValueCollection<T>` generic class, allowing for value addition and removal:

```
request.Headers.Date = DateTimeOffset.UtcNow;
request.Headers.Accept.Add(new MediaTypeWithQualityHeaderValue("text/html",1.0));
```

Figure 10-2 shows the three header container classes, one for each header context. These classes don't have public constructors and can't be easily instantiated in isolation. Instead, they are created when a message or content instance is created.

The properties exposed by each one of these classes are restricted to the headers defined by the HTTP RFC. For instance, `HttpRequestHeaders` contains only properties corresponding to the headers that can be used on an HTTP request. Specifically, it does not provide a way to add nonstandard headers. However, all three classes derive from an `HttpHeaders` abstract class, shown in Figure 10-3, which provides a set of methods for more low-level access to headers.

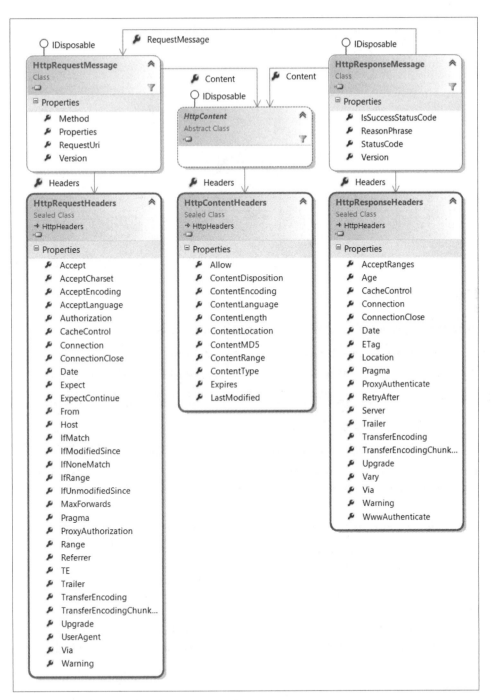

Figure 10-2. The three header container classes

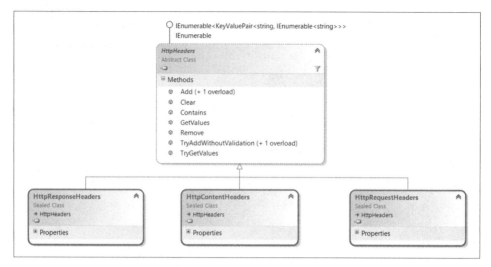

Figure 10-3. The HttpHeaders base class provides untyped access to a header collection

First, the HttpHeaders class implements the following interface:

```
IEnumerable<KeyValuePair<string,IEnumerable<string>>>
```

This provides access to all the headers as a sequence of pairs, where the header name is a string and the header value is a string sequence. This interface preserves the header ordering and takes into account that header values can be lists. The HttpHeaders class also contains a set of methods for adding and removing headers.

The Add method allows for the addition of headers to the container. If the header has a standard name, its value is validated prior to addition. The Add method also validates if the header can have multiple values:

```
[Fact]
public void Add_validates_value_domain_for_std_headers()
{
    var request = new HttpRequestMessage();
    Assert.Throws<FormatException>(() =>
        request.Headers.Add("Date", "invalid-date"));
    request.Headers.Add("Strict-Transport-Security", "invalid ;; value");
}
```

On the other hand, the TryAddWithoutValidation method does not perform header value validation. However, if the value is not valid, it will not be accessible via the typed properties:

```
[Fact]
public async void
    TryAddWithoutValidation_doesnt_validates_the_value_but_preserves_it()
{
```

```
var request = new HttpRequestMessage();
Assert.True(request.Headers
    .TryAddWithoutValidation("Date", "invalid-date"));
Assert.Equal(null, request.Headers.Date);
Assert.Equal("invalid-date", request.Headers.GetValues("Date").First());

var content = new HttpMessageContent(request);
var s = await content.ReadAsStringAsync();
Assert.True(s.Contains("Date: invalid-date"));
}
```

After seeing how message and content can be enriched with headers, in the next section we focus our attention on the content itself.

Message Content

In the new HTTP programming model, the HTTP message body is represented by the abstract HttpContent base class, shown in Figure 10-4. Both the HttpRequestMes sage and HttpResponseMessage have a Content property of this type, as previously depicted in Figure 10-1.

In this section, we will show how:

- Message content can be consumed via the HttpContent methods.
- Message content can be produced via one of the existing HttpContent-derived concrete classes or through the creation of a new class.

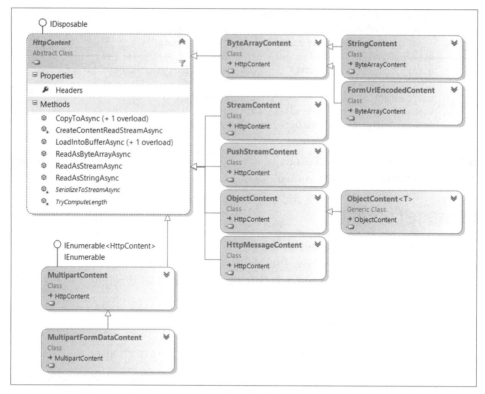

Figure 10-4. The HttpContent base class and associated hierarchy

Consuming Message Content

When producing message content, we can choose one of the available concrete HttpContent-derived classes. However, when consuming message content, we are limited to the HttpContent methods or extension methods.

In addition to the Headers property described in the previous section, the HttpContent contains the following public, nonvirtual methods:

- Task CopyToAsync(Stream, TransportContext)
- Task<Stream> ReadAsStreamAsync()
- Task<string> ReadAsStringAsync()
- Task<byte[]> ReadAsByteArrayAsync()

The first one allows for the consumption of the raw message content in a *push* style: we pass a stream to the CopyToAsync method that then writes (pushes) the message content into that stream. The returned Task can be used to synchronize with the copy termination:

```
[Fact]
public async Task HttpContent_can_be_consumed_in_push_style()
{
    using (var client = new HttpClient())
    {
        var response =
            await client.GetAsync("http://www.ietf.org/rfc/rfc2616.txt",
            HttpCompletionOption.ResponseHeadersRead
            );
        response.EnsureSuccessStatusCode();
        var ms = new MemoryStream();
        await response.Content.CopyToAsync(ms);
        Assert.True(ms.Length > 0);
    }
}
```

The previous example uses the HttpCompletionOptions.ResponseHeadersRead option to allow GetAsync to terminate immediately after the response headers are read. This allows the response content to be consumed without buffering, using the CopyToAsync method.

Alternatively, the ReadAsStreamAsync method allows for the consumption of the raw message content in a *pull* style: it asynchronously returns a stream, from where the content can then be pulled:

```
[Fact]
public async Task HttpContent_can_be_consumed_in_pull_style()
{
    using (var client = new HttpClient())
    {
        var response = await
            client.GetAsync("http://www.ietf.org/rfc/rfc2616.txt");
        response.EnsureSuccessStatusCode();
        var stream = await response.Content.ReadAsStreamAsync();
        var buffer = new byte[2*1024];
        var len = await stream.ReadAsync(buffer, 0, buffer.Length);
        var s = Encoding.ASCII.GetString(buffer, 0, len);
        Assert.True(s.Contains("Hypertext Transfer Protocol -- HTTP/1.1"));
    }
}
```

The last two methods, ReadAsStringAsync and ReadAsByteArrayAsync, asynchronously provide a buffered copy of the message contents: the latter returns the raw byte content while the former decodes that content into a string:

```
[Fact]
public async Task HttpContent_can_be_consumed_as_a_string()
{
    using (var client = new HttpClient())
```

```
{
    var response = await
        client.GetAsync("http://www.ietf.org/rfc/rfc2616.txt");
    response.EnsureSuccessStatusCode();
    var s = await response.Content.ReadAsStringAsync();
    Assert.True(s.Contains("Hypertext Transfer Protocol -- HTTP/1.1"));
}
}
```

In addition to the `HttpContent` instance methods, there are also extension methods defined in the `HttpContentExtensions` static class. All these methods are variations of the following:

```
public static Task<T> ReadAsAsync<T>(
    this HttpContent content,
    IEnumerable<MediaTypeFormatter> formatters,
    IFormatterLogger formatterLogger)
```

This method receives a sequence of media type formatters and tries to use one of them to read the message content as a T instance:

```
class GitHubUser
{
    public string login { get; set; }
    public int id { get; set; }
    public string url { get; set; }
    public string type { get; set; }
}

[Fact]
public async Task HttpContent_can_be_consumed_using_formatters()
{
    using (var client = new HttpClient())
    {
        var response = await
            client.GetAsync("https://api.github.com/users/webapibook");
        response.EnsureSuccessStatusCode();
        var user = await response.Content
            .ReadAsAsync<GitHubUser>(new MediaTypeFormatter[]
            {
                new JsonMediaTypeFormatter()
            });
        Assert.Equal("webapibook", user.login);
        Assert.Equal("Organization", user.type);
    }
}
```

Recall that media type formatters, presented in greater detail in Chapter 13, are classes that extend the abstract `MediaTypeFormatter` class and perform bidirectional conversions between objects and byte stream representations, as defined by *Internet media types*.

There is also an overload that doesn't receive the media type formatter sequence. Instead, it uses a set of *default* formatters, which currently are `JsonMediaTypeFormatter`, `XmlMe diaTypeFormatter`, and `FormUrlEncodedMediaTypeFormatter`.

Creating Message Content

When creating messages with nonempty payload, we assign the `Content` property with an instance of an `HttpContent` derived class, chosen in accordance with the content type. Figure 10-4 shows some of the available classes. For instance, if the message content is plain text, then the `StringContent` class can be used to represent it:

```
[Fact]
public void StringContent_can_be_used_to_represent_plain_text()
{
    var response = new HttpResponseMessage()
        {
            Content = new StringContent("this is a plain text representation")
        };
    Assert.Equal("text/plain", response.Content.Headers.ContentType.MediaType);
}
```

By default, the `Content-Type` header is set to `text/plain`, but this value can be over-riden.

The `FormUrlEncodedContent` class is used to produce name/value pair content, encoded according to the `application/x-www-form-urlencoded` rules—the same encoding rules used by HTML forms. The name/value pairs are defined via an `IEnumerable<Key ValuePair<string,string>>` passed in the `FormUrlEncondedContent` constructor:

```
[Fact]
public async Task FormUrlEncodedContent_can_represent_name_value_pairs()
{
    var request = new HttpRequestMessage
        {
            Content = new FormUrlEncodedContent(
                new Dictionary<string, string>()
                    {
                        {"name1", "value1"},
                        {"name2", "value2"}
                    })
        };
    Assert.Equal("application/x-www-form-urlencoded",
        request.Content.Headers.ContentType.MediaType);
    var stringContent = await request.Content.ReadAsStringAsync();
    Assert.Equal("name1=value1&name2=value2", stringContent);
}
```

The programming model also provides three additional classes for when the content is already available as a byte sequence. The `ByteArrayContent` class is used when the content is already contained in a byte array:

```
[Fact]
public async Task ByteArrayContent_can_represent_byte_sequences()
{
    var alreadyExistantArray = new byte[] { 0x48, 0x65, 0x6c, 0x6c, 0x6f};
    var content = new ByteArrayContent(alreadyExistantArray);
    content.Headers.ContentType = new MediaTypeHeaderValue("text/plain")
        { CharSet = "utf-8" };
    var readText = await content.ReadAsStringAsync();
    Assert.Equal("Hello", readText);
}
```

The StreamContent and PushStreamContent classes are both used for dealing with streams: the StreamContent is adequate for when the content is already available as a stream (e.g., reading from a file), while the PushStreamContent class is used when the content is produced by a *stream writer*.

The StreamContent instance is created with the stream defined in the constructor. Afterward, when serializing the HTTP message, the HTTP model runtime will *pull* the byte sequence from this stream and add it to the serialized message body:

```
[Fact]
public async Task StreamContent_can_be_used_when_content_is_in_a_stream()
{
    const string thisFileName = @"..\..\HttpContentFacts.cs";
    var stream = new FileStream(thisFileName, FileMode.Open, FileAccess.Read);
    using (var content = new StreamContent(stream))
    {
        content.Headers.ContentType = new MediaTypeHeaderValue("text/plain");

        // Assert
        var text = await content.ReadAsStringAsync();
        Assert.True(text.Contains("this string"));
    }
    Assert.Throws<ObjectDisposedException>(() => stream.Read(new byte[1], 0, 1));
}
```

The stream will be disposed when the wrapping StreamContent is disposed (e.g., by the Web API runtime).

There are, however, scenarios where the content is not already on a stream. Instead, the content is produced by a process that requires a stream into which to write the content. A typical example is XML serialization using a XmlWriter, which requires an output stream in which to write the serialized bytes. A solution would be to use an intermediary MemoryStream where the stream writer writes the contents, and then give this memory stream to a StreamContent instance. However, this solution implies an intermediate copy and is not well suited for streaming scenarios.

A better solution is to use the PushStreamContent class, which receives an Action<Stream, ...> and works in a *push-style* manner: when the runtime has a stream available (e.g., the underlying ASP.NET response context stream), it calls the action with the stream. It is the action's responsibility to write the contents to this final stream, without any intermediate buffering:

```
[Fact]
public async Task
    PushStreamContent_can_be_used_when_content_is_provided_by_a_stream_writer()
{
    var xml = new XElement("root",
                                new XElement("child1", "text"),
                                new XElement("child2", "text")
        );
    var content = new PushStreamContent((stream, cont, ctx) =>
        {
            using (var writer = XmlWriter.Create(stream,
                new XmlWriterSettings { CloseOutput = true }))
            {
                xml.WriteTo(writer);
            }
        });
    content.Headers.ContentType =
        new MediaTypeWithQualityHeaderValue("application/xml");

    // Assert
    var text = await content.ReadAsStringAsync();
    Assert.True(text.Contains("<child1"));
}
```

An important aspect to highlight is that the action does not need to write all the contents synchronously. In fact, the runtime considers the contents to be completely written only when the stream is closed, not when the action returns. This means that the contents can be written by code scheduled by the action (e.g., asynchronous task or timer callback), *after* the action has returned. The only requirement is that the stream's Close method be called, in order to signal that the content is completely written. Unfortunately, if an error occurs after the action returns, there is no way to signal it to the runtime. The only possible behavior is to close the stream, which does not distinguish success from failure. To address this problem, newer versions of the System.Net.Http.Format ting.dll assembly provide a PushStreamContent overload receiving a Func<Stream, HttpContent, TransportContext, Task>. This allows the asynchronous code to return a Task, providing a way to signal the ocurrences of exceptions back to the runtime. In the following example, note that the lambda expression is prefixed with async, meaning that it will return a Task:

```
[Fact]
public async Task PushStreamContent_can_be_used_asynchronously()
{
    const string text = "will wait for 2 seconds without blocking";
    var content = new PushStreamContent(async (stream, cont, ctx) =>
    {
        await Task.Delay(2000);
```

```
        var bytes = Encoding.UTF8.GetBytes(text);
        stream.Write(bytes, 0, bytes.Length);
        stream.Close();
    });
    content.Headers.ContentType =
        new MediaTypeWithQualityHeaderValue("text/plain");

    // Assert
    var sw = new Stopwatch();
    sw.Start();
    var receivedText = await content.ReadAsStringAsync();
    sw.Stop();
    Assert.Equal(text, receivedText);
    Assert.True(sw.ElapsedMilliseconds > 1500);
}
```

The previous content classes require the content to already be represented as a byte sequence. However, the new HTTP programming model also contains the `ObjectContent` and `ObjectContent<T>` classes, providing a way to define HTTP message content directly from an object. Internally, these classes use media type formatters to convert the object into the byte sequence.

The following example shows the production of a JSON representation for an anonymous object with three fields. Notice that the media type formatter used—`JsonMediaTypeFormatter`, in this case—must be explicitly defined in the `ObjectContent` constructor:

```
[Fact]
public async Task ObjectContent_uses_mediatypeformatter_to_produce_the_content()
{
    var representation = new
        {
          field1 = "a string",
          field2 = 42,
          field3 = true
        };
    var content = new ObjectContent(
        representation.GetType(),
        representation,
        new JsonMediaTypeFormatter());

    // Assert
    Assert.Equal("application/json",content.Headers.ContentType.MediaType);
    var text = await content.ReadAsStringAsync();
    var obj = JObject.Parse(text);
    Assert.Equal("a string", obj["field1"]);
    Assert.Equal(42, obj["field2"]);
    Assert.Equal(true, obj["field3"]);
}
```

The `ObjectContent` receives both the input object value and object type. The generic version, `ObjectContent<T>`, is just a simplification where the input type is given as a generic parameter.

The new programming model also has a set of extension methods, contained in multiple `HttpRequestMessageExtensions` classes, that aim to simplify the creation of responses from requests. For instance, you can create a response message that is automatically linked to the request message:

```
[Fact]
public void HttpRequestMessage_has_a_CreateResponse_extension_method()
{
    var request =
        new HttpRequestMessage(HttpMethod.Get,
            new Uri("http://www.example.net"));
    var response = request.CreateResponse(HttpStatusCode.OK);
    Assert.Equal(request, response.RequestMessage);
}
```

You can also use a `CreateResponse` overload to create a representation from an object, given a media type formatter, similarly to what you can do with `ObjectContent`:

```
public void CreateResponse_can_receive_a_formatter()
{
    var request =
        new HttpRequestMessage(HttpMethod.Get,
            new Uri("http://www.example.net"));

    var response = request.CreateResponse(
        HttpStatusCode.OK,
        new { String = "hello", AnInt = 42 },
        new JsonMediaTypeFormatter());

    Assert.Equal("application/json",
        response.Content.Headers.ContentType.MediaType);
}
```

The `CreateResponse` message is particularly useful in server-driven content negotiation scenarios, where the request information—namely, the request `Accept` header—is needed to decide the most appropriate media type:

```
[Fact]
public void CreateResponse_performs_content_negotiation()
{
    var request =
        new HttpRequestMessage(HttpMethod.Get,
            new Uri("http://www.example.net"));
    request.Headers.Accept.Add(
        new MediaTypeWithQualityHeaderValue("application/xml", 0.9));
    request.Headers.Accept.Add(
        new MediaTypeWithQualityHeaderValue("application/json", 1.0));
```

```
        var response = request.CreateResponse(
            HttpStatusCode.OK,
            "resource representation",
            new HttpConfiguration());

        Assert.Equal("application/json",
            response.Content.Headers.ContentType.MediaType);
    }
```

Notice how the used `CreateResponse` overload receives an `HttpConfiguration` with the configured formatters.

Finally, you also have the option of producing message content by creating custom `HttpContent`-derived classes. However, before we present this technique, it is useful to understand how an HTTP message content length is computed.

Content length and streaming

In HTTP, there are three major ways to define the payload body length:

- Explicitly, by adding the `Content-Length` header field with the message length
- Implicitly, by using *chunked transfer encoding*
- Implicitly, by closing the connection after all the content is transmitted (applicable only to response content)

The last option exists mainly for compatibility with HTTP 1.0 and should not be used, since an abnormal termination of the connection will result in undetected content corruption.

With chunked transfer encoding, the message body is divided in a series of *chunks*, each with its own size definition. This allows streaming content, where the length information is not known beforehand, to be transmitted without buffering.

The first option is the simpler one, but it requires a priori knowledge of the content length. For this purpose, the `HttpContent` class contains the following abstract method:

```
protected internal abstract bool TryComputeLength(out long length)
```

Each concrete content class must implement this method according to how the content is represented. For instance, the `ByteArrayContent` class implementation always returns `true`, providing the underlying array length. On the other hand, the `PushStream Content` class implementation returns `false`, since the contents are pushed dynamically by the registered action. Notice that there is no way for the `PushStreamContent` class to know how many bytes will be pushed by this action. Finally, the `StreamContent` class implementation delegates this query to the underlying `Stream`, defined in the constructor: if this stream is *seekable*, then the `TryComputeLength` method uses the

---

`Stream.Length` to compute the content length; otherwise, the `TryComputeLength` method returns `false`.

There is also a close relationship between the `TryComputeLength` method and the `long? HttpContentHeaders.ContentLength` property: when this property is not explicitly set, its value will query the `TryComputeLength` method. This means that there is no need to explicitly set the `Content-Length` header, except in scenarios where this information is obtained by external methods. Notice also that `HttpContentHeaders.ContentLength` is of type `long?`, allowing for the absence of value.

In Chapter 11, we will describe how this information is used by the hosting layer to determine the best way to handle the response message content (namely, to decide if buffering should be used or not).

Custom content classes

Now that we've seen how message content length is defined and what influences streaming, we will address the creation of custom content classes. The following code excerpt shows the definition of the `FileContent` class: a custom `HttpContent`-derived class to represent file contents:

```
public class FileContent : HttpContent
{
    private readonly Stream _stream;
    public FileContent(string path,
        string mediaType = "application/octet-stream")
    {
        _stream = new FileStream(path, FileMode.Open, FileAccess.Read);
        base.Headers.ContentType = new MediaTypeHeaderValue(mediaType);
    }
    protected override Task
        SerializeToStreamAsync(Stream stream, TransportContext context)
    {
        return _stream.CopyToAsync(stream);
    }
    protected override bool TryComputeLength(out long length)
    {
        if (!_stream.CanSeek)
        {
            length = 0;
            return false;
        }
        else
        {
            length = _stream.Length;
            return true;
        }
    }
    protected override void Dispose(bool disposing)
    {
```

```
        _stream.Dispose();
    }
}
```

Creating a custom `HttpContent` class requires us to define the following two abstract methods:

```
protected internal abstract bool TryComputeLength(out long length)
protected abstract Task SerializeToStreamAsync(
    Stream stream, TransportContext context);
```

As we saw in the last section, the first one—`TryComputeLength`—is used to try to obtain the content length. In the `FileContent` implementation, this method uses the `Stream.CanSeek` property to query if the file stream length can be computed. If so, it uses the `Stream.Length` property to return the content length.

The second method, `SerializeToStreamAsync`, is responsible for writing the contents to the passed-in `Stream`. This method can operate asynchronously, returning a `Task` before the write is concluded. This returned `Task` should be signaled when the write process is finally finished. This asynchronous ability is useful when the message contents are provided by another asynchronous process (e.g., reading from the filesystem or from an external system). For instance, the `FileContent` implementation takes advantage of the `CopyToAsync` method, introduced in .NET 4.5, to start the asynchronous copy and return a `Task` representing this operation.

Instead of deriving directly from `HttpContent`, you can take an alternative approach and use the `StreamContent` and `PushStreamContent` classes, either as a base class or via factory methods. The following class shows you how to build XML-based content without requiring any buffering, by creating a `PushStreamContent`-derived class:

```
public class XmlContent : PushStreamContent
{
    public XmlContent(XElement xe)
        : base(PushStream(xe), "application/xml")
    {
    }

    private static Action<Stream,HttpContent,TransportContext>
        PushStream(XElement xe)
    {
        return (stream, content, ctx) =>
            {
                using (var writer = XmlWriter.Create(stream,
                    new XmlWriterSettings(){CloseOutput = true}))
                {
                    xe.WriteTo(writer);
                }
            };
    }
}
```

Since the PushStreamContent constructor requires an Action<Stream, HttpContent, TransportContext>, in the previous example we use a private static method to create this action from the given XElement. Notice also the use of the XmlWriterSettings parameter in order to close the given stream. Recall that, since the action is assumed to be asynchronous, the close of the stream signals the conclusion of this process.

We can accomplish the same goal by using an extension method on XElement:

```
public static class XElementContentExtensions
{
    public static HttpContent ToHttpContent(this XElement xe)
    {
        return new PushStreamContent((stream, content, ctx) =>
            {
                using (var writer = XmlWriter.Create(stream,
                    new XmlWriterSettings(){CloseOutput = true}))
                {
                    xe.WriteTo(writer);
                }
            },"application/xml");
    }
}
```

Conclusion

In this chapter, our focus was on the new HTTP programming model, which was introduced in version 4.5 of the .NET Framework and is at the core of both Web API and the new HttpClient class. As we've shown, this new model provides a more usable and testable way of dealing with the core HTTP concepts of messages, headers, and content. The following chapters build upon this knowledge to provide a deeper understanding of Web API inner workings. Namely, Chapter 11 describes the interface between this model and a lower HTTP stack, such as the one provided by ASP.NET.

CHAPTER 11

Hosting

Web API meets its downstairs neighbors.

Chapter 4 divided the ASP.NET Web API processing architecture into three layers: hosting, message handler pipeline, and controller handling. This chapter addresses in greater detail the first of these layers.

The hosting layer is really a host *adaptation* layer, establishing the bridge between the Web API processing architecture and one of the supported *external* hosting infrastructures. In fact, Web API does not come with its own hosting mechanism. Instead, it aims to be host independent and usable in multiple hosting scenarios.

In summary, the host adapter layer is responsible for the following tasks:

- Creating and initializing the message handler pipeline, encapsulated in an `HttpServer` instance.
- Receiving HTTP requests from the underlying hosting infrastructure, typically by registering a callback function.
- Transforming HTTP requests from their native representation (e.g., ASP.NET's `HttpRequest`) into `HttpRequestMessage` instances.
- Pushing these instances into the message handler pipeline, effectively initiating the Web API request processing.
- When a response is produced and returned, the hosting adapter transforms the returned `HttpResponseMessage` instance into a response representation native to the underlying infrastructure (e.g., ASP.NET's `HttpResponse`) and delivers it to the underlying hosting infrastructure.

In version 1.0, two hosting adapters were available: *web hosting* and *self-hosting*. The former hosting option allows Web API to be used on top of the classic ASP.NET hosting infrastructure, supported by the IIS (Internet Information Services) server. The latter hosting option—self-hosting—enables the use of Web API on any Windows process, namely console applications and Windows services. These two hosting adapters are available as independent NuGet packages: `Microsoft.AspNet.WebApi.WebHost` and `Microsoft.AspNet.WebApi.SelfHost`. Version 2.0 of ASP.NET Web API introduces the OWIN host adapter, available via the `Microsoft.AspNet.WebApi.Owin` package. This new alternative allows the usage of any OWIN-compliant host.

Our aim in this chapter is to provide the knowledge required for fully using Web API in these hosting scenarios. So, with that in mind, we will now take a deeper look into these host adapters, with a focus on their internal behavior. We'll also detail how new hosting scenarios can be supported, by presenting a Azure Service Bus adapter, enabling the secure exposure of a privately hosted Web API application into the public web, via the Service Bus relay.

We end with the description of a special hosting option targeted at testing scenarios and usually designated by *in-memory hosting*. By directly connecting an `HttpClient` instance to a Web API `HttpServer` instance, this hosting option allows for direct in-memory HTTP communication between client and server.

By presenting the internal implementation structure, we provide the knowledge required for the correct configuration and optimization of Web API hosting aspects, such as message buffering. This chapter is also relevant for anyone trying to write a custom host or extend an existing one.

Addressing the Web API hosting mechanisms implies dealing with several external technologies, such as the classical ASP.NET pipeline, the WCF channel stack layer, or the OWIN specification. Aiming to be self-contained, this chapter also contains short introductions to these external technologies, focusing on the topics related to hosting.

Web Hosting

So-called *web hosting* uses the classic ASP.NET pipeline. In the following section, we start by reviewing the relevant aspects of this pipeline. Then, we briefly describe the ASP.NET routing infrastructure, used by both Web API and ASP.NET MVC. Finally, we describe how Web API integrates these two elements.

The ASP.NET Infrastructure

As shown in Figure 11-1, the ASP.NET infrastructure is composed of three main elements: applications, modules, and handlers.

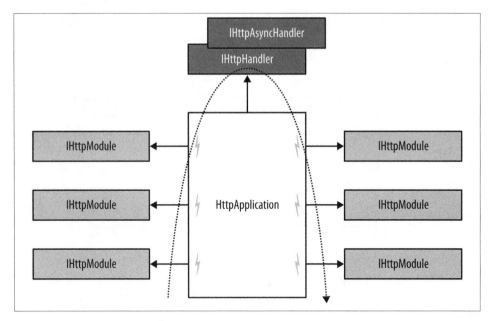

Figure 11-1. ASP.NET pipeline

Applications

In ASP.NET, the unit of deployment is the *application*, represented by the class HttpAp
plication. You can create a specific derived class for each application by defining a
custom *global.asax* file.

When a request is mapped to an application, the runtime creates or selects an HttpAp
plication instance to handle it. It also creates a *context* representing both the HTTP
request and response:

```
public sealed class HttpContext : IServiceProvider
{
    public HttpRequest Request { get {...} }
    public HttpResponse Response { get {...} }
    ...
}
```

The application then flows this context through a set of pipeline stages, represented by
HttpApplication member events. For instance, the HttpApplication.BeginRequest
event is triggered when a request begins its processing.

Modules

An application contains a set of registered *module* classes, implementing the IHttpMod
ule interface:

```
public interface IHttpModule
{
    void Dispose();
    void Init(HttpApplication context);
}
```

When a new application object is constructed, it creates an instance for each one of these module classes and calls the `IHttpModule.Init` method on those instances. Each module uses this call as an opportunity to attach itself to the pipeline events that it wants to process. A module can be attached to more than one event and an event can have more than one module attached.

These modules can then act as filters, processing both the HTTP request and response as they flow through the event pipeline. These modules also have the ability to short-circuit the request processing, immediately producing the response.

Handlers

After all the request events are triggered, the application selects a *handler*, represented by the `IHttpHandler` or the `IHttpAsyncHandler` interfaces, and delegates the processing of the request to it:

```
public interface IHttpHandler
{
    void ProcessRequest(HttpContext context);
    bool IsReusable { get; }
}
public interface IHttpAsyncHandler : IHttpHandler
{
    IAsyncResult BeginProcessRequest(HttpContext context,
        AsyncCallback cb, object extraData);
    void EndProcessRequest(IAsyncResult result);
}
```

When the handler processing ends, the context is then flowed back through the application pipeline, triggering the response events.

Handlers are *endpoints* on which the application ultimately delegates the request processing. They constitute the main integration point used by the multiple frameworks based on the ASP.NET infrastructure, such as Web Forms, ASP.NET MVC, or Web API.

For instance, in the ASP.NET Web Forms Framework, the `System.Web.UI.Page` class implements the `IHttpHandler` interface. This means that the class associated with an *.aspx* file constitutes a handler, called by the application if the request URI matches the *.aspx* filepath.

We make the handler selection by mapping the request URI to a file in the application's directory (e.g., an *.aspx* file) or by using the ASP.NET *routing* feature. The former technique is used by ASP.NET Web Forms,[1] while the latter is used by ASP.NET MVC. Web API also uses the ASP.NET routing functionality, as described in the next section.

ASP.NET Routing

In the ASP.NET infrastructure, we commonly configure routing by adding *routes* to the `RouteTable.Routes` static property, which holds a `RouteCollection`.

For instance, Example 11-1 shows the default mapping defined by the ASP.NET MVC project template, typically present in the *global.asax* file.

Example 11-1. ASP.NET MVC default route configuration

```
protected void Application_Start()
{
    ...
    RegisterRoutes(RouteTable.Routes);
    ...
}

public static void RegisterRoutes(RouteCollection routes)
{
    routes.IgnoreRoute("{resource}.axd/{*pathInfo}");

    routes.MapRoute(
        "Default", // Route name
        "{controller}/{action}/{id}", // URL with parameters
        new { controller = "Home", action = "Index",
                                id = UrlParameter.Optional }
    );
}
```

The `RouteTable.Routes` static property defines a route collection, global to the application, where specific routes are added. The `MapRoute` method, used in Example 11-1 to add a route, isn't a route collection instance method. Instead, it is an extension method, introduced by ASP.NET MVC, that adds MVC-specific routes. As we will see, Web API uses a similar approach.

---

1. Web Forms can also use routing via the `RouteCollection.MapPageRoute` method.

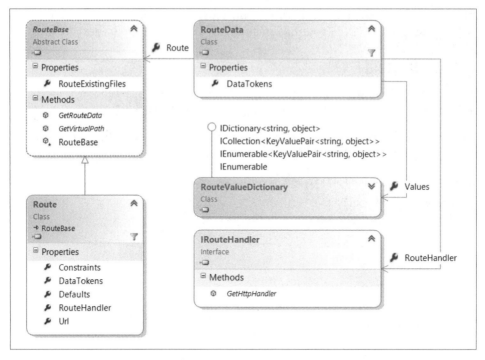

Figure 11-2. ASP.NET routing classes

Figure 11-2 shows some of the classes participating in the ASP.NET routing process. The general *route* concept is defined by the abstract RouteBase class, containing the GetRouteData instance method. This method checks if a request context, namely the request URI, matches the route. If so, it returns a RouteData instance containing a IRouteHandler, which is simply a handler factory. In addition, the RouteData also contains a set of extra values, produced by the matching process. For instance, an HTTP request matched by the Default route of Example 11-1 will result in a RouteData containing the controller and action route values.

The RouteBase class also contains the GetVirtualPath method, performing the inverse lookup process: given a set of values, it returns a URI that would match the route and produce those values.

The abstract RouteBase class is not associated with a specific route matching process, leaving this characterization open for the concrete derived classes. One of those is the Route class, which defines a concrete matching procedure, based on:

- A *URI template* defining the URI's structure (e.g., "{controller}/{action}/ {id}")

- A set of default values (e.g., `new { controller = "Home", action = "Index", id = UrlParameter.Optional })`
- A set of additional constraints

The URI template defines both the structure that the URIs must have to be matched by the route, and the placeholders used to extract the route data values from the URI's path segments.

On a request, the routing selection logic is performed by the `UrlRoutingModule` attached to the `PostResolveRequestCache` pipeline event. With each request, this module matches the current request against the routes in the global `RouteTable.Routes` collection. If there is a match, the associated HTTP handler is mapped to the current request. As a consequence, at the end of the pipeline, the application delegates the request processing to this handler. For instance, all the routes added by the MVC's `Map Route` extension method map to the special `MvcHandler`.

Web API Routing

The ASP.NET routing model and infrastructure is tied to the legacy ASP.NET model, namely the representation of requests and responses via `HttpContext` instances. Although it uses similar routing concepts, Web API uses the new HTTP class model and thus defines a new set of routing-related classes and interfaces, presented in Figure 11-3.

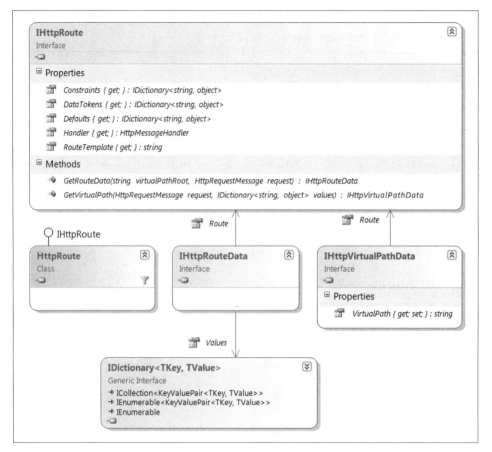

Figure 11-3. Web API routing classes

`IHttpRoute` represents a Web API route, and has characteristics similar to the classic ASP.NET `Route` class, including:

- A `GetRouteData` method that receives an HTTP request and the virtual path root and returns an `IHttpRouteData` containing a value dictionary

- A `GetVirtualPath` method that receives a value dictionary and a request message, and returns an `IHttpVirtualPath` with a URI

- A set of properties with the route template, the route defaults, and the constraints

An important distinction in Web API is the use of the new HTTP class model—specifically the `HttpRequestMessage` and `HttpMessageHandler` classes—instead of the old ASP.NET classes, such as `HttpRequest` and `IHttpHandler`.

Web API also defines a way of using the new routing classes on the classic ASP.NET routing infrastructure, as described in Figure 11-4. This *internal* adaptation layer is used when Web API is hosted on top of ASP.NET, and allows the simultaneous use of new and old routes in the same HTTP application.

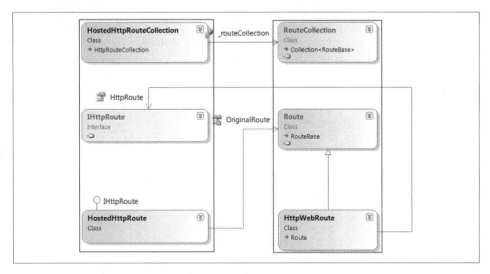

Figure 11-4. Web API routing adaptation classes

The HostedHttpRouteCollection class is an adapter, providing an ICollection<IHttp Route> interface on top of the classic ASP.NET RouteCollection. When a new IHttp Route is added to this collection, it wraps it into a special adapter Route (HttpWeb Route) and adds it to the ASP.NET route collection.

This way, the global ASP.NET route collection can have both classic routes and adapters for the new Web API routes.

Global Configuration

When hosting on ASP.NET, the Web API–specific configuration is defined on a single-ton HttpConfiguration object, accessible via the static GlobalConfiguration.Config uration property. This singleton object is used as the parameter to the default route configuration illustrated in Example 11-2.

Example 11-2. ASP.NET Web API default route configuration

```
// config equals GlobalConfiguration.Configuration
config.MapHttpAttributeRoutes();
config.Routes.MapHttpRoute(
    name: "DefaultApi",
    routeTemplate: "api/{controller}/{id}",
```

```
    defaults: new { id = RouteParameter.Optional }
);
```

The `Routes` property on this singleton configuration references a `HostedHttpRoute`
`Collection` that wraps the global `RouteTable.Routes` collection, as shown in
Figure 11-5. This means that all the Web API routes added to `GlobalConfigura`
`tion.Configuration.Routes` will end up being added as classical ASP.NET routes into
the global `RouteTable.Routes` collection. As a consequence, when the `UrlRoutingMod`
`ule` tries to find a route match, these Web API routes will also be taken into consider-
ation.

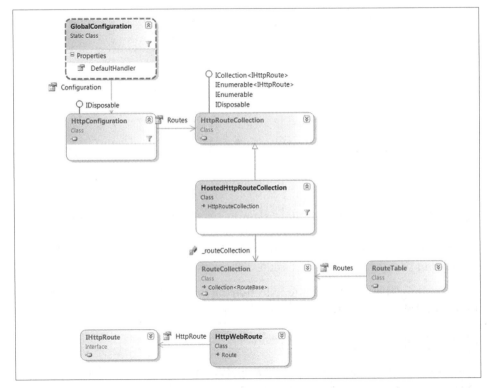

Figure 11-5. Web API global configuration

The routes added by an ASP.NET MVC configuration are associated with the `MvcHan`
`dler` class. This means that all the requests that match one of these routes will be delegated to this `MvcHandler` at the end of the pipeline. Then, this special handler performs
the MVC-specific request processing—that is, selecting the controller and calling the
mapped action.

The scenario with Web API is rather similar: the routes added via `GlobalConfiguration.Configuration.Routes` are associated with the `HttpControllerHandler` that will ultimately handle all the requests matched by one of these Web API routes.

Figure 11-6 illustrates this characteristic, showing the `RouteTable.Routes` collection holding both MVC and Web API routes. However, note that the MVC routes are associated with `MvcHandler`, while the Web API routes are associated with `HttpControllerHandler`.

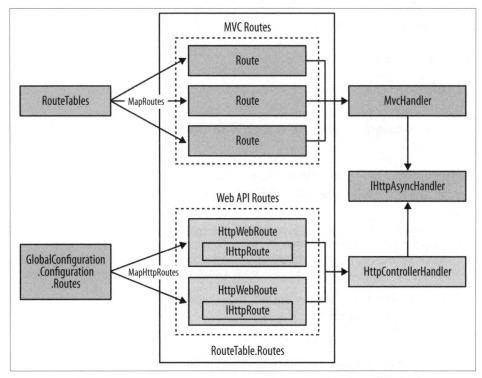

Figure 11-6. RouteTable.Routes containing both MVC and Web API routes

The Web API ASP.NET Handler

All ASP.NET requests that match a Web API route are handled by the new `HttpControllerHandler`, as we've been detailing. When called on its `BeginProcessRequest` method this handler performs the following actions:

- First, a singleton `HttpServer` instance is lazily created on the first handled request, via `GlobalConfiguration.Configuration`. This server instance contains the message handler pipeline, including the controller dispatching handler.

- Then, the ASP.NET `HttpRequest` message, present in the current `HttpContext`, is translated into a new `HttpRequestMessage` instance.
- Finally, this `HttpRequestMessage` is pushed into the singleton `HttpServer` instance, effectively starting the host-independent phase of the Web API processing, composed of the message handler pipeline and the controller layer.

The translation between the native ASP.NET message representation and the Web API message representation is configured by a *service object* that implements the `IHostBufferPolicySelector` interface. This interface has two methods, `UseBufferedInputStream` and `UseBufferedOutputStream`, that define whether the message body should be buffered. The `HttpControllerHandler` requests this service object from the global configuration and uses it to decide:

- If the `HttpRequestMessage` content uses the ASP.NET buffered or streamed request input stream
- If the `HttpResponseMessage` content is written to a ASP.NET buffered output stream

The web host policy registered by default always buffers the input stream. For the output stream, it uses the following rules based on properties of the returned `HttpResponseMessage`:

- If the content length is known, then the `Content-Length` is explicitly set and no *chunking* is used. The content is transmitted without buffering since its length was already determined.
- If the content class is `StreamContent`, then *chunked* transfer encoding will be used only if the underneath stream does not provide length information.
- If the content class is `PushStreamContent`, then *chunked* transfer encoding is used.
- Otherwise, the content is buffered before being transmitted to determine its length, and no chunking is used.

The translation of the ASP.NET `HttpRequest` message into a new `HttpRequestMessage` instance does more than just including the request message information. A set of contextual hosting information is also captured and inserted into the `HttpRequestMessage.Properties` dictionary. This information includes:

- The certificate used by the client, if the request was done on a SSL/TLS connection with client authentication
- A Boolean property stating if the request was originated in the same machine
- An indication if the custom errors are enabled

Note that this information does not originate from the request message. Instead, it is provided by the hosting infrastructure and reflects contextual aspects, such as the connection characteristics. For intance, the client certificate information, added as a message property, can be publicly accessed via a `GetClientCertificate` extension method. The remaining information is used privately by the Web API runtime.

Version 2.0 of the ASP.NET Web API introduces the concept of a *request context* as a way to group all this contextual information. Instead of being dispersed by different untyped request properties, the new `HttpRequestContext` class contains the following set of properties to represent this information:

- The client certificate
- The virtual path root
- The request's principal

The Web API ASP.NET handler creates a `WebHostHttpRequestContext` instance (`WebHostHttpRequestContext` derives from `HttpRequestContext`) and fills it with the request's contextual information. Upper layers can then access this information via the request's `GetRequestContext` extension method.

Figure 11-7 visually summarizes the web hosting architecture, presenting the route resolution process and the dispatch into the `HttpServer` instance. In conclusion:

- Web API can be hosted on top of the ASP.NET infrastructure and share the same application with other frameworks, such as ASP.NET MVC or Web Forms.
- The ASP.NET routing infrastructure is used to identify the requests that are bound to the Web API runtime. These requests are routed to a special handler that converts the native HTTP representations into the new `System.Net.Http` model.
- We configure Web API at the start of the application, typically by adding code to the `Application_Start` method within the *global.asax.cs* file, and use the `Global Configuration.HttpConfiguration` singleton object.
- When using web hosting, we must define some configuration aspects on the underlying host, not on the common Web API configuration. An example is the configuration of secure connections, using SSL or TLS, which we can do using the IIS Manager.

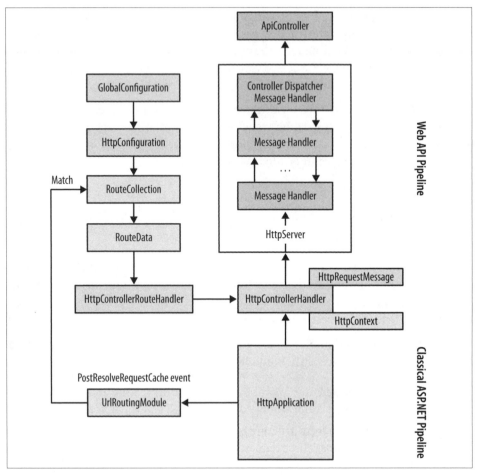

Figure 11-7. ASP.NET hosting architecture

Self-Hosting

Web API also contains an adapter for self-hosting (i.e., hosting on any Windows process, such as a console application or a Windows service). Example 11-3 shows the typical code required for this type of hosting.

Example 11-3. Self-hosting

```
var config = new HttpSelfHostConfiguration("http://localhost:8080");
config.Routes.MapHttpRoute("default", "{controller}/{id}",
                            new { id = RouteParameter.Optional });
var server = new HttpSelfHostServer(config);
server.OpenAsync().Wait();
Console.WriteLine("Server is opened");
```

```
Console.ReadLine();
server.CloseAsync().Wait();
```

Note that in this case, a server instance must be explicitly created, configured, and opened. This contrasts with web hosting, where the supporting `HttpServer` instance is implicitly and lazily created by the ASP.NET handler. Note also that Example 11-3 uses specific classes for the self-hosting scenario. The `HttpSelfHostServer` class derives from the general `HttpServer` class and is configured by an `HttpSelfHostConfigura tion`, which itself derives from the general `HttpConfiguration` class. The hosting base address is explicitly defined in the self-hosting configuration. Figure 11-8 shows the relationship between these classes.

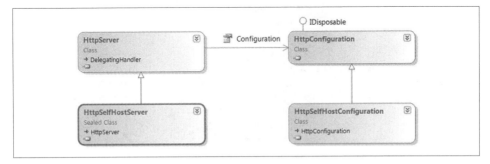

Figure 11-8. Self-host server and configuration classes

In version 1.0 of Web API, the `HttpSelfHostServer` internally uses the WCF (Windows Communication Foundation) *channel stack layer* to obtain request messages from the underlying HTTP infrastructure. The following section briefly presents the WCF high-level architecture, setting the groundwork for the description of Web API self-hosting characteristics.

WCF Architecture

The WCF architecture is divided into two layers: the *channel stack layer* and the *service model layer*, as depicted in Figure 11-9.

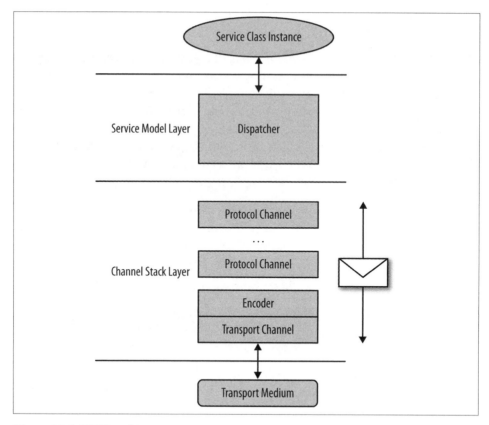

Figure 11-9. WCF architecture

The bottom channel stack layer is composed of a stack of *channels* and behaves similarly to a classical network protocol stack. The channels are divided into two types: transport channels and protocol channels. Protocol channels process the messages that flow up and down through the stack. A typical use case for a protocol channel is the addition of digital signatures at the sending side and the verification of those signatures at the receiving side. Transport channels handle interfacing with the transport medium (e.g., TCP, MSMQ, HTTP), namely by receiving and sending *messages*. They use *encoders* to convert between the transport medium byte streams and message instances.

The upper service model layer performs the interfacing between messages and method calls, dealing with tasks such as:

- Transforming a received message into a parameter sequence
- Obtaining the service instance to use
- Selecting the method to call

- Obtaining the thread at which to call the method

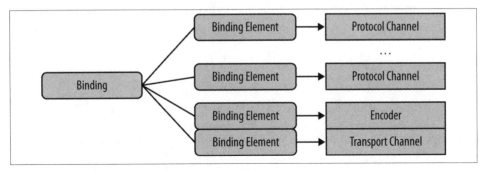

Figure 11-10. Binding, binding elements, and channels

The concrete channel stack layer organization is *described* by bindings, as shown in Figure 11-10. A binding is an ordered collection of binding elements, where each element roughly describes one channel or encoder. The first binding element describes the upper channel and the last element describes the lower channel, which is always a transport channel.

The HttpSelfHostServer Class

The HttpSelfHostServer class implements a self-hosted Web API server. As presented in Example 11-3, this server is configured by an instance of the HttpSelfHostConfigu ration class, which derives from the more general HttpConfiguration and adds specific configuration properties relevant for the self-host scenario.

Internally, the HttpSelfHostServer creates a WCF channel stack and uses it to listen for HTTP requests. This channel stack is described by an instance of the new HttpBind ing class, introduced by the Web API self-hosting support.

When starting the server, the HttpSelfHostserver.OpenAsync method creates an HttpBinding instance and asks the HttpSelfHostConfiguration instance to configure it. Then it uses this binding to asynchronously create the WCF channel stack. It also creates a *pump* that repeatedly pulls messages from this channel stack, converts them into HttpRequestMessage instances, and pushes these new requests into the message handler pipeline.

Similar to what happens in the web hosting scenario, the created HttpRequestMes sage is enriched with an HttpRequestContext instance, containing the set of properties obtained from the hosting context. One of them is the client certificate, when TLS/SSL is used with client-side authentication.

This pump is also responsible for taking the returned HttpResponseMessage and writing it into the channel stack. In terms of response streaming, the self-host behaves quite differently from the web host. It statically uses either an explicit Content-Length header or a chunked transfer encoding, based on the following HttpSelfHostConfiguration option:

```
public TransferMode TransferMode {get; set;}
```

If TransferMode.Buffered is chosen, then the Content-Length is *always explicitly set*, independently of what is returned by TryComputeLength or by the ContentLength header property. Namely, if the length information is not provided by the HttpCon tent instance, the host will *buffer in memory all the content* to determine the length, and send it only afterward. On the other hand, if TransferMode.Streamed is chosen, then the chunked transfer is always used, even if the content length is known.

The HttpSelfHostConfiguration Class

As we've stated, the HttpSelfHostConfiguration defined in the HttpSelfHostServ er has the task of configuring the internally used HttpBinding, which in turn configures the WCF message channel. As a consequence, the HttpSelfHostConfiguration class contains a set of public properties, as in Example 11-4, that reflect this internal implementation detail (i.e., are based on the WCF programming model). For instance, the MaxReceivedMessageSize, also available in the popular WCF BasicHttpBinding class, defines the maximum size of the received message. Another example is the X509Cer tificateValidator property, based on a type from the System.IdentityModel assembly and used to configure the validation of the client certificates received on SSL/TLS connections.

Example 11-4. HttpSelfHostConfiguration properties

```
public class HttpSelfHostConfiguration : HttpConfiguration
{
    public Uri BaseAddress {get;}
    public int MaxConcurrentRequests {get;set;}
    public TransferMode TransferMode {get;set;}
    public HostNameComparisonMode HostNameComparisonMode {get;set;}
    public int MaxBufferSize {get;set;}
    public long MaxReceivedMessageSize {get;set;}
    public TimeSpan ReceiveTimeout {get;set;}
    public TimeSpan SendTimeout {get;set}
    public UserNamePasswordValidator UserNamePasswordValidator {get;set;}
    public X509CertificateValidator X509CertificateValidator {get;set;}
    public HttpClientCredentialType ClientCredentialType {get;set;}

    // other members elided for clarity
}
```

Another way to configure the internal self-host behavior is to create an `HttpSelfHost Configuration` derived class and override the `OnConfigureBinding` method. This receives the `HttpBinding` instance created internally by the `HttpSelfHostServer` and can change the binding settings before they are used to configure the WCF channel stack. Figure 11-11 shows the self-hosting architecture, specifically the use of the WCF channel stack and the relation between the configuration and WCF binding.

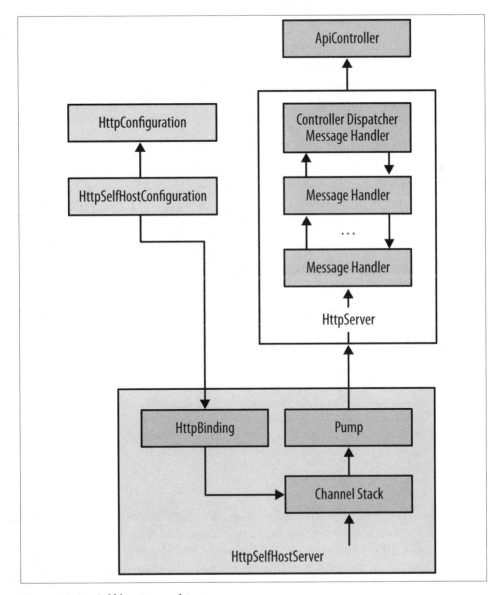

Figure 11-11. Self-hosting architecture

The Web API self-host's reliance on WCF has both advantages and disadvantages. The main advantage is the availability of most of the WCF HTTP binding capabilities, such as message limiting, throttling, and timeouts. The major disadvantage is that this WCF dependency is exposed on the `HttpSelfhostConfiguration` public interface, namely on some of its properties.

Note the message pump that retrieves messages from the underlying channel stack and converts them into `HttpRequestMessage` instances before pushing them into the `HttpServer`.

URL Reservation and Access Control

When starting a self-hosted web server from a nonadministrator account, you'll commonly encounter the following error:

```
HTTP could not register URL http://+:8080/.
Your process does not have access rights to this namespace
```

Why does this happen and how can we solve it? The answer to these questions requires a short introduction to the low-level HTTP handling architecture.

On Windows, a kernel-mode device driver, called HTTP.sys, listens for HTTP requests. Both IIS and the WCF self-hosting transport channel use this kernel-mode driver, via the user mode HTTP Server API. Server applications use this API to *register* their interest in handling requests for a given URL namespace. For instance, running Example 11-3 results in the registration of the `http://+:8080` namespace by the self-host application. The + in the hostname represents a *strong wildcard*, instructing HTTP.SYS to consider requests originating from all network adapters. However, this registration is subject to access control, and by default only a process with administrative privileges is authorized to perform it. The aforementioned error occurs for this reason.

One solution would be to start the self-host application using an account with those privileges. However, running a server with administrative rights is seldom a good idea. A better solution is to grant the required permissions to the account under which the application will run. We do this by *reserving* the URL namespace for that account, allowing the associated applications to register URLs in the reserved namespace. We can make this reservation using the `netsh` command-line tool (which requires administrative privileges):

```
netsh http add urlacl url=http://+:8080/ user=domain\user
```

The `domain\user` value should be replaced by the identity under which the self-host application will run. This identity can also be one of the Windows special accounts, such as `network service`, which is typically used when HTTP servers are hosted inside Windows services. In this case, `domain\user` can be replaced by `network service` or `local service`.

Hosting Web API with OWIN and Katana

At the beginning of the chapter, we learned that ASP.NET Web API is built in a manner that is host-agnostic, and that characteristic makes it possible to run a Web API in either a traditional ASP.NET and IIS host or a custom process (self-hosting). This enables new opportunities for building and running Web APIs; it also surfaces some new challenges. For example, in many cases, developers do not want to have to write a custom console application or Windows service in order to self-host their Web API. Many developers who have some experience with frameworks such as Node.js or Sinatra expect to be able to host their application in a presupplied executable. Additionally, a Web API is generally only one component of several in a modern web application. Other components include server-side markup generation frameworks like ASP.NET MVC, static file servers, and real-time messaging frameworks like SignalR. Additionally, an application can be made up of many smaller components that focus on specific tasks such as authentication or logging. While Web API currently provides for different hosting options, a Web API host is not able to simultaneously host any of these other components, meaning that each of the different technologies in a modern web application would require its own host. In the web-hosted scenario, IIS and the ASP.NET request pipeline mask this constraint, but it becomes much more apparent when self-hosting.

What we really need is an abstraction that enables many different types of components to form a single web application and then allows the entire application to run on top of a variety of servers and hosts, based on the unique requirements of the application and deployment environment.

OWIN

The Open Web Interface for .NET (OWIN) (*http://owin.org*) is a standard created by the open source community that defines how servers and application components interact. The goal of this effort is to change how .NET web applications are built—from applications as extensions of large, monolithic frameworks to loosely coupled compositions of small modules.

To accomplish this goal, OWIN reduces interactions between server and application components to the following simple interface, known as the application delegate or app func.:

```
Func<IDictionary<string, object>, Task>
```

This interface is the only requirement for an OWIN-compatible server or module (also known as *middleware*). Additionally, because the application delegate consists of a small number of .NET types, OWIN applications are inherently more likely to be portable to different framework versions and even different platforms, such as the Mono project.

The application delegate defines an interaction whereby a component receives all state —including server, application, and request state—via a dictionary object known as the environment or environment dictionary. As an OWIN-based application is assumed to be asynchronous, the application delegate returns a Task instance after performing work and modifying the environment dictionary. OWIN itself defines several of the keys and values that may or must exist in the environment dictionary, as shown in Table 11-1. Additionally, any OWIN server or host can supply its own entries in the environment dictionary, and these can be used by any other middleware.

Table 11-1. Environment entries for request data

Required	Key name	Value description
Yes	"owin.RequestBody"	A Stream with the request body, if any. Stream.Null *may* be used as a placeholder if there is no request body.
Yes	"owin.RequestHeaders"	An IDictionary<string, string[]> of request headers.
Yes	"owin.RequestMethod"	A string containing the HTTP request method of the request (e.g., "GET", "POST").
Yes	"owin.RequestPath"	A string containing the request path. The path *must* be relative to the "root" of the application delegate.
Yes	"owin.RequestPathBase"	A string containing the portion of the request path corresponding to the "root" of the application delegate.
Yes	"owin.RequestProtocol"	A string containing the protocol name and version (e.g., "HTTP/1.0" or "HTTP/1.1").
Yes	"owin.RequestQueryString"	A string containing the query string component of the HTTP request URI, without the leading "?" (e.g., "foo=bar&baz=quux"). The value may be an empty string.
Yes	"owin.RequestScheme"	A string containing the URI scheme used for the request (e.g., "http", "https"); see URI Scheme.

In addition to prescribing server and application interactions to the application delegate and environment dictionary, OWIN also provides guidance for host and server implementors related to subjects such as processing URIs and HTTP headers, application startup, and error handling. The simplicity of the application delegate combined with the flexibility of the loosely typed environment dictionary makes it easy for smaller, more focused components to be developed and assembled by a developer into a single application pipeline. As will be covered more in Chapter 15, several examples of these more focused components are already being incorporated in the next release of ASP.NET.

The complete OWIN specification is listed online (*http://bit.ly/owin-docs*).

The Katana Project

Whereas OWIN is the specification for defining how servers and application components interact to process web requests, the Katana project is a collection of OWIN-compatible components that are created by Microsoft and distributed as open source software.[2] Katana project components are organized by architecture layer, as illustrated in Figure 11-12. The HTTP data flow through the different layers and components is illustrated in Figure 11-13.

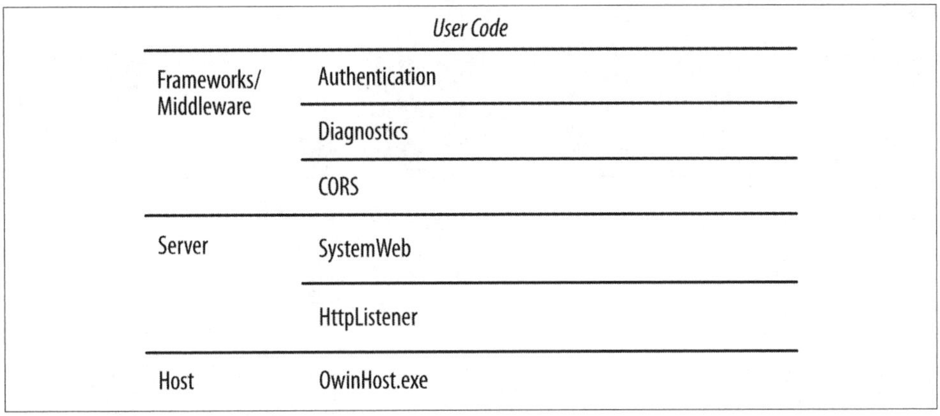

	User Code	
Frameworks/ Middleware	Authentication	
	Diagnostics	
	CORS	
Server	SystemWeb	
	HttpListener	
Host	OwinHost.exe	

Figure 11-12. Katana component architecture with example components

Katana components are divided into one of three layers: hosts, servers, and middleware. The responsibility for each type of component is as follows:

Host

> Hosts start and manage processes. A host is responsible for launching a process and initiating the startup sequence put forward in section 4 of the OWIN specification (*http://bit.ly/owin-doc-app*).

Server

> Servers listen for HTTP requests, ensure that values are correctly placed in the environment dictionary, and call the application delegate for the first middleware in a pipeline of middleware components.

Middleware

> Middleware are components that perform any number of different tasks on a request or response. They can be scoped to small tasks, such as implementing compression or enforcing HTTPS, or can function as adapters to an entire framework,

---

2. In addition to Microsoft's Katana components, many popular open source web frameworks, such as NancyFX, FUBU, ServiceStack, and others, can also be run in an OWIN pipeline.

such as ASP.NET Web API. Components are arranged in a pipeline structure, where each component has a reference to the next component in the pipeline. The host has the responsibility of constructing this pipeline during its startup sequence.

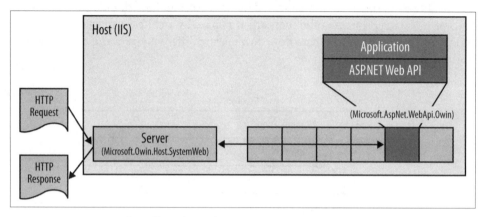

Figure 11-13. HTTP data flow through an ASP.NET Web API application running on an OWIN pipeline and Katana host

In a conventional, framework-based approach to running web applications, the host, server, and framework start independently of the application and then call into the application at designated points. In this model, a developer's code is effectively extending the underlying framework, and as a result, the level of control over the request processing that application code will be determined by the framework. Additionally, it means that the application will pay a performance penalty for features of the framework that it does not use, but are run as a part of the framework itself.

In an OWIN-based web application, the startup sequence is reversed. After the host has initialized an environment dictionary and selected a server, it immediately discovers and calls into the developer's application code to determine what components should be composed together in the OWIN pipeline. By default, Katana hosts discover a developer's startup code based on the following rules:

- Look up or find a startup class (in order of precedence).
- If present, use the `appSettings` value for key `owin:AppStartup`.
- If present, use the type defined in the assembly-level attribute `OwinStartupAttribute`.
- Scan all assemblies looking for a type named `Startup`.
- If a startup class is found, find and call a configuration method matching the signature `void Configuration(IAppBuilder app)`.

Following this default discovery logic, we simply need to add the following startup class definition to our project in order for the Katana host's loader to find and run it:

```
public class Startup
{
    public void Configuration(IAppBuilder app)
    {
        app.Use(typeof(MyMiddleware));
    }
}
```

Within the startup class's configuration method, we can construct the OWIN pipeline by calling the Use method of the supplied IAppBuilder object. The Use method is intended to be a generic means for allowing any component that implements the application delegate to be configured in the pipeline. Additionally, many middleware components and frameworks provide their own extension methods for simplifying pipeline configuration. For example, ASP.NET Web API provides the UseWebApi extension method, which enables the configuration code as follows:

```
var config = new HttpConfiguration();

// configure Web API
// ...

app.UseWebApi(config);
```

But what actually happens when you use Web API's configuration extension method? Going deeper into the Web API configuration method and the Web API middleware component will help you to better understand both the OWIN pipeline and Katana implementation, as well as the decoupled nature of Web API's host adapter design.

Web API Configuration

When the UseWebApi method is called from within a user's startup class, the method, which is found in the System.Web.Http.Owin assembly's WebApiAppBuilderExten sions class, constructs an instance of the HttpMessageHandlerAdapter class—the OWIN middleware component for Web API—and adds it to the IAppBuilder instance using the generic Use method. Looking at the UseWebApi method reveals more about how the Katana infrastructure binds middleware together to form the complete pipeline:

```
public static IAppBuilder UseWebApi(
    this IAppBuilder builder,
    HttpConfiguration configuration)
{
    IHostBufferPolicySelector bufferPolicySelector =
        configuration.Services.GetHostBufferPolicySelector()
            ?? _defaultBufferPolicySelector;

    return builder.Use(typeof(HttpMessageHandlerAdapter),
```

```
    new HttpServer(configuration), bufferPolicySelector);
}
```

The generic Use method takes the type of the Web API middleware as its first parameter, followed by an arbitrary array of additional parameters. In the case of the Web API middleware, we can see that there are two additional parameters: an HttpServer instance, which is configured with the supplied HttpConfiguration object, and an object that instructs the middleware on how to handle request and response streaming. The middleware itself is passed to Use as a type rather than an instance so that the infrastructure can, as a part of creating the middleware instance, configure it (via the middleware's constructor) with a reference to the next middleware object in the pipeline. We can see this in action by examining the HttpMessageHandlerAdapter constructor: the next reference is supplied as the first parameter and is then followed by the additional parameters that were passed to the generic Use method:[3]

```
public HttpMessageHandlerAdapter(OwinMiddleware next,
    HttpMessageHandler messageHandler,
    IHostBufferPolicySelector bufferPolicySelector) : base(next)
```

The output of the generic Use method is the modified IAppBuilder object, and therefore the extension method simply returns that object. Returning the IAppBuilder in this way enables us to use a fluid syntax when composing the OWIN pipeline in our startup class.

Web API Middleware

Once the Web API middleware has been added to the OWIN pipeline, an OWIN server can call the middleware's application delegate for HTTP requests. Recall the signature for the OWIN application delegate:

```
Func<IDictionary<string, object>, Task>
```

Web API's HttpMessageHandlerAdapter class exposes this function indirectly via its base class, OwinMiddleware, which is provided by the Microsoft.Owin NuGet package. This base class supplies the server with the application delegate function and then exposes a simpler API to its descendants:

```
public async override Task Invoke(IOwinContext context)
```

The context object provides a more strongly typed object model for accessing members of the environment dictionary like the HTTP request and response objects. The current list of accessors provided by IOwinContext is summarized in Table 11-2.

---

3. Details surrounding Web API's dispatching logic, including HttpServer and HttpMessageHandler, will be discussed at length in Chapter 12.

Table 11-2. Property accessors for IOwinContext

Request	A wrapper around the current request
Response	A wrapper around the current response
Environment	The wrapped OWIN environment dictionary
Authentication (.NET 4.5 and higher)	Accesses the authentication middleware functionality available for the current request

Each property in the context object provides strongly typed access to different members of the environment dictionary. To inspect each of the different wrapper types, see the `Microsoft.Owin` source (*http://bit.ly/katana-source*).

As a request flows through the OWIN pipeline, when it reaches the `HttpMessageHand lerAdapter Invoke` method, it is processed according to the data flow illustrated in Figure 11-14.

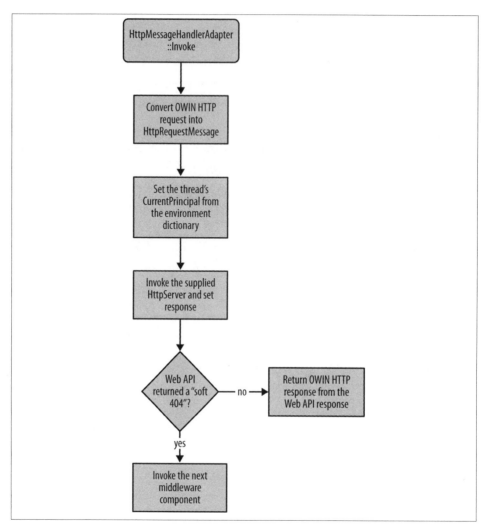

Figure 11-14. Web API middleware data flow

Because the HttpMessageHandlerAdapter's primary responsibility is to serve as a bridge between the OWIN pipeline and the Web API programming model, the first action that it performs is to convert the objects found in the OWIN environment dictionary into the fundamental types used by Web API. Not surprisingly, these are HttpRequestMessage and HttpResponseMessage. Prior to sending the HTTP request to Web API for processing, the middleware also extracts the user object, if it exists, from the environment dictionary (via IOwinContext.Request.User) and assigns it to the active thread's CurrentPrincipal property.

Once the middleware has an `HttpRequestMessage` representation of the request, it can invoke Web API in a manner similar to the previously described Web API hosting infrastructure components. As is discussed in Chapter 12, the `HttpServer` type is derived from `HttpMessageHandler` and acts as the entry point into the Web API message handler pipeline (there is also an extension method overload that enables the developer to specify an additional `HttpMessageHandler` object known as the dispatcher, which is the last node in the message handler pipeline). Because an `HttpMessageHandler` cannot be invoked directly, the middleware wraps it in an `HttpMessageInvoker` object and then calls it with the following:

```
response = await _messageInvoker.SendAsync(request, owinRequest.CallCancelled);
```

This initiates processing of the `HttpRequestMessage` through Web API's message handler pipeline and controller pipeline and sets a reference to the resultant `HttpRespon` `seMessage` on a local variable. The message handler and controller pipelines are discussed at length in Chapter 12.

One additional responsibility of the Web API middleware component is determining what to do with an HTTP `404 Not Found` status code on the `HttpResponseMessage`. This is important because in the context of the larger OWIN pipeline, this status code can mean one of two things:

- The request did not match any of the `HttpRoutes` that were specified in the `HttpConfiguration` object. In this case, the middleware should invoke the application delegate on its next middleware component.

- The application developer explicitly returned this status code as a part of the application's protocol implementation (e.g., for request `GET /api/widgets/123`, item 123 cannot be found in the widgets data store). In this case, the middleware should not invoke the next middleware component in the chain, but instead return the `404` response to the client.

In Web API middleware terms, a `404` response code that is set by Web API's route matching logic is called a "soft not found," and it is identified by the presence of an additional setting—`HttpPropertyKeys.NoRouteMatched`—in the response message's properties collection. A `404` response code without this setting will be assumed to be a "hard not found" and will result in an immediate `404` HTTP response to the client.

The OWIN Ecosystem

The full set of Katana components is broader than what has been discussed in this chapter. The most recent release of the Katana components includes components for authentication, including middleware for both social and enterprise providers, diagnostics middleware, the `HttpListener` server, and the `OwinHost.exe` host. OWIN-based authentication components will be covered in greater detail in Chapter 15. Over time, the list of OWIN-compatible components from Microsoft will continue to grow to include many of the common features currently in System.Web.dll. Additionally, the ecosystem of third-party components created by the community continues to grow, and at present includes many different HTTP frameworks and middleware components. We should expect to see the OWIN component space grow significantly over the next several years.

In-Memory Hosting

An additional Web API hosting option, mainly aimed at testing scenarios, is based on the direct connection between an HttpClient instance and an HttpServer instance. It is commonly designated by *in-memory hosting*.

As described in Chapter 14, an HttpClient instance can be configured by an HttpMes sageHandler passed in the constructor. The client then uses this handler to asynchronously obtain the HTTP request from the HTTP request. Typically, this handler is either an HttpClientHandler that uses an underlying network infrastructure to send and receive HTTP messages, or a DelegatingHandler that performs pre- and post-processing on the request and response, respectively.

However, the HttpServer class also extends from the HttpMessageHandler, meaning that you can use it when constructing an HttpClient. This results in the direct in-memory communication between the client and the server, without any network stack overhead, which is useful in testing scenarios. Example 11-5 shows how to use this capability.

Example 11-5. In-memory hosting

```
var config = new HttpConfiguration();
config.Routes.MapHttpRoute("default", "{controller}/{id}",
                                new { id = RouteParameter.Optional });
var server = new HttpServer(config);
var client = new HttpClient(server);
var c = client.GetAsync("http://can.be.anything/resource").Result
    .Content.ReadAsStringAsync().Result;
```

The can.be.anything hostname in Example 11-5 means exactly that: since no network layer is used, the URI's hostname part is ignored and therefore can be anything.

It is the symmetry between HttpClient and HttpServer—one is a message handler and the other receives a message handler—that allows the direct connection of the client to the server, as shown in Figure 11-15.

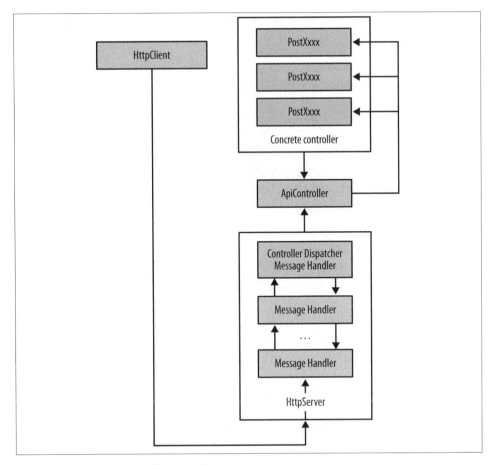

Figure 11-15. In-memory hosting diagram

Azure Service Bus Host

Finally, before we end this chapter, we are going to exemplify the development of a custom hosting adapter. As a motivator, we will use the Windows Azure *Service Bus*, which is a cloud-hosted infrastructure providing both *brokered* and *relayed* messaging capabilities. Brokered messaging includes mechanisms such as *queues* and *topics*, providing both temporal decoupling and message multicast between senders and receivers. Relayed messaging, which is the main topic in this section, allows the public exposure of APIs hosted on private networks.

Consider Figure 11-16, where an API (i.e., a set of resources) is hosted on a machine with the following characteristics:

- Located in a private network, without owning any public IP or a public DNS name

- Separated from the Internet by both NAT (network address translation) and firewall systems.

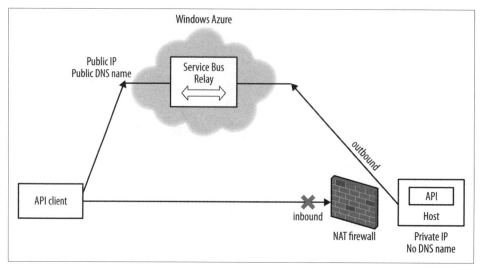

Figure 11-16. Service Bus usage scenario

A concrete example of such a setting is a home automation system providing a Web API. In a typical residential scenario, the Internet access (e.g., via DSL) has the characteristics depicted in Figure 11-16—that is, no public IP address or DNS name, and NAT and firewalls blocking inbound connections. However, it would be useful if this API could be consumed by external clients, located on the Internet. Consider, for instance, a scenario where a smartphone is used to remotely control the room temperature or view surveillance images.

As shown in Figure 11-16, the Service Bus relay feature solves these connectivity problems by acting as an intermediary between the client and the API host:

- First, the host establishes an *outbound* connection to the Service Bus relay. Since it is an outbound connection, not inbound, no public IP is required internally; the translation is performed by the NAT.

- As a consequence of this connection, the Service Bus relay creates and exposes a public endpoint using a domain name in its namespace (e.g., `webapibook.serv icebus.windows.net`).

- Every request sent to this public endpoint is then relayed to the API host via the opened outbound connection. The responses produced by the API host are also returned via this outbound connection and delivered to the client by the Service Bus relay.

The Azure Service Bus is multitenant, and each tenant *owns* a DNS name with the structure {tenant-namespace}.servicebus.windows.net. For instance, the example in this section uses the name webapibook.servicebus.windows.net. When a host establishes the connection with the service bus, instructing the relay to start listening for requests, it must authenticate itself—that is, prove that it is allowed to use the tenant's name. Also, the host must define a prefix path, which is combined with the tenant's DNS name to form the base address. Only requests with this prefix are forwarded to the host by the relay.

The Azure Service Bus provides a SDK (software development kit) that integrates into the WCF programming model and provides special bindings for hosting services via the Service Bus relay. Unfortunately, at the time of this writing, it does not contain any support for the ASP.NET Web API. However, based on the hosting independence capabilities of Web API and inspired by the WCF-based self-host, we can build the custom HttpServiceBusServer class that uses the Service Bus relay to host ASP.NET Web API.

Figure 11-17 shows the HttpServiceBusServer host server and associated classes.

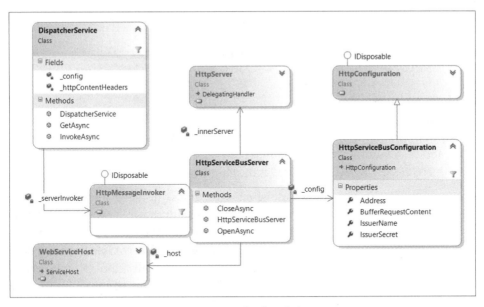

Figure 11-17. The HttpServiceBusServer and related classes

This new server is configured by an instance of the HttpServiceBusConfiguration class, which derives from the base HttpConfiguration, and adds the following properties specific to this hosting scenario:

- The public Service Bus relay address (e.g., *https://tenant-namespace.servicebus.windows.net/some/path*)
- The credentials required to establish the outbound connection to the Service Bus relay

This design, on which a specific configuration class derives from the base `HttpConfiguration`, is similar to the one used by the self-host and presented in Figure 11-8. Internally, the `HttpServiceBusServer` creates a WCF `WebServiceHost`, and adds an endpoint configured by the `WebHttpRelayBinding`, which is one of the new bindings in the Service Bus SDK. This new binding is similar to the WCF native `WebHttpBinding`, with the major difference that the service is exposed remotely on the Service Bus relay, instead of on the local hosting machine. All the requests received through this endpoint are handled by an instance of the `DispatcherService` class:

```
[ServiceContract]
[ServiceBehavior(InstanceContextMode = InstanceContextMode.Single,
                 ConcurrencyMode = ConcurrencyMode.Multiple)]
internal class DispatcherService
    [WebGet(UriTemplate = "*")]
    [OperationContract(AsyncPattern = true)]
    public async Task<Message> GetAsync()
    {...}

    [WebInvoke(UriTemplate = "*", Method = "*")]
    [OperationContract(AsyncPattern = true)]
    public async Task<Message> InvokeAsync(Message msg)
    {...}
}
```

This generic service implements two operations asynchronously: `Get` and `Invoke`. The `Get` operation handles all the HTTP requests with the `GET` method. The `Invoke` operation handles all the other request methods (`Method = "*"`). Notice that both operations have `UriTemplate = "*"`, meaning that they both handle requests for any path.

When a request is received by any of these two methods, the native message representation is transformed into a new `HttpRequestMessage` instance. This new instance is then pushed into an inner `HttpServer`, created in the `HttpServiceBusServer` constructor and configured by the passed `HttpServiceBusConfiguration`. Unfortunately, the `HttpServer.SendAsync` method cannot be called directly, since it is protected. However, the `HttpMessageInvoker` can wrap any message handler, namely the `HttpServer`, and expose a public `SendAsync` method:

```
public DispatcherService(HttpServer server, HttpServiceBusConfiguration config)
{
    _serverInvoker = new HttpMessageInvoker(server, false);
    _config = config;
}
```

When the `HttpServer` produces the `HttpResponseMessage`, the `DispatcherService` converts it back to the WCF message representation and returns it.

The overall design is inspired by the WCF-based self-host adapter. There are, however, two differences. The first and most important is that the Service Bus host sits on top of the WCF Service Model, while the self-host uses the WCF channel stack directly. This choice, which introduces additional overhead, was adopted because it results in a simpler implementation.

The second difference is that `HttpServiceBusServer` does not derive from `HttpServer`. Instead of using an inheritance-based design, like the one chosen by the `HttpSelfHostServer`, the `HttpServiceBusServer` uses a compositional approach: an `HttpServer` instance is created and used internally.

The `HttpServiceBusServer` is available in the source code (*http://bit.ly/service-bus-code*). The source code repository also includes an example showing the simplicity of using this new Web API host. The `ServiceBusRelayHost.Demo.Screen` project defines a Service Bus hosted service, containing only one resource:

```
public class ScreenController : ApiController
{
    public HttpResponseMessage Get()
    {
        var content = new StreamContent(ScreenCapturer.GetEncodedByteStream());
        content.Headers.ContentType = new MediaTypeHeaderValue("image/jpeg");
        return new HttpResponseMessage()
        {
            Content = content
        };
    }
}
```

where `ScreenCapturer` is an auxiliary class for capturing the desktop screen. The hosting of this resource controller is also straightforward:

```
var config = new HttpServiceBusConfiguration(
    ServiceBusCredentials.ServiceBusAddress)
{
    IssuerName = "owner",
    IssuerSecret = ServiceBusCredentials.Secret
};
config.Routes.MapHttpRoute(
    "default",
    "{controller}/{id}",
    new { id = RouteParameter.Optional });
var server = new HttpServiceBusServer(config);
server.OpenAsync().Wait();
...
```

First, an `HttpServiceBusConfiguration` instance is initialized with the Service Bus address, access credentials (`IssuerSecret`), and access username (`"owner"`). Then, the routes are added to the `Routes` property, just as in any other hosting scenario. Finally, an `HttpServiceBusServer` is configured with this configuration instance and then explicitly opened.

Figure 11-18 shows the result of accessing the screen resource, hosted via Azure Service Bus, through a plain old browser. Notice the use of a public DNS name in the browser's address bar.

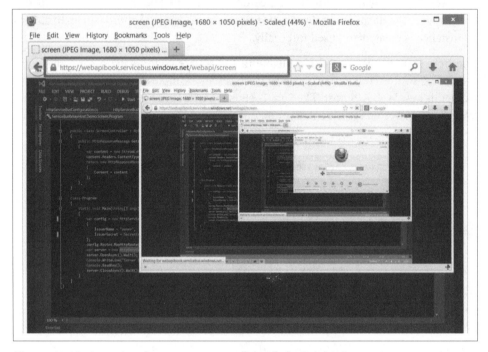

Figure 11-18. Accessing the screen resource hosted via Service Bus

Conclusion

This chapter focused on the way Web API interfaces with *external* hosting infrastructures. It described not only the originally available host adapters, web host and self-host, but also the new hosting options based on the OWIN specification and the Katana project. Finally, it also presented in-memory hosting and an example of a custom hosting adapter. In the following chapters, our focus will change to the upper layers of ASP.NET Web API, in particular routing and controllers.

CHAPTER 12

Controllers and Routing

*Knowing how home plumbing works is unnecessary much of the time—but when you need
to know it, you really need to know it.*

While ASP.NET Web API provides a litany of helpful high-level features ranging from
serialization and model binding to support for OData-style queries, the core job of all
Web APIs, and ASP.NET Web API as a result, is to process HTTP requests and provide
appropriate responses. Therefore, it is critical to understand the core mechanics of how
an HTTP request flows from a client through the various elements of the ASP.NET Web
API infrastructure and programming model, ultimately resulting in an HTTP response
that can be sent back to the client.

This chapter focuses on that message flow, exploring the fundamental mechanics and
supporting the programming model behind request handling and response generation.
In addition, this chapter will look at the key types and insertion points that enable the
framework to be extended to support custom message flow and processing schemes.

HTTP Message Flow Overview

The precise message flow through ASP.NET Web API will vary somewhat depending
on the choice of host, and hosting is discussed in much greater detail in Chapter 10.
However, at a high level, the framework components that participate in the HTTP message flow fall into two categories (as illustrated in Figure 12-1):

- Components that rely only on the HTTP message for context
- Components that rely on the higher-level programming model for context

The components that rely only on the core HTTP message context form the lower-level
"message handler" pipeline. These components receive an `HttpRequestMessage` object

from the hosting abstraction and are ultimately responsible for returning an `HttpRes
ponseMessage` object.

By contrast, components that rely on the higher-level programming model have visibility into and are able to take advantage of programming framework abstractions, such
as the controller and action methods as well as the parameters that map to the various
elements of the HTTP request.

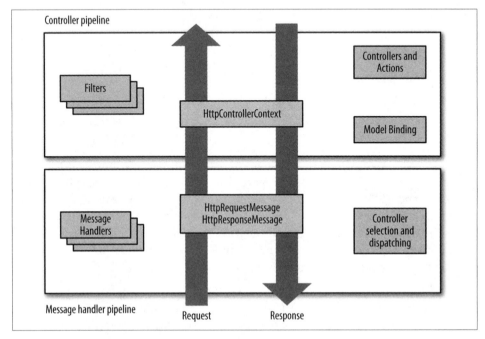

Figure 12-1. The message handler and controller pipelines

As mentioned, the low-level mechanics for activities such as selecting URL routes varies
depending on the host. For example, when a Web API is hosted as part of an MVC
application hosted on IIS, an HTTP message flows through the core routing infrastructure provided by ASP.NET. Conversely, when a Web API is self-hosted, the message
flows through a WCF channel stack built around an `HttpListener` object. Regardless
of the selected hosting option, a request will ultimately be converted to an instance of
`HttpRequestMessage` and will be passed to an instance of `HttpServer`.

The Message Handler Pipeline

`HttpServer` is the entry point into the message handler pipeline for host-specific components. It initializes the pipeline from the handlers supplied by both global and route

configuration data using the HttpClientFactory's CreatePipeline method, as shown in Example 12-1.

Example 12-1. Initializing the MessageHandler pipeline

```
protected virtual void Initialize()
{
    // Do final initialization of the configuration.
    // It is considered immutable from this point forward.
    _configuration.Initializer(_configuration);

    // Create pipeline
    InnerHandler = HttpClientFactory.CreatePipeline(_dispatcher,
        _configuration.MessageHandlers);
}
```

Finally, because HttpServer itself derives from the DelegatingHandler class, it acts as the first handler in a message handler pipeline. The complete pipeline consists of HttpServer followed by any number of custom DelegatingHandler objects that you register with HttpConfiguration; followed by another special handler called HttpRou tingDispatcher; and finally, either a custom route-specific message handler (or another message handler pipeline built up with HttpClientFactory.CreatePipeline) supplied during route registration, or the default HttpControllerDispatcher message handler. HttpControllerDispatcher selects, creates, and dispatches the message to a controller instance. The pipeline is illustrated in Figure 12-2.

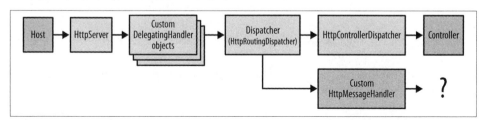

Figure 12-2. The MessageHandler Pipeline

HttpServer establishes itself as the first node in the pipeline by setting the value returned from HttpClientFactory.CreatePipeline to its own InnerHandler property. This enables HttpServer to pass control to the next handler in the pipeline by calling the SendAsync method on its base class. This approach is consistent with all message handlers in the pipeline:

```
return base.SendAsync(request, cancellationToken)
```

The DelegatingHandler base class simply calls SendAsync on the object's InnerHan dler value. The inner handler processes the message in its SendAsync method and then repeats the process by calling SendAsync on its own InnerHandler. This process of calling the inner handler's SendAsync method continues until the innermost handler is reached—which, in the case of a typical ASP.NET Web API, is the handler that dispatches the request to a controller instance. This style of pipeline, depicted in Figure 12-3, is sometimes referred to as a "Russian doll" because handlers are layered within one another, and request data flows from the outermost handler to the innermost handler (and then vice versa for response data) as a result of the outer handler directly calling its inner handler.[1]

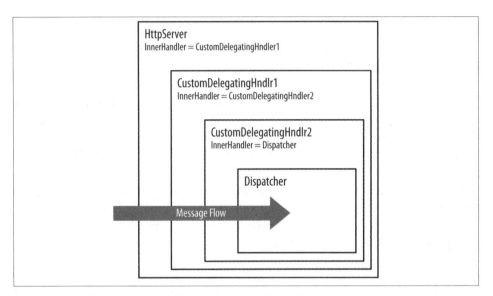

Figure 12-3. The MessageHandler "Russian doll" model

Keep in mind that this entire data flow is asynchronous and therefore the value returned from SendAsync is a Task. In fact, its complete signature is as follows:

```
Task<HttpResponseMessage> SendAsync(HttpRequestMessage request,
    CancellationToken cancellationToken)
```

Participating in a task-based async pipeline can take some getting used to, and that topic is discussed in much more depth in Chapter 10. However, some basic guidelines are as follows for creating a task-based message handler.

- To pass control on to the next, or inner, handler in the pipeline, simply return the value of calling SendAsync on the base class.

---

1. This pipeline style can be contrasted with a style whereby the pipeline is external to its components and data flows as the result of the pipeline calling a component, obtaining its response, calling the next component, and so on.

- To stop all further processing of the message and return a response (also known as "short-circuiting" the request processing), return a new `Task<HttpResponseMes sage>`.

- To process the HTTP response as it flows back from the innermost handler to the outermost handler, append a continuation (implemented with the `ContinueWith` method) to the returned task. The continuation should take a single parameter to hold the task that is being continued and should return an `HttpResponseMessage` object. With version 4.5 and later of the .NET Framework, you can simplify working with asynchronous code using the `async` and `await` keywords.

As an example, consider the message handler shown in Example 12-2, which examines an HTTP `GET` request and determines whether the request is a conditional `GET` request (that is, a request that contains an `if-none-match` header). If the request is a conditional request, and the entity tag (`ETag`) contained in the request cannot be found in a local cache, this indicates to the handler that the value of the underlying resource state has changed. Therefore, the handler lets the request continue to flow through the pipeline and to the appropriate controller by calling and returning the value of `base.SendAsync`. This will ensure that the response to this `GET` request will contain the most up-to-date representation of the resource.

Example 12-2. MessageHandler for processing conditional GET requests with ETags

```
protected override Task<HttpResponseMessage> SendAsync(
    HttpRequestMessage request,
    CancellationToken cancellationToken)
{
    if (request.Method == HttpMethod.Get &&
        request.Headers.IfNoneMatch.Count > 0 &&
        (!IfNoneMatchContainsStoredEtagValue(request)))

        return base.SendAsync(request, cancellationToken).ContinueWith(task => {
            var resp = task.Result;
            resp.Headers.ETag = new EntityTagHeaderValue(
                _eTagStore.Fetch(request.RequestUri));
            return resp;
        });
    }

    ...

    //by default, let the request keep moving through the message handler pipeline
    return base.SendAsync(request, cancellationToken);
}
```

The handler also adds a continuation to the returned task so that it can create and apply a new `ETag` value to the response message. This new `ETag` value can then be passed and validated for future requests to the resource.

Dispatcher

The final stage of the message handler pipeline is the dispatching stage. In earlier versions of ASP.NET Web API, this stage was predefined to select a controller from the information supplied by the route data, get an instance of the controller, and then pass the HTTP message and context to the controller for processing by the controller's execution logic. You could still circumvent the controller programming model by simply adding a custom message handler that returned a new Task object. However, that message handler needed to be added in the global HttpConfiguration object, meaning that it needed to process every HTTP request sent to the Web API.

To enable message handlers to be configured on a per-route basis, as well as to enable different Web API frameworks that may use a different higher-level abstraction than IHttpController, the team added a level of indirection to the dispatching process. HttpServer composes an instance of HttpRoutingDispatcher as the last node in the message handler pipeline. As the following excerpt from the product source code illustrates, HttpRoutingDispatcher is responsible for invoking either a custom message handler supplied by the route or, alternately, the default HttpControllerDispatcher. Because the dispatcher derives from HttpMessageHandler, which cannot be directly invoked, the `HttpRoutingDispatcher` code wraps the instance in an `HttpMessageIn voker` object so that it can be executed:

```
var invoker = (routeData.Route == null || routeData.Route.Handler == null) ?
    _defaultInvoker : new HttpMessageInvoker(routeData.Route.Handler,
        disposeHandler: false);
return invoker.SendAsync(request, cancellationToken);
```

Route-specific message handlers are declared as a part of the route configuration itself. For example, consider the following route registration code:

```
public static void Register(HttpConfiguration config)
{
    config.Routes.MapHttpRoute("customHandler", "custom/{controller}/{id}",
        defaults: new {id = RouteParameter.Optional},
        constraints: null,
        handler: HttpClientFactory.CreatePipeline(
                    new HttpControllerDispatcher(config),
            new[] {new MyHandler()})
    );

    ...
}
```

In addition to the standard route configuration and registration code, the `customHan dler` route provides a custom message handler as the last parameter to `MapHttpRoute`. However, the code actually does more than simply register an instance of the custom `MyHandler` message handler. It uses the `HttpClientFactory.CreatePipeline` helper method to compose `MyHandler` with the default `HttpControllerDispatcher` message handler. This is an important point to keep in mind when you're inserting route-specific message handlers. If a custom message handler is supplied to `HttpRoutingDispatch er`, that message handler becomes responsible for any and all further processing of the HTTP message. The `CreatePipeline` method accepts the desired "final destination" message handler as its first argument followed by a list of all the additional message handlers to be composed into the pipeline. The method then wires the message handlers together by setting the `InnerHandler` property of the individual message handlers, and returns the first message handler in the chain. In this example, the chain consists of `MyHandler` followed by `HttpControllerDispatcher`. Keep in mind that for a message handler pipeline to be created like this, all message handlers except for the innermost handler must derive from `DelegatingHandler` rather than directly from `HttpMessage Handler`, since the `DelegatingHandler` supports composition via its `InnerHandler` property.

HttpControllerDispatcher

By default, the final stop in the message handler pipeline will be the `HttpController Dispatcher`. This handler is the glue that binds together the message handler pipeline with the higher-level programming model elements of controllers and actions (we will call this the *controller pipeline*). The HttpControllerDispatcher has three responsibilities:

- Select a controller using an object that implements IHttpControllerSelector.
- Get an instance of a controller using an object that implements IHttpController Activator.
- Execute the controller instance, passing it a controller context object that is composed of the current configuration, route, and request context.

To fulfill these responsibilities, HttpControllerDispatcher relies on two noteworthy types. These are types that implement the IHttpControllerSelector interface and types that implement the IHttpControllerActivator interface.

Controller Selection

As its title suggests, the responsibility of the IHttpControllerSelector is to select the proper controller based on the HTTP request. ASP.NET Web API supplies a default implementation with the DefaultHttpControllerSelector class. This class uses the following algorithm for choosing the controller:

- Determine whether the controller can be identified directly from the route data. This condition is true when attribute-based routing is used.

-

- Check whether the controller name is valid. If it is either null or an empty string, throw a 404 response exception.

- Using the controller name, look for a matching HttpControllerDescriptor in its controller info cache and return it.

The controller info cache is a dictionary of controller names and HttpControllerDescriptor objects that is initialized when the cache is first accessed. During initialization, the controller info cache uses an instance of the HttpControllerTypeCache, which in turn uses an object that implements the IHttpControllerTypeResolver for iterating assemblies and types and building up a list of all valid controller types. By default, Web API uses DefaultHttpControllerTypeResolver, which selects as valid controllers any types that meet the following conditions:

- The type is a class.
- The class is public.
- The class is not abstract.

- The class implements or derives from a class that implements the `IHttpControl ler` interface.

- The class name ends with the string `"Controller"`.

Because controllers are discovered when the `DefaultHttpControllerSelector` info cache is first accessed, any failure to find exactly one match for the requested controller name indicates an error in the default controller selection logic. For example, if no entries are found for the requested controller name, the framework returns an HTTP `404 Not Found` response to the client. If, on the other hand, more than one entry is found for the requested controller name, then the framework throws an `InvalidOper ationException` for the ambiguous match.

Assuming that the requested controller name matches a single entry in the default controller selector's info cache, the controller selector returns the corresponding `HttpCon trollerDescriptor` value to the calling `HttpControllerDispatcher`.

One additional thing to note here is that the lifetime of the controller descriptor is the duration of the `HttpConfiguration` object, which practically speaking means that the controller descriptor lifetime is the lifetime of the application.

Supporting attribute-based routes

Web API 2 added the ability to specify routes as attributes. These attributes can be applied to both controller classes and action methods, and this declarative approach to routing adds to the purely convention-based approach of matching controllers and actions by route parameters and naming conventions.

Mechanically, using attribute-based routing is a two-step process. The first step is decorating controllers and/or actions with `RouteAttribute` and supplying the appropriate route template values. The second step is to have Web API map those attribute values to actual route data, which the framework can then use when processing requests.

For example, consider the following basic greeting Web API:

```
public class GreetingController : ApiController
{
    // mapped to GET /api/greeting by default
    public string GetGreeting()
    {
        return "Hello!";
    }
}
```

Using attribute-based routing, we could map this controller and action to a completely different URL without requiring a change to the global route configuration rules:

```
public class GreetingController : ApiController
{
```

```
// mapped to GET /services/hello
[Route("services/hello")]
public string GetGreeting()
{
    return "Hello!";
}
```
}

In order to ensure that attribute-based routes are correctly added to Web API's route configuration, we must call the `MapHttpAttributeRoutes` method on `HttpConfigura tion` as follows:

```
config.MapHttpAttributeRoutes();
```

The approach of integrating attribute routes at configuration time enables fewer modifications to the other framework components. For example, because all of the complexity for parsing and managing attribute-based route values is managed at the `Route Data` level, the impact to `DefaultHttpControllerSelector` is limited to the following:

```
controllerDescriptor = routeData.GetDirectRouteController();
if (controllerDescriptor != null)
{
    return controllerDescriptor;
}
```

As the code indicates, if a controller and/or action is explicitly known from the route as a result of matching an attribute-based route, the `HttpControllerDescriptor` is immediately selected and returned. Otherwise, the convention-based controller selection process attempts to find and select a controller based on the type name.

Plugging in a custom controller selector

While the default logic for selecting a controller will be sufficient for the majority of Web API development scenarios, there may be cases where it is beneficial to supply a custom selection strategy.

Overriding the default controller selection strategy requires creating a new controller selector service and then configuring it to be used by the framework. Creating a new controller selector is simply a matter of authoring a class that implements the `IHttp ControllerSelector` interface, which is defined as follows:

```
public interface IHttpControllerSelector
{
    HttpControllerDescriptor SelectController(HttpRequestMessage request);
    IDictionary<string, HttpControllerDescriptor> GetControllerMapping();
}
```

As the name indicates, the `SelectController` method has the primary responsibility of choosing a controller type for a supplied `HttpRequestMessage` and returning an `HttpControllerDescriptor` object. The `GetControllerMapping` method adds a secondary responsibility to the controller selector to return the entire set of controller names and their corresponding HttpControllerDescriptor objects as a dictionary. To date, however, this responsibility is exercised only by ASP.NET Web API's API explorer feature.

We configure a custom controller selector to be used by the framework through the HttpConfiguration object's Services collection. For example, the following code snippet illustrates how to replace the default controller selector logic, which looks for the suffix Controller in the class name, with a strategy that allows the developer to specify a custom suffix:[2]

```
const string controllerSuffix = "service";

config.Services.Replace(
    typeof(IHttpControllerSelector),
    new CustomSuffixControllerSelector(config, controllerSuffix));
```

What Are the Default Services?

If you browse through the ASP.NET Web API source, you will see many places where the framework components leverage the common services provided by the configuration object to get an object that implements one of the various framework service interfaces. You may be wondering, however, where the concrete types behind the interfaces are actually declared.

A brief look into the constructor for HttpConfiguration reveals the following declaration:

```
Services = new DefaultServices(this);
```

A further look into the DefaultServices class reveals an implementation of the ServicesContainer class, the type used to store common framework services, with default service objects set in its constructor via code such as the following:

```
public DefaultServices(HttpConfiguration configuration)
{
    if (configuration == null)
    {
        throw Error.ArgumentNull("configuration");
    }

    _configuration = configuration;

    SetSingle<IActionValueBinder>(new DefaultActionValueBinder());
    SetSingle<IApiExplorer>(new ApiExplorer(configuration));
```

2. The full code for overriding the default controller suffix is more involved than simply providing a new controller selector.

```
        SetSingle<IAssembliesResolver>(new DefaultAssembliesResolver());
        SetSingle<IBodyModelValidator>(new DefaultBodyModelValidator());
        SetSingle<IContentNegotiator>(new DefaultContentNegotiator());

        ...
    }
```

This list of default services can serve as a good starting point for exploring the default behaviors of the framework, help you determine whether you want to replace one or more of the default behaviors, and give you a clear sense of what component to replace in order to modify a specific behavior.

Controller Activation

Once the controller selector finds and returns an `HttpControllerDescriptor` object to the dispatcher, the dispatcher gets an instance of the controller by calling the `Create Controller` method on `HttpControllerDescriptor`. That method, in turn, delegates the responsibility of creating or getting a controller instance to an object that implements the `IHttpControllerActivator` interface.

The `IHttpControllerActivator` has the single responsibility of creating controller instances, and this is reflected in its definition:

```
public interface IHttpControllerActivator
{
    IHttpController Create(HttpRequestMessage request,
        HttpControllerDescriptor controllerDescriptor,
        Type controllerType);
}
```

Similarly to controller selection, the default logic for controller activation is implemented in the class `DefaultHttpControllerActivator` and registered with the framework in the `DefaultServices` constructor.

The default controller activator creates controller objects via one of two methods. It first attempts to create an instance using the ASP.NET Web API dependency resolver. The dependency resolver is an implementation of the `IDependencyResolver` interface, and provides a general mechanism for the framework to externalize tasks like creating objects and managing object lifetime. In ASP.NET Web API, this is also the mechanism used to plug in inversion-of-control (IOC) containers such as Ninject and Castle Windsor. An instance of a dependency resolver is registered with the framework through the `DependencyResolver` property on the `HttpConfiguration` object, and when the property is non-`null`, the framework will call methods such as `GetService(Type service Type)` in order to create object instances rather than create instances of those types directly. This facility can promote more loosely coupled and extensible designs, both for the ASP.NET Web API Framework itself and for your own services.

In the event that a dependency resolver has not been registered with the framework or if the dependency resolver cannot create an instance for the requested controller type, the default controller activator attempts to create an instance of the supplied controller type by executing the type's parameterless constructor.

After the instance of the controller is created by the controller activator, it is passed back to the controller dispatcher. The dispatcher then passes control flow into the controller pipeline by calling `ExecuteAsync` on the controller object as follows:

```
return httpController.ExecuteAsync(controllerContext, cancellationToken);
```

Like the majority of the components discussed, the controller's `ExecuteAsync` method is asynchronous and returns an instance of `Task`, thereby helping to improve the throughput of the Web API framework itself, as none of its components will block the thread of execution with I/O operations. This efficiency enables the framework to handle an increased number of requests given a finite number of computing resources.

The Controller Pipeline

While the message handler pipeline provides abstractions for the lower-level processing of HTTP requests and responses, the controller pipeline enables a developer to work with higher-level programming abstractions such as controllers, actions, models, and filters. Orchestrating all of the objects used in processing requests and responses is the controller instance itself—hence the term controller pipeline.

ApiController

At a foundational level, an ASP.NET Web API controller is any class that implements the `IHttpController` interface. This interface consists of a single, asynchronous execute method, which by default is called by the underlying dispatcher:

```
public interface IHttpController
{
    Task<HttpResponseMessage> ExecuteAsync(
        HttpControllerContext controllerContext,
        CancellationToken cancellationToken);
}
```

While this simple interface provides a great deal of flexibility in its simplicity, it is devoid of much of the functionality that ASP.NET developers have grown accustomed to. This kind of functionality includes capabilities like authorization, model binding, and validation. In order to provide these capabilities while preserving the simplicity of the interface and reducing the amount of coupling between the message handler pipeline and the controller pipeline, the ASP.NET Web API team created the `ApiController` base class. `ApiController` extends the core controller abstraction and provides two types of services to the controller classes that derive from it:

- A processing model that includes filters, model binding, and action methods.
- Additional context objects and helpers. These include objects for the underlying configuration, request message, model state, and others.

ApiController Processing Model

The processing model orchestrated by `ApiController` is made up of several different stages, and, like the lower-level message handler pipeline, provides many different points for extending the default data flow with custom logic.

In general, the controller pipeline enables an action method to be selected for processing a request, maps properties of the request to the parameters of the selected method, and allows for the execution of a variety of filter types. Request processing through `ApiController` looks similar to Figure 12-4.

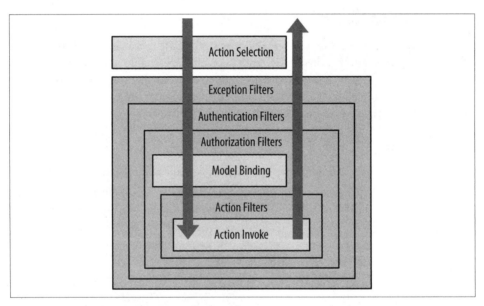

Figure 12-4. The controller pipeline

Similar to the message handler pipeline, the controller pipeline constructs a "Russian doll" structure wherein a request flows from an outermost scope through a series of nested scopes to the action method, which is the innermost scope. The action method generates a response, and that response flows back from the innermost scope to the outermost scope. Scopes in the controller pipeline are implemented via filters, and just as with the message handler pipeline, all components of the controller pipeline are implemented asynchronously via tasks. This is evident in pipeline interfaces such as `IActionFilter`:

```
public interface IActionFilter : IFilter
{
    Task<HttpResponseMessage> ExecuteActionFilterAsync(
        HttpActionContext actionContext,
        CancellationToken cancellationToken,
        Func<Task<HttpResponseMessage>> continuation);
    }
}
```

Filters will be described in more detail later in the chapter. First, we will explore the process for selecting the correct action method on the controller based on aspects of the request.

Action selection

One of the first steps taken inside of the `ApiController.ExecuteAsync` method is action selection. Action selection is the process of selecting a controller method based on the incoming `HttpRequestMessage`. As in the case of controller selection, action selection is delegated to a type whose primary responsibility is action selection. This type can be any class that implements the `IHttpActionSelector` interface. The signature for `IHttpActionSelector` looks as follows:

```
public interface IHttpActionSelector
{
    HttpActionDescriptor SelectAction(HttpControllerContext controllerContext);

    ILookup<string, HttpActionDescriptor> GetActionMapping(
        HttpControllerDescriptor controllerDescriptor);
}
```

As in the case of `IHttpControllerSelector`, the `IHttpActionSelector` technically has two responsibilities: selecting the action from the context and providing a list of action mappings. The latter responsibility enables the action selector to participate in ASP.NET Web API's API explorer feature.

We can easily supply a custom action selector by either explicitly replacing the default action selector (discussed next) or using a dependency resolver—generally in concert with an IoC container. For example, the following uses the Ninject IoC container to replace the default action selector with a custom selector, appropriately named `Custom ActionSelector`:

```
var kernel = new StandardKernel();
kernel.Bind<IHttpActionSelector>().To<CustomActionSelector>();

config.DependencyResolver = new NinjectResolver(kernel);
```

In order to decide whether it makes sense to supply a custom action selector, you must first understand the logic implemented by the default action selector. The default action selector provided by Web API is the `ApiControllerActionSelector`. Its implementation is effectively a series of filters that are expected to yield a single action from a list of candidate actions. The algorithm is implemented in `ApiControllerActionSelector`'s `FindMatchingActions` method and is illustrated in Figure 12-5.

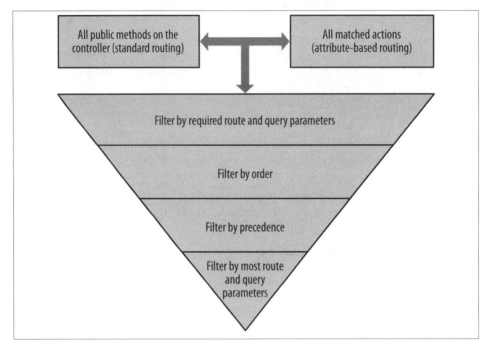

Figure 12-5. Default action selector logic

The initial and pivotal decision point in the default action selection algorithm is whether or not the matched routes are standard routes (i.e., those declared in global Web API configuration code via methods such as `MapHttpRoute`), or whether they are attribute-based routes created as a result of decorating an action with the `RouteAttribute` attribute.

```
public class ValuesController
{
    [ActionName("do")]
    public string ExecuteSomething() {
        ...
    }
}
```

If no action methods are found that match the value of the action route parameter, an HTTP 404 Not Found response is returned. Otherwise, the list of matched actions is then filtered once more to remove actions that are not allowed for the specific method associated with the incoming request and returned as the initial action candidate list.

If the route data does not have an explicit entry for the action method, then the initial action candidate selection logic tries to infer the action method name from the HTTP method name. For example, for a GET request, the selector will search for qualified action methods whose name begins with the string "Get".

If the request matches a route that has been declared via attribute-based routing, the initial candidate action list is provided by the route itself and then filtered to remove those candidate actions that are not appropriate for the HTTP method of the incoming request.

After establishing the initial list of candidate action methods, the default action selection logic executes a sequence of refinements to narrow down the list of candidate actions to exactly one. Those refinements are as follows:

- Filter out those methods that do not contain the set of parameters required for the matched route.
- Narrow the list of candidate actions to the actions with the lowest evaluation order. You can control the order of candidate actions for attribute-based routing using the RouteAttribute's Order property. By default, Order is set to zero, resulting in the entire set of candidate actions being returned from this refinement stage.
- Narrow the list of candidate actions to those with the highest precedence. Precedence is used for attribute-based routes and is determined algorithmically by the RoutePrecedence.Compute function based on the matched route.
- Group the remaining list of candidate actions by the number of parameters and then return the first candidate action from the group with the most parameters.

At this point, a single action method should be all that remains in the list of candidate actions. Hence, the default action selector performs a final check and takes one of the following three actions based on the number of candidate actions returned:

- If 0, return an HTTP 405 message if a candidate action exists but is not allowed for the HTTP method of the request; return an HTTP 404 message if there is no matching action.
- If 1, return the matching action descriptor so that it can be invoked.
- If > 1, throw an InvalidOperationException for an ambiguous match.

Filters

As depicted in Figure 12-4, filters provide a set of nested scopes that you can use to implement functionality that cuts across multiple controllers or actions. While conceptually similar, filters are broken down into four categories based on when they are run and what kind of data they have access to. The four categories are authentication filters, authorization filters, action filters, and exception filters. This factoring is illustrated in Figure 12-6.

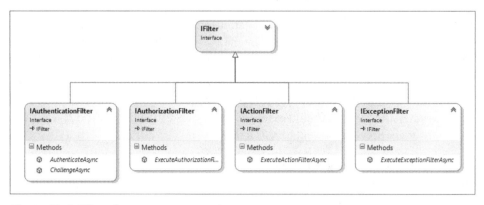

Figure 12-6. Filter classes

At a fundamental level, a filter in Web API is any class that implements the `IFilter` interface, which consists of a single method:

```
public interface IFilter
{
    bool AllowMultiple { get; }
}
```

In addition to providing the `IFilter` interface, Web API provides a base class that implements the interface and also derives from the .NET Framework's `Attribute` class. This enables all derived filters to be added in one of two ways. First, they can be added directly to the global configuration object's `Filters` collection as follows:

```
config.Filters.Add(new CustomActionFilter());
```

Alternately, filters that derive from `FilterAttribute` can be added as an attribute to either a Web API controller class or action method as follows:

```
[CustomActionFilter]
public class ValuesController : ApiController
{
    ...
}
```

Regardless of how filters are applied to a Web API project, they are stored in the `HttpConfiguration.Filters` collection, which stores them as a collection of `IFilter` objects. This generic design enables the `HttpConfiguration` object to contain many different types of filters, including filter types that go beyond the four current categories of authentication filter, authorization filter, action filter, and exception filter. Such new filter types can be created and added to `HttpConfiguration` without breaking the application or requiring changes to `HttpConfiguration`. They can then be later discovered and run by a new, custom controller class.

The ordering and execution of filters is orchestrated by `ApiController` based on the following criteria:

Filter type

> `ApiController` groups filters by type and executes each group as a different nested scope, as shown in Figure 12-4.

Where applied

> Filters added as a part of global configuration (`HttpConfiguration.Fil ters.Add(..)`) are added to the `Filters` collection before filters added as attributes (`ActionFilterAttribute`, `AuthorizationFilterAttribute`, `ExceptionFilterAt tribute`) at the class or action method level. Filters added via attribute to the controller class are added before filters added to action methods. When filters are run, they execute in the reverse order of how they were added. Therefore, filters added globally are run first, followed by filters added via attribute to the controller, followed by filters added to the action method.

Order added

> After filters have been grouped, they are executed within the group based on the order in which they were added.

Authentication filters

Authentication filters have two responsibilities. First, they examine a request as it flows through the pipeline and validate a set of claims to establish an identity for the calling user. In the event that the identity cannot be established from the provided claims, the authentication filter may also be used to modify the response to provide further instructions to the user agent for establishing a user's identity. This response is known as a challenge response. Authentication filters are discussed at greater length in Chapter 15.

Authorization filters

Authorization filters apply policy to enforce the level to which a user, client application, or other *principal* (in security terms) can access an HTTP resource or set of resources provided by Web API. The technical definition of an authorization filter is simply a class that implements the IAuthorizationFilter interface. This interface contains a single method for running the filter asynchronously:

```
Task<HttpResponseMessage> ExecuteAuthorizationFilterAsync(
    HttpActionContext actionContext,
    CancellationToken cancellationToken,
    Func<Task<HttpResponseMessage>> continuation);
```

While this interface is the only requirement for running authorization filters, it is not the most developer-friendly programming model—largely because of the complexities associated with asynchronous programming and the .NET Framework's task API. As a result, Web API provides the AuthorizationFilterAttribute class. This class implements the IAuthorizationFilter interface as well as the ExecuteAuthorizationFilterAsync method. It then provides the following virtual method, which can be overridden by derived classes:

```
public virtual void OnAuthorization(HttpActionContext actionContext);
```

The AuthorizationFilterAttribute calls OnAuthorization from its ExecuteAuthorizationFilterAsync method, which enables derived authorization filters to be written in a more familiar, synchronous style. After calling OnAuthorization, the base class then examines the state of the HttpActionContext object and decides whether to let request processing continue or whether to return a new Task with a new HttpResponseMessage indicating an authorization failure.

When you are authoring a custom authorization filter that is derived from AuthorizationFilterAttribute, the way to indicate an authorization failure is to set an HttpResponseMessage object instance on actionContext.Response, as follows:

```
public class CustomAuthFilter : AuthorizationFilterAttribute
{
    public override void OnAuthorization(HttpActionContext actionContext)
    {
        actionContext.Response = actionContext.Request.CreateErrorResponse(
            HttpStatusCode.Unauthorized, "denied");
    }
}
```

When the call to OnAuthorize is finished, the AuthorizationFilterAttribute class uses the following code to analyze the state of the context and either continue processing or return a response immediately:

```
if (actionContext.Response != null)
{
    return TaskHelpers.FromResult(actionContext.Response);
}
else
{
    return continuation();
}
```

Additionally, if an exception is thrown from within `OnAuthorize`, the `Authorization FilterAttribute` class will catch the exception and halt processing, returning an HTTP response with the `500 Internal Server Error` response code:

```
try
{
    OnAuthorization(actionContext);
}
catch (Exception e)
{
    return TaskHelpers.FromError<HttpResponseMessage>(e);
}
```

When you're designing and implementing a new authorization filter, a good starting point is the existing `AuthorizeAttribute` provided by Web API. This attribute uses `Thread.CurrentPrincipal` to get the identity (and optionally role membership information) for an authenticated user and then compares it to policy information provided in the attribute's constructor. Additionally, an interesting detail to note about the `Au thorizeAttribute` is that it checks for the presence of the `AllowAnonymousAttri bute` on both the action method and the containing controller, and exits successfully if the attribute is present.

Action filters

Action filters are conceptually very similar to authorization filters. In fact, the signature of the `IActionFilter` execute method looks identical to the corresponding method on `IAuthorizationFilter`:

```
Task<HttpResponseMessage> IActionFilter.ExecuteActionFilterAsync(
    HttpActionContext actionContext,
    CancellationToken cancellationToken,
    Func<Task<HttpResponseMessage>> continuation)
```

Action filters differ from authorization filters in a couple of respects, however. The first difference is when action filters will be called. As we discussed earlier, filters are grouped by type and different groups are executed at different times. Authorization filters are run first, followed by action filters, followed by exception filters.

The second, and more notable, difference between action filters and the other two filter types is that action filters give the developer the ability to process a request on both sides of the call to the action method. This capability is exposed by the following two methods on the `ActionFilterAttribute` class:

```
public virtual void OnActionExecuting(HttpActionContext actionContext);

public virtual void OnActionExecuted(
    HttpActionExecutedContext actionExecutedContext);
```

Just like in the case of the other filter types, `ActionFilterAttribute` implements the `IActionFilter` interface to abstract the complexities of working directly with the `Task` API as well as to derive from `Attribute`, thereby enabling action filters to be applied directly to controller classes and action methods.

As a developer, you can easily create action filters by simply deriving from `ActionFilterAttribute` and overriding either or both the `OnActionExecuting` and `OnActionExecuted` methods. For example, Example 12-3 performs some basic auditing of action methods.

Example 12-3. An example action filter that audits action methods

```
public class AuditActionFilter : ActionFilterAttribute
{
    public override void OnActionExecuting(HttpActionContext c)
    {
        Trace.TraceInformation("Calling action {0}::{1} with {2} arguments",
            c.ControllerContext.ControllerDescriptor.ControllerName,
            c.ActionDescriptor.ActionName,
            c.ActionArguments.Count);
    }

    public override void OnActionExecuted(HttpActionExecutedContext c)
    {
        object returnVal = null;
        var oc = c.Response.Content as ObjectContent;
        if (oc != null)
            returnVal = oc.Value;

        Trace.TraceInformation("Ran action {0}::{1} with result {2}",
            c.ActionContext.ControllerContext.ControllerDescriptor.ControllerName,
            c.ActionContext.ActionDescriptor.ActionName,
            returnVal ?? string.Empty);
    }
}
```

If an exception is thrown from within an action filter, a `Task<HttpResponseMessage>` containing the error is created and returned, thereby halting request processing by other components in the pipeline. This is consistent with the logic discussed for authorization filters. Because action filters enable processing both before and after the action method, `ActionFilterAttribute` contains additional logic to nullify the context of the response message if an exception is thrown in the `OnActionExecuted` side of the filter. It accomplishes this by simply wrapping the call to `OnActionExecuted` in a `try..catch` block and setting the response to `null` in the `catch` block:

```
try
{
    OnActionExecuted(executedContext);
    ...
```

```
   }
   catch
   {
      actionContext.Response = null;
      throw;
   }
```

Exception filters

Exception filters exist for the purpose of, as their name suggests, enabling the custom handling of exceptions that are thrown during the controller pipeline. As in the case of authorization and action filters, you define exception filters by implementing the IEx ceptionFilter interface. Additionally, the framework provides the base class, Excep tionFilterAttribute, which provides .NET Framework attribute capabilities and a more simplified programming model to classes that derive from it.

Exception filters can be extremely helpful in preventing the flow of potentially sensitive information outside of your service. As an example, database exceptions typically contain details identifying your database server or schema design. This kind of information could be used by an attacker to launch attacks against your database. The following is an example of an exception filter that logs exception details to the .NET Framework's diagnostics system and then returns a generic error response:

```
public class CustomExceptionFilter : ExceptionFilterAttribute
{
   public override void OnException(
      HttpActionExecutedContext actionExecutedContext)
   {
      var x = actionExecutedContext.Exception;

      Trace.TraceError(x.ToString());

      var errorResponse = actionExecutedContext.Request.CreateErrorResponse(
         HttpStatusCode.InternalServerError,
         "Please contact your server administrator for more details.");

      actionExecutedContext.Response = errorResponse;
   }
}
```

When you apply this filter (globally, or at the controller or action level), action methods such as the following:

```
[CustomExceptionFilter]
public IEnumerable<string> Get()
{
   ...
   throw new Exception("Here are all of my users credit card numbers...");
}
```

will return a sanitized error message to the client:

```
$ curl http://localhost:54841/api/values
{"Message":"Please contact your server administrator for more details."}
```

But what happens if your exception filter throws an exception? More broadly, what if you don't have an exception filter? Where are unhandled exceptions ultimately caught? The answer is the HttpControllerDispatcher. If you remember from earlier in the chapter, the HttpControllerDispatcher is by default the last component in the message handler pipeline, and it is responsible for calling the ExcecuteAsync method on a Web API controller. In addition, it wraps this call in a try..catch block, as shown here:

```
protected override async Task<HttpResponseMessage> SendAsync(
    HttpRequestMessage request, CancellationToken cancellationToken)
{
    try
    {
        return await SendAsyncCore(request, cancellationToken);
    }
    catch (HttpResponseException httpResponseException)
    {
        return httpResponseException.Response;
    }
    catch (Exception exception)
    {
        return request.CreateErrorResponse(HttpStatusCode.InternalServerError,
            exception);
    }
}
```

As you can see, the dispatcher is capable of returning the HttpResponseMessage object attached to an HttpResponseException. Additionally, in the case where an unhandled exception is caught, the dispatcher contains a generic exception handler that turns the exception into an HttpResponseMessage containing details of the exception along with an HTTP 500 Internal Server Error response code.

Model binding and validation

Chapter 13 will focus on model binding, so we will not spend a significant amount of time describing it here. However, the key point from the perspective of the controller pipeline is that model binding occurs just before the action filters are processed, as shown by the following fragment from the ApiController class source code:

```
private async Task<HttpResponseMessage> ExecuteAction(
    HttpActionBinding actionBinding, HttpActionContext actionContext,
    CancellationToken cancellationToken, IEnumerable<IActionFilter> actionFilters,
    ServicesContainer controllerServices)
{

    ...

    await actionBinding.ExecuteBindingAsync(actionContext, cancellationToken);
```

```
    _modelState = actionContext.ModelState;

    ...
}
```

The order is important here, as it means that the model state is available to action filters, making it trivial to, for example, build an action filter that automatically returns an HTTP 400 Bad Request response in the event of an invalid model. This enables us to stop inserting code like the following into every PUT and POST action method:

```
public void Post(ModelValue v)
{
    if (!ModelState.IsValid)
    {
        var e = Request.CreateErrorResponse(HttpStatusCode.BadRequest, ModelState);
        throw new HttpResponseException(e);
    }
}
```

Instead, this model state check can be pulled into a simple action filter, as shown in Example 12-4.

Example 12-4. Model state validation filter

```
public class VerifyModelState : ActionFilterAttribute
{
    public override void OnActionExecuting(HttpActionContext actionContext)
    {
        if (!actionContext.ModelState.IsValid)
        {
            var e = actionContext.Request.CreateErrorResponse(
                HttpStatusCode.BadRequest, actionContext.ModelState);
            actionContext.Response = e;
        }
    }
}
```

Action invocation

The final step in the controller pipeline is to invoke the selected action method on the controller. This responsibility falls to a specialized Web API component called the *action invoker*. An action invoker is any class that implements the IHttpActionInvoker interface. This interface has the following signature:

```
public interface IHttpActionInvoker
{
    Task<HttpResponseMessage> InvokeActionAsync(
        HttpActionContext actionContext, CancellationToken cancellationToken);
}
```

ApiController requests the action invoker from DefaultServices, which means that you can replace it using either the Replace method on DefaultServices or using

DependencyResolver in conjunction with a dependency injection framework. However, the default implementation supplied by the framework, ApiControllerActionInvok er, should be sufficient for most requirements.

The default invoker performs two primary functions, as illustrated here:

```
object actionResult = await actionDescriptor.ExecuteAsync(controllerContext,
    actionContext.ActionArguments,
    cancellationToken);

return actionDescriptor.ResultConverter.Convert(controllerContext, actionResult);
```

The first responsibility is, as you would expect, to invoke the selected action method. The second responsibility is to convert the result of the action method call into an HttpResponseMessage. For this task, the invoker uses a specialized object called an *action result converter*. An action result converter implements the IActionResult Converter interface, which contains a single method accepting some context and returning an HttpResponseMessage. Currently, Web API contains three action result converters:

ResponseMessageResultConverter
> Used when an action method returns an HttpResponseMessage directly; passes the responses message through.

ValueResultConverter<T>
> Used when an action method returns a standard .NET Framework type; creates an HttpResponseMessage using the associated HttpRequestMethod's CreateRes ponse<T> method.

VoidResultConverter
> Used when an action method has a void return value; creates a new HttpResponse Message with a status of 204 No Content.

Once the return value has been converted to an HttpResponseMessage, that message can begin the flow back out of the controller and message handler pipelines, and then over the wire to the client.

Conclusion

In this chapter, we explored in depth the two pipelines that handle request processing in ASP.NET Web API: the low-level message handler pipeline and the controller pipeline. Each has associated benefits as well as trade-offs. For example, the message handler pipeline is executed early in the handling of requests, so it can be advantageous to leverage when your component could prevent the needless execution of more expensive code paths. However, this comes at the cost of having to work at the level of HttpRe questMessage and HttpResponseMessage. The controller pipeline, on the other hand, provides its components access to the higher-level programming model objects, such as those that describe the controller, action methods, and associated attributes. Both of these pipelines provide a complete set of default components as well as a flexible model for extensibility using either `HttpConfiguration` or a custom `DependencyResolver`.

In the next chapter, we will take a much deeper look at the core building blocks that make up the message handler pipeline, including the message handlers themselves as well as the HTTP primitives, `HttpRequestMessage` and `HttpResponseMessage`.

Formatters and Model Binding

Anyone can write code that a computer can understand. Only good programmers write
code that humans can understand.

We previously discussed media types and their semantics as a way to represent concepts in the domain space of a system. Once we move to the implementation side, those abstractions must be translated somehow to a language that programmers speak. In the case of ASP.NET Web API, that final representation would be objects—or models, to give them a more precise name. Having said that, models represent a level of abstraction that developers use to map objects into media type representations or other different parts in an HTTP message.

The *model binding* infrastructure in ASP.NET Web API provides the necessary runtime services to perform many of these mappings for us. In that way, a developer can focus on the implementation details of Web API and leave all serialization concerns to the framework. There is an evident advantage in using this kind of architecture. The developer can work with a single level of abstraction, which is the model, and support a variety of media types according to the requirements of the different Web API consumers. For example, in our Issue Tracker application, we have a single model class representing an issue, which can optionally be converted to different media types like JSON or XML by the framework.

As part of this chapter, we will explore *model binding* in detail by looking at the different runtime components and extensibility hooks provided by the framework to customize or add new model binding functionality.

The Importance of Models in ASP.NET Web API

As a rule of thumb, controller actions that focus on single concerns are easier to test, extend, and maintain in the long run. Converting message representations into model objects is one of those concerns that you should try to move away from your action implementations in the first place. Consider Example 13-1, in which serialization concerns are mixed with the implementation of a Web API action.

Example 13-1. Action with serialization concerns

```
public HttpResponseMessage Post(HttpRequestMessage request) // <1>
{
  int id = int.Parse(request.RequestUri.ParseQueryString().Get("id")); // <2>

  var values = request.Content.ReadAsFormDataAsync().Result // <3>

  var issue = new Issue
  {
    Id = id,
    Name = values["name"],
    Description = values["description"]
  };

  // do something with the constructed issue
}
```

There are a few evident problems with this code:

- The generic signature in the controller method makes it really hard to infer its purpose without looking at the implementation details. It also limits our ability to overload the Post method with different arguments for supporting multiple scenarios.

- It is not checking whether the parameter in the query string really exists or can be converted to an integer.

- It is tying the implementation to a single media type (application/form-url-encoded) and also blocking the execution thread for reading the body content synchronously. To this last point, invoking the Result property directly on asynchronous tasks without checking if they are completed is not considered good practice and might prevent the execution thread from returning to the thread pool to attend to new requests.

We can easily rewrite this action to use a model class only and avoid all these issues, as illustrated in Example 13-2.

Example 13-2. Action with model binding

```
public void Post(Issue issue) // <1>
{
  // do something with the constructed issue
}
```

As you can see, all the serialization concerns literally disappeared from the implementation, leaving only what it matters most. The model binding infrastructure in the framework will take care of the rest at the moment of executing the action.

How Model Binding Works

At a very core level in the model binding infrastructure is a component called `HttpParameterBinding`, which knows how to infer the value of a parameter from a request message and is demonstrated in Example 13-3. Every `HttpParameterBinding` instance is tied to a single parameter, which is defined at the moment of the Web API with the `HttpConfiguration` object. How that instance is tied to a parameter is determined by another configuration class called `HttpParameterDescriptor`, which contains metadata for describing a parameter in terms of name, type, or any other attribute that could be used by the model binding infrastructure to select an `HttpParameterBinding`.

Example 13-3. Action with model binding

```
public abstract class HttpParameterBinding
{
  protected HttpParameterBinding(HttpParameterDescriptor descriptor);

  public abstract Task ExecuteBindingAsync(ModelMetadataProvider metadataProvider,
  HttpActionContext actionContext, CancellationToken cancellationToken); // <1>
}
```

Example 13-3 shows the basic structure of an `HttpParameterBinding` with the key method `ExecuteBindingAsync`, which every implementation must provide to perform the binding for a parameter.

As happens with many of the runtime components in ASP.NET Web API, an `HttpParameterBinding` also offers an asynchronous signature for its core method, `ExecuteBindingAsync`. This would be useful if you had, for example, an implementation that does not necessarily rely on values obtained from the current request message and performs some I/O operations such as querying a database or reading a file. Example 13-4 shows a basic implementation of an `HttpParameterBinding` for binding action parameters of the type `CultureInfo` from the culture set in the executing thread.

Example 13-4. HttpParameterBinding implementation

```
public class CultureParameterBinding : HttpParameterBinding
{
  public CultureParameterBinding(HttpParameterDescriptor descriptor) // <1>
    : base(descriptor)
  {
  }

  public override System.Threading.Tasks.Task
```

```
ExecuteBindingAsync(System.Web.Http.Metadata.ModelMetadataProvider
metadataProvider, HttpActionContext   actionContext,
System.Threading.CancellationToken cancellationToken)
{
  CultureInfo culture = Thread.CurrentThread.CurrentCulture; // <2>
  SetValue(actionContext, culture); // <3>

  var tsc = new TaskCompletionSource<object>(); // <4>
  tsc.SetResult(null);
  return tsc.Task;
}
}
```

An instance of our `HttpParameterBinding` is created with a descriptor. Our implementation just ignores that parameter, but other implementations might use some of
its information *<1>*. The `ExecuteBindingAsync` method gets the `CultureInfo` instance
from the current thread *<2>* and uses it to set the binding with the help of the `SetVal`
`ue` method in the base class *<3>*. As the last step in this method, a `TaskCompletion`
`Source` is created for returning a new task, already completed synchronously *<4>*. In an
asynchronous version of this method, `SetValue` would probably be called as part of the
returned task.

This `CultureParameterBinding` can now be used to inject a `CultureInfo` instance directly as a parameter of an action method, as shown in Example 13-5.

Example 13-5. A Web API action that receives a CultureInfo instance as a parameter

```
public class HomeController : ApiController
{
  [HttpGet]
  public HttpResponseMessage BindCulture(CultureInfo culture)
  {
    return Request.CreateResponse(System.Net.HttpStatusCode.Accepted,
        String.Format("BindCulture with name {0}.", culture.Name));
  }
```

Now you know what an `HttpParameterBinding` is, but we haven't discussed yet how it
is configured and selected by the framework when an action is executed. This selection
is made in one of the many pluggable services available in the
`System.Web.Http.ModelBinding.IActionValueBinder` framework, whose default implementation is `System.Web.Http.ModelBinding.DefaultActionValueBinder`. An
`IActionValueBinder` is reponsible for returning an `HttpActionBinding` instance,
which mainly contains a collection of `HttpParameterBinding` instances associated with
a given controller action that can be cached across requests:

```
public interface IActionValueBinder
{
  HttpActionBinding GetBinding(HttpActionDescriptor actionDescriptor);
}
```

The built-in implementation in `DefaultActionValueBinder` uses reflection to build a list of `HttpParameterDescriptors`, which is later used for querying the configuration and selecting the appropriate `HttpParameterBinding` instances (see Figure 13-1).

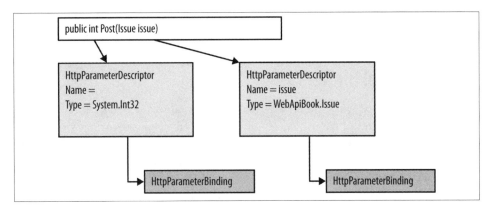

Figure 13-1. The HttpParameterBinding selection

This class currently supports two different ways to determine which `HttpParameter Binding` instances are associated with an action. In the first one, the association is done through configuration with the property `ParameterBindingRules` in the `HttpConfigu ration` object, which exposes a set of rules for choosing an binding instance for a given `HttpParameterDescriptor`. Those rules take the shape of a delegate, `Func<HttpPara meterDescriptor, HttpParameterBinding>`, that receives a descriptor as a parameter and returns a binding instance. That means you can either provide a method callback or a lambda expression to resolve the bindings. For our scenario with the `CulturePar ameterBinding`, we need a rule that returns our binding for an `HttpParameterDescrip tor` associated with the type `System.Globalization.CultureInfo`, as shown in Example 13-6.

Example 13-6. HttpParameterBinding configuration with a rule

```
config.ParameterBindingRules.Insert(0, (descriptor) => // <1>
{
    if (descriptor.ParameterType == typeof(System.Globalization.CultureInfo)) // <2>
      return new CultureParameterBinding(descriptor);

    return null;
});
```

The new rule is inserted with a lambda expression *<1>* that checks for the `Parameter Type` property in the descriptor and returns the binding only when the type is equal to `System.Globalization.CultureInfo` *<2>*.

A second mechanism, which is more declarative, involves the use of an attribute, `Pa rameterBindingAttribute`, that we need to derive (as we will explore in the next section).

If no mapping rule or `ParameterBindingAttribute` is found, this binder uses a default policy, which binds simple types to URI segments or query string variables and complex types to the request body.

Built-In Model Binders

The framework ships with several built-in implementations, but only three of them deserve special attention from a developer: `ModelBindingParameterBinder`, `Format terParameterBinder`, and `HttpRequestParameterBinding`, which implement completely different ways of binding a message part to a model. The first one, `ModelBin dingParameterBinder`, uses an approach borrowed from ASP.NET MVC in which the model is composed of different parts in the message, as if they are Lego building blocks. The second one, `FormatterParameterBinder`, relies on formatters that understand all the semantics and formatting of a given media type and know how to serialize or deserialize a model applying those semantics. Formatters represent a key part of content negotiation and are the preferred method for binding a message body to a model. Finally, the third one, `HttpRequestParameterBinding`, is used for supporting scenarios with generic actions that use `HttpRequestMessage` or `HttpResponseMessage` instances directly as part of the method signature.

The ModelBindingParameterBinder Implementation

The `ModelBindingParameterBinder` implementation reuses the same idea applied in ASP.NET MVC for doing model binding. It relies on value providers, which know how to obtain data from different parts of an HTTP message, and model binders for assembling those parts into a model.

This implementation is mainly focused on binding simple key/value pairs such as those found in HTTP headers, URL segments, query strings, or a body encoded with `appli cation/form-url-encoded` (the media type used for encoding an HTTP form). All these values are usually strings that can be found in the message and converted to primitive types. Modeling binders do not know anything specific about media types or how they can be interpreted; that's the job of the *formatters*, which we will discuss in detail in the next section.

The framework ships with several built-in model binder implementations that assemble different small pieces found in an HTTP message into fairly complex models. To be more precise, those implementations also take care of converting strings into simple data types such as `Timespan`, `Int`, `Guid`, `Decimal`, or other types decorated with a type converter before *hydrating* the model. Two examples of these built-in implementations are `Array ModelBinder` and `TypeConverterModelBinder`, both in the `System.Web.Http.Model Binding.Binders` namespace. It's worth mentioning that model binders are mostly used for rehydrating simple types, or as building blocks for composing more complex types. These built-in implementations typically cover the most common scenarios, so you will have to think twice before you start writing a new model binder from scratch.

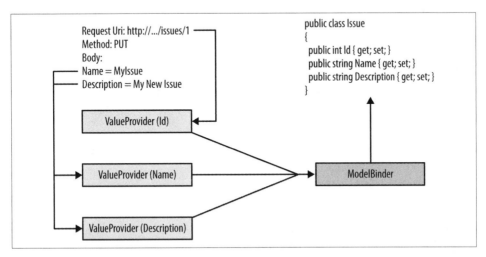

Figure 13-2. Model binding in action

In Figure 13-2, the configured value providers first take care of decomposing the message into pieces for getting different values such as the issue ID from the query string and the rest of the fields from the message body, which were submitted as a HTTP PUT with the URL form encoding media type. The selected model binder works closely with the value providers to request the data needed for initializing a new `Issue` class instance.

Value Providers

Value providers provide a thin abstraction layer for decoupling model binders from any messaging details. They do this by aggregating values from different parts of an HTTP message, and providing an uniform interface to consume them.

At a very core level, every value provider implements the `System.Web.Http.ValuePro viders.IValueProvider` interface, as shown in Example 13-7.

Example 13-7. IValueProvider interface definition

```
public interface IValueProvider
{
  bool ContainsPrefix(string prefix); // <1>
```

```
    ValueProviderResult GetValue(string key); // <2>
}
```

The first method, ContainsPrefix *<1>*, returns a Boolean value indicating whether the value provider implementation can provide a value for a key with the *prefix* passed as an argument, which typically represents a property name in the model being deserialized.

The second method, and probably the most important, GetValue *<2>*, searches the key passed as an argument in the HTTP message and returns the associated value. The value is not returned as a raw string directly but as a ValueProviderResult instance, which contains methods for getting the raw value or a value cast to an specific type.

You might want to create a new value provider or derive from an existing one for addressing new use cases such as searching values in the request message under specific name conventions or in other places such as custom cookies.

Example 13-8 shows a basic implementation of a value provider for searching headers with a vendor prefix X-.

Example 13-8. IValueProvider implementation

```
public class HeaderValueProvider : IValueProvider
{
  public const string HeaderPrefix = "X-";

  private HttpControllerContext context;

  public HeaderValueProvider(HttpControllerContext context) // <1>
  {
    this.context = context;
  }

  public bool ContainsPrefix(string prefix)
  {
    var contains = context.Request
      .Headers
      .Any(h => h.Key.Contains(HeaderPrefix + prefix)); // <2>

    return contains;
  }

  public ValueProviderResult GetValue(string key)
  {
    if (!context.Request.Headers.Any(h => h.Key == HeaderPrefix + key))
      return null;

    var value = context.Request
      .Headers
      .GetValues(HeaderPrefix + key).First(); // <3>
```

```
    var stringValue = (value is string) ? (string)value : value.ToString(); // <4>

    return new ValueProviderResult(value, stringValue,
        CultureInfo.CurrentCulture); // <5>
  }
}
```

The HeaderValueProvider implementation is constructed with an HttpController
Context instance that provides access to the execution context and also the request
message *<1>*. The ContainsPrefix method returns true for any key in the HTTP request headers starting with an X- prefix *<2>*, and the GetValue method gets its value
<3>. That value is returned in a new ValueProviderResult instance *<5>* and also as a
raw string *<4>*.

A IValueProvider implementation can be injected at runtime through a ValueProvi
derFactory, which is a class that derives from the abstract class System.Web.Http.Val
ueProviders.ValueProviderFactory and overrides the method GetValueProvider
for returning instances of the IValueProvider implementation. You can find the corresponding value provider factory implementation for HeaderValueProvider in
Example 13-9.

Example 13-9. ValueProviderFactory implementation
```
public class HeaderValueProviderFactory : ValueProviderFactory
{
  public override IValueProvider GetValueProvider(HttpActionContext actionContext)
  {
    return new HeaderValueProvider(actionContext.ControllerContext); // <1>
  }
}
```

The HeaderValueProviderFactory implementation instantiates a new HeaderValue
Provider using the current HttpActionContext as an argument in the constructor
<1>. We can register this factory in the HttpConfiguration object using the global
dependency resolver, as shown in Example 13-10.

*Example 13-10. The HeaderValueProviderFactory injected in the configuration for a
web host*
```
public static void RegisterValueProvider(HttpConfiguration config)
{
  var valueProviderFactories = config.ServiceResolver
    .GetValueProviderFactories().ToList();

  valueProviderFactories.Insert(0, new HeaderValueProviderFactory()); // <1>

  config.ServiceResolver.SetServices(typeof(System.Web.Http.ValueProviders
    .ValueProviderFactory),
```

```
                valueProviderFactories.ToArray()); // <2>
}
```

The factory is added to the existing list of factories in the first position *<1>*, so it takes precedence when a value needs to be provided, and is injected afterward as a service with the dependency resolver *<2>*.

The most important value providers shipped with the framework are `Sys tem.Web.Http.ValueProviders.Providers.QueryStringValueProvider` and `Sys tem.Web.Http.ValueProviders.Providers.RouteDataValueProvider`, and their corresponding factories, `System.Web.Http.ValueProviders.Providers.QueryStringVa lueProviderFactory` and `System.Web.Http.ValueProviders.Providers.RouteData ValueProvider`. While the first provider parses and provides values found in the query string, the second is responsible for obtaining values from the route parameters (i.e., the parameters that you define at the route level in the route configuration).

Model Binders

Model binders orchestrate all the actions for assembling a new model instance from the different data pieces requested to the configured value providers. A model binder implements the interface `System.Web.Http.ModelBinding.IModelBinder`, which contains only one method, `BindModel`, where all the magic happens (see Example 13-11).

Example 13-11. IModelBinder interface

```
public interface IModelBinder
{
  bool BindModel(HttpActionContext actionContext, ModelBindingContext
  bindingContext); // <1>
}
```

The `BindModel` method receives two objects *<1>*, an `HttpActionContext` instance with specific information about the current execution, and an instance of `ModelBindingCon tent` representing the context of the model binding process. This method also returns a Boolean value indicating whether the implementation could successfully assemble a new model instance. There are two important properties available as part of the binding context, `ModelState` and `ModelMetadata`. The former is a property bag class used by the model binder for storing the results of the binding model process or any error that might happen in that process. The latter provides access to the discovered metadata associated to the model, such as available properties or any component model attribute for performing data validations. Although this interface looks very simple at first glance, it hides a good deal of the complexity required for implementing a model binder and providing the right behavior at runtime. For that reason, the following sequence describes in detail all the steps performed by an `IModelBinder` implementation.

1. The implementation tries to get all the values it needs to assemble a new model from the value provider passed as part of the binding context. Although the binding context provides access to a single value provider, that instance usually represents a built-in value provider, `CompositeValueProvider`, which implements the IVa lueProvider interface but internally delegates the method calls to all the configured value providers.

2. A model is created and initialized with all the values obtained from the value provider. If some error happens during the model initialization, the exceptions are set on the binding context through the `ModelState` property.

3. The model is set on the binding context.

Example 13-12 shows a model binder implementation to create instances of the `Issue` model class previously discussed in this chapter.

Example 13-12. IssueModelBinder implementation

```
public class IssueModelBinder : IModelBinder
{
  public bool BindModel(HttpActionContext actionContext, ModelBindingContext
  bindingContext)
  {
    var model = (Issue)bindingContext.Model ?? new Issue();

    var hasPrefix = bindingContext.ValueProvider
      .ContainsPrefix(bindingContext.ModelName);

    var searchPrefix = (hasPrefix) ? bindingContext.ModelName + "." : "";

    int id = 0;
    if(int.TryParse(GetValue(bindingContext, searchPrefix, "Id"), out id)
    {
      model.Id = id; // <1>
    }

    model.Name = GetValue(bindingContext, searchPrefix, "Name"); // <2>
    model.Description = GetValue(bindingContext, searchPrefix, "Description"); // <3>

    bindingContext.Model = model;

    return true;
  }

  private string GetValue(ModelBindingContext context, string prefix, string key)
  {
    var result = context.ValueProvider.GetValue(prefix + key); // <4>
    return result == null ? null : result.AttemptedValue;
  }
}
```

This implementation uses the value provider available as part of the binding context *<1>* for requesting data, and binds those values to the model's properties afterward in *<2>*, *<3>*, and *<4>*. This is not something you would likely do in a real application, but it provides a simple demonstration of how an IModelBinder implementation might look.

A model binder implementation is finally configured and injected at runtime through a model binder provider, which works as a factory. A model binder provider derives from the base class System.Web.Http.ModelBinding.ModelBinderProvider and implements the method GetBinder for returning a new model binder instance, as shown in Example 13-13.

Example 13-13. A ModelBinderImplementation for returning IssueModelBinder instances

```
public class IssueModelBinderProvider : ModelBinderProvider
{
  public override IModelBinder GetBinder(HttpActionContext actionContext,
  ModelBindingContext bindingContext)
  {
    return new IssueModelBinder();
  }
}
```

You can register this provider by using the dependency resolver available as part of the HttpConfiguration object, or by decorating the model class with a Sys tem.Web.Http.ModelBinding.ModelBinderAttribute, as shown in Examples 13-14 and 13-15.

Example 13-14. A model class decorated with ModelBinderAttribute

```
[ModelBinder(typeof(IssueModelBinderProvider))]
public class Issue
{
  public int Id { get; set; }
  public string Name { get; set; }
  public string Description { get; set; }
}
```

Example 13-15. A parameter decorated with ModelBinderAttribute

```
public void Post([ModelBinder(typeof(IssueModelBinderProvider))]Issue issue)
{
}
```

An interesting fact about the ModelBinderAttribute is that it derives from the previously discussed attribute ParameterBindingAttribute. This attribute was used to declaratively attach an HttpParameterBinding instance to a parameter. In this case, the ModelBinderAttribute initializes a new instance of ModelBindingParameterBinder that internally uses the ModelBinderProvider passed as an argument (IssueModelBin derProvider, in our examples).

Model Binding Against URIs Only

The framework ships with another attribute, FromUriAttribute, that derives from the ModelBinderAttribute to force the runtime to perform the binding only against data available in the URL. This is useful for binding values found in the URL to properties in a model class, as the framework will bind values in the URL only against simple types by default.

Example 13-16 illustrates how the query string variables Lang and Filter are automatically mapped to the properties with the same name on the IssueFilters model.

Example 13-16. Model binding with query string variables

```
// Sample url: http://../Issues?Lang=en&Filter=2345

public class IssueFilters
{
  public string Lang { get; set; }
  public string Filter { get; set; }
}

public IEnumerable<Issue> Get([FromUri]IssueFilters)
{
  // Action implementation
}
```

The FormatterParameterBinder Implementation

This implementation relies on formatters, which were introduced in ASP.NET Web API for supporting better content-negotiation scenarios with the use of media types. In ASP.NET MVC, only the HTML (text/html) and JSON (application/json) media types were treated as first-class citizens and fully supported across the entire stack. Also, there was not a consistent model for supporting content negotiation. You could support different media types for the response messages by providing custom ActionResult implementations, but it was not clear how a new media type could be introduced and handled by the framework. Developers typically solved this by leveraging the model binding infrastructure with new model binders or value providers.

Fortunately, this inconsistency has been solved in ASP.NET Web API with the introduction of formatters. A formatter now unifies all the serialization concerns by providing a single entry point for serializing or deserializing a model using the format expressed by a media type. The formatters to use for a given message will be determined by the content negotiation algorithm.

Every formatter derives from the base class `MediaTypeFormatter` (see Example 13-17) and overrides the methods `CanReadType` and `ReadFromStreamAsync` for supporting deserialization, and `CanWriteType` and `WriteToStreamAsync` for supporting serialization of models following the semantics and format of a media type.

Example 13-17. MediaTypeFormatter class definition

```
public abstract class MediaTypeFormatter
{
  public Collection<Encoding> SupportedEncodings { get; }

  public Collection<MediaTypeHeaderValue> SupportedMediaTypes { get; }

  public Collection<MediaTypeMapping> MediaTypeMappings { get; }

  public abstract bool CanReadType(Type type);

  public abstract bool CanWriteType(Type type);

  public virtual Task<object> ReadFromStreamAsync(Type type, Stream readStream,
    HttpContent content, IFormatterLogger formatterLogger);

  public virtual Task WriteToStreamAsync(Type type, object value,
    Stream writeStream, HttpContent content, TransportContext transportContext);
}
```

The following list summarizes the principal characteristics of the `MediaTypeFormat` ter class:

- The `CanReadType` and `CanWriteType` methods receive a type as an argument, and must return a value indicating whether they can read or write an object of that type into an stream representing the message body. This means a formatter might know how to write a type but not how to read it from an stream, for example.

- The `SupportedMediaTypes` collection specifies the list of supported media types (e.g., `text/html`). This list is typically initialized in the formatter constructor method. The runtime will determine which formatter to use during the content negotiation handshake based on the value returned by the `CanReadType` or `CanWrite` `Type` methods and the supported media types. It's worth mentioning that a request message can mix different media types sometimes when the `Content-Type` header is set to multipart, so every part defines its media type. The runtime can handle this scenario as well by selecting one or more formatters for all the present media types.

- A `MediaTypeFormatter` adheres to the Task Parallel Library (TPL) programming model for the read and write operations. Most implementations will still run synchronously, as they involve only serialization.

- The `MediaTypeMappings` collection allows a formatter to define how to look for the media type associated with a request message. (e.g., query string, HTTP header).

For example, a client application might send the expected media type format for the response as part of the query string.

The framework includes a set of formatters out of the box for handling the most common media types such as form-encoded data (`FormUrlEncodedMediaTypeFormatter`), JSON (`JsonMediaTypeFormatter`), or XML (`XmlMediaTypeFormatter`). For other media types, you will have to write your own implementation, or use one of the many implementations provided by the open source community.

JsonMediaTypeFormatter and XmlMediaTypeFormatter

It is worth mentioning that the `JsonMediaTypeFormatter` implementation currently uses the Json.NET library internally to serialize/deserialize JSON payloads, and the `XmlMediaTypeFormatter` implementation uses either the `DataContractSerializer` or the `XmlSerializer` classes included in the .NET Framework. This class provides a Boolean property `UseXmlSerializer` to use the `XmlSerializer` class or not, which is set to `false` by default. You can extend these classes to use your libraries of preference for serializing XML or JSON.

Now we'll discuss the implementation of a `MediaTypeFormatter` for serializing a model as part of a RSS or ATOM feed (see Example 13-18).

Example 13-18. MediaTypeFormatter implementation

```
public class SyndicationMediaTypeFormatter : MediaTypeFormatter
{
  public const string Atom = "application/atom+xml";
  public const string Rss = "application/rss+xml";

  public SyndicationMediaTypeFormatter()
    : base()
  {
    this.SupportedMediaTypes.Add(new MediaTypeHeaderValue(Atom)); // <1>
    this.SupportedMediaTypes.Add(new MediaTypeHeaderValue(Rss));
  }

  public override bool CanReadType(Type type)
  {
    return false;
  }

  public override bool CanWriteType(Type type)
  {
    return true; // <2>
  }

  public override Task WriteToStreamAsync(Type type, object value, Stream
```

```
  writeStream, HttpContent content, TransportContext transportContext) // <3>
  {
    var tsc = new TaskCompletionSource<AsyncVoid>(); // <4>
    tsc.SetResult(default(AsyncVoid));

    var items = new List<SyndicationItem>();

    if (value is IEnumerable)
    {
      foreach (var model in (IEnumerable)value)
      {
        var item = MapToItem(model);
        items.Add(item);
      }
    }
    else
    {
      var item = MapToItem(value);
      items.Add(item);
    }

    var feed = new SyndicationFeed(items);

    SyndicationFeedFormatter formatter = null;
    if (content.Headers.ContentType.MediaType == Atom)
    {
      formatter = new Atom10FeedFormatter(feed);
    }
    else if (content.Headers.ContentType.MediaType == Rss)
    {
      formatter = new Rss20FeedFormatter(feed);
    }
    else
    {
      throw new Exception("Not supported media type");
    }

    using (var writer = XmlWriter.Create(writeStream))
    {
      formatter.WriteTo(writer);

      writer.Flush();
      writer.Close();
    }

    return tsc.Task; // <5>
  }

  protected SyndicationItem MapToItem(object model) // <6>
  {
    var item = new SyndicationItem();
```

```
    item.ElementExtensions.Add(model);

    return item;
  }

  private struct AsyncVoid
  {
  }
}
```

This implementation knows only how to serialize models according to the Atom and RSS media type definitions, so that is explicitly specified as part of the constructor <1>. It also returns true in the CanWrite method to specify that the implementation is write only <2>.

The WriteToStreamAsync method implementation <3> mainly relies on the syndication classes included with the WCF Web Programming model for serializing the models into Atom or RSS feeds. This programming model provides classes for constructing a syndication feed and all the associated entries, as well as the formatter classes for transforming those into a well-known syndication format such as Atom or RSS.

As we stated, the WriteToStreamAsync and ReadFromStreamAsync methods leverage the new Task Parallel Library for doing the asynchronous work. They both return a Task instance that internally wraps the asynchronous work. However, most of the time, serialization is a safe operation that can be done synchronously. In fact, many of the serializer classes you will find in the .NET Framework do their job synchronously. Creating a new task using the method Task.Factory.StartNew for all the serialization work would be the easiest thing to do, but there are some collateral effects associated with that action. After we invoke the StartNew method, a new job is scheduled, which might generate a thread context switch that hurts performance. The trick in this scenario is to use a TaskCompletionSource <4>. The TaskCompletionSource is marked as complete so all the work is done synchronously afterward, and the resulting task associated with the TaskCompletionSource is returned <5> The method MapToItem <6> simply uses the model instance as the content for a syndication item.

Synchronous Formatters

Most formatters are synchronous and use a TaskCompletionSource instance to return a completed task. However, if you want to make your implementation simpler, there is a base class, BufferedMediaTypeFormatter, that does all this for you internally. This base class provides two methods that you can override in an implementation, SaveTo Stream and ReadFromStream, which are the synchronous versions of SaveTo StreamAsync and ReadFromStreamAsync, respectively.

One more thing we might want to support in a formatter is the ability to negotiate the media type from additional sources rather than the Accept header. This is a very common requirement these days for clients where the HTTP client stack is not correctly implemented (as happens with browsers in some older mobile devices). In those cases, a client might want to provide the accepted media type in the query string, such as http://…/Issues?format=atom. The MediaTypeFormatter supports this scenario through the MediaMappings property, which represents a collection of MediaMapping instances indicating the locations where the media type can be found, such as query strings, headers, or URI segments. The framework provides several concrete implementations of the MediaMapping abstract class for addressing the most common scenarios. The following list provides a brief description of these mappings:

QueryStringMapping

This can be used to map the requested media type to a query string variable. For example, the format variable in the URL *http://localhost/issues?format=atom* would map to the atom media type.

UriPathExtensionMapping

This can be used to map a path in a URI to a media type. For example, *http://localhost/issues.atom* would map the path *.atom* to the atom media type.

RequestHeaderMapping

This maps a request header to a media type. This would be useful in case you do not want to use any of the standard HTTP request headers.

The media type mappings are injected in a formatter through the constructor. Example 13-19 shows how the constructor was modified to use a QueryStringMapping instance for searching the media type as part of a query string.

Example 13-19. Media type mapping from query string

```
public const string Atom = "application/atom+xml";
public const string Rss = "application/rss+xml";

public SyndicationMediaTypeFormatter()
  : base()
{
  this.SupportedMediaTypes.Add(new MediaTypeHeaderValue(Atom));
  this.SupportedMediaTypes.Add(new MediaTypeHeaderValue(Rss));

  this.MediaTypeMappings
        .Add(new QueryStringMapping("format", "atom",
              new MediaTypeHeaderValue(Atom))); // <1>
}
```

If the formatter found a query string variable format with a value atom, that would be mapped to the Atom media type (application/atom+xml) *<1>*.

Default HttpParameterBinding Selection

By default, the model binding infrastructure will try to use `FormatterParameterBind`
`er` for complex type parameters, and `ModelBindingParameterBinder` for simple .NET
types. If you have multiple complex type arguments, the binding will fail unless you
explicitly specify that any of these arguments must be bound from the URL or the body
with the `FromUriAttribute` or `FromBodyAttribute` attributes, respectively. The `From`
`BodyAttribute` is another mechanism you can use to force the use of a `FormatterPar`
`ameterBinder` for a given parameter. If an action contains multiple complex parameters,
only one of them can be read from the request body via the `FromBodyAttribute`. Otherwise, the runtime will throw an exception.

Model Validation

Model validation is another feature that you get in Web API with the model binding
infrastructure. You can use this feature to either enforce business rules or to make sure
the data sent by a client is correct. As the model validation is performed in a single place
while the model is bound, this centralization results in code that's easier to maintain
and test.

Another important aspect of model validation is to inform clients about any possible
errors in the data they sent with a chance to correct those errors. In practice, when this
aspect is not enforced, developers will simply stop adopting the API as part of their
applications.

As with all of the model binding infrastructure, model validation in ASP.NET Web API
is also completely extensible. The framework ships with a general-purpose validator
that uses attributes for validating the models. This validator works for most scenarios,
and reuses the data annotation attributes included in the `System.ComponentModel.Da`
`taAnnotations` namespace. Several validation attributes are provided out of the box in
that namespace—such as `Required` to mark a property as required or `RegularExpres`
`sion` to validate a property value with a regular expression. You are also free to create
your own custom data annotation attributes for use cases initially not covered by the
built-in ones.

Applying Data Annotation Attributes to a Model

Suppose we want have some validations applied to our issue model. We can start using
the data annotation attributes to decorate the model and enforce common validation
scenarios without having to write much code, and more importantly, without requiring
repetitive code. Example 13-20 shows how the issue model looks after we've applied
some data annotation attributes.

Example 13-20. An issue model with data annotation attributes

```
public class Issue
{
  [DisplayName("Issue Id")]
  [Required(ErrorMessage = "The issue id is required")]
  [Range(1, 1000, ErrorMessage = "The unit price must be between {1} and {2}")]
  public int Id { get; set; }

  [DisplayName("Issue Name")]
  [Required(ErrorMessage = "The issue name is required")]
  public string Name { get; set; }

  [DisplayName("Issue Description")]
  [Required(ErrorMessage = "The issue description is required")]
  public string Description { get; set; }
}
```

All the properties in the model have been labeled with attributes that clearly state their intention. Some properties, such as Name and Description, have been marked as required, and the Id property has been marked to require a value within a given range. The DisplayName attribute is not used for validation but affects how the output messages are rendered.

Querying the Validation Results

Once the model binding infrastructure validates a model based on the attributes that were defined on it, the results will become available to be used by a controller implementation or in a more centralized manner with a filter.

Adding a few lines in an action implementation is by far the simplest way to check whether the model has been correctly bound and all the validation results were successful (see Example 13-21).

Example 13-21. Checking the validation results in an action implementation

```
public class ValidationError
{
  public string Name { get; set; }
  public string Message { get; set; }
}

public class IssueController : ApiController
{
  public HttpResponseMessage Post(Issue product)
  {
    if(!this.ModelState.IsValid)
    {
      var errors = this.ModelState // <1>
               .Where(e => e.Value.Errors.Count > 0)
               .Select(e => new ValidationError // <2>
```

```
            {
                Name = e.Key,
                Message = e.Value.Errors.First().ErrorMessage
            }).ToArray();

        var response = new HttpResponseMessage(HttpStatusCode.BadRequest);
        response.Content = new ObjectContent<ValidationError[]>(errors,
                new JsonMediaTypeFormatter());

        return response;
    }

    // Do something
  }
}
```

As illustrated in Example 13-21, all the validation results become available in a controller action through the ModelState property *<1>*. In that example, the action simply converts all the validation errors into a model class, ValidationError *<2>*, that we can serialize into the response body as JSON, and returns that with a Bad Request status code.

This represents some generic code that you might want to reuse in multiple actions, so probably the best way to do that is to move it to a custom filter. Example 13-22 shows the same code in a filter implementation.

Example 13-22. ActionFilterAttribute implementation for doing validations

```
public class ValidationActionFilter : ActionFilterAttribute
{
    public override void OnActionExecuting(HttpActionContext actionContext)
    {
        if (!actionContext.ModelState.IsValid)
        {
          var errors = this.ModelState
                .Where(e => e.Value.Errors.Count > 0)
                .Select(e => new ValidationError
                {
                    Name = e.Key,
                    Message = e.Value.Errors.First().ErrorMessage
                }).ToArray();

        var response = new HttpResponseMessage(HttpStatusCode.BadRequest);
        response.Content = new ObjectContent<ValidationError[]>(errors,
                new JsonMediaTypeFormatter());

        actionContext.Response = response;
        }
    }
}
```

As you can see, the filter implementation is quite simple as well. When the filter detects that the model is not valid, the execution pipeline is automatically interrupted and a new response is sent to the consumer with the validation errors. If we send, for example, a message with an empty product name and invalid unit price, we will get the response shown in Example 13-23.

Example 13-23. Invalid request message and corresponding response message

```
Request Message in JSON

POST http://../Isssues HTTP/1.1
Content-Type: application/json

{
  Id: 1,
  "Name":"",
  "Description": "My issue"
}

Response Message

HTTP/1.1 400 Bad Request
Content-Type: text/plain; charset=utf-8

[{
  "Message": "The Issue Name is required.",
  "Name": "Name"
}]
```

Conclusion

The model binding infrastructure acts as a mapping layer between HTTP messages and object instances known as models. It mainly relies on `HttpParameterBinding` components for doing the parameter binding to different HTTP message parts like headers, query strings, or the body text. Two main implementations of `HttpParameterBind` `ing` are shipped out of the box in the framework: a `ModelBindingParameterBinder` implementation that uses the traditional binding mechanism brought from ASP.NET MVC (in which the models are composed from small pieces found in the HTTP messages), and a `FormatterParameterBinder` that uses formatters to convert a media type format to a model.

The `ModelBindingParameterBinder` implementation uses `IValueProvider` instances for collecting values from different parts in a HTTP message, and `IModelBinder` instances to compose all those values into a single model.

The `FormatterParameterBinder` implementation is a fundamental piece of content negotiation, as it understands how to transform the body of an HTTP message expressed with the semantics rules and format of a given media type into a model using formatters.

A formatter derives from the base class `MediaTypeFormatter` and typically knows how to manage a single media type. In addition to parameter binding, the model binding infrastructure also offers an extensibility point for validating the models once they are deserialized. The models are validated out of the box through rules defined as data annotation attributes.

CHAPTER 14

HttpClient

It is always easier to get a good result with good tools.

This chapter is a deeper exploration of the `HttpClient` library that is part of the `System.Net.Http` library discussed in Chapter 10.

The first incarnation of `HttpClient` was bundled with the REST Starter Kit (RSK) on CodePlex in early 2009. It introduced a number of concepts such as a request/response pipeline, an abstraction for the HTTP payload that was distinct from the request/response and strongly typed headers. Despite a big chunk of RSK making it into .NET Framework 4.0, `HttpClient` itself did not. When the Web API project started in 2010, a rewritten version of `HttpClient` was a core part of the project.

HttpClient Class

Simple things should be simple, and `HttpClient` tries to adhere to that principle. Consider the following:

```
var client = new HttpClient();
string rfc2616Text =
await client.GetStringAsync("http://www.ietf.org/rfc/rfc2616.txt");
```

In this example, a new `HttpClient` object is instantiated and an HTTP `GET` request is made, and the content of the response is translated to a .NET string.

This apparently trivial piece of code provides sufficient context for us to discuss a range of issues related to the usage of the `HttpClient` class.

Lifecycle

Although `HttpClient` does indirectly implement the `IDisposable` interface, the recommended usage of `HttpClient` is not to dispose of it after every request. The

HttpClient object is intended to live for as long as your application needs to make HTTP requests. Having an object exist across multiple requests enables a place for setting DefaultRequestHeaders and prevents you from having to respecify things like CredentialCache and CookieContainer on every request, as was necessary with HttpWebRequest.

Wrapper

Interestingly, HttpClient itself does not do any of the dirty work of making HTTP requests; it defers that job to an aggregated object that derives from HttpMessageHandler. The default constructor takes care of instantiating one of these objects. Alternatively, one can be passed in to the constructor, like this:

```
var client = new HttpClient((HttpMessageHandler) new HttpClientHandler());
```

HttpClientHandler uses the System.Net HttpWebRequest and HttpWebResponse classes under the covers. This design provides the best possible outcome. Today, we get a clean new interface to a proven HTTP stack, and tomorrow we can replace that HttpClientHandler with some improved HTTP internals and the application interface will not change. The implementation of HttpClientHandler uses a lowest common denominator of the System.Net library to allow usage on multiple platforms like WinRT and Windows Phone. As a result, certain features are not available, such as client caching, pipelining, and client certificates, as they are dependent on the desktop operating system. To use those features, it is necessary to do the following:

```
var handler = new WebRequestHandler {
            AuthenticationLevel = AuthenticationLevel.MutualAuthRequired,
            CachePolicy = new RequestCachePolicy(RequestCacheLevel.Default)
        };
var httpClient = new HttpClient(handler);
```

The WebRequestHandler class derives from HttpClientHandler but is deployed in a separate assembly, System.Net.Http.WebRequest.

The reason that HttpClient implements IDisposable is to dispose the HttpMessageHandler, which then attempts to close the underlying TCP/IP connection. This means that creating a new HttpClient and making a new request will require creating a new underlying socket connection, which is very expensive in comparison to just making a request.

It is important to realize that if an instance of the HttpMessageHandler class is instantiated outside of the HttpClient and then passed to the constructor, disposing of the HttpClient will render the handler unusable. If there is significant setup required to configure the handler, you might wish to be able to reuse a handler across multiple HttpClient instances. Fortunately, an additional constructor was added to support this scenario:

```
var handler = HttpHandlerFactory.CreateExpensiveHandler(};
var httpClient = new HttpClient(handler, disposeHandler:false);
```

Instructing HttpClient to not dispose the HttpMessageHandler allows the reuse of the message handler across multiple HttpClient instances.

Multiple Instances

One reason that you might want to create multiple HttpClient instances is because certain properties of HttpClient cannot be changed once the first request has been made. These include:

```
public Uri BaseAddress
public TimeSpan Timeout
public long MaxResponseContentBufferSize
```

Thread Safety

HttpClient is a threadsafe class and can happily manage multiple parallel HTTP requests. If these properties were to be changed while requests were in progress, then it might introduce bugs that are hard to track down.

These properties are relatively self-explanatory, but the MaxResponseContentBuffer Size is worth highlighting. This property is of type long but is defaulted and limited to the Int32.MaxValue, which is sufficiently large to start with for most scenarios. Fear not, though: just because the size is set to 4GB, HttpClient will not allocate more memory than is required to buffer the HTTP payload.

Beyond being a wrapper for the HttpMessageHandler, a host for configuration properties, and a place for some logging messages, HttpClient also provides some helper methods to make issuing common requests easy. These methods make HttpClient a good replacement for System.Net.WebClient.

Helper Methods

The first example introduced GetStringAsync. Additionally, there are GetStreamAsync and GetByteArrayAsync methods. All of the helper methods have the Async suffix to indicate that they will execute asynchronously, and they all return a Task object. This will also allow the use of async and await on platforms that support those keywords. In .NET 4.5, it has become policy to expose methods that could take longer than 50 milliseconds as asynchronous only. This policy is intended to encourage developers to take approaches that will not block an application's user interface thread and therefore create a more responsive application. Our example used the .Result property on the returned task to block the calling thread and return the string result. This approach circumvents the recommended policy and comes with some dangers that will be addressed later in this chapter. However, for simplicity's sake, we'll use the `.Result` shortcut to simulate a synchronous request.

Peeling Off the Layers

The helper methods are handy but provide little insight into what is going on under the covers. If we remove one layer of simplification we have the `GetAsync` method, which can be used as follows:

```
var client = new HttpClient();
HttpResponseMessage response;
response = await client.GetAsync("http://www.ietf.org/rfc/rfc2616.txt");
HttpContent content = response.Content;
string rfc2616Text = await content.ReadAsStringAsync();
```

In this example, we now get access to the response object and the content object. These objects allow us to inspect metadata in the HTTP headers to guide the process of consuming the returned content.

Completed Requests Don't Throw

The `HttpClient` behavior is different than `HttpWebRequest` in that, by default, no completed HTTP responses will throw an exception. An exception may be thrown if something fails at the transport level; however, unlike `HttpWebRequest`, status codes like 3XX, 4XX, and 5XX do not throw exceptions. The `IsSuccessStatusCode` property can be used to determine if the status code is a 2xx, and the `EnsureSuccessStatusCode` method can be used to manually trigger an exception to be thrown if the status code is not successful.

The status codes returned in response to an HTTP request often can be handled directly by application code and therefore do not warrant throwing an exception. For example, we can handle many 3xx responses automatically by making a second request to the URI specified in the location header. Error `503 Service Unavailable` can apply a retry mechanism to ensure temporary interruptions are not fatal to the application. Later in this chapter, there will be further discussion about building clients that intelligently react to HTTP status codes.

Content Is Everything

The `HttpContent` class is an abstract base class that comes with a few implementations in the box. `HttpContent` abstracts away the details of dealing with the bytes that need to be sent over the wire. `HttpContent` instances deal with the headaches of flushing and positioning streams, allocating and deallocating memory, and converting CLR types to bytes on the wire. They provide access to the HTTP headers that are specifically related to the HTTP payload.

You can access the content of an HttpContent object using the ReadAs methods discussed in Chapter 10. Although the HttpContent abstraction does shield you from most of the nasty details about reading bytes over the wire, there is one key detail that is not immediately apparent and is worth understanding. A number of the methods on HttpClient have a completionOption parameter. This parameter determines whether the asynchronous task will complete as soon as the response headers have been received or whether the complete response body will be completely read into a buffer first.

There are a couple reasons why you might want to have the task complete as soon as the headers are retrieved:

- The media type of the response may not be understood by the client, and where networks are metered, downloading the bytes may be a waste of time and money.
- You may wish to do processing work based on the response headers in parallel to downloading the content.

The following code is a hypothetical example of how this feature could be used:

```
var httpClient = new HttpClient();
httpClient.BaseAddress = new Uri("http://www.ietf.org/rfc/");
var tcs = new CancellationTokenSource();

var response = await httpClient.GetAsync("rfc2616.txt",
        HttpCompletionOption.ResponseHeadersRead, tcs.Token);
// Headers have been returned

if (!IsSupported(response.Content.ContentType)) {
        tcs.Cancel();
        return;
}
UIManager userInterfaceManager = new UIManager();

// Start building up the right UI based on the content-type
userInterfaceManager.PrepareTheUI(content.ContentType);

// Start pulling the payload data across the wire
var payload = await response.Content.ReadAsStreamAsync()

// Payload has been completely retrieved
userInterfaceManager.Display(payload);
```

To implement this technique, the UIManager has to do some thread synchronization because the Display method will likely be called on a different thread than Prepare TheUI, and the Display method will probably need to wait until the UI is ready. Sometimes the extra effort is worth the performance gain of being able to effectively do two things at once. Obviously, this technique is not much use if your client can't determine what you are trying to display without parsing the payload.

Cancelling the Request

The last parameter to discuss on the GetAsync method is the CancellationToken. Creating a CancellationToken and passing it to this method allows calling objects the opportunity to cancel the Async operation. Be aware that cancelling an operation will cause the Async operation to throw an exception, so be prepared to catch it.

The following example cancels a request if it does not complete within one second. This illustrates the use of Cancel only, as HttpClient has a built-in timeout mechanism:

```
[Fact]
    public async Task RequestCancelledByCaller()
    {
        Exception expectedException = null;

        bool done = false;

        var httpClient = new HttpClient();
        var cts = new CancellationTokenSource();

        var backgroundRequest = new TaskFactory().StartNew(async () =>
        {
            try
            {
                var request = new HttpRequestMessage()
                {
                    RequestUri = new Uri("http://example.org/largeResource")
                };

                var response = await httpClient.SendAsync(request,
                    HttpCompletionOption.ResponseHeadersRead, cts.Token);

                done = true;
            }
            catch (TaskCanceledException ex)
            {
                expectedException = ex;
            }
        }, cts.Token);

        // Wait for it to finish
        Thread.Sleep(1000);

        if (!done)
            cts.Cancel();

        Assert.NotNull(expectedException);
    }
```

SendAsync

All of the HttpClient methods we have covered so far are just wrappers around the single method SendAsync, which has the following signature:

```
public Task<HttpResponseMessage> SendAsync(
        HttpRequestMessage request,
        HttpCompletionOption completionOption,
        CancellationToken cancellationToken)
```

By creating an HttpRequestMessage and setting the Method property and the Content property, you can easily replicate the behavior of the helper methods using SendAsync. However, the HttpRequestMessage can be used only once. After the request is sent, it is disposed immediately to ensure that any associated Content object is disposed. In many cases this shouldn't be necessary; however, if an HttpContent object were wrapping a forward-only stream it would not be possible to resend the content without reinitializing the stream, and the HttpContent class does not have any such interface. Introducing a link class as a request factory (as we did in Chapter 9) is one way to work around this limitation:

```
var httpClient = new HttpClient();
httpClient.BaseAddress = new Uri("http://www.ietf.org/rfc/");

var request = new HttpRequestMessage() {
        RequestUri = new Uri("rfc2616.txt"),
        Method = HttpMethod.Get
}
var response = await httpClient.SendAsync(request,
        HttpCompletionOption.ResponseContentRead, new CancellationToken());
```

The SendAsync method is a core piece of the architecture of both HttpClient and Web API. SendAsync is the primary method of HttpMessageHandler, which is the building block of request and response pipelines.

Client Message Handlers

Message handlers are one of the key architectural components in both HttpClient and Web API. Every request and response message, on both client and server, is passed through a chain of classes that derive from HttpMessageHandler. In the case of HttpClient, by default there is only one handler in the chain: the HttpClientHandler. You can extend the default behavior by inserting additional HttpMessageHandler instances at the begining of the chain, as Example 14-1 demonstrates.

Example 14-1. Adding a handler to the client request pipeline

```
var customHandler = new MyCustomHandler()
        { InnerHandler = new HttpClientHandler()};
```

```
var client = new HttpClient(customHandler);

client.GetAsync("http://example.org",content);
```

The code in Example 14-1 creates an object graph that looks like Figure 14-1.

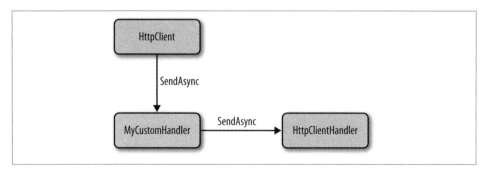

Figure 14-1. Extensibility with HttpMessageHandlers

Multiple message handlers can be chained together to compose additional functionality. However, the base HttpMessageHandler does not have a built-in chaining capability. A derived class, DelegatingHandler, provides the InnerHandler property to support chaining.

Example 14-2 shows how you can use a message handler to allow a client to use the PUT and DELETE methods against a server that does not support those methods and requires the use of the X-HTTP-Method-Override header.

Example 14-2. HttpMethodOverrideHandler

```
public class HttpMethodOverrideHandler: DelegatingHandler
    {
        protected override Task<HttpResponseMessage> SendAsync(
            HttpRequestMessage request,
            System.Threading.CancellationToken cancellationToken)
        {
            if (request.Method == HttpMethod.Put)
            {
                request.Method = HttpMethod.Post;
                request.Headers.Add("X-HTTP-Method-Override", "PUT");
            }
            if (request.Method == HttpMethod.Delete)
            {
                request.Method = HttpMethod.Post;
                request.Headers.Add("X-HTTP-Method-Override", "DELETE");
            }
            return base.SendAsync(request, cancellationToken);
        }
    }
```

Another class derived from `DelegatingHandler`, called `MessageProcessingHandler` (see Example 14-3), makes it even easier to create these handlers as long as the custom behavior will not need to do any long-running work that would require asynchronous operations.

Example 14-3. MessageProcessingHandler

```
public class HttpMethodOverrideMessageProcessor : MessageProcessingHandler {

    protected override HttpRequestMessage ProcessRequest(
            HttpRequestMessage request,
            CancellationToken cancellationToken) {

        if (request.Method == HttpMethod.Put)
        {
            request.Method = HttpMethod.Post;
            request.Headers.Add("X-HTTP-Method-Override", "PUT");
        }
        if (request.Method == HttpMethod.Delete)
        {
            request.Method = HttpMethod.Post;
            request.Headers.Add("X-HTTP-Method-Override", "DELETE");
        }
        return request;
    }

    protected override HttpResponseMessage ProcessResponse(
            HttpResponseMessage response,
            CancellationToken cancellationToken) {
        return response;
    }
}
```

When using these *message handlers* to extend functionality, you should be aware that they will often execute on a different thread than the thread that issued the request. If the handler attempts to switch back onto the requesting thread—for example, to get back onto the UI thread to update some user interface control—then there is a risk of deadlock. If the original request is blocking, waiting for the response to return, then a deadlock will occur. You can avoid this problem when using the .NET 4.5 `async` `await` mechanism, but it is a very good reason to avoid using `.Result` to simulate synchronous requests.

Proxying Handlers

There are many potential uses of `HttpMessageHandlers`. One is to act as a proxy for manipulating outgoing requests. The following example shows a proxy for the Runscope debugging service:

```
public class RunscopeMessageHandler : DelegatingHandler
{
    private readonly string _bucketKey;

    public RunscopeMessageHandler(string bucketKey,
            HttpMessageHandler innerHandler)
    {
        _bucketKey = bucketKey;
        InnerHandler = innerHandler;
    }

    protected override Task<HttpResponseMessage> SendAsync(
            HttpRequestMessage request,
            CancellationToken cancellationToken)
    {
        var requestUri = request.RequestUri;
        var port = requestUri.Port;

        request.RequestUri = ProxifyUri(requestUri, _bucketKey);
        if ((requestUri.Scheme == "http" && port != 80 )
                || requestUri.Scheme == "https" && port != 443)
        {
            request.Headers.TryAddWithoutValidation(
                "Runscope-Request-Port", port.ToString());
        }
        return base.SendAsync(request, cancellationToken);
    }

        private Uri ProxifyUri(Uri requestUri,
                        string bucketKey,
                        string gatewayHost = "runscope.net")
    {
      ...
    }
}
```

In this scenario, the request URI is modified to point to the proxy instead of the original resource.

Fake Response Handlers

You can use message handlers to assist with testing client code. If you create a message handler that looks like the following:

```
public class FakeResponseHandler : DelegatingHandler
  {
        private readonly Dictionary<Uri, HttpResponseMessage> _FakeResponses
            = new Dictionary<Uri, HttpResponseMessage>();

        public void AddFakeResponse(Uri uri, HttpResponseMessage responseMessage)
        {
                _FakeResponses.Add(uri,responseMessage);
```

```
        }

        protected async override Task<HttpResponseMessage> SendAsync(
                HttpRequestMessage request,
                CancellationToken cancellationToken)
        {
            if (_FakeResponses.ContainsKey(request.RequestUri))
            {
                return _FakeResponses[request.RequestUri];
            }
            else
            {
                return new HttpResponseMessage(HttpStatusCode.NotFound)
                    { RequestMessage = request};
            }

        }
    }
```

you can use it as a replacement for the HttpClientHandler:

```
[Fact]
public async Task CallFakeRequest()
{
    var fakeResponseHandler = new FakeResponseHandler();
    fakeResponseHandler.AddFakeResponse(
        new Uri("http://example.org/test"),
        new HttpResponseMessage(HttpStatusCode.OK));

    var httpClient = new HttpClient(fakeResponseHandler);

    var response1 = await httpClient.GetAsync("http://example.org/notthere");
    var response2 = await httpClient.GetAsync("http://example.org/test");

    Assert.Equal(response1.StatusCode,HttpStatusCode.NotFound);
    Assert.Equal(response2.StatusCode, HttpStatusCode.OK);
}
```

In order to test client-side services, you must ensure that they allow an HttpClient instance to be injected. This is another example of why it is better to share an HttpClient instance rather than instantiating on the fly, per request. The FakeResponseHandler needs to be prepopulated with the responses that are expected to come over the wire. This setup allows the client code to be tested as if it were connected to a live server:

```
[Fact]
public async Task ServiceUnderTest()
{
    var fakeResponseHandler = new FakeResponseHandler();
    fakeResponseHandler.AddFakeResponse(
            new Uri("http://example.org/test"),
            new HttpResponseMessage(HttpStatusCode.OK)
                    {Content = new StringContent("99")});
```

```
    var httpClient = new HttpClient(fakeResponseHandler);

    var service = new ServiceUnderTest(httpClient);
    var value = await service.GetTestValue();

    Assert.Equal(value, 99);
}
```

Creating Resuable Response Handlers

In Chapter 9, we discussed the notion of *reactive clients* that decoupled the response
handling from the context of the request.

Message handlers and the HttpClient pipeline are a natural fix for achieving this goal,
and have the side effect of simplifying the process of making requests.

Consider the message handler shown in Example 14-4.

Example 14-4. Pluggable response handler

```
public abstract class ResponseAction
    {
        abstract public bool ShouldRespond(
                ClientState state,
                HttpResponseMessage response);

        abstract public HttpResponseMessage HandleResponse(
                ClientState state,
                HttpResponseMessage response);
    }

public class ResponseHandler : DelegatingHandler
    {
        private static readonly List<ResponseAction> _responseActions
            = new List<ResponseAction>();


        public void AddResponseAction(ResponseAction action)
        {
            _responseActions.Add(action);
        }

        protected override Task<HttpResponseMessage> SendAsync(
                HttpRequestMessage request,
                CancellationToken cancellationToken)
        {
            return base.SendAsync(request, cancellationToken)
                .ContinueWith<HttpResponseMessage>(t =>
                    ApplyResponseHandler(t.Result));
        }
```

```
    private HttpResponseMessage ApplyResponseHandler(
            HttpResponseMessage response)
{

    foreach (var responseAction in _responseActions)
    {
        if (responseAction.ShouldRespond(response))
        {
            var response = responseAction.HandleResponse(response);
            if (response == null) break;
        }
    }
    return response;
}
}
```

In this example, we have created a delegating handler that will dispatch responses to a particular `ResponseAction` class if `ShouldRespond` returns `true`. This mechanism allows an arbitrary number of response actions to be defined and plugged in. The `Should dRespond` method's role can be as simple as looking at the HTTP status code, or it could be far more sophisticated, looking at *content type* or even parsing the payload looking for specific tokens.

Making HTTP requests then gets simplified to what you see in Example 14-5.

Example 14-5. Using response handlers

```
var responseHandler = new ResponseHandler()
        {InnerHandler = new HttpClientHandler()};

responseHandler.AddAction(new NotFoundHandler());
responseHandler.AddAction(new BadRequestHandler());
responseHandler.AddAction(new ServiceUnavailableRetryHandler());
responseHandler.AddAction(new ContactRenderingHandler());

var httpClient = new HttpClient(responseHandler);

httpClient.GetAsync("http://example.org/contacts");
```

Conclusion

`HttpClient` is a major step forward in the use of HTTP on the .NET platform. We get an interface that is as easy to use as `WebClient` but with more power and configurability than `HttpWebRequest`/`HttpWebResponse`. The same interface will support future protocol implementations. Testing is easier, and the pipeline architecture allows us to apply many cross-cutting concerns without complicating the usage.

CHAPTER 15

Security

The cowl does not make the monk.

In the broadest sense, the security of computer systems encompasses many subjects and techniques, ranging from encryption schemes to availability and disaster recovery systems. However, it is not the goal of this chapter to discuss such a wide range of themes. Instead, we'll focus our attention on the security aspects that are more specific to Web APIs—in particular, transport security, authentication, and authorization. So, in the following sections we will be addressing these subjects, from both theoretical and practical viewpoints, using ASP.NET Web API as the supporting technology.

This chapter is complemented by the following chapter, which will focus solely on the OAuth 2.0 Framework: a set of protocols and patterns addressing access control in HTTP-based APIs.

Transport Security

The confidentiality and integrity of transferred information are important security requirements that must be addressed when you are designing and implementing distributed systems. Unfortunately, the HTTP protocol provides little support in this area. For this reason, the common practice among developers is to address these requirements by using HTTP on top of a secure transport layer, as defined by RFC 1818, "HTTP Over TLS," resulting in what is informally known as HTTPS. Briefly, this specification states that when a client performs an HTTP request to a URI with the https scheme (e.g., *https://www.example.net*), then the HTTP protocol is layered on top of a secure transport (TLS or SSL) instead of directly over TCP, as depicted in Figure 15-1. This way, both the request and the response message bytes are protected by the transport protocol while being transferred between two transport endpoints.

The *Transport Layer Security protocol* (TLS), defined by RFC 5246, is an evolution of the *Secure Socket Layer protocol* (SSL).[1] Both these protocols aim to provide a *secure* bidirectional connection between two communicating entities, usually called *peers*, with the following properties:

Integrity

Each peer has the assurance that the received byte stream is equal to the byte stream transmitted by the remote peer. Any modifications to this stream by a third party, including replays, are detected and the connection is terminated.

Confidentiality

Each peer has the guarantee that the sent byte stream will be *visible* only to the remote peer.

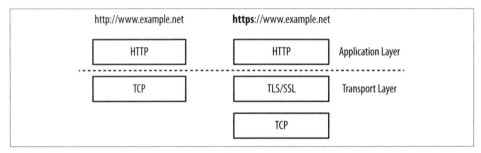

Figure 15-1. The https scheme and transport security

In addition to the integrity and confidentiality assurances, the TLS protocol can also perform peer authentication, providing the client or the server with the verified identity of the remote peer. Very importantly, when used in the HTTP context, TLS is also responsible for the fundamental task of server authentication, providing the client with the server's verified identity before the client sends any request message. We will address TLS-based authentication in more detail in the section "Authentication" on page 360.

The TLS protocol is itself divided into two major subprotocols. The *record subprotocol* provides the integrity and confidentiality properties, using symmetric encryption schemes and message authentication codes (MAC) to protect the exchanged byte stream. It operates over a reliable transport protocol (e.g., TCP), and is composed of three different layers. The first one divides the incoming stream into records, each one with a maximum length of 16 KB. The second layer applies compression to each one of these records. The last layer applies the cryptographic protection, using a *MAC-then-Encrypt* design: first a MAC is computed over the compressed record concatenated with a sequence number; then both the compressed record and the MAC value are encrypted.

---

1. In the remainder of this chapter, we will refer to both these protocols as TLS.

The *handshake subprotocol* is used to establish the TLS operation parameters, namely the cryptographic material used by the record subprotocol (e.g., encryption and MAC keys). It supports multiple key establishment techniques. However, in the web context, the most common ones are based on the use of public-key cryptography and certificates. In Appendix G, we present a brief introduction to this subject and also show how to create keys and certificates to use in development environments.

Using TLS in ASP.NET Web API

The TLS protocol operates on top of the transport layer, meaning that it is implemented by the low-level HTTP hosting infrastructure, which on Windows is the kernel-mode HTTP.SYS driver. As a consequence, most of its related configuration is done outside of ASP.NET Web API and also differs between IIS hosting and self-hosting.

Using TLS with IIS Hosting

On IIS, TLS is configured through the addition of an HTTPS *binding* to a *site*, as illustrated in Figure 15-2.

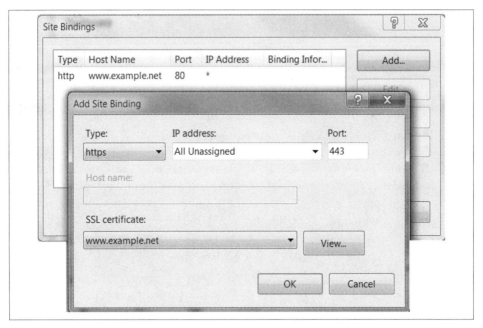

Figure 15-2. Adding an HTTPS binding to a site

This addition is configured by the server's certificate, which must be installed in the *Personal* store of the *Local Computer* location, have an associated private key, and also have a valid certification path to a trusted root certification authority. No further changes are required on the IIS configuration or on the Web API configuration.

Figure 15-3 shows the user interface presented by a browser performing a request via HTTPS. Notice that the presented information includes both the server's identity (*www.example.net*) and the certification authority name ("Demo Certification Authority").

Figure 15-3. Accessing ASP.NET Web API using HTTPS

In IIS 7.5, multiple sites may have HTTP bindings configured for the same IP address and port, since the request *demultiplexing* (dispatching the request for the selected site) uses the hostname present in the Host header. However, it is not possible to have multiple HTTPS bindings with *different* certificates configured for the *same* IP address and port (because the server certificate is needed when the TLS connection is established, well before the HTTP request is received). So, when hosting multiple HTTPS sites on the same server, the alternatives are:

- Use a different IP address or port for each HTTPS binding.

- Use the same certificate for all bindings, which typically implies using wildcards in the certificate's subject name. Alternatively, the *Subject Alternative Name* extension can be used to define multiple subject names for the same certificate.

Subject Alternative Names

The X.509 certificate specification includes an extension field named *Subject Alternative Name*, allowing for the inclusion of one or more subject names in a single certificate. For instance, at the time of writing, a connection to *https://www.google.com* uses a server X.509 certificate with 44 alternative names, including: **.google.com*, **.android.com*, **.google.com.ar*, **.google.ca*, and **.google.pt*.

RFC 4366 defines a new TLS extension, named *Server Name Indication* (SNI), which adds the name of the HTTP host into the TLS initial handshake. This extra information allows the server to use a different certificate for each hostname, even if the TCP connection is established for the same IP address and port. Unfortunately, this extension is supported by IIS 8.0 and greater versions but not by IIS 7.5 or previous versions.

Using TLS with Self-Hosting

When you are using self-hosting, TLS is configured using the `netsh` command-line tool:

```
netsh http add sslcert ipport=0.0.0.0:port certhash=thumbprint appid={app-guid}
```

where:

- `ipport` is the listening IP address and port (the special `0.0.0.0` IP address matches any IP address for the local machine).
- `certhash` is the server certificate SHA-1 hash value, represented in hexadecimal.
- `appid` is just a GUID used to identify the owning application.

The chosen server certificate has the same requirements as when you are hosting on IIS, namely that it must be installed in the *Personal* store of the *Local Computer* location, have an associated private key, and also have a valid certification path to a trusted root. The only change required on the ASP.NET Web API configuration is the usage of the `https` scheme in the self-host listening address:

```
var config = new HttpSelfHostConfiguration("https://www.example.net:8443");
```

This concludes the section on transport security. In the next section, we will address authentication.

Authentication

According to RFC 4949 (Internet Security Glossary), *authentication* is "The process of verifying a claim that a system entity or system resource has a certain attribute value." In the context of HTTP, the two obvious *system entities* are the client and the server, and this attribute verification is typically required by both these entities.

On one side, *server authentication* is required to preemptively ensure clients that request messages are sent only to *correct* origin servers—that is, the servers on which the identified resources reside or should be created. In this case, the message sender needs to authenticate the message receiver before sending the message, typically by authenticating the other side of the transport connection. Server authentication is also needed to check if the received response messages were indeed produced by the *correct* servers. Since clients are interacting with resources identified by http URIs, the main attribute checked by this authentication process is the possession of the URI's hostname (an IP address or DNS name).

On the other side, *client authentication* provides servers with identity information used to decide if the request message should be authorized—that is, if the requested methods can be applied to the identified resources. In this case, the attributes verified by the authentication process are more context dependent, and may range from simple opaque identifiers, such as usernames, to rich collections of attributes, such as emails, names, roles, addresses, and banking and social security numbers.

As we will see in the following sections, these authentication requirements can be accomplished at two levels:

- At the transport level, by sending and receiving HTTP messages over secure connections
- At the message level, by attaching security information to the messages in order to authenticate its origin

However, before presenting the details of these authentication mechanisms, we will first address how identity—that is, the output of the authentication process—can be represented in the .NET Framework.

The Claims Model

Since version 1.0, the .NET Framework contains two interfaces to represent identities, shown in Figure 15-4: IPrincipal and IIdentity. The IPrincipal interface "represents the security context of the user on whose behalf the code is running." For instance, in the HTTP request handling context, this interface represents the request message producer—the HTTP client. This interface contains an IsInRole method, used to query if the requester has a given role, and an `Identity` property, of type `IIdentity`. This last interface represents an identity via three properties:

- The `AuthenticationType` string
- The `Name` string
- The `IsAuthenticated` string

Figure 15-4. The IPrincipal and IIdentity interfaces

The *current* principal (i.e., the object representing the security context of the user on whose behalf the current code is running), can be accessed via the `Thread.Current Principal` static property. This information is also accessible via more context-specific properties, such as the ASP.NET MVC `System.Web.Mvc.Controller.User` property or WCF's `System.ServiceModel.ServiceSecurityContext.PrimaryIdentity`. In the ASP.NET Web API context, this role is played by the `ApiController.User` property, also containing an `IPrincipal`.

The .NET Framework also contains a set of concrete classes implementing the `IPrin cipal` and `IIdentity` interfaces:

- The `GenericPrincipal`, `WindowsPrincipal`, and `RolePrincipal` classes implement the `IPrincipal` interface.
- The `GenericIdentity`, `WindowsIdentity`, and `FormsIdentity` classes implement the `IIdentity` interface.

However, the previous model uses a rather limited view of what an identity can be, reducing it to a simple string and a role query method. Also, this model assumes an implicit identity authority, which does not fit a world where identity information can be provided by multiple providers, ranging from social sites to organizational directories.

The *claims model* aims to overcome these limitations by defining a new way of representing identities, based on the *claim* concept. *A Guide to Claims-Based Identity and*

Access Control (Microsoft Patterns & Practices) defines a claim as a "statement, such as a name, identity, key, group, permission or capability made by one subject about itself or another subject." We'll highlight two characteristics of this definition. First, this definition is broad enough to allow different identity attributes, ranging from simple name identifiers to authorization capabilities. Second, it makes explicit that claims can be issued by multiple parties, including the identified subject (self-issued claims).

With version 4.5, the .NET Framework adopted this claims model to represent identities and introduced the `System.Security.Claims` namespace, which contains several classes associated with this model. The `Claim` class, depicted in Figure 15-5, is composed of three core properties:

- `Issuer` is a string identifying the authority that asserted the identity claim.
- `Type` is a string characterizing the claim type.
- `Value` contains the claim value, also represented as a string.

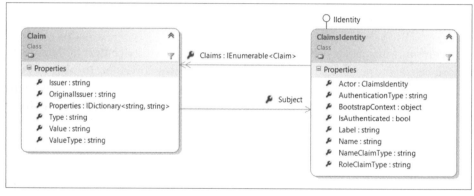

Figure 15-5. The Claim and ClaimsIdentity classes

The following code excerpt illustrates the three `Claim` core properties, for a claim obtained from the process's Windows identity:

```
[Fact]
public void Claims_have_an_issuer_a_type_and_a_value()
{
    AppDomain.CurrentDomain.SetPrincipalPolicy(
        PrincipalPolicy.WindowsPrincipal);
    var identity = Thread.CurrentPrincipal.Identity as ClaimsIdentity;
    Assert.NotNull(identity);
    var nameClaim = identity.Claims
        .First(c => c.Type == ClaimsIdentity.DefaultNameClaimType);
    Assert.Equal(identity, nameClaim.Subject);

    Assert.Equal("AD AUTHORITY", nameClaim.Issuer);
```

```
    Assert.Equal(ClaimTypes.Name, nameClaim.Type);
    Assert.Equal(
        "http://schemas.xmlsoap.org/ws/2005/05/identity/claims/name",
        nameClaim.Type);
    Assert.True(nameClaim.Value.EndsWith("pedro"));
}
```

The ClaimTypes class contains a set of commonly used claim type identifiers:

```
public static class ClaimTypes
{
    public const string Role = "http://schemas.microsoft.com/.../claims/role";
    public const string AuthenticationInstant = ...
    public const string AuthenticationMethod = ...
    public const string AuthorizationDecision = ...
    public const string Dns = ...
    public const string Email = ...
    public const string MobilePhone = ...
    public const string Name = ...
    public const string NameIdentifier = ...
    // other members elided for readability
}
```

NET Framework 4.5 also introduced two new claims-based concrete classes:

- The ClaimsIdentity class, also shown in Figure 15-5, represents an identity as a claim sequence.

- The ClaimsPrincipal class represents a principal as one or more claims-based identities.

Note that these new classes also implement the old IPrincipal and IIdentity interfaces, meaning they can be used with legacy code. In addition, the old concrete principal and identity classes, such as WindowsPrincipal or FormsIdentity, were also retrofitted to derive from these new claims-based classes, as shown in Figure 15-6.

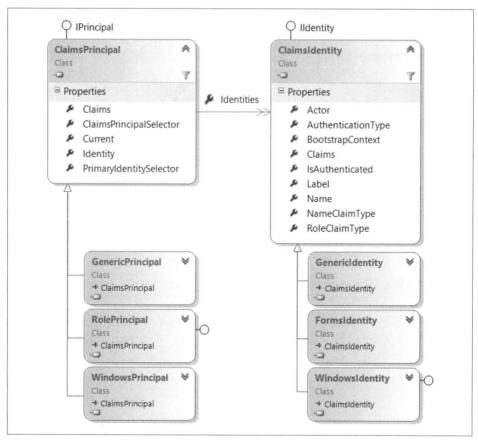

Figure 15-6. The ClaimsPrincipal and ClaimsIdentity classes

For the remainder of this chapter, we will be using the new claims-based classes to represent identities.

Windows Identity Foundation and the .NET Framework

The class model for claims-aware applications was initially introduced in 2009 as an extension to the .NET platform, called *Windows Identity Foundation*. This class model was mostly contained in the Microsoft.IdentityModel namespace. Starting with version 4.5, this class model became an integral part of the .NET Framework. This introduced some breaking changes, namely the migration to the System namespace.

In distributed systems, the source for the identity information and the party interested in it may not be the same. In these contexts, it is important to distinguish these two parties:

- An *identity provider* is an entity that issues identity claims about a subject, typically containing information for which it is authoritative or that it has verified.
- A *relying party* is an entity that uses (i.e., consumes or relies on) identity claims issued by an identity provider.

Figure 15-7 shows the relations between these two parties. The task of a distributed authentication protocol, such as WS-Federation, is to provide the mechanisms for:

- A relying party to request identity claims about a subject to an identity provider
- The identity provider to issue and make these claims available to the requesting relying party

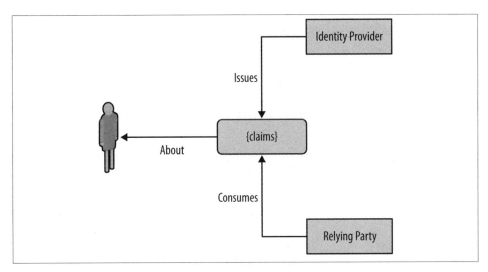

Figure 15-7. Identity providers and relying parties

Retrieving and Assigning the Current Principal

In the early days of the .NET Framework, the retrieving and assignment of the *current* principal was performed via the `Thread.CurrentPrincipal` static property. However, currently this technique presents two problems. First, a request isn't necessarily executed by a single thread. Specifically, the broad adoption of asynchronous programming models means that the affinity between a request and its single executing thread doesn't exist anymore. Secondly, several .NET Framework components, such as ASP.NET and WCF, created alternative ways to access and define this information. As an example, in ASP.NET, the HttpContext class contains a User static property holding an IPrincipal. This increases the probability of incoherence between the identities present in these multiple places.

In version 1.0 of ASP.NET Web API, the correct way of assigning the *current* principal inside the message handler pipeline depends on the used host. When you are self-hosting, it is sufficient to assign the Thread.CurrentPrincipal. However, when using the web host, you must assign *both* the Thread.CurrentPrincipal and the HttpContext.Current.User. A commonly used technique is to check if HttpContext.Current isn't null:

```
Thread.CurrentPrincipal = principalToAssign;
if (HttpContext.Current != null)
{
    HttpContext.Current.User = principalToAssign;
}
```

Unfortunately, this technique creates a dependency to the System.Web assembly, even in the self-host scenario.

In ASP.NET Web API version 2.0, you can solve this problem by using the new HttpRequestContext class. First, the *current* identity should be retrieved and assigned to the current request object, not to a static property. Secondly, different hosts can use different HttpRequestContext implementations:

- The self-host uses the SelfHostHttpRequestContext, which simply assigns the Thread.CurrentPrincipal property.

- The web host uses the WebHostHttpRequestContext, which assigns both the Thread.CurrentPrincipal and the HttpContext.User properties.

- Finally, the OWIN host uses the OwinHttpRequestContext, which assigns both the Thread.CurrentPrincipal and the current OWIN context.

Unfortunately, there isn't a way that works for both versions of Web API. In the remainder of this book, we will primarily use the version 2.0 method.

Transport-Based Authentication

As we stated previously in this chapter, the TLS protocol can also be used to perform authentication, providing each transport peer with the verified identity of the remote peer. In the following sections, we show how to use this feature to obtain both server authentication and client authentication.

Server Authentication

When a client sends an HTTP request with an `https` request URI, the used connection must always be protected by TLS or SSL, ensuring the integrity and confidentiality of the sent message. In addition, the client must check the server identity by comparing the URI hostname with the identity present in the server's certificate, received during the handshake negotiation. This verification solves the server authentication problem by ensuring that an HTTP request message is sent only to a properly identified server.

The server's identity is obtained from the certificate in one of two ways:

- If the certificate contains a *subject alternative name* extension of type *DNS name*, then its value is used.
- Otherwise, the *common name* in the certificate *subject* field is used instead.

If the *subject alternative name* extension contains multiple names, then the URI hostname can match any of them. This feature allows the use of the same certificate for different hostnames (e.g., `www.example.net` and `api.example.net`), which is very useful when these hostnames are bound to the same IP address. For instance, until version 7.5 of IIS, different `https` bindings that use the same IP and port must use the same certificate.

The name in the server's certificate can also contain wildcards (e.g., `*.example.net`). As an example, the hostname `www.example.net` is matched by `*.example.net`. This feature is useful in multitenancy scenarios, where the set of hostnames is not known in advance, namely when the server's certificate is issued. As an example, currently the Azure Service Bus uses a certificate containing two alternative names: `*.service bus.windows.net` and `servicebus.windows.net`. This allows a hostname such as `my-tenant-name.servicebus.windows.net` to be matched by this certificate.

Currently, TLS-based server authentication is based on the PKI trust model described in Appendix G, where the overall security depends on the correct behavior of a set of certificate authorities. Unfortunately, this model presents a rather significant surface area for MITM (*man-in-the-middle*) attacks. For instance, if a certificate authority's (CA) name verification practices are compromised, an attacker can obtain certificates that bind public keys under his control to names that he does not own. The same consequence can result if the attacker is able to use the CA private keys to issue rogue certificates.

This problem is amplified by the high number of trusted root certification authorities configured by default on several platforms. As an example, the list of root certificates used by the Mozilla projects (e.g., the Firefox browser) has more than 150 different entries (*http://bit.ly/mozilla-cert*). Note that if *any* of these certificate authorities is compromised, then a MITM attack can be mounted against any server, even if its certificate is not issued by the compromised authority.

A solution to this security problem is the addition of extra contextual requirements to the server certificate validation process. One of these extra requirements is called *certificate pinning*, where the certificates in the chain are compared with a fixed set of known certificates, called the *pinset*. In scenarios where the first interaction of a client with a server is guaranteed to be safe from MITM attacks, the certificate chain presented by the server can be used to build the pinset. The rationale behind this choice is based on the low probability of a server changing the root authority that it uses.

Another choice is to use a static context-based pinset. As an example, the Chromium browser (*http://bit.ly/chromium-blog*) limits the CAs that can be used when users connect to the Gmail and Google account servers. Another example is the Twitter API security best practices (*http://bit.ly/twitter-ssl*), which state that any client application should ensure that the certificate chain returned by the Twitter servers contains a subset of the approved CAs.

When using `HttpClient`, you can enforce certificate pinning by using the `WebRequestHandler` client handler and a custom certificate validation callback, as shown in the following example:

```
private readonly CertThumbprintSet verisignCerts = new CertThumbprintSet(
    "85371ca6e550143dce2803471bde3a09e8f8770f",
    "62f3c89771da4ce01a91fc13e02b6057b4547a1d",

    "4eb6d578499b1ccf5f581ead56be3d9b6744a5e5",
    "5deb8f339e264c19f6686f5f8f32b54a4c46b476"
    );

[Fact]
public async Task Twitter_cert_pinning()
{
    var wrh = new WebRequestHandler();
    wrh.ServerCertificateValidationCallback =
        (sender, certificate, chain, errors) =>
        {
            var caCerts = chain.ChainElements
                .Cast<X509ChainElement>().Skip(1)
                .Select(elem => elem.Certificate);

            return errors == SslPolicyErrors.None &&
                caCerts.Any(cert =>
                    verisignCerts.Contains(cert.GetCertHashString()));
        };

    using (var client = new HttpClient(wrh))
    {
        await client.GetAsync("https://api.twitter.com");
```

```
        var exc = Assert.Throws<AggregateException>(() =>
            client.GetAsync("https://api.github.com/").Result);
        Assert.IsType<HttpRequestException>(exc.InnerExceptions[0]);
    }
}
```

The `verisignCerts` field contains the pinset as a set of certificate thumbprints contained in the custom `CertThumbprintSet` class:

```
public class CertThumbprintSet : HashSet<string>
{
    public CertThumbprintSet(params string[] thumbs)
        :base(thumbs, StringComparer.OrdinalIgnoreCase)
    {}
}
```

The `HttpClient` used in this example is created with an explicitly instantiated `WebRe questHandler`. This handler exposes the `ServerCertificateValidationCallback` property, which can be assigned with a delegate that is called by the runtime after the standard built-in certificate validation process is finished. This delegate receives this validation result, including information on the occurrence of errors, and returns a Boolean with the final validation result. It can be used to override the built-in validation result or to perform additional verification steps.

In this case, we use it for this last goal. The server certificate is considered valid only if:

- The built-in validation was successful; that is, `errors == SslPolicyErrors.None`.
- The certificate chain contains at least one of the known CA certificates (the pinned certificates).

Notice that the leaf certificate is skipped in this process, since we are interested only in ensuring that the CA certificates belong to a well-known pinset. Notice also that this pinset is applicable only to the Twitter context. As `Assert.Throws` illustrates, connecting to a different server (`api.github.com`) using this configuration results in a certificate authentication exception.

At the time of this writing, the use of certificate pinning is still highly context-dependent and must typically be coordinated with the authority managing the servers. The Twitter security best practices are an example of the pinning strategy. There are, however, some specifications being developed that aim to make this technique more generic. One of them, called *Public Key Pinning Extension for HTTP*, enables a server to instruct clients to pin the provided certificates for a given period of time. It accomplishes this by adding a response header with the pinned certificates and the pinning time period:

```
Public-Key-Pins: pin-sha1="4n972HfV354KP560yw4uqe/baXc=";
        pin-sha1="qvTGHdzF6KLavt4PO0gs2a6pQ00=";
        pin-sha256="LPJNul+wow4m6DsqxbninhsWHlwfp0JecwQzYpOLmCQ=";
        max-age=2592000
```

Another aspect that you should enforce when authenticating a server is to ensure that none of the presented certificates was revoked. However, for this to happen the `Serv icePointManager` must be explicitly configured via the `CheckCertificateRevocation List` static property:

```
ServicePointManager.CheckCertificateRevocationList = true;
```

The `ServicePointManager` is the class used by the .NET HTTP client infrastructure to obtain connections to servers, via `ServicePoint` objects.

We can also use the `WebRequestHandler.ServerCertificateValidationCallback` to ensure that the proper revocation verification was performed.

```
return errors == SslPolicyErrors.None &&
    caCerts.Any(cert => verisignCerts.Contains(cert.GetCertHashString())) &&
    chain.ChainPolicy.RevocationMode == X509RevocationMode.Online;
```

The last condition in the previous code excerpt uses the `ChainPolicy` property of the `X509Chain` received by the callback delegate to ensure that the revocation verification was performed over an online mechanism. If this condition does not hold, then the server certificate is not accepted and an exception is thrown.

Client Authentication

The TLS transport security mechanism can also provide client authentication. However, it requires the use of *client certificates*, increasing the client complexity and infrastructure requirements: clients must store private keys and have certificates issued to them. Because of these requirements, this client authentication option is not very common. However, you should strongly consider its use in the following scenarios:

- The security requirements demand a higher-assurance client authentication method.
- There is already a public key infrastructure (PKI) in place that can be used to issue the client certificates.

For instance, several European countries are developing electronic identity initiatives (*https://www.eid-stork.eu/*), where each citizen has a smartcard containing a personal certificate (and associated private key). These certificates can be used to authenticate the citizen's TLS interactions with e-government sites. So, when developing an e-government Web API in these contexts, you should consider using TLS client authentication. Currently, the major limitation is the difficulty in using these smartcards in portable devices, such as smartphones or tablets.

As a concrete example , the *Windows Azure Service Management REST API* is a public Web API using TLS-based client authentication: client requests must use a *management certificate*, previously associated with the managed service. In this API, the certificates are self-generated by the client and no PKI is required, which simplifies its usage.

When hosting on top of IIS, you can configure TLS client authentication in the SSL Settings of the IIS Manager Features view, as shown in Figure 15-8.

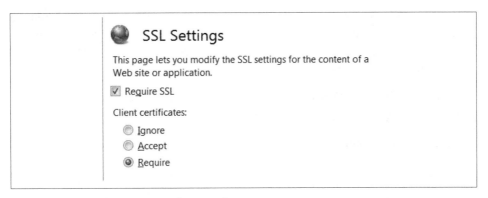

Figure 15-8. Configuring TLS client authentication

This setting is scoped to a folder and presents three options for the TLS handshake:

- Not requesting the client certificate (Ignore)
- Requesting the client certificate but allowing the client to not send one (Accept)
- Requesting the client certificate and requiring the client to send it (Require)

When self-hosting, you configure the client authentication using the `netsh` command-line tool, by using the `clientcertnegotiation` parameter when setting the server TLS certificate:

```
netsh http add sslcert (...) clientcertnegotiation=enable
```

The client certificate is not contained in the HTTP request sent by the client. Instead, this certificate is a property of the transport connection on which the request was received. This certificate is associated with the request object via the Web API hosting layer. If self-hosting, you must perform an additional configuration step: setting the configuration's `ClientCredentialType` property to `Certificate`:

```
var config = new HttpSelfHostConfiguration("https://www.example.net:8443");
config.ClientCredentialType = HttpClientCredentialType.Certificate;
```

This configuration is required only so that the certificate information is flowed up from the self-host WCF adapter into the request object. It *does not* influence the way the TLS connection is negotiated and established—namely, it does not replace the `netsh`-based configuration. When you're using web hosting, this configuration step isn't required.

The HttpSelfHostConfiguration also contains the X509CertificateValidator property, allowing the definition of an additional custom certificate validation procedure. Note that this definition *does not* change the certificate validation done by the TLS HTTP.SYS implementation; it simply adds another one. Also, it is available only when you're self-hosting.

When using TLS-based client-side authentication, you obtain the client's identity at the server side by inspecting the negotiated certificate, independently of the hosting scenario. This information is retrieved from the request message via the GetClientCertificate extension method, as shown in Example 15-1.

Example 15-1. Accessing the client certificate

```
public class HelloController : ApiController
{
    public HttpResponseMessage Get()
    {
        var clientCert = Request.GetClientCertificate();
        var clientName = clientCert == null ? "stranger" : clientCert.Subject;
        return new HttpResponseMessage
        {
            Content = new StringContent("Hello there, " + clientName)
        };
    }
}
```

In ASP.NET Web API 2.0, the new HttpRequestContext class can also be used to retrieve the client certificate:

```
var clientCert = Request.GetRequestContext().ClientCertificate;
```

However, a better approach is to create a message handler, such as the one shown in Example 15-2, that maps the received client certificate into a claims-based identity. This way, we obtain a homogeneous identity representation that is independent of the authentication mechanism. We can also use this message handler to perform additional certificate validation. By default, the TLS HTTP.SYS implementation will validate certificates using any of trusted root certification authorities present in the Windows Store. However, we may wish to limit this validation to a more restricted certification authority set.

Example 15-2. Message handler for certificate validation and claims mapping

```
public class X509CertificateMessageHandler : DelegatingHandler
{
    private readonly X509CertificateValidator _validator;
    private readonly Func<X509Certificate2, string> _issuerMapper;
    const string X509AuthnMethod =
        "http://schemas.microsoft.com/ws/2008/06/identity/authenticationmethod/x509";

    public X509CertificateMessageHandler(
```

```
        X509CertificateValidator validator,
        Func<X509Certificate2,string> issuerMapper)
{
    _validator = validator;
    _issuerMapper = issuerMapper;
}

protected override async Task<HttpResponseMessage> SendAsync(
    HttpRequestMessage request,
    CancellationToken cancellationToken)
{
    var cert = request.GetClientCertificate();
    if (cert == null) return await base.SendAsync(request, cancellationToken);
    try
    {
        _validator.Validate(cert);
    }
    catch (SecurityTokenValidationException)
    {
        return new HttpResponseMessage(HttpStatusCode.Unauthorized);
    }
    var issuer = _issuerMapper(cert);
    if (issuer == null)
    {
        return new HttpResponseMessage(HttpStatusCode.Unauthorized);
    }

    var claims = ExtractClaims(cert, issuer);
    var identity = new ClaimsIdentity(claims, X509AuthnMethod);
    AddIdentityToCurrentPrincipal(identity, request);

    return await base.SendAsync(request, cancellationToken);
}

private static IEnumerable<Claim> ExtractClaims(
    X509Certificate2 cert,
    string issuer)
{
    ...
}

private static void AddIdentityToCurrentPrincipal(ClaimsIdentity identity)
{
    ...
}
}
```

First, the client certificate is obtained from the request message via the GetClientCer
tificate extension method. Afterward, the validator defined in the constructor is used
to perform the additional certificate validation. The X509CertificateValidator is an

abstract base class, belonging to the .NET Framework, that represents a certificate validation process. It contains a set of static classes with commonly used validators:

```
public abstract class X509CertificateValidator : ICustomIdentityConfiguration
{
        // members and implementation elided for clarity
        public static X509CertificateValidator None {get{...}}
        public static X509CertificateValidator PeerTrust {get{...}}
        public static X509CertificateValidator ChainTrust {get{...}}
        public static X509CertificateValidator PeerOrChainTrust{get{...}}
}
```

If the certificate passes the additional verification, then the Func<X509Certificate2, string> is used to obtain an issuer name, which will be used when the extracted claims are created. The two common strategies for this are:

- Use the certificate's issuer name (e.g., CN=Demo Certification Authority, O=Web API Book).

- Map the CA certificate that issued the client's certificate to an issuer string, using a previously defined registry.

The IssuerNameRegistry is a .NET Framework class providing this last behavior.

After the issuer name is obtained, the claim set representing the requester is computed from the client certificate:

```
private static IEnumerable<Claim> ExtractClaims(
    X509Certificate2 cert,
    string issuer)
{
    var claims = new Collection<Claim>
        {
            new Claim(ClaimTypes.Thumbprint,
                    Convert.ToBase64String(cert.GetCertHash()),
                ClaimValueTypes.Base64Binary, issuer),
            new Claim(ClaimTypes.X500DistinguishedName,
                cert.SubjectName.Name,
                ClaimValueTypes.String, issuer),
            new Claim(ClaimTypes.SerialNumber, cert.SerialNumber,
                ClaimValueTypes.String, issuer),
            new Claim(ClaimTypes.AuthenticationMethod, X509AuthnMethod,
                ClaimValueTypes.String, issuer)
        };
    var email = cert.GetNameInfo(X509NameType.EmailName, false);
    if (email != null)
    {
        claims.Add(new Claim(ClaimTypes.Email, email,
            ClaimValueTypes.String, issuer));
    }
```

```
        return claims;
    }
```

In the previous example, we mapped several certificate fields into individual claims—namely, the certificate hash thumbprint, the subject's name, the certificate serial number, and the subject's email, if present. A claim with the authentication method is also added.

Finally, a claims identity is created and added to the current claims-based principal. If there isn't a current principal, then a new one is created:

```
private static void AddIdentityToCurrentPrincipal(ClaimsIdentity identity)
{
    private void AddIdentityToCurrentPrincipal(
        ClaimsIdentity identity,
        HttpRequestMessage request)
    {
        var principal = request.GetRequestContext().Principal as ClaimsPrincipal;
        if (principal == null)
        {
            principal = new ClaimsPrincipal(identity);
            request.GetRequestContext().Principal = principal;
        }
        else
        {
            principal.AddIdentity(identity);
        }
    }
}
```

Using a message handler to map the client certificate into a claims-based identity allows the downstream Web API runtime components to always consume identity information in the same manner. For instance, the previous `HelloController` presented in Example 15-1 can now be rewritten as:

```
public class HelloController : ApiController
{
    public HttpResponseMessage Get()
    {
        var principal = User as ClaimsPrincipal;
        var name = principal
            .Identities.SelectMany(ident => ident.Claims)
            .FirstOrDefault(c => c.Type == ClaimTypes.Email).Value ?? "stranger";
        return new HttpResponseMessage
        {
            Content = new StringContent("Hello there, " + name)
        };
    }
}
```

The `ApiController` class contains a `User` property with the requester's principal, similar to what happens in ASP.NET MVC. Note also that the consuming code deals only with claims and does not depend on the transport-based client mechanism. As an example, the use of a new authentication mechanism, such as the ones we'll address in the next section, will not require changes on the action's code. However, before we move on to message-based authentication, we must see how transport-based client authentication is used on the client side.

On the client side, the configuration of TLS-based authentication requires you to deal directly with one of the available HttpClient handlers presented in Chapter 14: HttpClientHandler or WebRequestHandler.

The first option is to explicitly configure the HttpClient with an HttpClientHandler instance, containing its ClientCertificateOptions property set to Automatic:

```
var client = new HttpClient(
    new HttpClientHandler{
        ClientCertificateOptions = ClientCertificateOption.Automatic
    });
// ...
```

The resulting HttpClient can then be used normally: if during a connection handshake the server requires the client certificate, the HttpClientHandler instance will automatically select a compatible client certificate. This option is the only one available for Windows Store applications.

For *classic* scenarios (e.g., console, WinForms, or WPF applications) there is a second option: using the WebRequestHandler:

```
var clientHandler = new WebRequestHandler()
clientHandler.ClientCertificates.Add(cert);
var client = new HttpClient(clientHandler)
```

Here, cert is a X509Certificate2 instance representing the client certificate. This instance can be constructed directly from a PFX file or obtained from a Windows certificate store:

```
X509Store store = null;
try
{
    store = new X509Store(StoreName.My, StoreLocation.CurrentUser);
    store.Open(OpenFlags.OpenExistingOnly | OpenFlags.ReadOnly);
    // select the certificate from store.Certificates ...
}
finally
{
    if(store != null) store.Close();
}
```

Having explored the use of the transport security mechanism to provide client and server authentication, we will now see how these security requirements can also be addressed at the HTTP message level.

The HTTP Authentication Framework

As we saw in Chapter 1, the HTTP protocol specification includes a generic *authentication framework*, upon which concrete mechanisms can be defined. The *basic authentication* and *digest access authentication* schemes are examples of such mechanisms, both defined by RFC 2617. This authentication framework defines both response status codes, message headers, and a challenge-response sequence that can be used by the concrete mechanisms, as illustrated in Chapter 1 and Appendix E.

The basic authentication scheme uses a simple username and password pair to authenticate the client. These credentials are added to the request message in the following manner:

1. The username and the password are concatenated, separated by a : (colon).

2. The concatenation result is Base64-encoded to produce a string that is placed after the `Basic` scheme identifier in the `Authorization` header.

Example 15-3 presents a code fragment for obtaining user information from the GitHub API, using basic authentication. Notice the addition of the `Authorization` header to the request message.

Example 15-3. Obtaining user information from GitHub using basic authentication

```
using (var client = new HttpClient())
{
    var req = new HttpRequestMessage(
        HttpMethod.Get, "https://api.github.com/user");
    req.Headers.UserAgent.Add(new ProductInfoHeaderValue("webapibook","1.0"));
    req.Headers.Authorization = new AuthenticationHeaderValue(
        "Basic",
        Convert.ToBase64String(
            Encoding.ASCII.GetBytes(username + ':' + password))
        );
    var resp = await client.SendAsync(req);
    Console.WriteLine(resp.StatusCode);
    var cont = await resp.Content.ReadAsStringAsync();
    Console.WriteLine(cont);
}
```

On the server side, the use of basic authentication can be enforced by a message handler, such as the one presented in Example 15-4. This handler checks for the presence of an `Authorization` header with the `Basic` scheme and tries to extract the username and password in order to validate it. If this verification succeeds, a principal describing the requester is created and added to the request message, before the processing is delegated to the next handler. If any of the preceding conditions fails, the handler short-circuits the request by producing a response message with a 401 status code.

In any of the former cases, if the response message has a 401 status code, then a WWW-Authenticate header containing the required scheme and the realm name is added.

Example 15-4. Basic authentication message handler

```
public class BasicAuthenticationDelegatingHandler : DelegatingHandler
{
    private readonly Func<string, string, Task<ClaimsPrincipal>> _validator;
    private readonly string _realm;

    public BasicAuthenticationDelegatingHandler(string realm, Func<string, string,
        Task<ClaimsPrincipal>> validator)
    {
        _validator = validator;
        _realm = "realm=" + realm;
    }

    protected async override Task<HttpResponseMessage> SendAsync(
        HttpRequestMessage request,
        CancellationToken cancellationToken)
    {
        HttpResponseMessage res;
        if (!request.HasAuthorizationHeaderWithBasicScheme())
        {
            res = await base.SendAsync(request, cancellationToken);
        }
        else
        {
            var principal = await
                request.TryGetPrincipalFromBasicCredentialsUsing(_validator);
            if (principal != null)
            {
                request.GetRequestContext().Principal = principal;
                res = await base.SendAsync(request, cancellationToken);
            }
            else
            {
                res = request.CreateResponse(HttpStatusCode.Unauthorized);
            }
        }

        if (res.StatusCode == HttpStatusCode.Unauthorized)
        {
            res.Headers.WwwAuthenticate.Add(
                new AuthenticationHeaderValue("Basic", _realm));
        }
        return res;
    }
}
```

If the authentication is successful, the resulting principal is added to the request via the `HttpRequestContext.Principal`. The extraction and validation is performed by an extension method:

```
public static async Task<ClaimsPrincipal>
    TryGetPrincipalFromBasicCredentialsUsing(
        this HttpRequestMessage req,
        Func<string,string,Task<ClaimsPrincipal>> validate)
{
    string pair;
    try
    {
        pair = Encoding.UTF8.GetString(
            Convert.FromBase64String(req.Headers.Authorization.Parameter));
    }
    catch (FormatException)
    {
        return null;
    }
    catch (ArgumentException)
    {
        return null;
    }
    var ix = pair.IndexOf(':');
    if (ix == -1) return null;
    var username = pair.Substring(0, ix);
    var pw = pair.Substring(ix + 1);
    return await validate(username, pw);
}
```

This function is decoupled from the username and password validation login, which is passed in as a delegate in the handler constructor.

Implementing HTTP-Based Authentication

In the previous example, we implemented server-side HTTP authentication as a Web API message handler. However, there are other architectural options: authentication can be implemented up in the pipeline as a Web API filter, or down in the hosting layer. Next we'll discuss the advantages and disadvantages of each option.

Implementing authentication on a Web API filter has the advantage of giving you access to a richer set of request information, namely:

- The selected controller and routes
- The routing parameters
- The action's parameters (if implemented as a action filter)

This option is relevant when the authentication depends on this information. In addition, Web API filters may be selectively applied to only a subset of controllers or actions.

However, implementing authentication at the filter level also has some important disadvantages:

- Improperly authenticated requests are detected later in the pipeline, increasing the computational cost of rejected requests.

- The requester's identity is available only later in the pipeline. This means that other middleware components, such as caching middleware, may not have access to the identity information. If the caching should be private (i.e., segregated by user), then this is a severe limitation.

An alternative option is to implement authentication on a message handler, as shown previously. Since a message handler runs immediately after the hosting adaptation layer, the cost of rejected requests is smaller. Also, the identity information is immediately available to all the following handlers. Since message handlers are also available on the client side, when you use HttpClient, this approach exhibits an interesting symmetry.

However, the use of the OWIN specification, described in Chapter 11, introduces another option for implementing authentication: OWIN middleware. This option presents important advantages:

- It broadens the usage scope, since the same authentication middleware can now be used by multiple frameworks, not only ASP.NET Web API.

- The identity information is immediately available to other downstream OWIN middleware, such as caching or logging.

In fact, the introduction of the OWIN specification means that all intermediary layers that are not specific to a framework should probably be best implemented as OWIN middleware. This is the approach being followed by the Katana project, which includes a set of authentication middleware implementations.

Obviously, this approach is applicable only when you're hosting Web API on top of an OWIN server. However, the increasing OWIN adoption makes this scenario much more plausible.

Katana Authentication Middleware

Version 2.0 of the Katana project includes a set of middleware implementations, providing multiple authentication mechanisms with different usage scopes, ranging from classical cookie-based authentication to OAuth 2.0–based authorization. These middleware implementations are based on an extensible class infrastructure, which we'll describe in the following paragraphs.

At the root of this infrastructure it is the base abstract AuthenticationMiddleware<TOp tion> class, shown in Example 15-5, from which concrete authentication middleware can derive.

Example 15-5. The authentication middleware base class

```
public abstract class AuthenticationMiddleware<TOptions> : OwinMiddleware
        where TOptions : AuthenticationOptions
{
    protected AuthenticationMiddleware(OwinMiddleware next, TOptions options)
        : base(next)
    { ... }

    public TOptions Options { get; set; }

    public override async Task Invoke(IOwinContext context)
    {
        AuthenticationHandler<TOptions> handler = CreateHandler();
        await handler.Initialize(Options, context);
        if (!await handler.InvokeAsync())
        {
            await Next.Invoke(context);
        }
        await handler.TeardownAsync();
    }

    protected abstract AuthenticationHandler<TOptions> CreateHandler();
}
```

This class is parameterized by a TOption type that defines the authentication middleware configuration options, such as credential validation. Typically, the development of custom authentication middleware includes the definition of a specific options class, such as the one presented in Example 15-6.

Example 15-6. Basic authentication options

```
public class BasicAuthenticationOptions : AuthenticationOptions
{
    public Func<string, string, Task<AuthenticationTicket>>
        ValidateCredentials { get; private set; }
    public string Realm { get; private set; }

    public BasicAuthenticationOptions(
        string realm,
        Func<string, string, Task<AuthenticationTicket>> validateCredentials)
        : base("Basic")
    {
        Realm = realm;
        ValidateCredentials = validateCredentials;
    }
}
```

The `OwinMiddleware.Invoke` method, called when the request is being passed through the middleware pipeline, delegates the authentication behavior into an *authentication handler* instance, provided by the `CreateHandler` method. So, the main task of a custom authentication middleware is typically just the definition of this method, as illustrated by Example 15-7.

Example 15-7. Basic authentication middleware

```
class BasicAuthnMiddleware : AuthenticationMiddleware<BasicAuthenticationOptions>
{
    public BasicAuthnMiddleware(
        OwinMiddleware next,
        BasicAuthenticationOptions options)
        : base(next, options)
    {}

    protected override AuthenticationHandler<BasicAuthenticationOptions>
        CreateHandler()
    {
        return new BasicAuthenticationHandler(Options);
    }
}
```

To better understand the handler's responsibilities, you'll find it useful to see how it is used by the base middleware. As shown in Example 15-5, after creating the handler, the base middleware's `Invoke` method performs three steps. First, it calls the handler's `Initialize` method. As we will see briefly, it is this method that triggers most of the authentication behavior. Afterward, it calls the handler's `InvokeAsync` method. If the return value is `false`, then the next middleware in the chain is called. Otherwise, the request processing is short-circuited, meaning that no more downstream middleware is called. Finally, at the end, the `TeardownAsync` method is called to finalize the handler's instance. Notice that the middleware and the handler objects have different lifetimes: the middleware lasts for the duration of the application, while the handler instance is specific to single-request processing. This is one of the reasons that justifies the existence of these two separate concepts.

The `AuthenticationHandler` abstract class, shown in Figure 15-9, is where most of the common authentication coordination resides. The specific authentication logic is delegated to hook methods implemented by concrete derived classes. In the context of the HTTP framework-based authentication, two of these hook methods are particularly relevant: `AuthenticateCoreAsync` and `ApplyResponseChallengeAsync`.

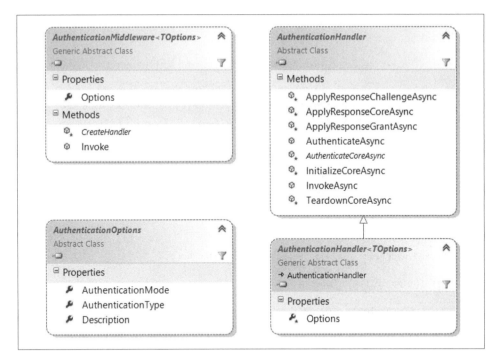

Figure 15-9. Katana authentication middleware

The `AuthenticateCoreAsync` method is called by the handler's `Initialize` method to try to authenticate the current request. Example 15-8 shows an `Authentication CoreAsync` implementation that tries to get and validate the `Basic` credentials from the request's `Authorization` header. If it's sucessful, an identity is returned, which will be added by the base `Initialize` method to the request—more specifically, to the `serv er.User` context entry. If not, `null` is returned to signal that no sucessful authentication was achieved.

`ApplyResponseChallengeAsync` is registered by the handler's `Initialize` method to be called on the response's `OnSendingHeaders` event, which is triggered just before the response's headers start to be sent to the connection. Example 15-8 also shows a `Ap plyResponseChallengeAsync` implementation that adds a `WWW-Authenticate` challenge header, with the `Basic` scheme, if the response is a `401`.

Example 15-8. Basic authentication handler

```
class BasicAuthenticationHandler : AuthenticationHandler<BasicAuthenticationOptions>
{
    private readonly string _challenge;

    public BasicAuthenticationHandler(BasicAuthenticationOptions options)
    {
```

```
        _challenge = "Basic realm=" + options.Realm;
    }

    protected override async Task<AuthenticationTicket> AuthenticateCoreAsync()
    {
        var authzValue = Request.Headers.Get("Authorization");
        if (string.IsNullOrEmpty(authzValue) || !authzValue.StartsWith("Basic ",
            StringComparison.OrdinalIgnoreCase))
        {
            return null;
        }
        var token = authzValue.Substring("Basic ".Length).Trim();
        return await
            token.TryGetPrincipalFromBasicCredentialsUsing(
                Options.ValidateCredentials);
    }

    protected override Task ApplyResponseChallengeAsync()
    {
        if (Response.StatusCode == 401)
        {
            var challenge = Helper.LookupChallenge(
                Options.AuthenticationType, Options.AuthenticationMode);
            if (challenge != null)
            {
                Response.Headers.AppendValues("WWW-Authenticate", _challenge);
            }
        }
        return Task.FromResult<object>(null);
    }
}
```

The AuthenticationTicket type, asynchronously returned by the Authentication Ticket hook method, is a new type introduced by the Katana project to represent an identity. It is composed of a claims identity and a set of additional authentication properties:

```
public class AuthenticationTicket
{
    public AuthenticationTicket(
        ClaimsIdentity identity, AuthenticationProperties properties)
    {
        Identity = identity;
        Properties = properties;
    }

    public ClaimsIdentity Identity { get; private set; }
    public AuthenticationProperties Properties { get; private set; }
}
```

To facilitate the middleware registration, it is typical for custom authentication implementations to also provide an extension method such as the one shown in Example 15-9. This enables usages such as this one:

```
app.UseBasicAuthentication(
    new BasicAuthenticationOptions("webapibook", (un, pw) => {
    /* some credential validation logic */
}));
```

Example 15-9. Extension method used to register the basic authentication middleware

```
public static class BasicAuthnMiddlewareExtensions
{
    public static IAppBuilder UseBasicAuthentication(
        this IAppBuilder app, BasicAuthenticationOptions options)
    {
        return app.Use(typeof(BasicAuthnMiddleware), options);
    }
}
```

Active and Passive Authentication Middleware

In the OWIN specification, middleware accesses the request before it reaches the web framework. This means that the authentication requirements may not be known at the time the middleware is run. As an example, consider a classical web application and a Web API hosted on the same OWIN host. The former may use cookies and forms-based authentication, while the latter may use basic authentication. Using cookies to inadvertently authenticate a Web API request may result in security problems such as CSRF (cross-site request forgery) attacks, since cookies are automatically sent by browser-based user agents.

For this reason, Katana introduced the concept of active and passive authentication modes. When in *active* mode, an authentication middleware will *actively* try to authenticate the request, adding an identity to the request context if successful. It also will add a challenge to the responses if they have 401 status codes. On the other hand, a middleware in *passive* mode registers itself only on a *authentication manager*. Only if explicitly asked does the handler try to authenticate the request and produce an identity. Authentication middleware operating in passive mode will also add challenges only if explicitly instructed by the authentication manager.

The *authentication manager* is yet another concept introduced by Katana and defines an interface through which other components, such as web applications, can interact with authentication middleware. In the next section, when describing Web API's authentication filters, we will present a concrete example of such usage.

The operation mode of an authentication middleware is defined by the `AuthenticationOptions.AuthenticationMode` property. For the most part, concrete authentication implementations don't have to be aware of the configured authentication mode. Instead, the behavioral differences are located in the common code located in the base `AuthenticationHandler` class. For instance, `AuthenticateCoreAsync` will be called only if the authentication mode is active.

One notable exception to this rule is the addition of challenges to the response. `ApplyR esponseChallengeAsync` is always called by the infrastructure, independently of the configured mode. However, the challenge should be added only if the mode is active or if the authentication scheme was added to the authentication manager.

The `ApplyResponseChallengeAsync` implementation in Example 15-8 uses the `Help er.LookupChallenge` utility method to decide if the challenge should be added.

Web API Authentication Filters

As stated before, an alternative architectural decision is to place authentication behavior on Web API filters. Version 2.0 of Web API introduces a new action pipeline stage, specifically designed to handle authentication. This stage is composed of *authentication filters* and precedes the authorization filters stage, meaning that it is the first one in the action pipeline.

An authentication filter is defined by the following interface, which contains two asynchronous methods:

```
public interface IAuthenticationFilter : IFilter
{
    Task AuthenticateAsync(
        HttpAuthenticationContext context,
        CancellationToken cancellationToken);

    Task ChallengeAsync(
        HttpAuthenticationChallengeContext context,
        CancellationToken cancellationToken);
}
```

This authentication pipeline stage is divided into two phases: request processing and response processing. In the first one, the Web API runtime calls the `AuthenticateAsync` method for each one of the registered filters, passing an *authentication context* containing both the action context and the request:

```
public class HttpAuthenticationContext
{
    public HttpActionContext ActionContext { get; private set; }
    public IPrincipal Principal { get; set; }
    public IHttpActionResult ErrorResult { get; set; }
    public HttpRequestMessage Request { get { ... }}
    ...
}
```

Each filter's `AuthenticateAsync` method is responsible for authenticating the context's request. If no credentials of the appropriate scheme are present in the message, then the context should be left unchanged. If credentials are present and valid, then the context's `Principal` property is assigned with the authenticated principal. Otherwise, if the credentials are invalid, a 401 status response message should be assigned to the context's `ErrorResult`, signaling to the runtime that there was an authentication error. As a consequence, the request processing phase is immediately stopped, without calling any further `AuthenticateAsync` method, and the response phase is started.

If no filter assigned the context's `ErrorResult`, then the runtime continues to the next action pipeline phase. This happens independently of the context's principal being assigned or not, delegating to upper layers the decision of whether or not to authorize the anonymous request.

The response processing phase of the authentication stage starts when a response is returned from the upper layer or if an error response was produced by an authentication filter. In this response phase, the `ChallengeAsync` method is called for each one of the registered filters, passing a *challenge context*:

```
public class HttpAuthenticationContext
{
    public HttpActionContext ActionContext { get; private set; }
    public IPrincipal Principal { get; set; }
    public IHttpActionResult ErrorResult { get; set; }
    public HttpRequestMessage Request { get { ... }}
    // members and definitions elided for clarity
}
```

This gives the authentication filters the opportunity to inspect the result message and add an authentication challenge if appropriate. Note that this method is always called for *all* authentication filters, independently of what happened in the request processing phase.

Example 15-10 shows a concrete authentication filter for the basic authentication scheme. Since the credential validation process may involve communication with external systems (e.g., a credential database), we use a function returning a `Task<Claim sPrincipal>`. If no `Authorization` header is present or if the scheme is not `Basic`, then `AuthenticateAsync` leaves the context unchanged. If credentials are present but are invalid, then an `UnauthorizedResult` representing a 401 status response is assigned to the `ErrorResult`. This `UnauthorizedResult` has an empty challenge list, since this challenge information is added to the response processing phase by the `ChallengeAsync` method.

`ChallengeAsync` simply checks if the response has a 401 status, and if so adds the appropriate challenge. The use of the `ActionResultDelegate` helper is required because the context's `Response` property is an `IHttpActionResult`, not directly an `HttpRespon` seMessage. This helper combines a sequence of IHttpActionResult instances into a single one.

Example 15-10. Basic authentication message handler

```
public class BasicAuthenticationFilter : IAuthenticationFilter
{
    private readonly Func<string, string, Task<ClaimsPrincipal>> _validator;
    private readonly string _realm;
    public bool AllowMultiple { get { return false; } }

    public BasicAuthenticationFilter(
        string realm, Func<string, string, Task<ClaimsPrincipal>> validator)
    {
        _validator = validator;
        _realm = "realm=" + realm;
    }

    public async Task AuthenticateAsync(
        HttpAuthenticationContext context,
        CancellationToken cancellationToken)
    {
        var req = context.Request;
        if (req.HasAuthorizationHeaderWithBasicScheme())
        {
            var principal = await
                req.TryGetPrincipalFromBasicCredentialsUsing(_validator);
            if (principal != null)
            {
                context.Principal = principal;
            }
            else
            {
                // challenges will be added by the ChallengeAsync
                context.ErrorResult = new UnauthorizedResult(
                    new AuthenticationHeaderValue[0], context.Request);
            }
        }
    }

    public Task ChallengeAsync(
        HttpAuthenticationChallengeContext context,
        CancellationToken cancellationToken)
    {
        context.Result = new ActionResultDelegate(context.Result, async (ct, next) =>
        {
            var res = await next.ExecuteAsync(ct);
            if (res.StatusCode == HttpStatusCode.Unauthorized)
            {
                res.Headers.WwwAuthenticate.Add(
                new AuthenticationHeaderValue("Basic", _realm));
            }
```

```
            return res;
        });
        return Task.FromResult<object>(null);
    }
}
```

ASP.NET Web API 2.0 also includes a concrete IAuthenticationFilter implementation, named HostAuthenticationFilter, that uses Katana's authentication middleware, via the Katana authentication manager.

On the AuthenticateAsync method, this filter starts by trying to obtain the Katana authentication manager from the request context. If the authentication manager is present, the filter then uses it to authenticate the request, passing the configured authentication type. Internally, the authentication manager checks if a compatible middleware was registered and, if so, invokes it to authenticate the request (passive mode) or returns the result of the previous authentication already done on the middleware pipeline (active mode).

Similarly, the HostAuthenticationFilter.ChallengeAsync method also tries to obtain the Katana authentication manager and uses it to add the challenge information, which will then be used by Katana's authentication middleware to add the challenge WWW-Authenticate header.

Token-Based Authentication

Unfortunately, the password-based HTTP basic authentication method described and used in the previous sections has several problems. The first set results from the password having to be sent on *every* request:

- The client must store the password or obtain it from the user on every request, which is rather impractical. Notice also that this storage must be done in clear text or through a reversible protection method, which increases the risk of password exposure.

- Similarly, the server has to validate the password on every request, which can have a significant cost.

- The validation information is typically stored on external systems.

- The validation process has a high computational cost due to the techniques used to protect against dictionary attacks.

- The probability of accidental exposure to an unauthorized party is increased.

Passwords also typically have low uncertainty and are subject to dictionary attacks. This means that any publicly available system that validates passwords must have protections against this type of attack, for instance by limiting the number of incorrect validations that are performed in a given time period.

Passwords also typically have broad scopes, meaning that the same password is used to authenticate a client when accessing any resource on a given system. Most of the time, it would be useful to have a credential that's usable only on a resource or HTTP method subset.

Password-based mechanisms are also not compatible with distributed scenarios, where the authentication process is delegated to external systems, such as organizational or social identity providers. Finally, they are not adequate for delegation scenarios, which we will see in Chapter 16.

A better approach to Web API authentication is to use *security tokens*, which are defined by RFC 4949 as "a data object (…) used to verify an identity in an authentication process." A concrete token example is the use of authentication cookies on a typical web application:

1. An initial bootstrap authentication is performed, eventually using a password-based mechanism, which results in the creation of a cookie that is returned to the client.

2. Every subsequent request made by the client is authenticated via this cookie and does not require the bootstrapping credentials.

Security tokens are a rather general and abstract concept; they may be instantiated in different ways and possess different characteristics. Next we present some of the most relevant design alternatives.

First, security tokens can *contain* the represented security information or just be a *reference* to that information. In the latter case, a token simply contains a nonforgeable reference to a security store entry, typically managed by the token issuer. These reference-based tokens are also called *artifacts* and have two main benefits:

- They have shorter dimensions, which is important when they have to be embedded in URIs.

- They are easier to revoke or cancel; the issuer just has to delete the referenced store entry.

However, they are not self-contained: obtaining the represented security information typically requires an query to the token issuer or external store. Thus, they are more commonly used when the issuing and consuming entities are the same or when there are length restrictions.

A nonforgeable reference token can be made of a random bit string with sufficient length (e.g., 256 bits), created by the token issuer. The associated token security information is then stored, keyed by the hash value of this reference. The use of a cryptographic hash function means that:

- It is easy to compute the store key and access the security information, given the token contents.

- It is hard to compute a valid token given the store key, which is an extra layer of defense in case an attacker can read the store contents.

The alternative option to references is for tokens to contain the security information, securely packaged for communication between two or more parties. This packaging requires the use of cryptographic mechanisms and ensures properties such as:

Confidentiality
  Only the authorized receiver should be able to access the contained information.

Integrity
  The consuming party should be able to detect any modifications to the token while in transit between the two parties.

These tokens are commonly called *assertions* and have the advantage of being self-contained: the token consumer can obtain the security information without having to access an external system or store. The downside is that they have higher dimensions, which can exceed the practical URI limits. They also require the use of cryptographic mechanisms for their production and consumption. The SAML (Security Assertion Markup Language) assertions are a broadly used example of self-contained tokens, where the security information is represented in a XML idiom and protected via XML-Signature and XML-Encryption. This type of security token is commonly used by classical federation protocols such as the SAML protocols, WS-Federation, or WS-Trust.

The JSON Web Token (JWT) is a more recent format for self-contained tokens, based on the JSON syntax. This token type aims to be usable in "space constrained environments such as HTTP Authorization headers and URI query parameters."

The following example represents a signed JWT token:

```
eyJ0eXAiOiJKV1QiLCJhbGciOiJIUzI1NiJ9.eyJpc3MiOiJodHRwOi8vaXNzdWVyLndlYmFwaWJvb
2submV0IiwiYXVkIjoiaHR0cDovL2V4YW1wbGUubmV0IiwibmJmIjoxMzc2NTcxNzAxLCJleHAiOjE
zNzY1NzIwMDEsInN1YiI6ImFsaWNlQHdlYmFwaWJvb2submV0IiwiZW1haWwiOiJhbGljZUB3ZWJhc
Glib29rLm5ldCIsIm5hbWUiOiJBbGljZSJ9.fCO6l0k_hey40kqEVuvMfiM8LeXJtsYLfNWBOvwbU-I
```

The JWT token is composed of a sequence of parts, separated by the . character. Each part is the *base64url* encoding of an octet stream: the first two octet streams result from the UTF-8 encoding of two JSON objects and the last one is the output of a signature scheme. The first object (encoded in the first part) is the JWT *header*:

```
{"typ":"JWT","alg":"HS256"}
```

It defines the token type and applied cryptographic protection. In this case, only integrity protection was added via a MAC scheme (HS256 stands for HMAC-SHA256). However, the JWT header also supports the encryption of its contents.

The second object is the JWT *claims set* (line breaks added for clarity):

```
{
  "iss":"http://issuer.webapibook.net",
  "aud":"http://example.net",
  "nbf":1376571701,
  "exp":1376572001,
  "sub":"alice@webapibook.net",
  "email":"alice@webapibook.net",
  "name":"Alice"
}
```

The JWT claims set object contains claims for a *subject* asserted by an *issuer* and intended to be used by an *audience*. Each property corresponds to the claim type and the property's value contains the claim value, which can be any JSON value (e.g., a string or an array). Some claim types are defined by the JWT specification, namely:

- iss (issuer) identifies the token issuer.
- sub (subject) is an unique identifier for the token subject—that is, the entity to which the token claim applies.
- aud (audience) identifies the allowed claim consumers.
- exp (expiration) and nbf (not before) define a valid time period.

Example 15-11 shows how a JWT token can be created and consumed, using the JwtSecurityTokenHandler class available in the System.IdentityModel.Tokens.Jwt NuGet package.

Example 15-11. Creating and consuming a JWT token

```
[Fact]
public void Can_create_and_consume_jwt_tokens()
{
    const string issuer = "http://issuer.webapibook.net";
    const string audience = "the.client@apps.example.net";
    const int lifetimeInMinutes = 5;

    var tokenHandler = new JwtSecurityTokenHandler();

    var symmetricKey = GetRandomBytes(256 / 8);
    var signingCredentials = new SigningCredentials(
        new InMemorySymmetricSecurityKey(symmetricKey),
        "http://www.w3.org/2001/04/xmldsig-more#hmac-sha256",
        "http://www.w3.org/2001/04/xmlenc#sha256");

    var now = DateTime.UtcNow;

    var claims = new[]
    {
        new Claim("sub", "alice@webapibook.net"),
```

```
        new Claim("email", "alice@webapibook.net"),
        new Claim("name", "Alice"),
    };

    var token = new JwtSecurityToken(issuer, audience, claims,
        new Lifetime(now, now.AddMinutes(lifetimeInMinutes)), signingCredentials);

    var tokenString = tokenHandler.WriteToken(token);

    var parts = tokenString.Split('.');
    Assert.Equal(3, parts.Length);

    var validationParameters = new TokenValidationParameters()
    {
        AllowedAudience = audience,
        SigningToken = new BinarySecretSecurityToken(symmetricKey),
        ValidIssuer = issuer,
    };

    tokenHandler.NameClaimType = ClaimTypes.NameIdentifier;
    var principal = tokenHandler.ValidateToken(tokenString, validationParameters);

    var identity = principal.Identities.First();

    Assert.Equal("alice@webapibook.net", identity.Name);
    Assert.Equal("alice@webapibook.net",
        identity.Claims.First(c => c.Type == ClaimTypes.NameIdentifier).Value);
    Assert.Equal("alice@webapibook.net",
        identity.Claims.First(c => c.Type == ClaimTypes.Email).Value);
    Assert.Equal("Alice", identity.Claims.First(c => c.Type == "name").Value);
    Assert.Equal(issuer, identity.Claims.First().Issuer);
}
```

On the validation side, `TokenValidationParameters` defines the token consumption parameters, such as the allowed destinations (audiences) and issuers. These parameters also define the signature validation key. Since the example uses a symmetrical signature scheme, the same key must be used both on the production and consumption sides. If the validation is successful, a claims principal with the token's claims is also produced.

Another token classification characteristic is the way they are bound to a message. The two most common alternatives are *bearer* and *holder-of-key*.

Bearer tokens are defined by RFC 6750 as:

> *A security token with the property that any party in possession of the token (a "bearer") can use the token in any way that any other party in possession of it can. Using a bearer token does not require a bearer to prove possession of cryptographic key material (proof-of-possession).*

A bearer token is simply added to a message without any additional binding between the two. This means that any party that has access to the plain-text message can get the contained token and use it on another message without any additional knowledge. In this regard, bearer tokens are similar to bearer checks: they can be used by a subject without any additional identity proof.

Bearer tokens are easy to use; however, their security fully depends on:

- The confidentiality of the message where they are contained
- The guarantee that they are never sent to the wrong parties

An alternative approach is the *holder-of-key* method, where, for each authenticated message, the client must prove the knowledge of a cryptographic key bound to the token. The client typically does this by adding a symmetric signature (a message authentication code) of selected parts of the message, computed with the cryptographic key.

As in the basic authentication scheme, a secret is also shared between the client and the server. However, this secret is really a key that is used to sign and validate messages and *is never transmitted*:

- The client uses the shared key to sign some carefully chosen parts of the request message and then attaches this signature to the message before sending it to the server, alongside the token (similar to a username).
- The server uses the token to retrieve the client's shared secret and then uses it to validate the signature.

This scheme is based on the assumption that, for a cryptographic signature mechanism, only a party that knows the shared key can produce valid signatures. This way, the client proves the knowledge of a shared secret, without having to reveal it.

A malicious third party that manages to observe the request message has access only to the signature value, not to the shared secret, so it cannot authenticate new messages. It can, however, replay the observed message since the same signature will be valid. To protect against this, you use a combination of timestamps and nonces.

A *timestamp* is a temporal value indicating the moment when the original message was produced. The timestamp is added to the sent message and is also protected by the signature. On the server side, messages are accepted only if the timestamp is in an acceptance window (e.g., current time plus or minus five minutes). This window exists to tolerate message transmission delays and clock deviations.

A *nonce* (contraction of the sentence "number used only once") is typically a random number that is used only one time. Nonces are used in conjunction with timestamps to avoid replays inside the server acceptance window: the nonces of all received messages are stored and a message is refused if its nonce already exists in the store. When used with timestamps, nonces only have to be stored for the duration of the acceptance window.

Signature mechanisms can be divided into two types. *Asymmetric* mechanisms use different keys for the signature production and the signature validation algorithms—the signature production uses a private key and the signature verification uses a public key. *Symmetric* mechanisms, usually designated by message authentication codes, use the same key for both the signature production and the signature validation. This symmetry means that any party able to verify the signatures can also produce them, which is different from what happens with conventional signatures. As a consequence of this symmetry, nonrepudiation isn't provided. However, symmetric mechanisms exhibit much better performance characteristics and so are typically used when the extra properties provided by asymmetrical mechanisms are not needed. When the key holding proof is based on message authentication codes, these tokens are designated as MAC tokens. Symmetric mechanisms are also typically deterministic: the signature of the same message with the same key always produces the same value. This means that we can verify the signature by computing the signature value and comparing it with the value in the received message.

A popular method of building MAC algorithms is HMAC (hash-based message authentication code), defined by RFC 2104, which internally uses a cryptographic hash function. For instance, Amazon S3 uses a combination of HMAC with the SHA-1 function, designated by HMAC-SHA1. Windows Azure Blob Service also uses the HMAC algorithm, but with the more recent SHA-256 hash function (HMAC-SHA256).

The MAC token technique is used by several authentication schemes, namely:

- The Amazon Simple Storage Service (S3) (*http://bit.ly/amzn-s3*)
- The Windows Azure Storage Services (*http://bit.ly/azure-storage*)
- The OAuth 1.0 protocol (*http://bit.ly/oauth-1*)
- The Hawk HTTP authentication scheme (*http://bit.ly/hawk-hub*), proposed by Eran Hammer

All four schemes use artifact tokens, meaning that the token is just an unique identifier used by the server to retrieve the client's identity claims as well as the token key.

Figure 15-10 illustrates the signature-based authentication process. The sending side extracts a *message representative* (defined shortly) from the message and signs it using the shared key. The resulting signature value is inserted in the sent request message. The receiving side validates this signature by extracting the message representative, signing it, and comparing the signature values.

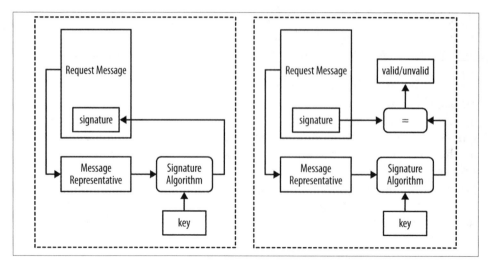

Figure 15-10. Message signature computation

Due to the presence of HTTP intermediaries that can change parts of the request message (e.g., remove proxy headers), the signature cannot be performed over the complete message. Instead, it is performed over the *message representative*, which is a string built from the message such that:

- It is not affected by the message changes typically performed by HTTP intermediaries.

- It captures all the important parts of the message; it should not be possible to have two *semantically* different messages with the same representative.

The Hawk Authentication Scheme

To make things more concrete, in this section we provide a brief description of the Hawk authentication scheme. In this scheme, the message representative is composed on the client side of the concatenations of the following elements, separated by a newline character:

- The constant string `"hawk.1.header"`

- A timestamp string representing the number of seconds since January 1, 1970, 00:00:00 GMT

- A nonce

- The request HTTP method

- The request URI path and query

- The request URI host name (excluding the port)
- The request URI port
- The optional payload hash or the empty string
- The optional application-specific extension data or the empty string

After being constructed, this message representative is converted into a byte sequence through UTF8 encoding and then supplied to the MAC scheme, configured with the token's key. In contrast with the Amazon and Azure schemes, the Hawk authentication scheme supports multiple MAC algorithms (currently HMAC-SHA1 and HMAC-SHA256). The output of the MAC scheme (a byte sequence) is then converted back into a string through the Base64-encoding algorithm.

The `Authorization` header uses the `Hawk` scheme string, followed by this set of key/value pairs:

`id`
> The token ID

`ts`
> The used timestamp

`nonce`
> The used nonce

`mac`
> The Base64 encoding of the MAC output

`hash`
> (Optional) The hash of the payload representative

`ext`
> (Optional) The optional extension data

The timestamp, nonce, and extension data must be explicitly added to the message `Authorization` header in order to allow the server to re-create the message representative. Using this message representative, the server recomputes the MAC output, using the key identified by the `id` field, and compares it with the received `mac` field. If the MAC values are diferent, that means that the message was tampered with and should be rejected. However, comparing the MAC values is not sufficient, because the attacker may be replying to past valid messsages. To protect against this, the server should:

- Check that the received nonce wasn't used on a previous message.
- Check that the received timestamp is inside an acceptance time window, which by default is more or less one minute.

The server should also store the received nonce, at least for the length of the acceptance time window.

The Hawk scheme allows for optional protection of the request message payload by allowing the message representative to include a hash of the payload representative, computed as the newline separated concatenation of:

- The constant string `"hawk.1.payload"`
- The request content type (e.g., `application/xml`), with the parameters removed
- The request payload, prior to any content or transfer encoding

When using payload protection, the hash of the payload representative string is also included in the `Authorization` header (`hash` field). This allows the server to verify the message representative before computing the payload hash.

For more detailed information about the Hawk scheme, refer to the *https://github.com/hueniverse/hawk* repository, which contains both the Hawk informal description and a Node.JS-based implementation. This book's GitHub repository also includes a C# implementation called HawkNet.

The following chapter, focusing on the OAuth 2.0 Framework, provides more concrete examples of token-based authentication, namely protocols for obtaining and using these tokens.

Authorization

As we've seen, authentication deals with the problem of collecting and validating information about a subject, namely its identity claims. Authorization, on the other hand, deals with the complementary problem of controlling the *actions* that these *subjects* may perform over protected *resources*. Figure 15-11 illustrates this problem, identifying the core concepts of subject, action, and resource.

Figure 15-11. The basic authorization model: subjects, actions, and resources

What constitutes a subject, action, and resource depends largely on the context. For instance, the .NET Framework includes a code access authorization model where the resources are class methods, actions correspond to method invocations, and the subjects are the identities associated with the running thread. On the other hand, in the context of Web APIs the mapping of this concept is rather straightforward:

- Protected resources correspond to the HTTP resources targeted by request messages.
- The actions are the HTTP methods (e.g., GET or DELETE).
- Finally, subjects correspond to the HTTP clients performing the HTTP requests.

It is often useful to divide authorization into the following parts: policy, decision, and enforcement. *Authorization policy* is the specification of what is allowed. For instance, the following statements are examples of an authorization policy expressed in natural language:

- "Nonsafe HTTP methods cannot be performed by anonymous subjects."
- "Issues can only be closed by their creators or by project managers."
- "The ticket title can only be changed by its creator."

Authorization decision is the process of evaluating whether an access, characterized by a (subject, action, resource) triple, is allowed by the defined policy. Finally, *authorization enforcement* is the mechanism used to ensure that only allowed accesses are performed. Authorization enforcement is typically coupled with the runtime mechanisms available to intercept accesses (e.g., Web API filters), whereas authorization decision is dependent on the policy. Figure 15-12 illustrates these concepts and their relationships.

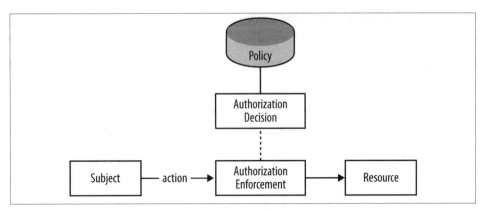

Figure 15-12. Authorization enforcement, decision, and policy

In a distributed system, the decision and enforcement components may be performed by different nodes or at multiple levels. For instance, when using the OAuth 2.0 Framework (presented in the following chapter), you can make the authorization decisions on an external *authorization server*, leaving to the *resource server* the task of ensuring that only allowed accesses are performed.

Authorization can also be performed at multiple levels, namely near the connector to the external world (the Web API) or near the domain objects and methods. These multiple levels are often complementary. Authorization performed at the Web API level allows unauthorized requests to be terminated as early as possible, but the policy decision point may not have access to all the domain information required to make a final decision. On the other hand, authorization performed at the domain level has access to a richer set of information. However, this also means that unauthorized requests use more computational resources. In this chapter, the focus is given to authorization at the Web API level.

Authorization Enforcement

ASP.NET Web API provides multiple ways of intercepting HTTP requests. One of these ways is authorization filters, which are located in the controller layer, after authentication filters but before model binding and action filters. As the name suggests, authorization filters can be used to perform authorization enforcement. ASP.NET Web API includes a concrete authorization filter, named `AuthorizeAttribute`, which can be used to annotate controller classes or actions. This `AuthorizeAttribute` class has two properties for defining the authorization policy:

- `Users` is a comma-separated list of usernames; when not empty, the access is allowed only if the user's name belongs to that list.

- `Roles` is a comma-separated list of roles; when not empty, the access is allowed only if the user has a role in that list.

Example 15-12 shows this attribute in use:

- The `AuthorizeAttribute`, targeting the `ResourceController` class, requires all requests to be authenticated. The only exception is `GET` requests, since the `Get` action is annotated with `AllowsAnonymous`.

- `Authorize(Roles = "ProjectManager")`, targeting `Delete` actions, requires all `DELETE` requests to be performed by subjects in the `ProjectManager` role.

Example 15-12. Using the AuthorizeAttribute

```
[Authorize]
public class ResourceController : ApiController
{
    [AllowAnonymous]
    public HttpResponseMessage Get()
    {
        return new HttpResponseMessage
        {
            Content = new StringContent("resource representation")
        };
```

```
    }
    public HttpResponseMessage Post()
    {
        return new HttpResponseMessage()
        {
            Content = new StringContent("result representation")
        };
    }
    [Authorize(Roles = "ProjectManager")]
    public HttpResponseMessage Delete(string id)
    {
        return new HttpResponseMessage(HttpStatusCode.NoContent);
    }
}
```

Unfortunately, having the authorization policy directly defined in the `AuthorizeAttri`
bute ties the authorization policy to the resource controller class. As a consequence,
any change on the policy (e.g., "QA engineers also can delete tickets") implies a change
and recompilation in the code.

A better approach would be to have the authorization attribute delegate the authorization decision to an external component, which could then be evolved and deployed
independently. One way to achieve this is by using the *claims authorization manager*
concept, provided in .NET 4.5 via the `ClaimsAuthorizationManager` base class and
summarized in Example 15-13. The main role of this task is to perform authorization
decisions via its `CheckAccess` method. By default, it always returns `true`, but derived
classes can override it to implement custom authorization policies.

Example 15-13. The ClaimsAuthorizationManager base class

```
public class ClaimsAuthorizationManager : ICustomIdentityConfiguration
{
        public virtual bool CheckAccess(AuthorizationContext context)
        {
          return true;
        }
        ...
}
```

The `CheckAccess` method receives an `AuthorizationContext` class, described in
Example 15-14, representing an access via the (subject, action, resource) triple, where
the subject is represented by a `ClaimsPrincipal`. Interestingly, both the action and the
resource are also represented as claims. Note also that this class is decoupled from the
authorization enforcement mechanism. Namely, it is not tied to Web API or other similar technology.

Example 15-14. The AuthorizationContext class, characterizing an access

```
public class AuthorizationContext
{
```

```
    public ClaimsPrincipal Principal
    {
        get {...}
    }

    public Collection<Claim> Action
    {
        get {...}
    }

    public Collection<Claim> Resource
    {
        get {...}
    }

    public AuthorizationContext(ClaimsPrincipal principal,
                               Collection<Claim> resource,
                               Collection<Claim> action)
    {...}
}
```

The Thinktecture.IdentityModel.45 (*http://bit.ly/thinktecture-id*) library provides a ClaimsAuthorizeAttribute that uses this strategy: when the Web API runtime calls this attribute to check whether the request is allowed, the attribute delegates this decision to the registered singleton ClaimsAuthorizationManager. The call to the ClaimsAu thorizeAttribute contains an authorization context with the request's claims principal, action name, and controller name. Example 15-15 shows a custom authorization manager, evaluating the same authorization policy as the one defined in Example 15-12. The main difference is that the policy is now externalized to a separate component that can be evolved and built independently.

Example 15-15. A custom ClaimsAuthorizationManager class

```
public class CustomPolicyClaimsAuthorizationManager : ClaimsAuthorizationManager
{
    public override bool CheckAccess(AuthorizationContext context)
    {
        var subject = context.Principal;
        var method = context.Action
            .First(c => c.Type == ClaimsAuthorization.ActionType).Value;
        var controller = context.Resource
            .First(c => c.Type == ClaimsAuthorization.ResourceType).Value;

        if (controller == "ClaimsResource")
        {
            if (method.Equals("GET", StringComparison.OrdinalIgnoreCase))
                return true;

            if (method.Equals("DELETE", StringComparison.OrdinalIgnoreCase)
                    && !subject.IsInRole("ProjectManager"))
                return false;
```

```
            return subject.Identity.IsAuthenticated;
        }
        return false;
    }
}
```

We will return to the subject of authorization in the next chapter, where we describe the OAuth 2.0 Framework. Until then, we shift our focus to a different kind of authorization: controlling browser access to cross-origin resources.

Cross-Origin Resource Sharing

User agents, such as browsers, combine and process content (e.g., HTML documents and script programs) from multiple sources. Typically, these sources have different trustworthiness levels, and may include malicious sites trying to compromise both the confidentiality and integrity of other sites' content. The *same-origin policy* is a set of security polices enforced by user agents, which uses the content's origin to impose restrictions on how these contents can interact, namely via the user agent internal APIs (e.g., DOM access and networking).

The origin concept, described by RFC 6454, groups URIs based on their scheme, host, and port. Simplifying a little, two URIs have the same origin if they have the same (scheme, host, port) triple. For instance, *http://example.com/* and *http://example.com: 80/path* have the same origin; however, *http://example.com* and *http://www.example.com* have different origins.

The XMLHttpRequest API is an example of a user agent API using the same-origin policy. When a request is initiated via the open method, the XMLHttpRequest object compares the origin of both:

- The requested URI
- The URI of the document that instantiated the XMLHttpRequest

The request is allowed only if these two URIs have the same origin, thereby forbidding *cross-origin* requests.

Same-origin policies are particularly important for browser contexts, due to the way cookie-based credentials are automatically attached to every sent request. For instance, if a browser has valid authentication cookies for *https://banking.example.net*, these cookies will be automatically attached to any request to that origin. As a consequence, if a malicious script from an external origin were allowed to perform a request on *https:// banking.example.net*, that request would automatically be authenticated and the script would have access to protected resources on *https://banking.example.net*. Same-origin policies are a method to protect against this type of attack.

However, the *cross-origin* request limitation also forbids some legitimate scenarios, where a resource would like to authorize access by contents from other origins. *Cross-Origin Resource Sharing* (CORS) is a W3C recommendation that enables this scenario, by defining a mechanism to permit cross-origin requests subject to authorization by the accessed resource. It is based on additional HTTP request and response headers, as well as a set of processing rules for user agents, namely for CORS-enabled XMLHttpRe quest implementations.

Briefly, the CORS specification stipulates that a cross-origin request should be executed by XMLHttpRequest in one of two ways. With the *simple cross-origin request algorithm*, requests are preemptively sent but the results are made visible to the calling script only if explicitly authorized by the resource. With the *cross-origin request with preflight algorithm*, a OPTIONS request (the preflight) is previously performed to query the resource if it authorizes the cross-origin request. The original request is performed only if the response to this query is positive.

The *simple* algorithm is an optimization applied only to cross-origin requests that could already be made by a script even without CORS. For instance, a script program can use dynamically generated and submitted HTML forms to initiate cross-origin GET or POST requests. This means that resources must already be prepared to correctly handle attacks based on this feature, commonly named cross-site request forgery (CSRF) attacks. In this case, a CORS-enabled XMLHttpRequest just has to ensure that the request's response is not visible to the script, except if explicitly authorized by the resource.

A cross-origin request can use the *simple* algorithm if:

- The request method is GET, HEAD, or POST (the so-called *simple* methods).
- The headers explicitly added by the script to the request are all *simple* headers (Accept, Accept-Language, Content-Language, or Content-Type).
- The content type is application/x-www-form-urlencoded, multipart/form-data, or text/plain.

For instance, consider a script running on a document loaded from *http://www.example.net* that wants to access a resource located at *https://api.example.net*, using the XMLHttpRequest API (different origin because the hostname and the scheme are different). If all the *simple* algorithm restrictions are met, then a CORS-enabled user agent preemptively sends the request, adding an Origin header with the document's origin (*http://www.example.net*):

```
GET https://api.example.net/api/resource HTTP/1.1
Host: api.example.net
Origin: http://www.example.net
Referer: http://www.example.net/
```

It is now the responsibility of the resource to evaluate whether the access is authorized for the *http://www.example.net/* origin. If so, the response must contain an Access-Control-Allow-Origin granting access to that origin:

```
HTTP/1.1 200 OK
Content-Length: 23
Content-Type: text/plain; charset=utf-8
Access-Control-Allow-Origin: http://www.example.net

resource representation
```

When the user agent receives this response and confirms that it contains an Access-Control-Allow-Origin with the requester's origin, it presents the response to the calling script. If the response's Access-Control-Allow-Origin is absent or does not include the caller's origin, then a network error is signaled to the calling script. Note that if the resource is not CORS-aware, the response will not contain the Access-Control-Allow-Origin and the user agent will interpret that as a denied authorization.

If any of the *simple* algorithm conditions does not hold (e.g., the request uses the PUT or DELETE method), the CORS specification uses a *preflight request*, wherein the user agent first performs an OPTIONS request on the resource to check whether a cross-origin request is authorized. This request contains an Origin header with the caller origin as well as an Access-Control-Request-Method with the required HTTP method:

```
OPTIONS https://api.example.net/api/resource HTTP/1.1
Host: api.example.net
Access-Control-Request-Method: PUT
Origin: http://www.example.net
Access-Control-Request-Headers: origin
Referer: http://www.example.net/
```

A CORS-aware resource uses this origin and method information to evaluate if the cross-origin is allowed. If so, it produces a response message containing both the Access-Control-Allow-Origin and the Access-Control-Allow-Methods headers:

```
HTTP/1.1 200 OK
Access-Control-Allow-Origin: http://www.example.net
Access-Control-Allow-Methods: PUT
Content-Length: 0
```

Only after receiving this response allowing the access does the user agent perform the original request:

```
PUT https://api.example.net/api/resource HTTP/1.1
Host: api.example.net
Connection: keep-alive
Origin: http://www.example.net
Referer: http://www.example.net/
```

Once again, the response is made visible to the calling script only if it includes the `Access-Control-Allow-Origin` header with the script's origin.

```
HTTP/1.1 204 No Content
Access-Control-Allow-Origin: http://www.example.net
```

For optimization purposes, the resource can also include an `Access-Control-Max-Age` in the preflight response, allowing the user agent to cache this response on a *preflight result cache* for the time defined by this header. This feature helps to reduce the number of preflight requests needed.

CORS Support on ASP.NET Web API

ASP.NET Web API version 2.0 adds support for the CORS specification by providing abstractions to define cross-origin policies and mechanisms to enforce them. Globally, you activate cross-origin support by calling the `EnableCors` extension method on the `HttpConfiguration` object:

```
config.EnableCors();
```

Then, you can use the `EnableCorsAttribute` to explicitly annotate the controllers or actions on which CORS support should be enabled:

```
[EnableCors(...)]
public class ResourceController : ApiController
{
     ...
}
```

You can also define the cross-origin support globally by passing an `EnableCorsAttri bute` instance to the `EnableCors` method:

```
config.EnableCors(new EnableCorsAttribute(...));
```

The `EnableCorsAttribute` not only enables but also defines the allowed cross-origin *policy* (for instance, the set of allowed origins or request methods). For that, this attribute is parameterized in its constructor with the allowed origins, the allowed request methods, and the allowed and exposed headers. It is also possible to define the preflight max age:

```
[EnableCors(origins:"https://localhost", headers:"*", methods:"GET",
    PreflightMaxAge = 60)]
public class ResourceController : ApiController
{
    ...
}
```

As expected, the policies defined by attributes targeting actions have higher precedence that those defined by attributes targeting controller classes. The attribute passed into `config.EnableCors` will define the default policy, applied when the request's controller and action don't have any associated policy.

Despite this simple attribute model, under the hood Web API has an extensible infrastructure, displayed in Figure 15-13, allowing alternate ways for cross-origin policy definition.

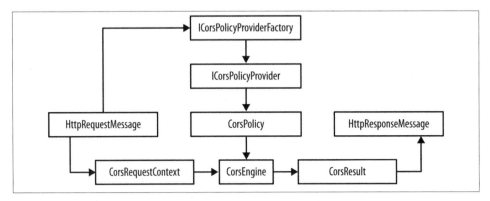

Figure 15-13. CORS runtime

Cross-origin policy is enforced by the `CorsMessageHandler`, inserted in the request pipeline by the `EnableCors` method. When an HTTP request reaches it, this handler checks the `Origin` header to see if it is CORS enabled. If so, the handler builds a `Cors RequestContext` with the CORS-related request information:

```
public class CorsRequestContext
{
    public Uri RequestUri { get; set; }
    public string HttpMethod { get; set; }
    public string Origin { get; set; }
    public string Host { get; set; }
    public string AccessControlRequestMethod { get; set; }
    public bool IsPreflight {get;}
    // ...
}
```

Afterward, it uses the `ICorsPolicyProviderFactory` registered in the configuration to try to locate the *policy provider*, which then provides the policy for the request:

```
public interface ICorsPolicyProviderFactory
{
    ICorsPolicyProvider GetCorsPolicyProvider(HttpRequestMessage request);
}

public interface ICorsPolicyProvider
{
    Task<CorsPolicy> GetCorsPolicyAsync(HttpRequestMessage request,
```

```
        CancellationToken cancellationToken);
    }
```

This double indirection is required because the factory is statically defined, while the policy provider may be different for each request.

The cross-origin policy is just an instance of the following value class:

```
public class CorsPolicy
{
    public bool AllowAnyHeader { get; set; }
    public bool AllowAnyMethod { get; set; }
    public bool AllowAnyOrigin { get; set; }
    public IList<string> ExposedHeaders { get; private set; }
    public IList<string> Headers { get; private set; }
    public IList<string> Methods { get; private set; }
    public IList<string> Origins { get; private set; }
    public long? PreflightMaxAge { get; set; }
    public bool SupportsCredentials { get; set; }
}
```

The CorsMessageHandler uses this CorsPolicy to convert the request's CorsRequest Context into a CorsResult that will then be applied to the HTTP response. So, by defining a new ICorsPolicyProviderFactory and registering it in the configuration (there's a SetCorsPolicyProviderFactory extension method for that), it is possible to completely change the way the CORS policy is defined.

By default, the ICorsPolicyProviderFactory interface is implemented by the Attrib uteBasedPolicyProviderFactory class, which looks into the controller and action descriptors for the presence of the EnableCorsAttribute instances. The way this is done depends on the CORS request type. For nonpreflight requests, the handler first forwards the request up the stack to its inner handler. When the response is finally returned, it uses the selected action descriptor (saved into a request property) to find out if there is any EnableCorsAttribute associated with the action or the controller. If so, it uses it to obtain the policy—EnableCorsAttribute implements ICorsPolicyProvider—and then applies the resulting CorsResult into the returned response. This will enrich the returned response message with the extra CORS headers.

However, for preflight requests, the behavior is slightly different. Remember that these are requests using the Options HTTP method, meant to probe the server for CORS support on a given request URI and method pair (the method is passed on the Access-Control-Request-Method). Namely, no action should be ever called when handling such requests. So, when a preflight request is received, the CorsMessageHandler replaces the OPTIONS method with the one in the Access-Control-Request-Method, and then uses the Web API resolution services to find the controller and action mapped to the request. However, this controller and action are never called. Instead, they are just used to locate and extract the CORS policy (provided by the EnableCorsAttribute). Finally, the preflight response is created and returned, short-circuiting any upper stack processing. In short, these preflight requests never reach the controller layer.

Conclusion

In this chapter, we described some of the security concerns that you must address when designing, implementing, and consuming Web APIs. Our focus was on the security concepts and technologies that are specific to Web APIs: transport security, authentication, and authorization. We continue with the security theme in the next chapter, where we address the OAuth 2.0 Framework. However, there are other security subjects that shouldn't be neglected, despite not being a subject of this book. Similar to web applications, most of the time a Web API is a connector between the public Internet and business-critical internal systems. So, secure coding practices such as input validation, proper output encoding, and *-injection mitigation (e.g., SQL injection) are still critically important.

CHAPTER 16

The OAuth 2.0 Authorization Framework

Delegata potestas non potest delegari.

The OAuth 2.0 Authorization Framework, defined by RFC 6749, is an evolution of the OAuth 1.0 protocol. At the time of writing, it is used by several popular Web APIs such as the Google APIs, Facebook, and GitHub. Its main usage scenario is *delegated constrained authorization*. As an example, consider the fictional scenario depicted in Figure 16-1.

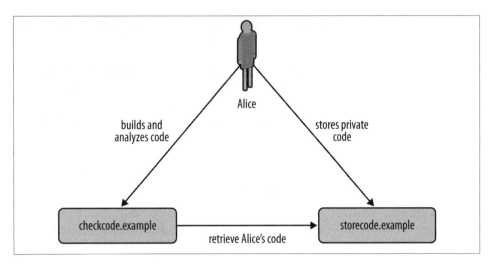

Figure 16-1. Delegated authorization scenario

In the figure, you can see that:

- *storecode.example* is a website for storing and managing code repositories, with an associated Web API.

- *checkcode.example* is a service for building and analyzing code, providing functionalities such as continuous integration, coding rules checking, error estimation, and test coverage.
- Alice uses the *storecode.example* site to store and manage her private code.

Alice wants to use the *checkcode.example* service to analyze the code she's stored at *storecode.example*. The fact that *storecode.example* provides an API is an important enabler for this scenario, but a problem remains: how can Alice allow *checkcode.example* to access some of her private code repositories?

A solution to this problem would be for Alice to provide her *storecode.example* credentials (e.g., username and password) to *checkcode.example*, so that this service could access her private code. However, this solution has several disadvantages:

- With these credentials, the *checkcode.example* service can do any action allowed for Alice, including accessing all her code and also changing it. In other words, this solution grants the *checkcode.example unconstrained authorization* over *storecode.example*.
- A compromise of the *checkcode.example* service would reveal Alice's password, allowing an attacker to have full access to her resources.
- The only way for Alice to revoke the *checkcode.example* access would be for her to change her credentials. As a side effect, all other applications that are authorized to access Alice's code (e.g., *www.hostcode.example*, a hosting service) would also have their access revoked.

A better solution is for Alice to grant *checkcode.example* a *constrained authorization* that allows this service to perform only a subset of operations (e.g., read from the master branch of only one repository), for a delimited time period. Alice should also be able to revoke this authorization grant at any time, without disturbing other services that access her resources.

Less Fictional Scenarios

For less fictional examples, as we write, both the AppHarbor PaaS (platform as a service) (*http://bit.ly/app-harbor*) and the Travis CI (*http://bit.ly/trav-started*) continuous integration service use OAuth 2.0 and delegated authorization to integrate with GitHub repositories.

This previous example illustrates the inadequacy of the simple client-server model to express the authorization requirements of Web APIs. Namely, since a Web API is an interface for application consumption, the distinction between client applications and human users is an important feature of an authorization model. Following this, the OAuth 2.0 Framework introduces a model with four roles:

- Alice plays the *resource owner* role—the entity owning or able to grant authorizations to a protected resource. In the remainder of this chapter, we will refer to the resource owner as simply the *user*.
- *storecode.example* plays the *resource server* role—the entity that provides the interface for accessing the protected resources.
- *checkcode.example* plays the *client* role—the application accessing the protected resource on behalf of the resource owner.
- The *authorization server* is a fourth role, and is responsible for managing authorizations and access grants. Typically, this role is also played by the *resource server*. However, the OAuth 2.0 Framework allows for separate deployments of these roles.

One of the main aspects of this model is that *user* and *client* are *not* synonymous in this scenario. Instead, they are separate entities, each one having its own well-defined identity and most of the time belonging to different security boundaries. For instance, access to a protected resource is frequently associated with the resource owner (the user) and the application performing the access (the client) on its behalf. This is a distinctive feature of this model when compared to the simpler client-server scenarios addressed previously. However, despite the focus on delegated authorization and on the *user-client-server* model, the OAuth 2.0 Framework also supports simpler scenarios where the client is acting on its own behalf and there isn't a user involved.

Thinktecture Authorization Server

Thinktecture Authorization Server (*http://bit.ly/thinktecture-gh*) is an open source OAuth 2.0 authorization server, written in C# over the .NET platform. It is decoupled from specific resource servers and user identity providers, making it usable on a wide range of scenarios. Being open source also makes it a good learning source for OAuth 2.0 design and implementation aspects. For that reason, in this chapter, we will be using Thinktecture Authorization Server as a source of illustrative examples. For simplicity, we will refer to it simply as *T.AS*.

Client Applications

The OAuth 2.0 Framework aims to be usable with different kinds of client applications, such as:

- Classic server-side web applications
- Native applications, particularly mobile ones
- JavaScript-based, client-side web applications, such as single-page applications (SPA)

This wide range of client types presents different challenges, particularly concerning the long-term storage of authentication secrets. To be able to participate in an OAuth 2.0 deployment, a client must be previously registered on the authorization server. In a typical OAuth 2.0 scenario, the client owner provides a set of information, such as:

- Descriptive information, intended for human consumption, such as the application name, logos, home page, or version information
- Technical information, used on the protocol steps, such as redirect URIs or required authorization scopes

On the other hand, the authorization server assigns a `client_id` string to the client, uniquely identifying it. Some clients may also receive a `client_secret` string that allows them to authenticate to the authorization server during some protocol steps. In this context, the OAuth 2.0 divides clients into two types:

- *Confidential* clients can securely store the `client_secret` and use it in protocol steps. The typical example is classic server-side web applications, where the client credentials are stored on the server side.
- *Public* clients aren't able to securely store credentials. These clients don't have `client_secret`, but they still have an assigned `client_id`. A typical example is client-side JavaScript applications, which are unable to securely store long-term secrets, since they are executed entirely in the user's browser.

Clients are typically classified as confidential or public during registration, based on the input provided by the client owner.

At the time of this writing, the typical scenario is for the client owner to register via web forms, such as the one shown in Figure 16-2.

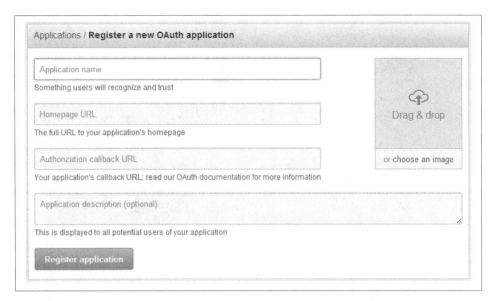

Figure 16-2. Client registration form at GitHub (2013)

However, a specification to define the dynamic registration of clients, using a Web API, is also being developed by the OAuth IETF working group (*http://bit.ly/oauth-ietf*).

An authorization server can also associate authorization polices with a registered client, limiting its permissions. As an example, Figure 16-3 depicts the T.AS class model for representing clients, where we can see that a client is associated with:

- The OAuth 2.0 flow where it can participate
- The set of authorizations—named scopes, as we will see shortly—that can be delegated to it

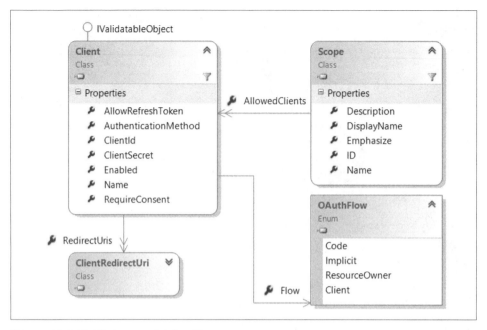

Figure 16-3. T.AS class model for clients

Accessing Protected Resources

In the OAuth 2.0 Framework, a client's access to a protected resource must include an *access token*, as illustrated in Figure 16-4. At the time of writing, the framework defines only bearer token usage,[1] meaning that the access token is simply added to the request message without any further binding. As we have seen before, bearer tokens are simpler to use but have several security drawbacks. In particular, they should always be used with transport security and the client must ensure that they are sent only to the associated resource server. Because of these limitations, the OAuth IETF group is also working on a specification (*http://bit.ly/oauth-status*) for MAC-based access tokens: the use of the access token must be combined with the proof of possession of a cryptographic key, via the computation of a MAC (message authentication code).

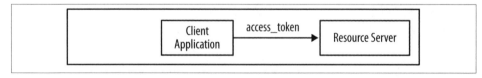

Figure 16-4. Accessing resources using access tokens

---

1. See RFC 6750.

The `access_token` is a representation of an authorization grant and is used by the resource server to obtain information about the requester, namely to enforce the resource's authorization policy. This may sound rather vague, but we will return to this subject later in the chapter and provide concrete examples of access tokens and of the contained information. We will also see how an ASP.NET-based resource server can extract a token from the request message and transform it into identity and authorization information.

The recommended way of binding a access token to a request message is by using the `Authorization` header with the `Bearer` scheme:

```
GET https://storecode.example/resource HTTP/1.1
Authorization: Bearer the.access.token
```

This recommended method follows the generic HTTP authentication framework, presented in Chapter 1. However, it's also possible to send the access token in an `application/x-www-form-urlencoded` body or in the request URI query string, using the `access_token` field, but it's not recommended. The use of access tokens in request URIs is particularly sensitive, since this information is typically logged and therefore can easily be leaked.

Obtaining Access Tokens

A client application obtains access tokens by requesting them from the *token endpoint*, which is part of the authorization server, as illustrated by Figure 16-5.[2] The token request includes an *authorization grant*, which is an abstract concept representing the information on which the authorization decision is based. This authorization grant can take multiple implementations.

---

2. The *implicit flow* is an exception to this rule; the token is not obtained from the token endpoint.

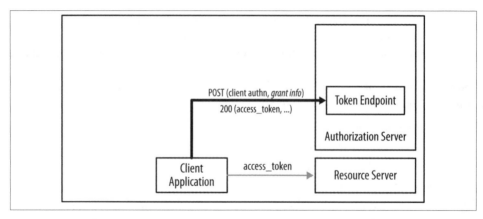

Figure 16-5. Obtaining access tokens using the token endpoint of the authorization server

In simple scenarios, where the client application is accessing the resource server on its own behalf (there is no user involved), the authorization grant can just be the client credentials. In OAuth 2.0 terminology, this is called the *client credentials grant* flow—the authorization is completely based on the client credentials. This option requires the client to be of the confidential type—that is, to have an assigned `client_secret`.

If there is a user involved, this authorization grant can be based on the user's password credentials, provided by the user to the client, as depicted in Figure 16-6.

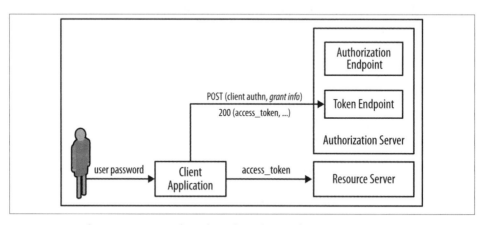

Figure 16-6. Obtaining access tokens based on the user's password credentials

This is called the *resource owner password credentials grant* flow in the OAuth 2.0 Framework. At first sight, the availability of this option in OAuth 2.0 may seem unreasonable, since one of its goals was to avoid this exact credentials disclosure. However, it can make sense in some scenarios, particularly when the user has a high trust level on the client application (e.g., enterprise scenarios). First, in OAuth 2.0, the password does not need to be persisted by the client application and used on every request. Instead, it is just used to request the access token and can be removed immediately after. So, if the user changes the password, the access token may remain valid. Another advantage of this authorization grant type is that it is simpler to implement than the alternatives, especially when the client is a native mobile application.

Another option is the use of an *authorization code* that represents a delegated authorization performed by the user without revealing her password. This option is called *authorization code grant* flow and will be described in detail in the next section.

The token request is handled via a POST to the token endpoint URI with an `applica tion/x-www-form-urlencoded` body containing the authorization grant type and values. For instance, on the authorization code grant flow, the grant type is `authoriza tion_code` and the grant value is the authorization code:

```
POST https://authzserver.example/token_endpoint HTTP/1.1
Content-Type: application/x-www-form-urlencoded
Host: authzserver.example

grant_type=authorization_code&
code=the.authorization.code
```

If the client is confidential (the client has an assigned `client_secret`), this token request must also include client authentication information. The OAuth 2.0 Framework defines two alternatives for this:

- Using the `Basic` HTTP authentication scheme, where the `client_id` and the `cli ent_secret` are used as the username and password, respectively
- Inserting the `client_id` and `client_secret` as fields of the token request body

If the request is successful, the response contains a `application/json` body including the access token value, its type (e.g., `bearer`), and validity:

```
HTTP/1.1 200 OK
Content-Type: application/json; charset=utf-8
Cache-Control: private, max-age=0, must-revalidate

{"access_token":"the.access.token","token_type":"bearer", "expires_in":3600,
    ... other info ...}
```

Authorization Code Grant

The authorization code grant provides a way for a user to delegate a constrained authorization to a client application, without revealing his credentials to the client. Instead, the user interacts directly with the authorization endpoint of the authorization server via a user agent (e.g., a web browser or web view). This flow starts with the client application redirecting the user agent to this authorization endpoint, as shown in Figure 16-7. The client uses the query string of the authorization endpoint request URI to embed a set of *authorization request parameters*:

```
https://authzserver.example/authorization_endpoint?
  client_id=the.client.id&
  scope=user+repo&
  state=crCMc3d0acGdDiNnXJigpQ%3d%3d&
  response_type=code&
  redirect_uri=https%3a%2f%2fclient.example%2fcallback&
```

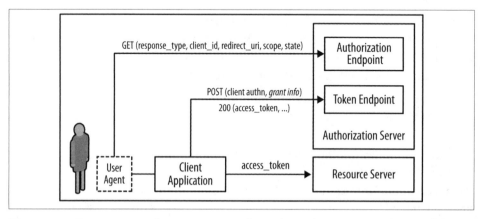

Figure 16-7. Requesting authorization grant from the authorization endpoint of the authorization server

For instance, the `response_type` parameter defines the authorization grant that is being requested, since the authorization endpoint can be used with a different flow, while the `scope` parameter characterizes the authorization that is being requested. After receiving this request, the authorization server starts an *out-of-protocol* user interaction with the aim of authenticating the user and optionally requesting her consent for the client requested authorization.

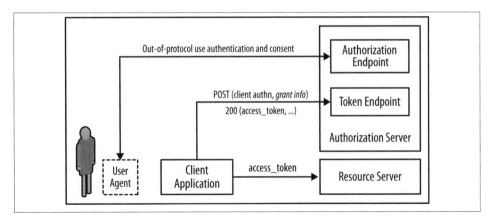

Figure 16-8. Direct interaction between the user and the authorization endpoint for au-thentication and authorization consent

The user authentication protocol is not defined by the OAuth 2.0 protocol, leaving the authorization server free to choose the most appropriate one, ranging from a simple form-based username and password scheme to a distributed federation protocol.

After a successful authentication, the authorization server can also ask the user if she consents to the authorization requested by the client application. Here, the authorization server uses the client's descriptive information (e.g., application name, logo, and home URI), defined during the registration process, to better inform the user. Finally, the authorization server redirects the user to the client application, using the value of the `redirect_uri` request parameter, with an authorization code embedded in the request URI, as depicted in Figure 16-9 and in the following URI:

```
https://client.example/callback?
    code=52...e4&
    state=cr...3D
```

For security reasons, the set of redirect URIs used by a client should be preconfigured. T.AS does exactly that, as shown earlier in Figure 16-3, where each client is related to a collection of redirect URIs.

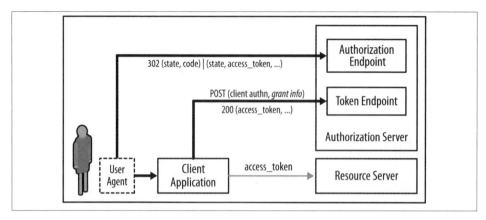

Figure 16-9. Authorization endpoint response containing the authorization grant

A final flow of the OAuth 2.0 Framework, named *implicit grant*, returns the access token immediately in the authorization response from the authorization endpoint. This is the only OAuth 2.0 flow where the access token is not returned from the token endpoint.

OAuth 2.0 Authorization Code Flow Example

The *OAuth2.Demos.AuthzCodeGrant* repository, available at *https://github.com/weba-pibook*, contains a console self-hosted OAuth 2.0 client application that uses the au-thorization code flow. It is preconfigured to use GitHub API v3, but can be used with another authorization server and resource server. To use it with the GitHub API, just provision a "developer application" at the GitHub "account settings" and assign the `client_id` and `client_secret` in the code. This sample is highly commented and can also be used to capture the OAuth 2.0 protocol messages.

Scope

As stated before, one of the goals of OAuth 2.0 is to allow clients to access resources, under a *constrained* authorization, eventually delegated by a user. For this, the frame-work uses the concept of *scope* as a way to define these authorization constraints. For-mally, a scope is a list of space-delimited identifiers, where each one defines a type of authorization. For instance, the following is a list of some scope identifiers used by the GitHub Web API:

- `user` authorizes the client to read/write to the user's profile information.
- `user:email` authorizes the client to read the user's email.

- `public_repo` authorizes the client to read/write to the user's public repositories.

This means that the string `user:email public_repo` defines a scope with the read email authorization and the read/write repositories authorization.

Typically, these scope identifiers and associated semantics are defined by the resource servers. They typically also have an associated human-readable description, used when presenting users with authorization consent forms.

As an example, in T.AS a scope is modeled by the following fields, as shown in Figure 16-3:

- The scope identifier
- The scope display name and description, used for human interface purposes, such as when requesting the user's authorization consent
- The list of clients allowed to request this scope

The set of scopes available for a client may be restricted, as also shown in Figure 16-3.

Scopes are intensively used by the protocol, typically via a `scope` parameter. When using the client credentials or resource owner password grants, the client can include the `scope` parameter in the token request sent to the token endpoint, as a way to define the request authorization. Similarly, when using the authorization code or implicit grant flows, the client can include the `scope` parameter in the authorization request sent to the authorization endpoint. The authorization server is free to concede an authorization scope that is different from the one requested, namely based on the user's consent. Accordingly, the `scope` parameter is also present on the token response to inform the client of the granted authorizations.

Front Channel Versus Back Channel

To better understand the OAuth 2.0 Framework, it is important to realize that the client communicates with the authorization server in two distinct ways: via the *back channel* and via the *front channel*. The *back channel* is the direct communication between the client and the token endpoint, such as the one depicted in Figure 16-5, whereas the front channel is the indirect communication between the client and the authorization endpoint via the user's agent and based on HTTP redirects (Figure 16-7). Therefore, the front channel has some significant limitations. Since it's based on redirects, it imposes restrictions on the HTTP features that can be used. The request method must be a `GET`, and the request information must be passed in the request URI, namely in the URI's query string:

```
https://authz_server.example/authorization_endpoint?
  client_id=the.client.id&
  scope=user+repo&
```

```
state=crCMc3d0acGdDiNnXJigpQ%3d%3d&
response_type=code&
redirect_uri=https%3a%2f%2fclient.example%2fcallback&
```

Also, the response must always be a redirect, so the response information is also passed in the redirected request URI:

```
https://client.example/callback?
  code=52...e4&
  state=cr...3D
```

In case of error, the standard HTTP status codes cannot be used (the response must always be a redirect). Instead, the `error` and `error_description` parameters are used to convey this information on the URI's query string:

```
https://client.example/callback?
  error=access_denied&
  error_description=authorization+not+granted
```

Also, because the front channel runs via the user agent, it is not safe for the client credentials (`client_secret`) transmission, since then they would be visible to the user. Thus, in all front-channel requests the client is identified (the `client_id` is sent) but not authenticated. Since the `client_id` is public, it is very easy for an attacker to forge valid authorization requests.

Finally, the front channel also does not ensure any correlation between the requests from the client to the authorization server and the corresponding responses. It is subject to CSRF (cross-site request forgery) attacks, where a third-party malicious site instructs the user's browser to make a request back to the client, thereby simulating an OAuth 2.0 front-channel response. Using this technique, the attacking site can control the access token that will be used by the client—for instance, by using an authorization code issued to the attacker account.

To address this, the OAuth 2.0 Framework uses a state parameter, present in both the request and the response, to ensure this correlation. The client creates a random state value and includes it in the request via the front channel. At the end, the authorization server includes the same value in the response returned via the front channel. This way, the client has a mechanism to correlate a received response with a previous request. RFC 6819—OAuth 2.0 Threat Model and Security Considerations—provides more information on how to adequately use this protection mechanism.

With all these restrictions and problems, you may wonder why the front channel is used at all. The main reason is that it allows for the authorization server to directly interact with the user, without any client intervention or visibility. Figure 16-8 shows how this feature can be used for the authorization server to authenticate the user and ask for her consent.

On the other hand, since the back channel connects the client directly to the token endpoint, the protocol is not limited to HTTP redirects. For instance, the token request is a POST HTTP request where the parameters are represented in the body and the response may use HTTP status codes to represent different error conditions (e.g., 400 for a bad request or 401 for invalid client authentication).

If the client possesses a client_secret (confidential client), it must use it in the back channel to authenticate itself. For that purpose, the OAuth 2.0 Framework recommends using the HTTP basic scheme, where the username and password are replaced by the client_id and client_secret, respectively:

```
POST https://authz_server.example/token_endpoint HTTP/1.1
Content-Type: application/x-www-form-urlencoded
Authorization: Basic dGhlLmNsaWVudC5pZDp0aGUuY2xpZW50LnNlY3JldA==
Host: authz_server.example

grant_type=authorization_code&
code=the.authorization.code
```

Back Channel and Front Channel

The terms *back channel* and *front channel* are not really used by the OAuth 2.0 RFCs. Instead, we borrowed these terms from the SAML glossary (*http://bit.ly/saml-glossary*) because we think they are really useful for describing the different ways in which the client communicates with the authorization server.

Refresh Tokens

Because bearer access tokens are very sensitive, their usage lifetime should be limited. To address that, the OAuth 2.0 Framework includes refresh tokens, which can be used to obtain new access tokens. When an authorization grant is exchanged for the access token at the token endpoint, the response may also include a refresh token:

```
HTTP/1.1 200 OK
Content-Type: application/json; charset=utf-8
Cache-Control: private, max-age=0, must-revalidate

{"access_token":"the.access.token","token_type":"bearer", "expires_in":3600,
 "refresh_token":"the.refresh.token"}
```

The client application can use this refresh token to obtain a new access token—for instance, when the older one is about to expire. This is also done by using the token endpoint, with the refresh_token value on the grant_type field:

```
POST https://authzserver.example/token_endpoint HTTP/1.1
Content-Type: application/x-www-form-urlencoded
```

```
Host: authzserver.example

grant_type=refresh_token&
refresh_token=the.refresh.token
```

A successful response will include the new access token and associated lifetime. It can also contain a new refresh token.

The use of refresh tokens imposes additional requirements on a client application, which will have to securely store this new information, monitor the access token lifetime, and refresh it periodically. However, refresh tokens have some useful properties. From a security viewpoint, reducing the access token lifetime limits the consequences of malicious access to this information.

From an implementation and optimization viewpoint, the use of refresh tokens allows hybrid approaches wherein refresh tokens are revocable artifact tokens, pointing to entries on a repository, while access tokens are short-lived and nonrevocable stateful assertions. This makes access token verification more easily scalable, since no repository access is required. The fact that they are nonrevocable is compensated for by their reduced lifetime. On the other hand, you can easily revoke refresh tokens by simply removing or disabling the associated entry in the repository.

Resource Server and Authorization Server

The OAuth 2.0 Framework explicitly identifies two server-side responsibilities:

- The *resource server* exposes the HTTP interface to the protected resources and is a consumer of access tokens.
- The *authorization server* is responsible, among other things, for issuing the access tokens that are used in the protected resource access.

This does not mean that the resource server and the authorization server must be two independent entities. It is perfectly acceptable for these two roles to be implemented by the same physical servers and software component. However, the framework does allow decoupled architectures in which the authorization server is run by a separate software component (e.g., Thinktecture Authorization Server). It is even possible for a resource server to rely on an external authorization server run by another entity (e.g., Windows Azure Active Directory).

Despite allowing for these decoupled architectures, the OAuth 2.0 Framework does not specify how separate resource servers and authorization servers can cooperate. Aspects such as access token format and validation procedures are left completely open by the OAuth 2.0 Framework and must be defined for each scenario. Note that from a user or client viewpoint, this does not have any impact, since the access tokens are meant to be opaque to these parties.

Also, the information conveyed by the authorization server to the resource server, via the access token, is left undefined by the OAuth 2.0 Framework. The immediate option is for this to be a representation of the token request and associated grant, including:

- The resource owner identity, when the client is not accessing on its own behalf
- The requesting client, identified by its `client_id`
- The requested authorization scope, identified by a `scope` string

The information associated with an access token should also include its temporal validity (tokens are not valid forever) and the token audience; that is, some identification of the resource server for whom the token was issued.

As an example, T.AS uses the JWT format to represent access tokens. Example 16-1 shows the payload of such a JWT token, containing:

- The `sub` claim, with the user unique identifier, as well as the `role` claim containing additional user's claims
- The `client_id` claim, with the client application identity
- The `scope` claim, with the granted authorization scope

The token payload also contains the issuer identity (`iss` claim) and the token's intended destination or audience (`aud` claim).

Example 16-1. JWT payload of an access token issued by the Thinktecture AuthorizationServer

```
{
    "exp": 1379284015,
    "aud": "http://resourceserver.example",
    "iss": "http://authzserver.example",
    "role": [
            "fictional_character",
            "student"
    ],
    "client_id": "client2",
    "scope": [
            "scope1",
            "scope2"
    ],
    "nbf": 1379280415,
    "sub": "Alice"
}
```

As illustrated by Example 16-1 with the inclusion of the `role` claim, the user's identity can be more than just a simple identifier, which fits nicely into the claims model presented in "The Claims Model" on page 360.

Processing Access Tokens in ASP.NET Web API

As noted in "Katana Authentication Middleware" on page 380, the Katana project includes a set of authentication middleware classes. One of these classes is the OAuthBear erAuthenticationMiddleware, which implements the OAuth 2.0 Bearer scheme. The OAuthBearerAuthenticationMiddleware behavior is configured via the OAuthBearer AuthenticationOptions class, depicted in Figure 16-10. When a request is received, the associated authentication handler performs the following steps:

1. Token extraction. If the request contains an Authorization header with the Bear er scheme, then its value is used as the access token. Otherwise, the authentication method returns without any identity.

2. Authentication ticket extraction. After the token is obtained from the message, the Options.AccessTokenFormat.Unprotect method is used to extract an authentication ticket from the access token. As we saw before, this ticket contains both a claims-based identity and additional authentication properties.

3. Authentication ticket validation. Finally, the ticket's validity period is checked.

At the end, if all the steps were performed successfully, the request's access token is converted into a returned identity. Using both the Options.Provider and the Op tions.AccessTokenProvider, you can customize the previous steps. For instance, if defined, the Options.Provider can be used to retrieve the access token from other message locations and also to validate or modify the extracted identity.

By default, Katana uses a custom access token format, coupled to its own authorization server. However, by changing the Options.AccessTokenFormat you can also configure Katana to accept JWT-based access tokens. The Katana's UseJwtBearerAuthentica tion extension method does exactly this:

1. Receives a JwtBearerAuthenticationOptions with information on how to validate JWT tokens, including the allowed audiences and the signature validation information

2. Internally creates an OAuthBearerAuthenticationOptions configured with a JwtFormat, which is an ISecureDataFormat that uses the JWT format

   • Registers an OAuthBearerAuthenticationMiddleware using these options

Figure 16-10 illustrates the classes involved in this process. Taking advantage of this, Example 16-2 shows the configuration of a Katana-based resource server:

   • The AllowedAudiences property is configured with the resource server's URI.

- The `IssuerSecurityTokenProviders` property is configured with the authorization server symmetric signature key.

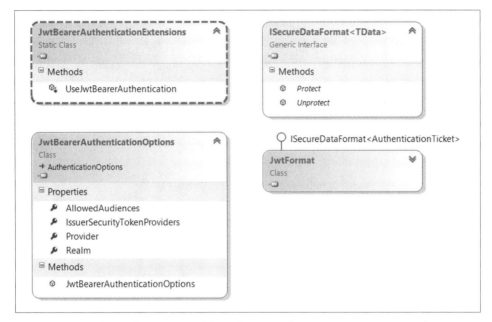

Figure 16-10. Classes for using JWT-based access tokens

Example 16-2. Configuring a Katana-based resource server to use T.AS

```
config.Filters.Add(new HostAuthenticationFilter("Bearer"));

app.UseJwtBearerAuthentication(new JwtBearerAuthenticationOptions
{
    AllowedAudiences = new []
    {
        "http://resourceserver.example"
    },
    IssuerSecurityTokenProviders = new []
    {
        new SymmetricKeyIssuerSecurityTokenProvider(
                "http://authzserver.example",
                "the.authorization.symmetric.signature.key")
    },

    Realm = "resourceserver.example",

    AuthenticationMode = AuthenticationMode.Passive
});
```

OAuth 2.0 and Authentication

As indicated in the name of RFC 6749, the primary focus of OAuth 2.0 is *authorization*, not *authentication*. Its main goal is to enable client applications to access a subset of resources exposed by a Web API, on its own behalf or on an user's behalf. However, *implementations* of this framework can also provide some forms of authentication.

As we stated at the beginning of this chapter, a request made by a client application to a resource server contains an access token. The primary aim of this token is to prove to the resource server that its bearer (i.e., the requesting client application) is authorized by the user to access a protected resource. A common way to achieve this is by having the access token:

- Authenticate the sending client application
- Authenticate the authorizing user
- Define the authorization scope

Figure 16-11 illustrates this authentication scenario, where the authorization server is the identity provider, the resource server is the relying party, and both the client and the user are the identity subjects. For instance, the JWT token issued by T.AS and presented in Example 16-1 contains exactly these three pieces of information: the `cli ent_id`, the user's claims (`role` and `sub`), and the authorized scope. Note also that, when you're using the Katana middleware, the access token information is transformed into an identity and propagated that way to the upper layers. However, as we've seen before, the OAuth 2.0 Framework does not define the access token format and information, leaving that as an implementation-dependent aspect. An OAuth 2.0 deployment where the access token contains only the authorized resources and HTTP methods, without any information about the client or the user, is perfectly conceivable. So, most of the times an access token is also an authentication token, authenticating both the client and user to the resource server, but this depends on the concrete implementation of the framework.

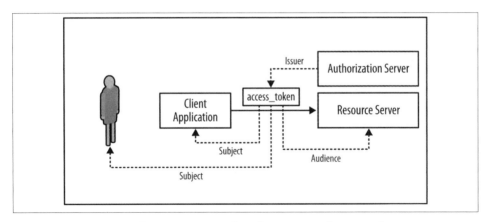

Figure 16-11. Access tokens as a way of authenticating clients and users to resource servers

The OAuth 2.0 Framework can also be used as the basis for a different kind of authentication: authenticating the user to the client application. The idea is to use context-specific resources, which we will call *user info* resources, that expose the user's identity as a way for the client to authenticate the user. Consider, for instance, the GitHub API v3: a successful GET on the *https://api.github.com/user* protected resource will return a representation with the email and the name of the user on whose behalf the used access token was issued. This allows the client application to obtain the user's identity, asserted by the resource server and authorization server, as illustrated in Figure 16-12.

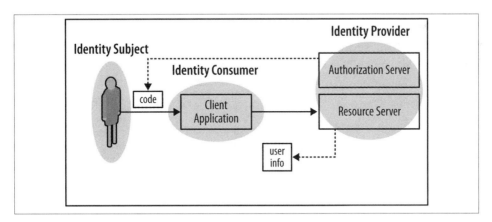

Figure 16-12. Protected resources as a way of authenticating users to clients

At the time of this writing, it is rather common for web applications to use this OAuth 2.0-based technique to authenticate their users against social identity providers such as Facebook or GitHub. However, there are two shortcomings to this approach. First, it depends on context-specific *user info* resources, which aren't defined by the OAuth 2.0 Framework. This implies that customization must be done for each different resource server. Secondly, and most important, this authentication usage is not secure for all of the OAuth 2.0 Framework flows—namely, the implicit flow and authorization code flow with public clients. For instance, in some flows, it is possible for a client application to use the authorization code or token to authenticate itself as the user on another client application. Consider, for instance, the implicit flow, where the token is delivered directly from the authorization endpoint to the client application via the user agent. After receiving this token, a malicious client can now present itself as the user to a different client and provide it with the same token. When the second client accesses the user info resource, it will receive the identity of the original user.

The OpenID Connect (*http://openid.net/connect/*) specification aims to solve these two problems by providing an identity layer on top of the OAuth 2.0 Framework.[3] First, it standardizes the concept of the user info resource (called *UserInfo Endpoint* in the specification) and the representation returned by it: a JSON object whose members are claims whose meaning is also defined by OpenID Connect. Example 16-3 shows the claims for our fictional Alice, returned by the Google UserInfo resource located at *https://www.googleapis.com/oauth2/v3/userinfo*.

Example 16-3. Representation returned by the UserInfo resource

```
{
  "sub": "104107606523710296052",
  "email": "alice4demos@gmail.com",
  "email_verified": true
}
```

OpenID Connect also extends the OAuth 2.0 token response definition, adding an id_token field, as shown in Example 16-4. The value of this field is a signed JWT token containing the user claims intended to be consumed by the client. Notice that this contrasts with the access token, which is opaque to the client. Example 16-5 shows the payload of a ID token containing identity claims about the user (the email claim) but also the intended audience of the token: the aud claims, whose value is the client_id of the relying client application. This aud field binds an ID token to a consumer, preventing a malicious client from reusing the token on another client.

Example 16-4. Token response containing an ID token

```
{
  "access_token" : "ya..8s",
  "token_type" : "Bearer",
  "expires_in" : 3599,
```

---

3. Despite its name, OpenID Connect is much more similar to OAuth 2.0 than to the *classic* OpenID protocol.

```
  "id_token" : "ey..OQ"
}
```

Example 16-5. Payload of an ID token returned in the token response

```
{
    "sub": "104107606523710296052",
    "iss": "accounts.google.com",
    "email_verified": "true",
    "at_hash": "G_...hQ",
    "exp": 1380480238,
    "azp": "55...ve.apps.googleusercontent.com",
    "iat": 1380476338,
    "email": "alice4demos@gmail.com",
    "aud": "55...ve.apps.googleusercontent.com"
}
```

OpenID Connect Authorization Code Flow Example

The `WebApiBook.Security` repository, available at *https://github.com/webapibook*, contains a console self-hosted OpenID Connect client application that uses the authorization code flow. It is preconfigured to use Google authorization server, but can be used with another OpendID Connect implementation.

By adding an identity layer upon OAuth 2.0, OpenID Connect provides an *unified* protocol for a client application to:

- Authenticate its users by obtaining a signed set of identity claims
- Obtain an access token that allows the client to access protected resources on the user's behalf

Notice that classical identity federation protocols, such as SAML, WS-Federation, or the classical OpenID protocol, provide only the first feature. On the other hand, the OAuth 2.0 Framework provides only the second.

Scope-Based Authorization

When using the OAuth 2.0 Framework, you can remove the authorization decision from the resource server and externalize it to the authorization server. As we've seen before, a scope is associated with an access token to define exactly what is being authorized to the client. So, in such a scenario, the resource server's task is simply to enforce the authorization decision expressed in the scope.

The `Thinktecture.IdentityModel.45` library that we saw in Chapter 15 also provides an authorization attribute with this purpose, named `ScopeAttribute`. This attribute receives an array of scope identifiers in its constructor and authorizes the request only if the associated claims principal has scope claims matching each one of these identifiers.

Example 16-6 illustrates the ScopeAttribute: POST requests require an access token with the create scope identifier, while DELETE requests require an access token containing the delete identifier.

Example 16-6. Using the ScopeAttribute

```
public class ScopeExampleResourceController : ApiController
{
    public HttpResponseMessage Get()
    {
        return new HttpResponseMessage
        {
            Content = new StringContent("resource representation")
        };
    }

    [Scope("create")]
    public HttpResponseMessage Post()
    {
        return new HttpResponseMessage()
        {
            Content = new StringContent("result representation")
        };
    }

    [Scope("delete")]
    public HttpResponseMessage Delete(string id)
    {
        return new HttpResponseMessage(HttpStatusCode.NoContent);
    }
}
```

Conclusion

In this chapter you were introduced to the OAuth 2.0 Authorization Framework, its protocols, and its patterns. There are several features of this framework that we want to highlight. First, it introduces a model where there is a clear distinction between users, clients, and resource servers. This separation is particularly important when these three actors belong to distinct trust boundaries and will have a profound impact on the way we model security in web-based systems. OAuth 2.0 also introduces the authorization server as the entity issuing and managing access tokens used by clients to access resources, namely on the user's behalf.

As we write, most of the OAuth 2.0 deployments use authorization servers that are coupled to the resource servers that use them. However, projects such as Thinktecture's Authorization Server and Windows Azure Active Directory are starting to provide authorization servers that can be used in multiple contexts and with different resource servers. The OAuth 2.0 Framework also provides concrete patterns and protocols for different scenarios, ranging from clients accessing resources on their own behalf (the *client credentials grant* flow) to constrained authorization delegation via front-channel interaction (the *authorization code grant* flow).

OAuth 2.0 is also the foundation of the new OpenID Connect protocol, which provides decentralized authentication capabilities. The overall result is an integrated way to solve some of the authentication and authorization challenges on Web APIs.

Despite its significant current adoption, there are many critics of the OAuth 2.0 Framework. First, it hinders interoperability by providing so many protocol options and alternatives. This flexibility also has a negative security impact: by leaving so many options available, it increases the probability of insecure implementations. The use of bearer tokens[4] is another relevant critique of OAuth 2.0, namely due to all the problems that we described in Chapter 15.

However, even with these problems, the OAuth 2.0 Framework is an important part of the current Web API security landscape.

---

4. Bearer tokens are the only complete specification as we write this chapter; the MAC specification is still a work in progress.

CHAPTER 17

Testability

The problem with troubleshooting is that trouble shoots back.

As developers, we often find ourselves in situations where we spend a significant amount of time trying to troubleshoot issues that might occur in our Web API implementation. In many cases, we just use a trial-and-error method with a browser or an HTTP debugger, but this sort of manual testing is time-consuming, irreproducible, and error-prone. To make things worse, as the number of scenarios that our Web API can cover increases, manually testing every possible path becomes a daunting task.

Over the years, different tools and practices have emerged to improve our lives as developers. Automated testing, for example, is one of the areas in which a lot of improvement has been made. Automated testing in this context consists of creating or configuring a piece of software to perform testing for us. There are some obvious advantages with this approach: a test becomes reproducible, and it can be run at any time, or we can even schedule it to run automatically with no interaction whatsoever.

As part of this chapter, we will explore the two most popular choices for developers to automate software testing in ASP.NET Web API: unit testing and integration testing. For those who are not familiar with these concepts, we have included a brief introduction to the subject, which also mentions test-driven development (TDD) as a core practice. Since this could be a very extensive subject, we have constrained it to ASP.NET Web API and how you can leverage it for testing all the components you build with the framework.

Unit Tests

A unit test is code that we typically write for verifying the expected behavior of some other code in isolation. We start the process of writing unit tests by splitting the application code into discrete parts, such as class methods, that are easy to manage and can be tested in isolation without affecting one another. For example, in the context of ASP.NET Web API, you might want to write different unit tests for every public method exposed in an `ApiController` implementation. "In isolation" means that there is no dependency between tests, so the order in which they run should not alter the final result. In fact, you should be able to run all the unit tests simultaneously.

A unit test is typically organized into three parts:

1. Arrange: set one or more objects in a known state.
2. Act: manipulate the state of those objects by calling some methods on it, for example.
3. Assert: check the results of the tests and compare them against an expected outcome.

As with any piece of source code, unit tests should also be treated as a development artifact that can be stored in a source repository. By having the tests in a repository, you can use them for multiple purposes such as documenting the expected behavior of certain code or ensuring that behavior is still correct as different changes in the implementation are made. They should also be easy and fast to run; otherwise, developers would be less likely to run them.

Unit Testing Frameworks

Unit testing frameworks help simplify the process of writing unit tests by enforcing certain aspects of the test structure and also providing tools to run them. As with any framework, they are not something strictly necessary, but they can certainly speed up the process of getting the unit tests done and working.

The most common unit testing frameworks used nowadays by developers are typically part of the xUnit family, including the Visual Studio unit testing tool (which is included in the paid version of Visual Studio), or xUnit.Net, a open source initiative that we will use in this chapter to cover both integration testing and unit testing. Most of the frameworks in the xUnit family are either a direct port of JUnit or use some of its concepts or ideas, which were initially originated and became popular in extreme programming.

Getting Started with Unit Testing in Visual Studio

To make things easier for developers, the ASP.NET team has included unit testing support in the New Project dialog in Visual Studio for ASP.NET Web API applications, as shown in Figure 17-1.

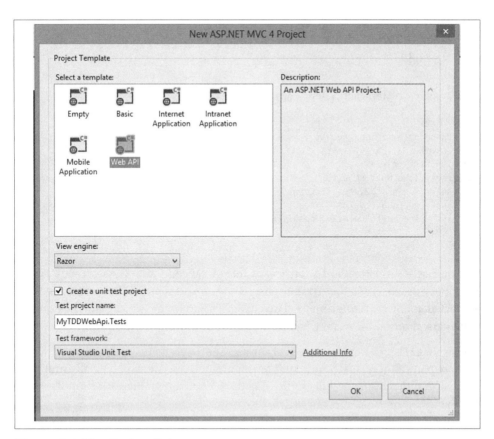

Figure 17-1. New Project dialog

By selecting the Create Unit Test project checkbox, you are instructing the Visual Studio project wizard to include a new Unit Test project using the testing framework of your preference (the Visual Studio Unit Testing tool is the only one available by default). When you select the Visual Studio Unit Testing tool, Visual Studio will also generate a project with a set of unit tests for the ASP.NET Web API controllers included in the default template. For other testing tools, this behavior will change based on the project template definition registered in Visual Studio for that tool.

In the case of the ASP.NET Web API project template, which includes a `ValuesController`, you will also find the unit test counterpart in the testing project, `ValuesControllerTest`. The code in Example 17-1 illustrates the `Get` method generated by Visual Studio in that class.

Example 17-1. Unit test generated by the ASP.NET Web API project template

```
[TestClass]
public class ValuesControllerTest
```

```
{
  [TestMethod]
  public void Get()
  {
    // Arrange
    ValuesController controller = new ValuesController(); // <1>

    // Act
    IEnumerable<string> result = controller.Get(); // <2>

    // Assert // <3>
    Assert.IsNotNull(result);
    Assert.AreEqual(2, result.Count());
    Assert.AreEqual("value1", result.ElementAt(0));
    Assert.AreEqual("value2", result.ElementAt(1));
  }
}
```

As you can see, this method is organized into Arrange, Act, and Assert parts, as we previously discussed. In the Arrange part *<1>*, the `ValuesController` under test is instantiated, follow by the `Get` method invocation as part of the Act *<2>* and the expected values assertions in the `Assert` part *<3>*.

The `Assert` class, as well as the `TestClass` and `TestMethod` attributes used by this unit test, are part of the Visual Studio unit testing framework. You will typically find these three with different names but similar functionality in any framework from the xUnit family.

While Example 17-1 shows how to unit test a particular controller, you will also find yourself writing unit tests for the rest of the components, such as the ones encapsulating data access or business logic as well as others that make sense only in the context of a Web API like message handlers.

xUnit.NET

xUnit.NET is another alternative in the xUnit family that began as an open source initiative from Brad Wilson and James Newkirk, also one of the authors of NUnit, the first port of JUnit in the .NET world. This framework was conceived with the goal of applying many of the best practices and lessons learned from previous experiences in unit testing and better aligning with the recent changes in the .NET platform. For example, this framework provides a nice way to check exceptions in a test compared to the other traditional frameworks. While most frameworks handle this scenario with the use of attributes, xUnit.NET uses delegates, as shown in Example 17-2.

Example 17-2. A unit test for checking an expected exception

```
[TestClass]
public class ValuesControllerTest
{
```

```
[TestMethod]
public void Get()
{
    // Arrange
    ValuesController controller = new ValuesController();

    // Assert // <1>
    controller.Throws<HttpException>(() => controller.Get("bad")) // <2>
}
}
```

As you can see in `assert_throws`, the `Throws` method provides a simple way to express the Assert *<1>* and Act *<2>* sections in a single line, where the delegate being passed to this method is responsible for throwing the exception.

Unit test organization

As a rule of thumb, a unit test should test only a single functionality or behavior; otherwise, it would be very complicated to get real feedback about what specifically was wrong. In addition, the unit test by itself wouldn't provide any value because it would be hard to determine what the expected behavior should be. For that reason, unit tests are typically organized in methods that provide fine-grained feedback. Each method should demonstrate only one expected behavior, but it might do so by using one or more assertions. In the case of xUnit.net, these methods must be decorated with a `Fact` attribute to identify them as unit tests. You might also want to organize unit tests in groups using different criteria, such as unit tests for a specific component or for a specific use case. xUnit just uses classes for grouping all the tests together in what is typically called a *test suite* in unit testing jargon.

The Assert class

Most xUnit frameworks, including xUnit.net, use an `Assert` class with common static methods for doing comparisons or checking results using a fluent interface, which helps to express intent explicitly. For example, if you express that the returning value of a method call should not be `null`, `Assert.IsNotNull(result)` probably communicates that intent better than `Assert.IsTrue(result == null)`, but this is just a personal preference of the developer writing the tests. All the methods in this `Assert` class throw exceptions when the condition evaluates to `false`, making it possible to detect whether a unit test failed.

The Role of Unit Testing in Test-Driven Development

Test-driven development (TDD) is a design technique in which you use unit tests to drive the design of production code by writing the tests first, followed by the necessary application code to make the tests pass. When TDD is applied correctly, the resulting artifacts are the application code along with the unit tests describing the expected behavior, which you can also use at any time later to make sure the behavior of the production code is still correct. However, TDD is focused not only on using unit tests to reduce the number of bugs in the production code, but also in improving that code's design. Since you are writing unit tests first, you are describing how the production code should behave *before* it is actually written. You are writing the application code that you need, and only that, with no chance of writing any unnecessary implementation.

A common mistake is to assume that writing some unit tests implies TDD. While TDD requires unit tests for driving the design of your code, the opposite is not necessarily true. You can write unit tests after the code is written, which is typically done for increasing the percentage of code that you have covered with tests, but that does not mean you are using TDD, as your application code already exists.

The red and green cycle

When you are writing unit tests, the words *red* and *green* can be used as a replacement for *failure* and *success*, respectively. These are the colors most test runners also use to help developers quickly identify which tests are passing or failing. TDD also makes extensive use of these two colors for driving the development of new functionality. Because you write a test for code that does not exist yet, your first test run will fail. You then write code designed to pass the test and rerun the test. You will get a green light if the behavior of the production code is correct, a red one if your production code still needs some work. In that way, you are constantly moving through a red/green cycle. However, once a test passes, you should stop writing new production code until you have a new test, with new requirements, that fails. You basically write enough application code to make the test pass, which might not be perfect at first glance, but you have a tool to verify that any improvement made to the production code does not affect the expected behavior. If you want to improve or optimize certain aspects of the production code, you can do it as long as you don't modify the public interface of your components. The tests can still be used as backup to make sure the underlying behavior is still the same.

Code refactoring

The term *code refactoring* refers to the act of changing the internal implementation of a component while leaving its observable behavior intact—for example, reducing a large public method to a set of individually concise and single-purpose methods, which are easier to maintain. When you are refactoring your production code, you don't modify the existing unit tests, which would imply you are adding, removing, or modifying existing functionality. The existing unit tests are used to make sure the observable behavior of the application code is still the same after the refactoring. If you have, for example, an action in a controller that returns a list of customers and a unit test for verifying that behavior, that test will only expect to receive the same list of customers no matter how the internal implementation is getting that list. If you detect some inconsistencies in that code, you can use refactoring to improve it and use the existing unit tests to make sure nothing was broken with the introduced changes.

Example 17-3 shows some code that can be improved through internal refactoring.

Example 17-3. Two methods instantiating an HttpClient instance

```
public abstract class IssueSource : IIssueSource
{
  HttpMessageHandler _handler = null;

  protected IssueSource(HttpMessageHandler handler = null)
  {
    _handler = handler;
  }

  public virtual Task<IEnumerable<Issue>> FindAsync()
  {
    HttpClient client;

    if (_handler != null)
      client = new HttpClient(_handler);
    else
      client = new HttpClient();

    // Do something with the HttpClient instance ...
  }

  public virtual Task<IEnumerable<Issue>> FindAsyncQuery(dynamic values)
  {
    HttpClient client;

    if (_handler != null)
      client = new HttpClient(_handler);
    else
      client = new HttpClient();

    // Do something with the HttpClient instance ...
  }
}
```

Both methods are initializing a new HttpClient instance. If that code requires some changes, such as the addition of new settings, it has to be changed in the two methods. That code can be moved to a common method, which is kept internal to the implementation, as shown in Example 17-4.

Example 17-4. HttpClient initialization moved to a common method

```
public abstract class IssueSource : IIssueSource
{
  HttpMessageHandler _handler = null;
```

```
protected IssueSource(HttpMessageHandler handler = null)
{
  _handler = handler;
}

public virtual Task<IEnumerable<Issue>> FindAsync()
{
  HttpClient client = GetClient();

  // Do something with the HttpClient instance ...
}

public virtual Task<IEnumerable<Issue>> FindAsyncQuery(dynamic values)
{
  HttpClient client = GetClient();

  // Do something with the HttpClient instance ...
}

protected HttpClient GetClient()
{
  HttpClient client;

  if (_handler != null)
    client = new HttpClient(_handler);
  else
    client = new HttpClient();

  return client;
}
}
```

We've removed the duplicated code without modifying the external interface of this class. The expected behavior is still the same, so the unit tests don't have to be changed, and they can be used to verify this change did not break anything.

Dependency injection and mocking

Dependency injection is another practice that usually goes hand in hand with unit testing in static languages where depedencies cannot be easily replaced at runtime. Since unit testing focuses on testing the behavior of certain code in isolation, you would want to minimize the impact of any external dependency during testing. By using dependency injection, you replace all the hardcoded dependencies and inject them at runtime, so their behavior can be faked. For example, if a Web API controller relies on a data access class for querying a database, we will not want to unit test the controller with that explicit dependency. That would imply a database is initialized and ready to be used every time the test is run, which might not always be the case. The controller is first decoupled from the real data access class implementation via an interface or an abstract class, which is later injected into the controller through either an argument in the constructor or a property setter. As part of the unit test, the only pending task is to create a fake class that implements the interface or abstract class and also satisfies the requirements of the test. That fake class could simply mimic the same interface and return the expected data for the test from a memory list previously initialized in the same test. In that way, we get rid of the database dependency in the tests. There are multiple open source frameworks, such as Moq or RhinoMocks, for automatically generating a fake or mock from an interface or base class, and setting expectations for how that mock class should be behave. Example 17-5 shows a fragment of a unit test for our Issue Tracker Web API that instantiates a mock (from the Moq framework) for emulating the behavior of a data access class.

Example 17-5. A unit test that uses a mock class

```
public class IssuesControllerTests
{
  private Mock<IIssueSource> _mockIssueSource = new Mock<IIssueSource>(); // <1>
  private IssuesController _controller;

  public IssuesControllerTests()
  {
    _controller = new IssuesController(_mockIssueSource.Object); // <2>
  }

  [Fact]
  public void ShouldCallFindAsyncWhenGETForAllIssues()
  {
    _controller.Get();
    _mockIssueSource.Verify(i=>i.FindAsync()); // <3>
  }
}
```

A mock for the IIssueSource interface is instantiated via the Mock class provided by the Moq framework *<1>* and injected into the IssuesController constructor *<2>*. The unit test invokes the Get method on the controller and verifies that the FindAsync method on the Mock object was actually called *<3>*. Verify is a method also provided by the Moq framework for checking if a method was invoked or not, and how many times it was invoked (invoking the method FindAsync more than once would imply a bug in the code, for example). If this framework isn't used, a lot of manual and repetitive code would be needed to implement a similar functionality.

Unit Testing an ASP.NET Web API Implementation

There are several components in an ASP.NET Web API implementation that you will want to test in isolation. As part of this chapter, we will cover some of them, such as ApiController, MediaTypeFormatter, and HttpMessageHandler. Toward the end of the chapter, we will also explore the idea of using the HttpClient class and in-memory hosting for doing integration testing.

Unit Testing an ApiController

An ApiController in the context of ASP.NET Web API acts as an entry point to your Web API implementation. It serves as a bridge for exposing application logic to the external world via HTTP. One of the main things you will want to test is how the controller reacts to different request messages in isolation. You can pick which messages to use based on the supported scenarios or use cases for the Web API. Isolation is also a key aspect for unit testing, as you cannot assume that everything is correctly set up in the Web API runtime before running the tests. For example, if your ApiController relies on the authenticated user for doing certain operations, the configuration of that user should also be done within the unit tests. The same idea applies for the initialization of the request messages.

As part of this section, we will use the ApiController that we built for managing issues as the starting point. We will try to write unit tests against that code for covering some of the supported use cases. Let's start with Example 17-6.

Example 17-6. Our IssuesController implementation

```
public class IssuesController : ApiController
{
  private readonly IIssueSource _issueSource;

  public IssuesController(IIssueSource issueSource )
  {
    _issueSource = issueSource;
  }

  public async Task<Issue> Get(string id) // <1>
  {
    var issue = await _issueSource.FindAsync(id);
    if(issue == null)
      throw new HttpResponseException(HttpStatusCode.NotFound);
    return issue;
  }

  public async Task<HttpResponseMessage> Post(Issue issue) // <2>
  {
    var createdIssue = await _issueSource.CreateAsync(issue);
    var link = Url.Link("DefaultApi", new {Controller = "issues",
      id = createdIssue.Id});
    var response = Request.CreateResponse(HttpStatusCode.Created, createdIssue);
    response.Headers.Location = new Uri(link);
    return response;
  }
}
```

Example 17-6 shows our first implementation of the IssuesController, which does not look too complex at first glance. It contains a Get method for retrieving an existing issue *<1>*, and a Post method for adding a new issue *<2>*. It also depends on an IIssueSource instance for handling persistence concerns.

Testing the Get method

Our first Get method, shown in Example 17-7, looks very simple and returns an existing issue by delegating the call to the IIssueSource implementation. As the unit tests should not rely on a concrete IIssueSource implementation, we will use a Mock instead.

Example 17-7. Our first unit test for the Get method

```
public class IssuesControllerTests
{
  private Mock<IIssueSource> _mockIssueSource = new Mock<IIssueSource>();
  private IssuesController _controller;

  public IssuesControllerTests()
  {
    _controller = new IssuesController(_mockIssueSource.Object); // <1>
  }

  [Fact]
  public void ShouldReturnIssueWhenGETForExistingIssue()
  {
    var issue = new Issue();

    _mockIssueSource.Setup(i => i.FindAsync("1"))
        .Returns(Task.FromResult(issue)); // <2>

    var foundIssue = _controller.Get("1").Result; // <3>

    Assert.Equal(issue, foundIssue); // <4>
  }
}
```

Example 17-7 mainly checks that the controller invokes the FindAsync method in the IIssueSource instance to return an existing issue. The controller is first initialized with a mock instance of IIssueSource *<1>* as part of the test initialization. That mock instance is set up to return an issue when it receives an argument equal to "1" *<2>*, which is the same argument that gets passed to the Get method controller *<3>*. Finally, the issue returned by the controller is compared with the issue injected in the mock to make sure they are the same *<4>*.

That's the happy path when an issue is returned by the IIssueSource implementation, but we will also want to test how the controller reacts when a requested issue is not found. We will create a new test for verifying that scenario, as shown in Example 17-8.

Example 17-8. Unit test for covering the nonexisting issue path

```
[Fact]
public void ShouldReturnNotFoundWhenGETForNonExistingIssue()
{
  _mockIssueSource.Setup(i => i.FindAsync("1"))
    .Returns(Task.FromResult((Issue)null)); // <1>

  var ex = Assert.Throws<AggregateException>(() =>
  {
    var task = _controller.Get("1");
    var result = task.Result;
  }); // <2>

  Assert.IsType<HttpResponseException>(ex.InnerException); // <3>
  Assert.Equal(HttpStatusCode.NotFound,
    ((HttpResponseException) ex.InnerException).Response.StatusCode); // <4>
}
```

The controller is throwing an `HttpException` with a status code equal to 404 when the issue is not found. The unit test is initializing the `Mock` for returning a `Task` with a `null` result when the issue ID is equal to 1. As part of the Assert section in the unit test, we are using the `Throws` method (provided in xUnit.NET) in the `Assert` class for checking whether a method returns an exception or not *<2>*. The `Throws` method receives a delegate that might throw an exception, and it tries to capture it. Finally, we are checking if the thrown exception is of the type `HttpResponseException` *<3>* and the status code on that exception is set to 404 *<4>*.

Testing the Post method

The `Post` method in the controller will create a new issue. We need to verify that the issue is correctly passed to the `IIssuesSource` implementation, and also that the response headers are correctly set before leaving the controller. Since this controller method relies on the `HttpRequestMessage` and `UrlHelper` instances in the controller context for generating a response and the link to the new resource, some tedious work is required to initialize the runtime configuration and the routing table, as shown in Example 17-9.

Example 17-9. Unit test for covering the nonexistent issue path

```
_controller.Configuration = new HttpConfiguration(); // <1>

var route = _controller.Configuration.Routes.MapHttpRoute(
  name: "DefaultApi",
  routeTemplate: "api/{controller}/{id}",
  defaults: new { id = RouteParameter.Optional }
); // <2>

var routeData = new HttpRouteData(route,
```

```
new HttpRouteValueDictionary
{
  { "controller", "Issues" }
}
);

_controller.Request = new HttpRequestMessage(HttpMethod.Post,
   "http://test.com/issues");  // <3>
_controller.Request.Properties.Add(HttpPropertyKeys.HttpConfigurationKey,
controller.Configuration);
_controller.Request.Properties.Add(HttpPropertyKeys.HttpRouteDataKey,
   routeData); // <4>
```

A new `HttpConfiguration` object is instantiated and set in the controller instance *<1>*. The route is set up in *<2>* and added to the existing configuration object. A new request object is created and set up with the HTTP verb and URI expected by the test *<3>*. Finally, the routing data and configuration object are associated with the request object through the generic property bag `Properties`, which is the one used by `UrlHelp er` to look up these objects *<4>*.

The ASP.NET Web API team already simplified this scenario in Web API, as we will see in the next section. In the meantime, if you are still using the first Web API release, there is a set of extension methods provided as part of the WebApiContrib project (*http:// bit.ly/nuget-testing*), which configures the controller with a single line of code (see Example 17-10).

Example 17-10. Extension methods for configuring the ApiController in a test

```
public static class ApiControllerExtensions
{
  public static void ConfigureForTesting(this ApiController controller,
    HttpRequestMessage request,
    string routeName = null,
    IHttpRoute route = null);

  public static void ConfigureForTesting(this ApiController controller,
    HttpMethod method,
    string uri,
    string routeName = null,
    IHttpRoute route = null);
}
```

These extension methods receive the request instance or HTTP method to use, and optionally a URL or default route to use in the test. We will be using these extension methods in the rest of the chapter for simplifying the code in the tests. Our first unit test is shown in Example 17-11.

Example 17-11. First test to verify that the CreateAsync method was invoked

```
[Fact]
public void ShouldCallCreateAsyncWhenPOSTForNewIssue()
{
  //Arrange
  _controller.ConfigureForTesting(HttpMethod.Post, "http://test.com/issues"); // <1>
  var issue = new Issue();
  _mockIssueSource.Setup(i => i.CreateAsync(issue))
    .Returns(() => Task.FromResult(issue)); // <2>

  //Act
  var response = _controller.Post(issue).Result; // <3>

  //Assert
  _mockIssueSource.Verify(i=>i
    .CreateAsync(It.Is<Issue>(iss => iss.Equals(issue)))); // <4>
}
```

The HttpRequestMessage and the UrlHelper instances in the IssuesController are initialized with the extension method ConfigureForTesting instances in the instances in the *<1>*. Once the controller is initialized, the IIssueSource mock instance is set to return an asynchronous task, which emulates the work of persisting the issue in the backend *<2>*. The Post method in the controller is invoked with a new issue *<3>*. The test verifies that the CreateAsync method in the mock instance was actually invoked *<4>*.

An additional test is needed to verify that a valid response is returned after we invoke the CreateAsync method in the IIssueSource implementation Example 17-12.

Example 17-12. Second test to verify the response message

```
[Fact]
public void ShouldSetResponseHeadersWhenPOSTForNewIssue()
{
  //Arrange
  _controller.ConfigureForTesting(HttpMethod.Post, "http://test.com/issues");
  var createdIssue = new Issue();
  createdIssue.Id = "1";
  _mockIssueSource.Setup(i => i.CreateAsync(createdIssue)).Returns(() =>
  Task.FromResult(createdIssue)); // <1>

  //Act
  var response = _controller.Post(createdIssue).Result; // <2>

  //Assert
  response.StatusCode.ShouldEqual(HttpStatusCode.Created); // <3>
  response.Headers.Location.AbsoluteUri.ShouldEqual("http://test.com/issues/1");
}
```

The IIssueSource mock instance is set up to return a task with the created issue *<1>*. The created issue is passed as an argument to the controller instance *<2>*. The test verifies that the expected HTTP status code is equal to `Created` and the new resource location is *http://test.com/issues/1*. At this point, you should have a pretty good idea of what is involved in unit testing a controller in ASP.NET Web API. In the next sections, we will discuss what needs to be done for testing a `MediaTypeFormatter` and an `HttpMessage Handler` *<3>*.

IHttpActionResult in Web API 2

Web API 2 introduces a new interface `IHttpActionResult` (equivalent to `ActionRe sult` in ASP.NET MVC) that greatly simplifies the unit testing story for controllers. A controller method can now return an implementation of `IHttpActionResult`, which internally uses the `Request` or the `UrlHelper` for link generation, so the unit test cares only about the returned `IHttpActionResult` instance. The following code shows the equivalent version of the `Post` method using an instance of `IHttpActionResult`:

```
public async Task<IHttpActionResult> Post(Issue issue)
{
  var createdIssue = await _issueSource.CreateAsync(issue);
  var result = new CreatedAtRouteNegotiatedContentResult<Issue>(
    "DefaultApi",
    new Dictionary<string, object> { { "id", createdIssue.Id } },
      createdIssue,
      this);

  return result;
}
```

`CreatedAtRouteNegotiatedContentResult` is an implementation also included in the framework for handling this scenario. A new resource is created and the location is set in the response message. The unit test is much simpler too, as illustrated in Example 17-13.

Example 17-13. Second test to verify the response message

```
[Fact]
public void ShouldSetResponseHeadersWhenPOSTForNewIssue()
{
  //Arrange
  var createdIssue = new Issue();
  createdIssue.Id = "1";
  _mockIssueSource.Setup(i => i.CreateAsync(createdIssue)).Returns(() =>
  Task.FromResult(createdIssue));

  //Act
  var result = _controller.Post(createdIssue).Result as
  CreatedAtRouteNegotiatedContentResult; // <1>

  //Assert
  result.ShouldNotBeNull(); // <2>
```

```
    result.Content.ShouldBeType<Issue>(); // <3>
}
```

The unit test just casts the returned result to the expected type, which is `CreateAtRou teNegotiatedContentResult` in this test *<1>*, and verifies that the result is not `null` *<2>* and the content set in that result is an instance of the `Issue` type *<3>*. No previous initialization code was required, as all the content negotiation and link management logic is now encapsulated in the `IHttpActionResult` implementation, which is a concern this unit test does not care about.

Unit Testing a MediaTypeFormatter

As a central piece for handling new media types or content negotiation, a `MediaType Formatter` implementation involves several aspects you'll want to address during unit testing. Those aspects include correct handling of the supported media types, converting a model from or to a given media type, or optionally checking the correct configuration of some settings such as encoding or mappings.

We can get a rough idea of what unit testing a `MediaTypeFormatter` implementation involves by looking at its class definition in Example 17-14.

Example 17-14. MediaTypeFormatter class definition

```
public abstract class MediaTypeFormatter
{
  public Collection<Encoding> SupportedEncodings { get; }

  public Collection<MediaTypeHeaderValue> SupportedMediaTypes { get; }

  public Collection<MediaTypeMapping> MediaTypeMappings { get; }

  public abstract bool CanReadType(Type type);

  public abstract bool CanWriteType(Type type);

  public virtual Task<object> ReadFromStreamAsync(Type type, Stream readStream,
    HttpContent content, IFormatterLogger formatterLogger);

  public virtual Task WriteToStreamAsync(Type type, object value,
    Stream writeStream, HttpContent content, TransportContext transportContext);
}
```

The following conditions can be checked with different unit tests:

- The supported media types (see Example 17-15) were correctly configured in the `SupportedMediaTypes` collection. In the example we built in Chapter 13 for supporting syndication media types such as Atom or RSS, this test would imply that the collection contains `application/atom+xml` and `application/rss+xml` for supporting those media types, respectively.

Example 17-15. Unit tests for checking the supported media types

```
[Fact]
public void ShouldSupportAtom()
{
  var formatter = new SyndicationMediaTypeFormatter();

  Assert.True(formatter.SupportedMediaTypes
    .Any(s => s.MediaType == "application/atom+xml"));
}

[Fact]
public void ShouldSupportRss()
{
  var formatter = new SyndicationMediaTypeFormatter();

  Assert.True(formatter.SupportedMediaTypes
    .Any(s => s.MediaType == "application/rss+xml"));
}
```

- The implementation supports serializing or deserialization of a given model type in the `CanReadType` and `CanWriteType` methods (see Example 17-16).

Example 17-16. Unit tests for checking whether an implementation can read or write a type

```
[Fact]
public void ShouldNotReadAnyType()
{
  var formatter = new SyndicationMediaTypeFormatter();

  var canRead = formatter.CanReadType(typeof(object));

  Assert.False(canRead);
}

[Fact]
public void ShouldWriteAnyType()
{
  var formatter = new SyndicationMediaTypeFormatter();

  var canWrite = formatter.CanWriteType(typeof(object));

  Assert.True(canWrite);
}
```

- The code for writing or reading a model into/out to stream using one of the supported media types is working correctly (see Example 17-17). That implies testing the WriteToStreamAsync and ReadFromStreamAsync methods, respectively.

Example 17-17. Unit tests for verifying the behavior of the WriteToStreamAsync method

```
[Fact]
public void ShouldSerializeAsAtom()
{
  var ms = new MemoryStream();

  var content = new FakeContent();
  content.Headers.ContentType = new MediaTypeHeaderValue("application/atom+xml");

  var formatter = new SyndicationMediaTypeFormatter();

  var task = formatter.WriteToStreamAsync(typeof(List<ItemToSerialize>),
    new List<ItemToSerialize> { new ItemToSerialize { ItemName = "Test" }},
    ms,
    content,
    new FakeTransport()
  );

  task.Wait();

  ms.Seek(0, SeekOrigin.Begin);

  var atomFormatter = new Atom10FeedFormatter();
  atomFormatter.ReadFrom(XmlReader.Create(ms));

  Assert.Equal(1, atomFormatter.Feed.Items.Count());
}

public class ItemToSerialize
{
  public string ItemName { get; set; }
}

public class FakeContent : HttpContent
{
  public FakeContent()
    : base()
  {
  }

  protected override Task SerializeToStreamAsync(Stream stream, TransportContext
      context)
  {
    throw new NotImplementedException();
  }
```

```
  protected override bool TryComputeLength(out long length)
  {
    throw new NotImplementedException();
  }
}

public class FakeTransport : TransportContext
{
  public override ChannelBinding GetChannelBinding(ChannelBindingKind kind)
  {
    throw new NotImplementedException();
  }
}
```

Example 17-17 shows a unit test that serializes a list of items of the type `ItemToSerial` `ize`, also defined in the test as an Atom feed. The test mainly verifies that the `Syndica` `tionMediaTypeFormatter` can serialize the list of items when the content type is equal to `application/atom+xml`. As the `WriteToStreamAsync` method expects instances of `HttpContent` and `TransportContext`, and those are not used at all in the implementation with the exception of the headers, two fake classes were defined that don't do anything special. The test also deserializes the stream back to an Atom feed using the WCF syndication class to make sure the serialization was done properly.

- All the required settings are correctly initialized. For example, if you have a requirement for supporting the media type mappings in the query string, a unit test could check that this mapping was correctly configured in the `MediaTypeMap` `pings` collection, as Example 17-18 demonstrates.

Example 17-18. Unit test for checking the supported media type mappings

```
[Fact]
public void ShouldMapAtomFormatInQueryString()
{
  var formatter = new SyndicationMediaTypeFormatter();

  Assert.True(formatter.MediaTypeMappings.OfType<QueryStringMapping>()
    .Any(m => m.QueryStringParameterName == "format" &&
              m.QueryStringParameterValue == "atom" &&
              m.MediaType.MediaType == "application/atom+xml"));
}
```

Example 17-18 illustrates a sample of a test that checks if a `MediaTypeMapping` was defined as a query string argument for mapping a query string variable `format` with value `atom` to the media type `application/atom+xml`.

Unit Testing an HttpMessageHandler

An HttpMessageHandler is a generic interception mechanism for the Web API runtime pipeline. It's asynchronous by nature, and typically contains a single method, SendAsync, for processing a request message (HttpRequestMessage) that returns a Task instance representing some work to obtain a response (HttpResponseMessage). See Example 17-19.

Example 17-19. HttpMessageHandler class definition

```
public abstract class HttpMessageHandler
{
  protected internal abstract Task<HttpResponseMessage> SendAsync(
    HttpRequestMessage request, CancellationToken cancellationToken);
}
```

The SendAsync method cannot be directly called in a unit test, as it is not public, but the framework provides a class, System.Net.Http.MessageInvoker, that you can use for that purpose. This class receives the HttpMessageHandler instance in the constructor and provides a public method, SendAsync, for invoking the method with the same name on the handler. Example 17-20 simply illustrates how the SendAsync method in a sample HttpMessageHandler is unit tested. However, an HttpMessageHandler might receive external dependencies or contain some other public methods you will want to test as well.

Example 17-20. Unit testing an HttpMessageHandler

```
[Fact]
public void ShouldInvokeHandler()
{
    var handler = new SampleHttpMessageHandler();

    var invoker = new HttpMessageInvoker(handler);
    var task = invoker.SendAsync(new HttpRequestMessage(), new CancellationToken());

    task.Wait();

    var response = task.Result;

    // Assertions over the response
    // ......
}
```

Unit Testing an ActionFilterAttribute

Action filters are not any different from the HTTP message handlers when it comes to message interception, but they run much deeper in the runtime pipeline once the action context has been initialized and the action is about to execute. The action filter base class System.Web.Http.Filters.ActionFilterAttribute (see Example 17-21) pro-

vides two methods that can be overridden, OnActionExecuting and OnActionExecu
ted, for intercepting the call before and right after the action has been executed.

Example 17-21. ActionFilterAttribute class definition

```
public abstract class ActionFilterAttribute : FilterAttribute,
  IActionFilter,
  IFilter
{
  public virtual void OnActionExecuted(HttpActionExecutedContext
    actionExecutedContext);

  public virtual void OnActionExecuting(HttpActionContext
    actionContext);
}
```

Both methods are public, so they can be called directly from a unit test. Example 17-22
shows a very basic implementation of a filter for authenticating clients with an application key. The idea is to use this concrete implementation to show how the different
scenarios can be unit tested.

Example 17-22. Action filter for authenticating clients with an application key

```
public interface IKeyVerifier
{
  bool VerifyKey(string key);
}

public class ApplicationKeyActionFilter : ActionFilterAttribute
{
  public const string KeyHeaderName = "X-AuthKey";

  IKeyVerifier keyVerifier;

  public ApplicationKeyActionFilter()
  {
  }

  public ApplicationKeyActionFilter(IKeyVerifier keyVerifier) // <1>
  {
      this.keyVerifier = keyVerifier;
  }

  public Type KeyVerifierType // <2>
  {
      get;
      set;
  }

  public override void OnActionExecuting(HttpActionContext
    actionContext)
  {
```

```
        if (this.keyVerifier == null)
        {
            if (this.KeyVerifierType == null)
            {
                throw new Exception("The keyVerifierType was not provided");
            }

            this.keyVerifier = (IKeyVerifier)Activator
                .CreateInstance(this.KeyVerifierType);
        }

        IEnumerable<string> values = null;

        if (actionContext.Request.Headers
            .TryGetValues(KeyHeaderName, out values)) // <3>
        {
            var key = values.First();

            if (!this.keyVerifier.VerifyKey(key)) // <4>
            {
                actionContext.Response =
                    new HttpResponseMessage(HttpStatusCode.Unauthorized);
            }
        }
        else
        {
            actionContext.Response =
                new HttpResponseMessage(HttpStatusCode.Unauthorized);
        }

        base.OnActionExecuting(actionContext);
    }
}
```

This action filter receives an instance of IKeyVerifier, which is used to verify whether a key is valid *<1>*. Because an action filter can also be used as an attribute, the implementation provides a property, KeyVerifierType *<2>*, to set the IKeyVerifier in that scenario. This filter only implements the OnActionExecuting method, which runs before the action is executed. This implementation checks for an X-Auth header in the request message set in the context *<3>*, and tries to pass the value of that header to the IKeyVerifier instance for authentication *<4>*. If the key cannot be validated or it is not found in the request message, the filter sets a response message with an HTTP status code of 401 Unauthorized in the current context, and the pipeline execution is interrupted.

The first unit test, shown in Example 17-23, will test the scenario in which a valid key is passed in the request message.

Example 17-23. Unit test for a valid key

```
[Fact]
public class ApplicationKeyActionFilterFixture
{
  public void ShouldValidateKey()
  {
      var keyVerifier = new Mock<IKeyVerifier>();
      keyVerifier
          .Setup(k => k.VerifyKey("mykey"))
          .Returns(true); // <1>

      var request = new HttpRequestMessage();
      request.Headers.Add("X-AuthKey", "mykey"); // <2>

      var actionContext = InitializeActionContext(request); // <3>

      var filter = new ApplicationKeyActionFilter(keyVerifier.Object);
      filter.OnActionExecuting(actionContext); // <4>

      Assert.Null(actionContext.Response); // <5>
  }
}

private HttpActionContext InitializeActionContext(HttpRequestMessage request)
{
    var configuration = new HttpConfiguration();

    var route = configuration.Routes.MapHttpRoute(
      name: "DefaultApi",
      routeTemplate: "api/{controller}/{id}",
      defaults: new { id = RouteParameter.Optional }
    );

    var routeData = new HttpRouteData(route,
        new HttpRouteValueDictionary
        {
            { "controller", "Issues" }
        }
    );

    request.Properties[HttpPropertyKeys.HttpRouteDataKey] = routeData;

    var controllerContext = new HttpControllerContext(configuration, routeData, request);

    var actionContext = new HttpActionContext
    {
        ControllerContext = controllerContext
    };

    return actionContext;
}
```

As a first step *<1>*, the unit test initializes a mock or fake instance of the IKeyVerifi er that will return true when the key passed to the VerifyKey method is equal to mykey. Secondly *<2>*, a new HTTP request message is created and the custom header X-AuthKey is set to the value expected by the IKeyVerifier instance. The Action context expected by the filter is initialized in the method InitializeActionContext *<3>*, which requires a lot of common boilerplate code to inject the routing configuration and the request message into the constructor of the HttpControllerContext class. Finally, the method OnActionExecuting is invoked *<4>* with the initialized context and an assertion is made for a null response *<5>*. If nothing fails in the action filter implementation, the response will never be set in the context, so the test will pass.

Example 17-24 will test the next scenario, in which a key is not valid and a response is returned with the status code 401 (Unauthorized).

Example 17-24. Unit test for an invalid key

```
[Fact]
public void ShouldNotValidateKey()
{
    var keyVerifier = new Mock<IKeyVerifier>();
    keyVerifier
        .Setup(k => k.VerifyKey("mykey"))
        .Returns(true);

    var request = new HttpRequestMessage();
    request.Headers.Add(ApplicationKeyActionFilter.KeyHeaderName, "badkey"); // <1>

    var actionContext = InitializeActionContext(request);

    var filter = new ApplicationKeyActionFilter(keyVerifier.Object);
    filter.OnActionExecuting(actionContext);

    Assert.NotNull(actionContext.Response); // <2>
    Assert.Equal(HttpStatusCode.Unauthorized,
        actionContext.Response.StatusCode); // <3>
}
```

The main difference with the previous test is that the application set in the request message *<1>* is different from the one expected by the IKeyVerifier mock instance. After the OnActionExecuting method is invoked, two assertions are made to make sure the response set in the context is not null *<2>* and its status code is equal to 401 (Un authorized) *<3>*.

Unit Testing Routes

Route configuration is another aspect that you might want to cover with unit testing. Although it's not a component itself, a complex route configuration that does not follow the common conventions might lead to some problems that you will want to figure out sooner rather than later, and far before the implementation is deployed. The bad news is that ASP.NET Web API does not offer any support for unit testing routes out-of-the-box, so custom code is required. That custom code will basically use some of the built-in Web API infrastructure components, like the `DefaultHttpControllerSelector` and `ApiControllerActionSelector`, to infer the controller type and action name for a given `HttpRequestMessage` and routing configuration. See Example 17-25.

Example 17-25. A generic method for testing routes

```
public static class RouteTester
{
  public static void TestRoutes(HttpConfiguration configuration,
    HttpRequestMessage request,
    Action<Type, string> callback)
  {
    var routeData = configuration.Routes.GetRouteData(request);
    request.Properties[HttpPropertyKeys.HttpRouteDataKey] = routeData;

    var controllerSelector = new DefaultHttpControllerSelector(configuration); // <1>
    var controllerContext = new HttpControllerContext(configuration, routeData,
        request);

    controllerContext.ControllerDescriptor = controllerSelector
      .SelectController(request); // <2>

    var actionSelector = new ApiControllerActionSelector(); // <3>

    var action = actionSelector.SelectAction(controllerContext).ActionName; // <4>
    var controllerType = controllerContext.ControllerDescriptor
      .ControllerType; // <5>

    callback(controllerType, action); // <5>
  }
}
```

Example 17-25 illustrates a generic method that receives an instance of `HttpConfigu ration` with the routing configuration and an `HttpRequestMessage`, and invokes a callback with the selected controller type and action name. This method first instantiates a `DefaultHttpControllerSelector` class using the `HttpConfiguration` received as an argument to determine the controller type *<2>*. The controller is selected afterward with the `HttpRequestMessage` also passed as an argument *<3>*. Once the controller is selected, an `ApiControllerActionSelector` is instantiated next to infer the action name *<4>*. The action name and controller type are obtained in *<5>* and *<6>*. Finally, a callback is called with the inferred controller type and action name. This callback will be used by the unit test to perform the assertions. See Example 17-26.

Example 17-26. A unit test that uses the RouteTester implementation

```
[Fact]
public void ShouldRouteToIssueGET()
{
  var config = new HttpConfiguration();
  config.Routes.MapHttpRoute(name: "Default",
    routeTemplate: "api/{controller}/{id}"); // <1>

  var request = new HttpRequestMessage(HttpMethod.Get,
  "http://www.example.com/api/Issues/1"); // <2>

  RouteTester.TestRoutes(config, request, // <3>
    (controllerType, action) =>
    {
      Assert.Equal(typeof(IssuesController), controllerType);
      Assert.Equal("Get", action);
    });
}
```

Example 17-26 illustrates how the RouteTester class can be used in a unit test to verify a route configuration. An HttpConfiguration is initialized and configured with the routes to test *<1>*, and also an HttpRequestMessage with the HTTP verb and URL to invoke *<2>*. As the final step, the RouteTester is used with the configuration and request instances to determine the controller type and action name. As part of the callback, the test defines the assertions for comparing the inferred controller type and action name with the expected ones *<3>*.

Integration Tests in ASP.NET Web API

Thus far we have discussed unit testing, which focuses on testing components in isolation, but what happens if you would like to test how all your components collaborate in a given scenario? This is where you will find integration testing very useful. In the case of a Web API, integration testing focuses more on testing a complete call end to end from the client to the service, including all the components in the stack such as controllers, filters, message handlers, or any other component configured in your Web API runtime. For example, you might want to use an integration test to enable basic authentication with an HttpMessageHandler and verify how that handler behaves with your existing controllers from the point of a view of a client application. Ideally, you will also unit test those components to make sure they behave correctly in isolation.

For doing integration testing in ASP.NET Web API, we will use HttpClient, which can handle requests in an in-memory hosted server. This has some evident advantages for simplifying the tests, as there is no need to open ports or send messages across the network. As shown in Example 17-27, the HttpClient class contains several constructors that receive an HttpMessageHandler instance. As covered in Chapter 4, the

HttpServer class is an `HttpMessageHandler` implementation, which means it can be directly injected in an `HttpClient` instance to automatically handle any message sent by the client in a test.

Example 17-27. HttpClient constructors

```
public class HttpClient : HttpMessageInvoker
{
    public HttpClient();
    public HttpClient(HttpMessageHandler handler);
    public HttpClient(HttpMessageHandler handler, bool disposeHandler);
}
```

We can configure an `HttpServer` instance with the `HttpMessageHandler` from our previous implementation and use it with an `HttpClient` instance within an integration test to verify how the scenario works end to end. See Example 17-28.

Example 17-28. Integration tests for basic authentication

```
public class BasicAuthenticationIntegrationTests
{
  [Fact]
  public ShouldReturn404IfCredentialsNotSpecified()
  {
      var config = new HttpConfiguration();
      config.Routes.MapHttpRoute(name: "Default",
        routeTemplate: "api/{controller}/{action}/{id}",
        defaults: new { id = RouteParameter.Optional }); // <1>

      config.MessageHandlers.Add(new BasicAuthHttpMessageHandler()); // <2>

      var server = new HttpServer(config);

      var client = new HttpClient(server); // <3>

      var task = client.GetAsync("http://test.com/issues"); // <4>
      task.Wait();

      var response = task.Result;

      Assert.AreEqual(HttpStatusCode.Unauthorized, response.StatusCode); // <5>
  }
}
```

As shown in Example 17-28, we can still use a unit testing framework for automating the integration tests. Our test is configuring a server in-memory with a default route *<1>* and a `BasicAuthHttpMessageHandler` *<2>*, which internally implements basic authentication. That server is injected in the `HttpClient` *<3>*, so the call to *http://test.com/issues* with `GetAsync` will be routed to that server *<4>*. In the case of this test, no authorization header was set in the `HttpClient`, so the expected behavior is that the

`BasicAuthHttpHandler` returns a response message with status code 404 (`Unauthor`
`ized`) *<5>*. Authentication is just a scenario where integration testing makes sense, but
as you can imagine, this idea can be extended to any scenario that requires coordination
between multiple components.

Conclusion

TDD can be used as a very effective tool to drive the design and implementation of your
Web API. As a side effect, you will get unit tests reflecting the expected behavior of the
implementation that you can also use to make progressive enhancements in the existing
code. Those tests can be used to make sure that nothing broke with the introduction of
new changes and that the implementation still satisfies the expected behavior. There are
two commonly used practices with TDD: dependency injection and code refactoring.
While the former focuses on generating more testable code by removing explicit dependencies, the latter is used to improve the quality of the existing code. In addition to
unit testing, which focuses on testing specific pieces of code in isolation, you can also
use integration testing for testing a scenario end to end, and see how the different components in the implementation interact.

Media Types

Table A-1. Media types

Media type	Description	Reference
`text/html`	Used for exchanging HTML documents.	*http://www.iana.org/assignments/media-types/text/html*
`application/xhtml+xml`	Used for exchanging HTML documents that use well-formed XML.	*http://tools.ietf.org/html/rfc3236*
`application/xml`	Used for exchanging XML documents and schemas.	*http://www.rfc-editor.org/rfc/rfc3023.txt*
`application/json`	Used for exchanging JSON documents.	*http://www.ietf.org/rfc/rfc4627.txt*
`application/x-www-form-urlencoded`	Used for exchanging form key/value data.	*http://www.w3.org/TR/html401/interact/forms.html#h-17.13.4.1*
`multipart/mixed`	Used for exchanging multiple sets of data combined into a single body.	*http://tools.ietf.org/html/rfc1521#section-7.2.2*
`multipart/form-data`	Used primarily for exchanging files.	*http://tools.ietf.org/html/rfc2388*
`image/jpeg`	Used for exchanging JPEG documents.	*http://tools.ietf.org/html/rfc2046*
`image/gif`	Used for exchanging GIF documents.	*http://tools.ietf.org/html/rfc2046*
`image/png`	Used for exchanging PNG documents.	*http://tools.ietf.org/html/rfc2083*
`image/svg+xml`	Used for exchanging SVG (*http://www.w3.org/TR/SVG11/*) documents.	*http://www.w3.org/TR/SVG/mimereg.html*
`application/atom+xml`	Used for exchanging Atom feeds.	*http://tools.ietf.org/html/rfc4287*
`application/vnd.hal+json`	Used for exchanging data that contains links to related resources	*http://stateless.co/hal_specification.html*
`application/vnd.collection+json`	Used for managing collections of data.	*http://amundsen.com/media-types/collection/*

HTTP Headers

Table B-1. Message headers

Header	Description	Reference
Cache-Control	Gives instructions to caching mechanisms that the request/response passes through related to its cachability.	*http://tools.ietf.org/html/draft-ietf-httpbis-p6-cache-21#section-7.2*
Connection	Gives options that are specific to the current connection and should not be passed on to proxies.	*http://tools.ietf.org/html/draft-ietf-httpbis-p1-messaging-21#section-6.1*
Date	Specifies the date and time the message originated.	*http://tools.ietf.org/html/draft-ietf-httpbis-p2-semantics-21#section-8.1.1.2*
Pragma	Specifies to caches that they should always revalidate a response they have cached. It exists for backward compatibility with HTTP 1.0 clients and is deprecated in HTTP 1.1 by the Cache-Control header.	*http://tools.ietf.org/html/draft-ietf-httpbis-p6-cache-21#section-7.4*
Transfer-Encoding	Indicates if the message body has had any transformation applied to it in order to transfer it between the sender and the recepient.	*http://tools.ietf.org/html/draft-ietf-httpbis-p1-messaging-21#section-3.3.1*
Upgrade	Allows the client to specify that it would like to use additional protocols if the server is willing to switch.	*http://tools.ietf.org/html/draft-ietf-httpbis-p1-messaging-21#section-6.3*
Via	Used by gateways and proxies, it contains the intermediate protocols and recepients between the client and the server on requests, and the server and client on responses. This header is very useful in a response from a TRACE request.	*http://tools.ietf.org/html/draft-ietf-httpbis-p1-messaging-21#section-5.7*
Warning	Used to carry additional information about the message that may not be reflected in the mesage itself.	*http://tools.ietf.org/html/draft-ietf-httpbis-p1-messaging-21#section-5.7*

Table B-2. Request headers

Header	Description	Reference
Host	Provides the host and port information in the target URI.	*http://tools.ietf.org/html/draft-ietf-httpbis-p1-messaging-21#section-5.4*
Max-Forwards	For use with debugging with TRACE and OPTION methods, this header allows the client to limit the number of times that the request can be forwarded by proxies.	*http://tools.ietf.org/html/draft-ietf-httpbis-p2-semantics-21#section-6.1.1*
Expect	Tells the server expected behavior from the client. For example, Expect: 100-Continue tells the server the client expects it to process the request before it starts sending the body.	*http://tools.ietf.org/html/draft-ietf-httpbis-p2-semantics-21#section-6.1.2*
Range	Specifies that the server should perform a byte-range operation and return only the requested bytes.	*http://tools.ietf.org/html/draft-ietf-httpbis-p5-range-21#section-5.4*
If-Match	Used to make a conditional request that should be performed only if the value of the entity tag matches one or more representations of the resource	*http://tools.ietf.org/html/draft-ietf-httpbis-p4-conditional-21#section-3.1*
If-None-Match	Used to make a conditional request that should be performed only if the value of the entity tag does not match one or more representations of the resource.	*http://tools.ietf.org/html/draft-ietf-httpbis-p4-conditional-21#section-3.2*
If-Modified-Since	Used to make a conditional request that should be performed only if the resource has been modified since the specified date.	*http://tools.ietf.org/html/draft-ietf-httpbis-p4-conditional-21#section-3.3*
If-Unmodified-Since	Used to make a conditional request that should be performed only if the resource has not been modified since the specified date.	*http://tools.ietf.org/html/draft-ietf-httpbis-p4-conditional-21#section-3.4*
If-Range	Used to make a conditional request that allows a client to get a partial representation returned as long as the entity tag matches.	*http://tools.ietf.org/html/draft-ietf-httpbis-p4-conditional-21#section-3.5*
Accept	Contains a prioritized list of acceptable response media types for the response.	*http://tools.ietf.org/html/draft-ietf-httpbis-p2-semantics-21#section-6.3.2*
Accept-Charset	Contains a prioritized list of acceptable character encodings for the response.	*http://tools.ietf.org/html/draft-ietf-httpbis-p2-semantics-21#section-6.3.3*
Accept-Encoding	Contains a prioritized list of acceptable transfer codings.	*http://tools.ietf.org/html/draft-ietf-httpbis-p2-semantics-21#section-6.3.4*
Accept-Language	Contains a prioritized list of languages.	*http://tools.ietf.org/html/draft-ietf-httpbis-p2-semantics-21#section-6.3.5*
From	Specifies the email for the human who is making the request.	*http://tools.ietf.org/html/draft-ietf-httpbis-p2-semantics-21#section-6.5.1*
Referer	Specifies the URI for the resource that provided the target URI for the current request.	*http://tools.ietf.org/html/draft-ietf-httpbis-p2-semantics-21#section-6.5.2*
TE	Indicates acceptable transfer codings, besides "chunked."	*http://tools.ietf.org/html/draft-ietf-httpbis-p1-messaging-21#section-4.3*

Header	Description	Reference
User-Agent	Specifies information about the client generating the request.	*http://tools.ietf.org/html/draft-ietf-httpbis-p2-semantics-21#section-6.5.3*
Authorization	Contains credentials for the realm being accessed.	*http://tools.ietf.org/html/draft-ietf-httpbis-p7-auth-21#section-4.1*

Table B-3. Response headers

Header	Description	Reference
Age	Specifies how much time has elapsed since the response was generated.	*http://tools.ietf.org/html/draft-ietf-httpbis-p6-cache-21#section-7.1*
Date	Specifies the date and time when the message was generated.	*http://tools.ietf.org/html/draft-ietf-httpbis-p2-semantics-21#section-8.1.1.2*
Location	Specifies a resource that is associated with the response (either a resource that was created or one that the client should redirect to).	*http://tools.ietf.org/html/draft-ietf-httpbis-p2-semantics-21#section-8.1.1.2*
Retry-After	Indicates how long the client should wait before retrying a request to the resource. In the case of a redirect, it relates to the redirect URI.	*http://tools.ietf.org/html/draft-ietf-httpbis-p2-semantics-21#section-8.1.1.3*
Last-Modified	Specifies the date and time at which the origin server believes the representation was modified.	*http://tools.ietf.org/html/draft-ietf-httpbis-p4-conditional-21#section-2.2*
ETag	Specifies an identifier that is unique to the currently selected representation.	*http://tools.ietf.org/html/draft-ietf-httpbis-p4-conditional-21#section-2.3*
Vary	Indicates which header fields were used as part of selecting the representation returned to the client.	*http://tools.ietf.org/html/draft-ietf-httpbis-p2-semantics-21#section-8.2.1*
WWW-Authenticate	Indicates one or more authentication challenges informing the client how they must authenticate to the target resource.	*http://tools.ietf.org/html/draft-ietf-httpbis-p7-auth-21#section-4.4*
Proxy-Authenticate	Specifies one or more authentication challenges informing the client how they must authenticate to the proxy for the target resource.	*http://tools.ietf.org/html/draft-ietf-httpbis-p7-auth-21#section-4.2*
Accept-Ranges	Specifies the acceptable ranges clients may use with a range request.	*http://tools.ietf.org/html/draft-ietf-httpbis-p5-range-21#section-5.1*
Allow	Specifies which HTTP methods are acceptable to the target resource.	*http://tools.ietf.org/html/draft-ietf-httpbis-p2-semantics-21#section-8.4.1*
Server	Contains information about the server environment for the origin server.	*http://tools.ietf.org/html/draft-ietf-httpbis-p2-semantics-21#section-8.4.2*

Table B-4. Representation headers

Header	Description	Reference
Content-Type	Specifies the media type of the representation.	*http://tools.ietf.org/html/draft-ietf-httpbis-p2-semantics-21#section-3.1.1.5*
Content-Encoding	Specifies the content codings that have been applied to the representation.	*http://tools.ietf.org/html/draft-ietf-httpbis-p2-semantics-21#section-3.1.2.2*
Content-Language	Indicates the language for the intended audience of the current representation.	*http://tools.ietf.org/html/draft-ietf-httpbis-p2-semantics-21#section-3.1.1.5*
Content-Location	Specifies a URI for specifically retrieving the current representation.	*http://tools.ietf.org/html/draft-ietf-httpbis-p2-semantics-21#section-3.1.4.2*
Expires	Gives the date and time for when the response is considered stale.	*http://tools.ietf.org/html/draft-ietf-httpbis-p6-cache-21#section-7.3*

Content Negotiation

There are two types of content negotiation (conneg): proactive and reactive.

Proactive Negotiation

This type of negotiation occurs when the server is responsible for selection and contains logic that executes per request in order to find the best representation. It makes the selection based on matching up against client preferences or additional headers and the server's available representations. The client expresses its preference through the previously mentioned `Accept*` headers (see Table B-2). Each of these headers allows for sending multiple values or ranges along with a *qualifier* (also known as a *q-value*) that contains prioritization. The server can use additional fields, though, like `User-Agent` or any other.

If the server determines that the client hasn't sent it enough information to make a selection it can make a default selection, return a status `406 Not Acceptable`, or perform *reactive negotiation* (see next section). Once it makes the selection the server should return to the client the chosen representation. The response should include a `Vary` header, which indicates exactly which header fields were used to make the selection. The server can also include a `Content-Location` header containing the URI of the negotiated content. It is important to remember that the server is not bound by the client preferences, but it should try to adhere to them as much as it can.

Figure C-1 indicates the steps of the process.

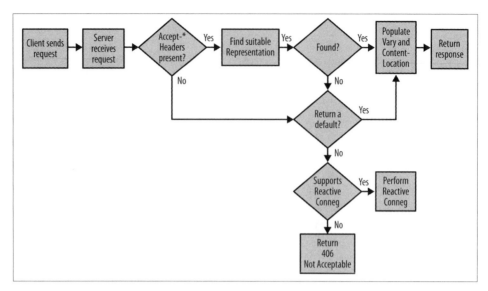

Figure C-1. Proactive conneg

Notice in the figure that in cases where the client has not sent client preferences, or a suitable match cannot be found, the server at its discretion can either return a default representation or return a 406 Not Acceptable response.

Web browsers conventionally use this type of negotiation. Whenever you make a request to a server, your browser sends a list of preferences of things that it supports. In some cases, it may send additional media types that are supported via browser plug-ins. The following is a request using Chrome; notice the various Accept headers that the browser is sending. Different browsers will also have different preferences.

```
GET http://www.yahoo.com/ HTTP/1.1
Host: www.yahoo.com
Connection: keep-alive
Accept: text/html,application/xhtml+xml,application/xml;q=0.9,*/*;q=0.8
Accept-Encoding: gzip,deflate,sdch
Accept-Language: en-US,en;q=0.8
Accept-Charset: ISO-8859-1,utf-8;q=0.7,*;q=0.3
```

Reactive Negotiation

With this type of negotiation (also referred to as *agent-driven negotiation*), the choice of selection is moved to the client. The way it works is that when the client sends a request to the server for a resource, the server returns a list of representations with a status code of 300 Multiple Choices. The client then chooses from the list based on its own logic and then sends a second request to get the selected representation.

This flow is depicted in Figure C-2.

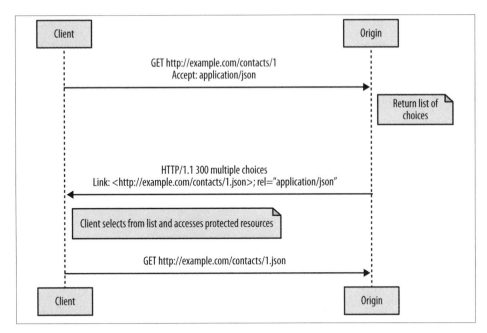

Figure C-2. Reactive conneg

As to the representation itself, which contains the choices, the spec is not at all prescriptive. Mike Amundsen has a nice article on this type of negotiation called "Agent-Driven conneg in HTTP." (*http://bit.ly/agent-conneg*)

In his post he recommends several different fully supported approaches. One approach is to return an XHTML representation using <a hrefs> for each option, as in the following example:

```
HTTP/1.1 300 Multiple Choices
Host: www.example.org
Content-Type: application/xhtml
Content-Length:XXX

<p>
  Select one:
</p>
<a href="/results/fr" hreflang="fr">French</a>
<a href="/results/en-US" hreflang="en-US">US English</a>
<a href="/results/de" hreflang="de">German</a>
```

An alternative approach is to use Link headers. This has the advantage of being a standard header that any client can understand. Here is an example:

```
HTTP/1.1 300 Multiple Choices
Host: www.example.org
```

```
Content-Length: 0
Link: <http://www.example.org/results/png>; type="image/png",
      <http://www.example.org/results/jpeg>;type="image/jpeg",
      <http://www.example.org/results/gif>;type="image/gif"
```

The benefit of using an established mechanism is that any HTTP client can be expected to understand it. You could return application/json and just embed the links in JSON, but unless your client has that knowledge out-of-band, it won't know how to parse it. Using the profile header helps because the client can be pointed to a spec that defines the link format (without your having to introduce a new media type). In this example, the profile document would specify to use an alternate JSON array for the list:

```
HTTP/1.1 300 Multiple Choices
Host: www.example.org
Content-Type: application/json
Content-Length: XXX
Link: <http://www.example.org/profile>; rel="profile"

{
  "alternates" : [
    {"href": "http://www.example.org/results/png", "type":"image/png"},
    {"href": "http://www.example.org/results/jpeg", "type": "image/jpeg"},
    {"href", "http://www.example.org/results/gif", "type": "image/gif"}
  ]
}
```

Caching in Action

As we've seen, there are quite a few moving parts involved with HTTP caching. To illustrate how everything works together, let's take a look at a common scenario involving two clients, an HTTP cache and the origin server. For the sake of brevity the body and all headers are not shown in the responses.

First, Client A does an initial request, as shown in Figure D-1.

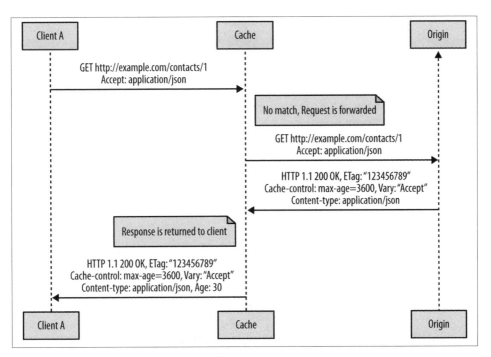

Figure D-1. Client A does an initial GET

1. The cache receives the request, and seeing that it is a GET request checks whether it has a cached response. It doesn't, so the cache forwards it on to the origin server.

2. The origin server generates a response, including ETag and max-age headers.

3. The cache receives the response and caches the result using a hash of the request URI and the Accept header value.

4. The cache then returns the response, including an additional AGE header to inform the client of the age of the representation.

5. Client A receives the representation and stores the ETag and Expires information.

Fifteen minutes later, Client B makes a request to the same resource, as shown in Figure D-2.

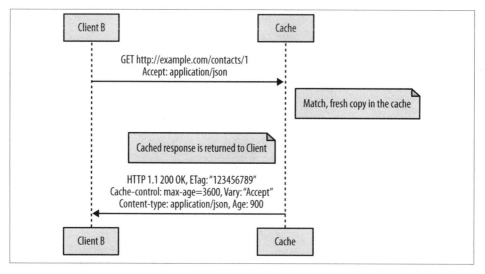

Figure D-2. Client B does an initial GET

1. The cache receives the request and checks whether it has a copy of the representation.

2. It sees from the matching on the URI and Accept that the representation is there and it is still fresh (based on the expiration), so it returns it immediately with the updated age.

3. Client B receives the representation and stores the ETag and Expires information.

An hour later, Client A does a conditional GET request back to the same resource, including the If-None-Match header, as shown in Figure D-3.

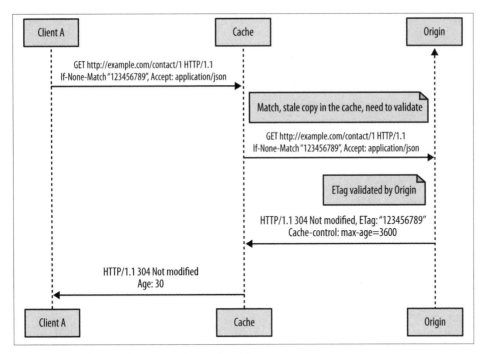

Figure D-3. Client A does a conditional GET

1. The cache receives the request and checks whether it has a copy of the representation. It finds the representation and sees that it is no longer fresh. It then forwards on the conditional GET request to the origin server to see if the copy it has is still valid.

2. The origin server receives the request and determines that the ETAG is still valid. It returns a 304 Not Modified with a new max-age.

3. The cache receives the request and returns the 304 to the client, along with an updated age calculation.

Time passes, and Client B does a conditional PUT against the contact resource, updating its state as shown in Figure D-4.

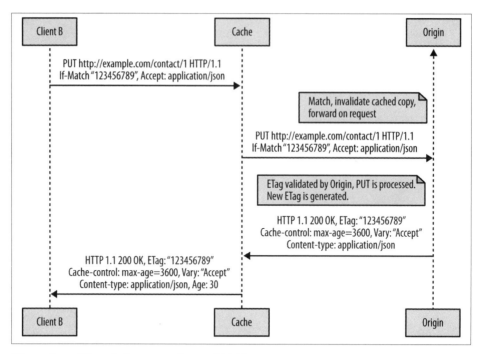

Figure D-4. Client B does a conditional PUT

1. The cache receives the request and seeing that it is a PUT, checks its cache to see if a copy exists for that resource, and if the ETag matches. Finding the copy, it invalidates the ETag for future requests. It then forwards on the request verbatim to the origin server.

2. The server applies the update and generates a new response with an updated ETag.

3. The cache receives the response and caches it. It then returns the response to Client B.

Client A comes along 10 minutes later and tries to also do a conditional PUT on the same resource as shown in Figure D-5.

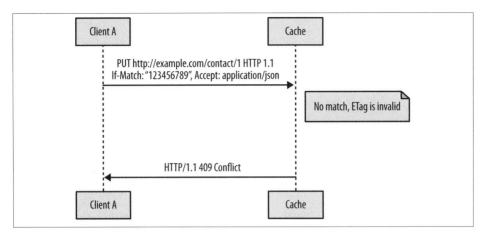

Figure D-5. Client B does a conditional PUT

1. The cache receives its request and looks in its cache. It sees that it does not have a match on the ETag, as it was previously updated.

2. It returns a 409 Conflict to the client, informing it that the ETag it has is no longer valid.

Authentication Workflows

The client-to-origin workflow involves a client authenticating to an origin server, as shown in Figure E-1.

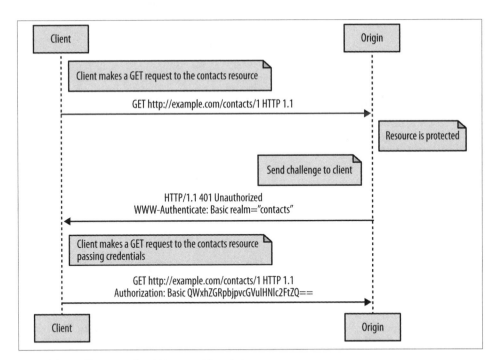

Figure E-1. Client authenticates with origin

The client attempts to access a protected resource from an origin server. The server, seeing that the resource is protected, sends back a challenge to the client via a 401 Unauthorized response. The response contains a WWW-Authenticate header (see

Table B-3) that contains one or more challenges that the client must respond to in order to access the resource.

The client then sends back a request to the resource providing an `Authorization` header with the requested credentials.

In the client-to-proxy workflow, a client attempts to access a resource via a secure proxy that it must authenticate against. This is shown in Figure E-2.

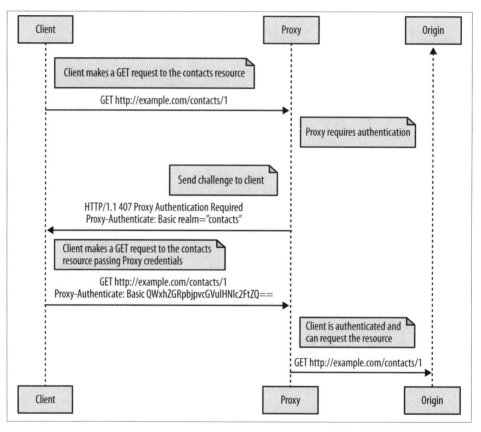

Figure E-2. Client authenticates with proxy

The client attempts to access a protected resource via an authenticated proxy. The proxy, seeing the request, sends back a challenge to the client via a `407 Proxy Authentication Required` response. The response contains a `Proxy-Authenticate` header (see Table B-3) that contains one or more challenges for accessing the proxy itself. The client then sends back the request, including the `Proxy-Authorization` header with the requested credentials. If, after authenticating with the proxy, the resource the user is attempting to access is protected, origin server authentication will also kick in. Figure E-3 illustrates this, showing the origin server responding with a challenge after proxy authentication is complete.

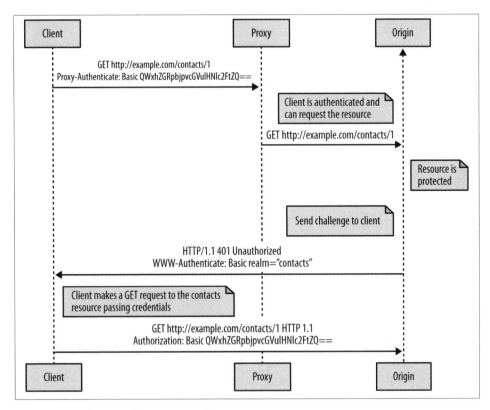

Figure E-3. Client authenticates with proxy

Media Type Specification for application/issue+json

During the lifecycle of many complex engineering projects and the subsequent maintenance of those products, we need to track the discovery and resolution of issues related to those projects. This media type specification describes a document format that has a very low barrier of entry for interoperability. The current specification is a minimal definition with the expectation that additional capabilities will be added over time.

Notational Conventions

The keywords MUST, MUST NOT, REQUIRED, SHALL, SHALL NOT, SHOULD, SHOULD NOT, RECOMMENDED, MAY, and OPTIONAL in this document are to be interpreted as described in RFC 2119 (*http://bit.ly/rfc-2119*).

Issue Documents

The Issue document, shown in Example F-1, uses the format described in RFC 4627 and has the media type application/issue+json.

Example F-1. Minimal Issue document

```
{
        "title" : "This is a very simple issue"
}
```

Issue documents may contain the properties listed in Table F-1.

Table F-1. Semantics of properties

Property name	Description
id	A unique numeric identifier for the issue

Property name	Description
title	A short textual summary of the issue (required)
description	A detailed description of the issue
status	A textual representation of the issue state containing one of the following values: open, closed.

issue+json also supports hypermedia using links that conform to the semantics of a link, as described by RFC 5988 (*http://bit.ly/rfc-5988*). Links are defined by a set of objects within an array named links.

Security Considerations

issue+json has some security issues common to all JSON content types. See RFC 4627 Section #6 (*http://bit.ly/rfc-4627*) for additional information. issue+json does not provide executable content. Information contained in issue+json documents does not require privacy or integrity services.

Interoperability Considerations

Unrecognized document content should be ignored and should not invalidate the document.

IANA Considerations

This specification defines a new Internet media type (RFC 6838) (*http://bit.ly/rfc-6838*):

```
Type name: application
Subtype name: issue+json
Required parameters: None
Optional parameters: None; unrecognised parameters should be ignored
Encoding considerations: Same as [RFC4627]
Security considerations: see [this document]
Interoperability considerations: None.
Published specification: [this document]
Applications that use this media type: HTTP
Additional information:
  Magic number(s): n/a
  File extension(s): n/a
  Macintosh file type code(s): n/a
Person & email address to contact for further information:
    Darrel Miller <darrel@tavis.ca>
Intended usage: COMMON
Restrictions on usage: None.
Author: Darrel Miller <darrel@tavis.ca>
Change controller: IESG
```

Public-Key Cryptography and Certificates

The introduction in 1976 of *public-key cryptography* by Whitfield Diffie and Martin Hellman represented a major breakthrough in the design of large-scale, secure communication systems. The main idea behind their proposal is the generation and usage of one or more key pairs by each entity, each composed of a private key and a public key. The private keys must remain confidential and never have to be sent to other parties. On the other hand, the public keys can be openly distributed without any confidentiality requirements. These distributed public keys can then be used by third parties to:

- Send encrypted messages that can be decrypted only by the private key holder.
- Validate signatures that can only have been produced by the private key holder.

Public-key cryptography is also called *asymmetric cryptography* since its mechanisms use two keys with different confidentiality requirements and different purposes:

- Private keys must remain confidential and are used to decrypt messages or to produce digital signatures.
- Public keys can be openly distributed without any confidentiality requirements and are used to encrypt messages or to validate signatures.

This contrasts with *classical cryptography*, also called *symmetric cryptography*, where the same key, which must remain secret, is used for all operations (e.g., encrypt and decrypt). Since the currently known asymmetric mechanisms have lower performance than their symmetric counterparts, it is common to use hybrid techniques. For instance, in TLS the asymmetric mechanism is used by the handshake protocol to establish a set of confidential symmetric *session* keys, which are then used by the record protocol to protect the bulk of the exchanged messages using a symmetric mechanism.

However, public-key cryptography introduces a new problem: public key *authentication*. Even if public keys can be openly distributed, the receiving parties must have some secure way of knowing to whom they belong (i.e., who is the holder of the associated private keys). Failure to correctly authenticate public keys makes them vulnerable to *man-in-the-middle* (MITM) attacks, where an attacker replaces an entity public key with its own. This allows the attacker to decrypt every message sent to that entity, since it is in possession of the private key associated with the used public key.

A common way of authenticating public keys is by using public key certificates, which are statements binding a public key to a subject, issued and signed by *certification authorities* (CA). These CAs are third parties on which a set of entities recognizes authority and competence to verify this binding; that is, they check whether the holder of the private key associated with a public key is also the owner of a name (e.g., DNS name).

To make things a little more concrete, let's consider the example where a client performs an HTTP request to the resource identified by *https://webapi-book.blob.core.windows.net/*. Since the URI has the `https` scheme, the HTTP request message must be sent on a TLS- or SSL-protected connection. The secure connection is established by the handshake protocol, which starts with the client sending a `client hello` message to the server, including the client-supported cryptographic mechanisms. The server responds with a `server hello` message with the chosen cryptographic mechanisms and also with a `certificate` message containing the server's certificate, represented in Figure G-1.

This certificate follows the X.509 specification (*http://bit.ly/x509-spec*) and is composed of several fields, such as:

- The *public key field*, containing the server's public key
- The *subject* field with the server's name, which in this case is the `*.blob.core.win dows.net` wildcard
- The *issuer* field containing the issuing entities' name (the CA name), which is Microsoft Secure Server Authority

The certificate also contains a signature produced by its issuer, so that it can be stored and distributed via unsafe channels.

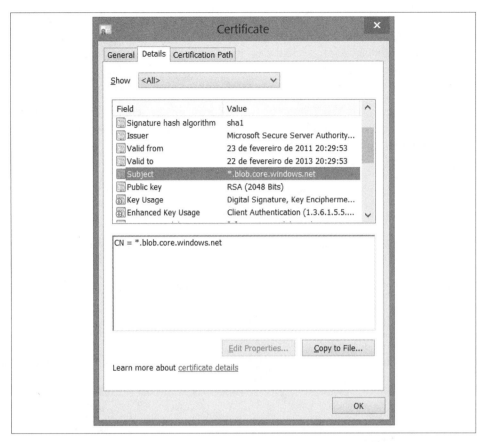

Figure G-1. The *.blob.core.windows.net certificate

Upon receiving this certificate, the client can then use the contained public key to encrypt a secret random seed value and send it to the server. This random seed is a secret value that will be used by both the client and the server to deterministically derive the set of session keys used to protect the exchanged byte stream. However, first the client must ensure that (among other things):

- The certificate's subject matches the `https` URI hostname.

- The certificate was not tampered with while in transit from the server to the client (the handshake protocol is done over an unprotected connection).

- The issuing CA (Microsoft Secure Server Authority, in the previous example) is trusted, in this context, to perform the binding between public keys and entity names.

The last verification is usually accomplished through a comparison of the certificate issuer's field against a *trust store* containing the trusted issuer's names and their public keys. The second task involves validating the certificate's signature using the issuer's public key, also present in this store.

Trust stores are typically composed of self-issued certificates, each one holding a trusted CA name and its public key. These self-issued certificates are created by CAs and distributed out-of-band, via an authenticated mechanism. The decision to add a self-issued certificate to this trust store means that the consuming entity:

- Has decided to trust the CA identified in the subject's field—that is, assumes that every certificate issued by the CA will contain a true public key binding
- Has checked that the contained public key does indeed belong to the CA

We stress this last requirement, since a self-signed certificate is not sufficient to bind a public key to a name: this verification must be done by alternative means.

Figure G-2 represents an example for the model we just described.

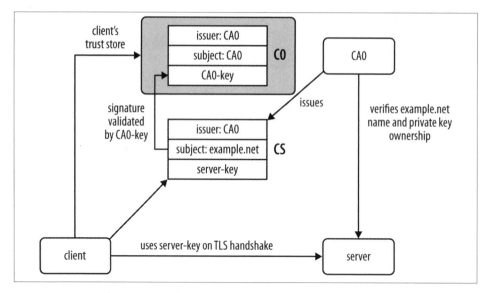

Figure G-2. Certificate issued directly by a trusted CA

In the figure:

- CA0 issues the CS certificate after checking that the entity running the server is the holder of the private key associated with server-key and also the legal owner of the example.net domain name.

- The client trusts CA0 for certificate purposes and so installs the CA0 self-issued certificate in its trust store, after checking the correctness of the certificate information, namely its public key.

- During the TLS handshake protocol, the client receives the CS certificate and validates it by checking that (1) it was issued by a trusted CA and (2) its signature is successfully validated through the CA's public key. After this, the client uses server-key to encrypt a secret seed that can be decrypted only by the *example.net* name (according to CA0).

Certificate issuance by a CA should be preceded by a secure verification of the certified information, particularly the binding of the public key to a name. Typically, CAs describe this secure verification procedures in a document called *Certification Practice Statements* (*http://cybertrust.omniroot.com/repository/*). Depending on the name scope (DNS name, email, citizen's identifier), the verification can be expensive (e.g., verifying official records to ensure that an entity is the owner of a registered name) or difficult to perform (the CA does not have any relation to the naming authority). Hence, CAs can delegate their certification capability to other CAs, called *intermediate* CAs or *subordinate* CAs. They do so by issuing a certificate, where the issuer is the directly trusted CA and the subject is the intermediate CA. This certificate serves two purposes: in addition to binding the intermediate CA name to its public key, it also states that a subset of the issuer's certification capabilities are delegated to the intermediate CA.

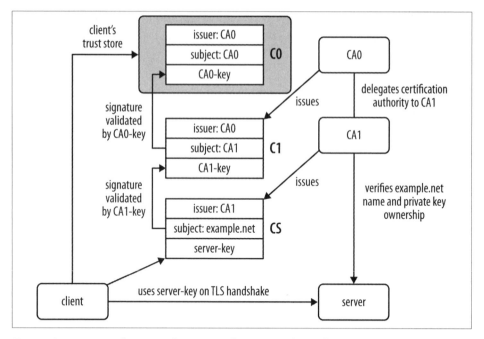

Figure G-3. Intermediate certification authorities and certification paths

Figure G-3 shows this extended model, where:

- CA0, usually called the *root* CA because it is directly trusted by the client, delegates its certification capability to CA1 by issuing the intermediate C1 certificate.
- It is CA1, not CA0, that checks if the entity running the server is the holder of the private key associated with server-key and also the legal owner of the *example.net* domain name.

In this model, the server certificate validation requires building a *certificate chain*—composed of all the certificates from the directly trusted C0 certificate (present in the trust store)—to the server's certificate, via the intermediate certificate C1.

Returning to our concrete scenario, Figure G-4 shows the **.blob.core.windows.net* certification path, composed of two intermediate CAs. Only the root CA (GTE CyberTrust Global Root) is directly trusted by the client. However, this CA has delegated its certification authority to Microsoft Internet Authority, which in turn redelegated it to Microsoft Secure Server Authority. It is this last CA that issues the server certificate.

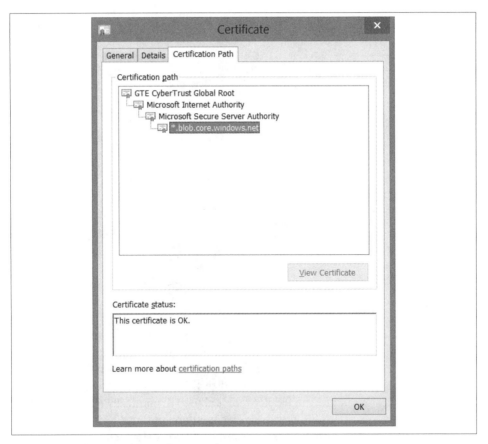

Figure G-4. The server's certificate path

On Windows systems, certificates are managed via stores, such as the ones represented in Figure G-5. These stores are grouped by store location (*current user*, *local computer*) and have specific semantics. For instance:

- The *Personal* store contains the certificates for which the private key associated with the public key is also stored.

- The *Trusted Root Certification Authorities* store contains the *trusted certificates* that can be used as roots for the certification paths.

- The *Intermediate Certification Authorities* store contains CA certificates that are not directly trusted but that can be used to build a certification path.

Figure G-5. Windows certificate stores

When the Windows certificate management system has to validate a certificate, it considers a certification path valid only if the root is in the Trusted Root Certification Authorities store. You must take great care before adding certificates to this store, since its contents define who is allowed to issue valid certificates. As an example, by adding a certificate to this trust store, the Fiddler tool is able to dynamically issue valid certificates for any server name. This allows Fiddler to intercept the HTTPS traffic by impersonating the remote server. This is an example of a MITM attack, used in this case for benign development and debugging purposes.

Revocation

The validity of the certificate information can change over time. Namely, if an attacker is able to obtain an entity's private key, then the associated public key should not be used anymore.

One way of accomplishing this is by using *certificate revocation lists* (CRL) containing invalidated (revoked) certificates. For instance, in the previous example the **.blob.core.windows.net* certificate contains a *CRL distribution point* field with a CRL URI (*http://mscrl.microsoft.com/pki/mscorp/crl/Microsoft%20Secure%20Server %20Authority(8).crl*). When validating the certificate, this URI can be used to retrieve the CRL and check if the certificate hasn't been revoked.

An alternative method is to check the certificate's current validity state by using the *Online Certificate Status Protocol* (OCSP), where the client directly asks the CA for the current certificate state. The validation of a certification should include one of these forms of revocation checking.

To know more about the use of X.509 certificates in Internet scenarios, including the certification path construction and validation details, we recommend the set of RFCs issued by the PKIX IETF working group, namely RFC 5280.

Creating Test Keys and Certificates

When you are developing clients and servers that use the TLS protocol, it is useful to have a set of keys and certificates for testing purposes. In the following paragraphs we show how to create this infrastructure using a set of Windows command-line tools. However, before we start, there is something we should emphasize: never use these keys and certificates in a production scenario; they are only for testing purposes.

The first step is to create a root certification authority, using the makecert tool:[1]

```
makecert -r -n "CN=Demo Certification Authority;O=Web API Book" ^
  -sv webapibook-ca.pvk ^
  -len 2048 -e 01/01/2020 -cy authority webapibook-ca.cer
```

The -r option instructs makecert to generate a self-signed certificate—that is, a certificate signed with the private key associated with the contained public key. This certificate will be used as the certification path root.

The certification authority will have the X.500 name CN=Demo Certification Author ity;O=Web API Book, where CN and O are name attributes: CN stands for *common name* and O stands for *organization*. The private key will be stored in the *webapibook-ca.pvk* file, encrypted by a key derived from a given password. This private key will be used to sign each issued certificate.

The second step is to generate an asymmetric key pair and certificate for a fictional server named *www.example.net*. We also accomplish this via the makecert tool:

```
makecert.exe -iv webapibook-ca.pvk -ic webapibook-ca.cer -n "CN=www.example.net" ^
  -sv example.pvk -len 2048 -e 01/01/2020 ^
  -sky exchange example.cer -eku 1.3.6.1.5.5.7.3.1

pvk2pfx.exe -pvk example.pvk -spc example.cer -pfx example.pfx
```

This certificate is issued by the previously generated CA, so makecert requires both the CA certificate (for naming) and the CA private key (for signing). The -eku 1.3.6.1.5.5.7.3.1 option adds an *enhanced key usage* extension to the generated certificate, indicating that it can be used with TLS server authentication.

---

1. Available in the .NET Framework tools.

The *.pvk* file contains the server's private key and the *.cer* file contains its certificate, including the public key. The last line in the previous example uses the `pvk2pfx` tool to encapsulate both the private key and the certificate into a single *.pfx* (*personal information exchange*) file. This last file uses the PKCS#12 interoperability format for exchanging cryptographic material, such as private keys and certificates, and is the most commonly used format in Windows for this purpose.

The final step is to generate client-side certificates for the two famous cryptography fictional characters, Alice and Bob (*http://bit.ly/alice-bob*):

```
makecert.exe -iv webapibook-ca.pvk -ic webapibook-ca.cer ^
    -n "CN=Alice;O=Web API book fictional characters" ^
    -sv alice.pvk -len 2048 -e 01/01/2020 -sky exchange ^
    alice.cer -eku 1.3.6.1.5.5.7.3.2
pvk2pfx.exe -pvk alice.pvk -spc alice.cer -pfx alice.pfx

makecert.exe -iv webapibook-ca.pvk -ic webapibook-ca.cer ^
    -n "CN=Bob;O=Web API book fictional characters" ^
    -pe -sv bob.pvk -len 2048 -e 01/01/2020 -sky exchange ^
    bob.cer -eku 1.3.6.1.5.5.7.3.2
pvk2pfx.exe -pvk bob.pvk -spc bob.cer -pfx bob.pfx
```

This process is similar to the one we used to generate the host cryptographic material, with only one exception: the generated certificates will have the 1.3.6.1.5.5.7.3.2 extension, which indicates that they can be used for TLS *client*-side authentication.

After completing this process, we should have generated two types of files. The *webapibook-ca.cer* file contains the CA certificate and should be used by every party that chooses to trust the certifications performed by this entity. On Windows, this trust decision results in adding the certificate to the *Trusted Root Certificate Authorities* user's store. The *.pfx* files contain both certificates *and* private keys for each of the parties (*www.example.net*, Alice and Bob) and should be installed in the *Personal* certificate store of each party.

Index

A

acceptance criteria, 151, 181
access tokens, 417
action filters, 309
action invocation, 313
action result converter, 314
action selection
    default vs. custom, 303
    matched vs. attribute-based routes, 304
    refinements to, 305
actions, 398
active authentication, 385
Advanced Research Projects Agency Network
    (ARPANET), 1, 6
affordances, 36, 37
agile software development, 84
Amazon Simple Storage Service (S3), 395
Amundsen, Mike, 38
API contracts
    breaking vs. nonbreaking changes to, 89
    link relation types
        extended link relation types, 117
        indirection layer, 119
        link hints, 117
        reference data, 120
        semantics, 116
        standard registry of, 116
        static vs. embedded resources, 118
        syntax, 122
        workflow, 120
    media types
        fear of new types, 110
        generic media types/profiles, 110–115
        hypermedia types, 110
        new formats, 108
        new hypermedia types, 115
        platform-independence of, 104
        popular formats, 107
        primitive formats, 105
    new link relations design
        basic characteristics, 130
        embedded, 132
        extension, 132
        registration, 132
        standard, 130
    new media type design
        basic characteristics, 124
        conveying semantics, 126
        embedded vs. external metadata, 127
        enabling hypermedia, 126
        extensibility and, 128
        format selection, 125
        registration, 130
    self-description in, 103
API styles
    HTTP verbs (RMM level 2), 33
    hypermedia (RMM level 3), 36
    resource-centric, 36

We'd like to hear your suggestions for improving our indexes. Send email to index@oreilly.com.

resources (RMM level 1), 31
REST, 41
REST constraints, 41
Richardson Maturity Model (RMM), 29
RPC (remote procedure call), 30
API wrappers (see wrapper libraries)
ApiController class, 56, 75, 301
AppHarbor PaaS (platform as a service), 412
applicability, 126
application delegates, 273
application element, 255
application keys, 194
application state, 144
application-level profile semantics (ALPS), 111
ArrayModelBinder, 323
artifacts, 390
ASP.NET infrastructure
    application element, 255
    global configuration, 261
    handler element, 256
    hosting architecture, 265
    module element, 255
    processing access tokens in, 428
    routing in, 257
    Web API message translation, 263
    web hosting with, 254
ASP.NET MVC, 46
ASP.NET Web API
    authentication filters in, 386
    benefits of, 46
    code-based configuration mode of, 48
    CORS support on, 406
    creating a new project, 50
    expressiveness of, 46
    flexible format support in, 48
    Hello Web API example, 58–66
    integration tests in, 462
    key goals of, 45
    model binding infrastructure in, 317
    multiple hosting options in, 50
    NuGet package management for, 52
    processing architecture (see processing architecture)
    routing, 259
    strongly typed HTTP views in, 47
    symmetric client/server programming in, 48
    TLS protocol in, 357
    unit test for ActionFilterAttribute, 457
    unit test for ApiController, 446

unit test for HttpMessageHandler, 456
unit testability in, 49
ValuesController.cs file, 56
WebApiConfig.cs file, 55
.aspx files, 256
assertions, 391
asymmetric cryptography, 487
asymmetric signature mechanisms, 395
Asynchronous Programming Model (APM), 228
Atom media type definition, 333
attribute groups, 95
attribute-based routing, 297
auditing (see change auditing)
authentication
    active/passive middleware, 385
    authentication context, 386
    authentication manager, 385
    basics of, 20
    challenge context, 387
    claims model, 360–365
    client authentication, 370–376
    current principal retrieval/assignment, 365
    filters, 307
    for change auditing, 194
    Hawk authentication scheme, 396
    HTTP authentication framework, 377
    HTTP authentication implementation, 379
    in OAuth 2.0 framework, 430
    Katana project, 380
    public-key authentication, 487
    schemes for, 21
    server authentication, 367
    server vs. client-side, 360
    signature-based, 395
    token-based, 389
    transport-based, 366
    Web API authentication filters, 386
    workflows for, 481–483
authorization
    authorization code, 419
    authorization decisions, 399
    authorization enforcement, 399–403
    authorization grant, 417
    authorization policies, 399
    basic model of, 398
    cross-origin resource sharing, 403
    OAuth 2.0 framework
        accessing protected resources, 416

authentication, 430
authorization code grant, 419, 419
basics of, 411
client applications, 414
code flow example, 422
front channel vs. back channel, 423
obtaining access tokens, 417
overview of, 434
processing access tokens in ASP.NET, 428
refresh tokens, 425
resource server/authorization server, 426
RFC 6819, 424
scope, 422
scope-based authorization, 433
authorization code grant, 419
authorization filters, 308
authorization servers, 413, 426
automated testing, 437
AWS authentication, 22
Azure Blob Service, 395
Azure Service Bus, 283
Azure Service Management REST API, 371
Azure Storage services, 22

B

back channel vs. front channel, 423
basic authentication scheme, 21, 377
BDD (behavior-driven development), 140
bearer tokens, 393, 416
Berners-Lee, Tim, 1, 8, 37
boilerplate code, 206
bookmarks, links as, 214
bootstrap authentication, 390
browser contexts, 223

C

cachable methods, 14
caching
adding tests for output caching, 184
benefits of, 17, 183
cache behaviors, 20
cache revalidation, 187
client dictation of, 208
conditional GETs for cache revalidation, 188
ETags, 19
expiration, 18
illustration of, 475–479
implementation steps, 183

invalidation, 19
negotiated responses, 20
stale responses, 18
validation, 18
certificates
certificate pinning, 368
certificate revocation lists (CRL), 494
creating for testing, 495
public key certificates, 488
self-issued, 490
stores system for, 493
Windows certificate management system, 494
certification authorities (CA), 367, 488
Certification Practice Statements, 491
challenge context, 387
change auditing
application key authentication, 194
HAWK authentication, 195–199
HMAC authentication, 194
security token authentication, 195
changes, breaking vs. nonbreaking, 89
channel stack layer, 267
channels, 268
chunked transfer encoding, 248, 264
claims authorization managers, 401
claims model, 360–365
classical cryptography, 487
client application state, 223
client authentication, 360, 370–376, 414
(see also authentication)
client credentials grant, 418
client development
application workflow
adapting to change, 219
adding/removing resources, 216
client state, 223
feature detection, 218
interactive missions, 220
workflow control, 216
client libraries
ease of use vs. quality, 205
links as functions, 210–216
purpose of, 206
wrapper libraries, 206–210
loose vs. tight coupling, 205, 224
cloud-hosted infrastructure, 283
code refactoring, 443
collection resources, 33, 99

Collection+Json, 115
common names, 367
conditional requests, 14
confidential clients, 414
conflict management, 191–194
constrained authorization, 411
content delivery networks (CDNs), 12
content negotiation
    basics of, 17
    FormatterParameterBinder+ implementa-
        tion, 339
    media type preferences and, 26
    proactive, 471
    reactive, 472
    server-driven approach to, 48, 247
controller dispatcher handler, 73
controller pipeline
    action invocation, 313
    action selection, 303
    ApiController, 301
    controller activation, 300
    controller selection, 296
    custom controller selectors, 298
    diagram of, 290, 302
    filters, 306
    HttpControllerDispatcher, 296
    model binding/validation, 312
    responsibilities of, 301
    Russian doll structure, 302
cool URIs, 5
coupling
    decoupling, 216
    loose vs. tight, 205, 224
Cross-Origin Resource Sharing (CORS), 403–
    409
cross-site request forgery (CSRF) attacks, 404,
    424
CRUD (create-read-update-delete), 151
cryptographic hash functions, 395
current identity, 366
current principal, 361, 365
current state attributes, 100
custom message handlers, 295

D

data model, 144
data volatility, 100
deadlock, 349

debugging
    Fiddler tool for, 59
    tracing, 199
        (see also testability)
Defense Advanced Research Projects Agency
    (DARPA), 1
delegated constrained authorization, 411
DELETE method, 13
demultiplexing, 358
dependency injection, 444
descriptive attributes, 100
digest access authentication scheme, 377
digest authentication scheme, 21
dispatcher, 294
dynamic types, 170

E

e-government Web APIs, 370
electronic identity initiatives, 370
encoders, 268
endpoints, 256
entity bodies, 9
entity-tags (ETags), 19, 293
environment dictionary, 273
evolvability
    barriers to, 85
    Issue Tracker example API, 91–101
    need for, 84
    price of, 83, 86
    vs. overspecification, 86
    vs. versioning, 88
exception filters, 311
expiration, 18
extended link relation types, 117
extensibility, 128, 335

F

feature detection, 86, 218
Fiddler debugging tool, 59
Fielding, Roy, 8, 37, 41
filter pipeline
    conversion into HttpResponseMessage, 79
    filter interfaces, 80
    overview of, 76
    parameter binding, 77
filters
    action, 309
    authentication, 307, 386

authorization, 308
creating new, 307
exception, 311
filter classes, 306
in model validation, 338
ordering/execution of, 307
storage of, 307
Flickr API, 32
FormatterParameterBinder, 329
formatters/model binding
benefits of models, 318
built-in model binders
architecture of, 323
HttpParameterBinding, 335
model binding against URIs only, 329
ModelBindingParameterBinder, 322
overview of, 322
role of, 326
value providers, 323
controller pipeline and, 312
default formatters, 242
formatters
role of, 322, 329
synchronous formatters, 333
JSONMediaTypeFormatter, 331
media type formatters, 242, 330
model binding operation, 319
model validation
applying data annotation attributes, 335
importance of, 335
querying validation results, 336
overview of, 338
use in mapping, 317
XmlMediaTypeFormatter, 331
forms, 37
front channel vs. back channel, 423

G

gateways, 12
geolocated resources, 119
GET method
basics of, 12
conditional, 293
Gherkin syntax, 140, 151
GitHub API, 35
Google Web Accelerator incident, 24

H

H-factors, 38
Hammer, Eran, 22
handler element, 256
handshake subprotocol, 357
HAWK authentication, 22, 195–199, 396
HEAD method, 12
Hello World example API
client for, 65
configuration details, 59
content negotiation, 61
controller addition, 58
creating, 58
error handling, 63
greeting addition, 61
host for, 65
method addition, 59
testing, 64
testing with Fiddler, 59
HMAC (hash-based message authentication
code), 194, 395
holder-of-key authentication, 394
homogeneous APIs, 132
hosting
Azure Service Bus host, 283
hosting layer responsibilities, 253
in-memory
basics of, 254
diagram of, 282
HttpClient/HttpServer instances, 282
in Issue Tracker API, 154
OWIN hosting
authentication in, 380
basics of, 70, 254
interface for, 273
Katana project, 275, 380
open standard for, 273
OWIN ecosystem, 282
Web API configuration, 277
Web API middleware, 278
self-hosting
basics of, 70, 254
flexibility of, 50
HttpSelfHostConfiguration class, 270
HttpSelfHostServer class, 269, 269
in Issue Tracker API, 142
typical code for, 266
URL reservation and access control, 272
WCF architecture, 267

web hosting
    ASP.NET infrastructure, 254
    ASP.NET routing, 257
    basics of, 70, 254
    global configuration, 261
    Web API ASP.NET handler, 263
    Web API routing, 259
HTTP (Hypertext Transfer Protocol)
    authentication, 20, 377, 379
    basics of, 8
    cache behaviors, 20
    caching, 17
    common methods, 12
    conditional requests, 14
    content negotiation, 17
    ETags, 19
    expiration, 18
    header types, 15
    httpbis, 8
    intermediaries, 11
    invalidation, 19
    media type identifiers, 90
    message exchange, 8
    method properties, 14
    negotiated responses, 20
    status codes, 16
    validation, 18
HTTP headers
    basics of, 9
    consumption/production of, 235
    content header collection, 234
    header container classes/properties, 234, 236
    list of, 467
    registry for, 234
    specifications for, 233
    types of, 15
HTTP methods, 9
HTTP Over TLS (HTTPS), 355
HTTP programming model
    assembly availability, 227
    earlier models, 227
    goals for new model, 227
    headers
        consumption/production of, 235
        content header collection, 234
        header container classes/properties, 234, 236
        registry for, 234
        specifications for, 233

message abstraction
    composition of, 228
    diagram of, 229
    message classes, 230
    requests, 229
    responses, 229
message content
    base class for, 239
    consuming, 240
    creating, 243–251
HTTP verbs (RMM level 2) API style, 33
HttpClient library
    client message handlers
        chaining capability, 348
        fake response handlers, 350
        HttpMessageHandler, 347
        HttpMethodOverrideHandler, 348
        MessageProceesingHandler, 349
        proxying handlers, 349
        reusable response handlers, 352
    history of, 341
    HttpClient Class
        content access with, 344
        exceptions and, 344
        GetAsync method, 344
        helper methods for, 344
        lifecycle of, 342
        multiple instances of, 343
        request cancellation, 346
        SendAsync method, 347
        simplicity of, 341
        thread safety in, 343
        wrapper for, 342
HttpControllerDispatcher, 296
HttpMessageInvoker, 294
HttpParameterBinding
    configuration with a rule, 321
    default selection of, 335
    implementation of, 319
    selection of, 320
hydrating, 323
hypermedia
    affordances, 37
    benefits of, 41, 106, 110
    client support for, 209
    Collection+Json, 115, 165
    definition of, 36
    enabling in media type design, 126
    H-factors, 38

implementation of, 41
origins of, 37
proper place to handle, 165
Siren, 115
workflow definition with, 120
Hypermedia Application Language (HAL), 113
hypertext, 37

I

IANA (Internet Assigned Numbers Authority)
    Internet-related specification, 116
    media type registration, 6, 26, 130
    public media type catalog, 48
idempotent methods, 14
identity providers, 365
IETF (Internet Engineering Task Force)
    dynamic registration of clients, 414
    header approval by, 16
    httpbis working body, 8
    Internet-related specifications, 116
IHttpController, 301, 451
in-memory hosting
    basics of, 254
    diagram of, 282
    HttpClient/HttpServer instances, 282
    in Issue Tracker API, 154
indirection layer, 119
information model
    attribute group collections, 96
    attribute groups, 95
    basic design, 93
    diagram of, 97
    media types vs. list capabilities, 98
    related resources, 94
    subdomains of, 93
    vs. media types, 96
integration tests, in ASP.NET Web API, 462
intermediaries, 11
Internet, 1
Internet Information Services (IIS), 50
Internet media types, 242
Internet protocol suite (TCP/IP), 1, 356
invalidation, 19
ISAM (indexed sequential access method) data-
    bases, 106
Issue Tracker example API
    building the API
        acceptance criteria, 151–154
        design overview, 139

downloading implementation/unit tests,
    140
    issue creation, 169–172
    issue deletion, 175–177
    issue retrieval, 154–169
    issue updating, 172–175
    models and services, 143–151
    navigating the solution, 141
    packages and libraries, 141
    self-host for, 142
    using behavior-driven development, 140
improving the API
    acceptance criteria, 181
    auditing, 194–199
    caching, 183–190
    conflict management, 191–194
    tracing, 199–202
information model
    attribute group collections, 96
    attribute groups, 95
    basic design, 93
    diagram of, 97
    issue collections, 98
    related resources, 94
    subdomains, 93
    vs. media types, 96
media types in
    discovery resources, 136
    item resources, 135
    list resources, 133
    search resource, 137
objectives for
    challenges faced by, 92
    goals, 91
resource models
    collection resources, 99
    diagram of, 100
    goals of, 98
    item resources, 99
    root resource, 98
    search resources, 98
item resources, 34

J

JSON numeric values, 129
JSON Web Token (JWT), 391
JSONMediaTypeFormatter, 331

K

Katana project, 275, 380, 385, 428
kernel-mode device drivers, 272

L

leaf certificates, 369
link relation types
    designing new
        basic characteristics, 130
        embedded, 132
        extension, 132
        registration, 132
        standard, 130
    extended link relation types, 117
    indirection layer, 119
    link hints, 117
    purpose of, 116
    reference data, 120
    semantics, 116
    standard registry of, 116
    static vs. embedded resources, 118
    syntax, 122
    workflow, 120
links
    as bookmarks, 214
    as functions
        deserializing links, 213
        link relation type, 210
        request/response separation, 213
        service antipattern, 211
    hypermedia affordance, 37
    media type profiles and, 26
load balancing, 119
loose coupling, 205, 224

M

MAC tokens, 395, 416
MAC-then-Encrypt design, 356
man in the middle (MITM) attacks, 367, 488
management certificates, 371
mandatory properties, 126
media types
    catalog of, 48
    dedicated vs. multiple, 132
    definition of, 6
    designing new contracts
        basic characteristics, 124

conveying semantics, 126
        embedded vs. external metadata, 127
        enabling hypermedia, 126
        extensibility and, 128
        format selection, 125
        registration, 130
    domain-specific, 25, 108
    fear of new types, 110
    generic media types/profiles, 110–115
    hypermedia types, 110
    Internet media types, 242
    list capabilities of, 98
    list of, 465
    new formats, 108
    new hypermedia types, 115
    opaque identifiers, 90
    origin of, 6
    out-of-band knowledge and, 104
    parts of, 6
    popular formats, 107
    primitive formats, 105
    profile link relation, 26
    purpose of, 104
    registration of, 6
    service-specific, 108
    specification for application/issue+json, 485
    versioning and, 90
    vs. information models, 96
MediaTypeFormatter, 331, 452
message authentication codes (MAC), 356
message exchange protocol, 8
message flow (see routing)
message handler pipeline
    attribute-based routes, 297
    conditional GET requests with Etags, 293
    controller activation, 300
    controller selection, 296
    custom controller selectors, 298
    custom message handler, 295
    default services, 299
    diagram of, 290, 291
    dispatcher, 294
    HttpMessageInvoker, 294
    initializing, 291
    role of, 71
    route-specific, 295
    Russian doll model, 292
    task-based guidelines, 292
message headers, 15

message representatives, 396
messaging
    brokered, 283
    relayed, 283
    self-descriptive, 86, 103
    WCF architecture for, 268
methods
    additional properties, 14
    basics of, 9
    types of, 12
middleware, 11, 273, 380, 385, 428
MIME (Multipurpose Internet Mail Extensions), 6
missions, 220
mocking, 444
model binding infrastructure, 317
    (see also formatters/model binding)
ModelBindingParameterBinder, 322
module element, 255
MVC 4 Web Application project, 50

N

negotiated responses, 20
.NET Framework HTTP programming model
    (see HTTP programming model)
Nielsen, Henrik Frystyk, 8
nonce, 394
nontransforming proxies, 11
noun-centric/non-object-oriented style, 36
NuGet package management application, 52

O

OAuth 2.0 authorization framework
    accessing protected resources, 416
    authentication, 430
    authorization code grant, 419, 419
    basics of, 22, 411
    change auditing with, 195
    client applications, 414
    code flow example, 422
    front channel vs. back channel, 423
    obtaining access tokens, 417
    overview of, 434
    processing access tokens in ASP.NET, 428
    refresh tokens, 425
    resource server/authorization server, 426
    RFC 6819, 424
    scope, 422

scope-based authorization, 433
object relational mapping (ORM) libraries, 209
omitted properties, 126
online certificate status protocol (OCSP), 495
opaque identifiers, 90
OpenID Connect, 432, 435
optional properties, 126
OPTIONS method, 13
origin concept, 403
out-of-band knowledge, 104
output caching, 184
overspecification, 86
OWIN (Open Web Interface for .NET) hosting
    authentication in, 380
    basics of, 70, 254
    interface for, 273
    Katana project, 275
    open standard for, 273
    OWIN ecosystem, 282
    Web API configuration, 277
    Web API middleware, 278

P

parameter binding, 77
passive authentication, 385
passwords, 389
PATCH method, 12
payload-based versioning, 89
peers, 356
per-route message handlers, 295
pinsets, 368
policy providers, 407
POST method, 12
preflight requests, 405
processing architecture
    ApiController base class, 75
    controller handling, 75
    hosting layer, 70
    hosting layer alternatives, 70
    HTTP request sample message, 67
    message handler pipeline, 71
    overview of, 68
    route dispatching, 73
    sample controller, 67
profile link relation, 26
programming model (see ASP.NET Web API;
    HTTP programming model)
properties, applicability of, 126
protected internal calls, 294

proxies, 11
public clients, 414
public key infrastructure (PKI), 370
public key pinning extension for HTTP, 369
public-key cryptography, 487–496
pull/push-style messaging, 241
PUT method, 13

Q

query strings, 5
querying, 137, 165, 213
QueryStringMapping, 334
queues, 283

R

reactive behavior, 218, 352
record subprotocol, 356
red and green (failure/success) cycle, 442
reference data, 120
reference-based tokens, 390
refresh tokens, 425
rehydrating, 323
relying party, 365
representation headers, 16
request context, 265
request headers, 15
RequestHeaderMapping, 334
resource class, 99
Resource Description Framework (RDF), 111
resource models
    attribute subsets, 100
    collection resources, 99
    diagram of, 100
    goals of, 98
    item resources, 99
    root resource, 98
    search resources, 98
resource owner password credentials grant, 418
resource servers, 413, 426
resource state, 144
resource-centric APIs, 36
resources
    accessing protected, 416
    collection resources, 33
    concept vs. implementation of, 99
    cross-origin resource sharing, 403
    definition of, 3
    discovery resources, 136

in authorization model, 398
item resources, 34, 135
list resources, 133
multiple representations, 27
related resources in information model, 94
representations, 5
search resources, 137
static vs. embedded, 118, 219
typelessness and, 170
resources (RMM level 1) style, 31
response headers, 16
REST (Representational State Transfer)
    constraints of, 41
    definition of, 41
    hypermedia and, 37
    RESTful APIs vs. REST architectural style, 83
REST architectural style
    application workflow, 120
    breaking vs. nonbreaking changes, 89
    vs. RESTful APIs, 83
revalidation, 187
RFC (Request for Comments)
    RFC 181, 355
    RFC 2104, 395
    RFC 2617, 377
    RFC 4366, 359
    RFC 4949, 360, 390
    RFC 5246, 356
    RFC 5861, 19
    RFC 6454, 403
    RFC 6749, 411
    RFC 6750, 393
    RFC 6819, 424
Richardson Maturity Model (RMM), 29–41
Richardson, Leonard, 29
root certification, 367
root resource, 98
route-specific message handlers, 295
routing
    ASP.NET routing classes, 257
    configuration in ASP.NET, 257
    controller pipeline
        action invocation, 313
        action selection, 303
        ApiController, 301
        diagram of, 302
        filters, 306
        model binding/validation, 312
        responsibilities of, 301

Russian doll structure, 302
HTTP message flow overview, 289
message handler pipeline
    controller activation, 300
    controller selection, 296
    dispatcher, 294
    HttpControllerDispatcher, 296
    HttpMessageInvoker, 294
    initializing, 291
    Russian doll model, 292
route declaration methods, 55
RouteConfig, 55
routing dispatcher handler, 73
unit testing of, 461
Web API routing adaptation classes, 261
Web API routing classes, 259
RPC (remote procedure call) style, 30
RSS media type definition, 333

S

safe methods, 14
same-origin security policies, 403
SAML (Security Assertion Markup Language), 391, 425
scalability, 183
scope
    authorization constraint definition, 422
    scope-based authorization, 433
search resources, 98
searching, 137, 167
Secure Socket Layer protocol (SSL), 356
security issues
    auditing, 194–199
    authentication
        active/passive middleware, 385
        claims model, 360–365
        client authentication, 370–376
        current principal retrieval/assignment, 365
        Hawk authentication scheme, 396
        HTTP authentication framework, 377
        HTTP authentication implementation, 379
        Katana project, 380
        server authentication, 367
        server vs. client-side, 360
        token-based, 389
        transport-based, 366
        Web API authentication filters, 386

authorization
    authorization decisions, 399
    authorization enforcement, 399–403
    authorization policies, 399
    basic model of, 398
    cross-origin resource sharing, 403
exception filters, 311
OAuth 2.0 framework
    accessing protected resources, 416
    authentication, 430
    authorization code grant, 419
    basics of, 411
    client applications, 414
    code flow example, 422
    drawbacks of, 435
    front channel vs. back channel, 423
    obtaining access tokens, 417
    overview of, 434
    processing access tokens in ASP.NET, 428
    refresh tokens, 425
    resource server/authorization server, 426
    RFC 6819, 424
    scope, 422
    scope-based authorization, 433
tracing, 199–202
Transport Layer Security (TLS)
    in ASP.NET Web API, 357
    subprotocols of, 356
    with IIS hosting, 357
    with self-hosting, 359
transport security
    bearer tokens, 416
    goals of, 356
    HTTPS, 355
security tokens, 390
self-descriptive messaging, 86, 103
self-hosting
    basics of, 70, 254
    flexibility of, 50
    HttpSelfHostConfiguration class, 270
    HttpSelfHostServer class, 269
    in Issue Tracker API, 142
    TLS configuration, 359
    typical code for, 266
    URL reservation and access control, 272
    WCF architecture, 267
serialization, 318
server authentication, 360, 367
    (see also authentication)

Server Name Indication (SNI), 359
Service Bus, 283
service interruptions, 207
service model layer, 267
service objects, 264
session keys, 487
sessions, 209
Should library, 158
signature-based authentication, 395
Single Responsibility Principle, 178
single-page applications (SPA), 414
Siren, 115
smartcards, 370
SOAP web services, 23, 46, 85, 170
software development models
    classic browser-based applications, 84
    conventional vs. agile, 84
    design by URL, 100
    evolvable APIs, 84
    homogeneous APIs, 132
    loosely vs. tightly-coupled clients, 205, 224
    performance-critical systems, 110
    representation design, 219
    versioning, 88
    waterfall approach, 85
SPDY protocol, 8
stale responses, 18
state model, 144
status codes, 10, 16
stream writers, 244
strong wildcards, 272
style, definition of, 29
    (see also API styles)
Subject Alternative Names, 359, 367
subjects, 398
subtypes, 6
symmetric cryptography, 487
symmetric signature mechanisms, 395
syntax, 122
system entities, 360

T

Task Asynchronous Pattern (TAP), 228
task-based message handlers, 292
tasks, 220
TDD (test-driven development), 140, 441
temporary service interruptions, 207
test keys, creating, 495

testability
    automated testing, 437
    fake response handlers, 350
    Fiddler debugging tool, 59
    integration tests in ASP.NET Web API, 462
    overview of, 464
    support in ASP.NET Web API, 49
    tracing, 199
    unit testing routes, 461
    unit tests
        frameworks for, 438
        in Visual Studio, 438
        organization of, 438
        role in test-driven development (TDD),
            442
        with xUnit.NET, 440
    unit tests for ASP.NET Web APIs
        ActionFilterAttribute, 457
        ApiController, 446
        HttpMessageHandler, 456
        MediaTypeFormatter, 452
Thinktecture Authorization Server (T.A.S.), 413,
    427
tight coupling, 205
timestamps, 394
token-based authentication
    access tokens, 417
    artifacts vs. assertions, 390
    bearer tokens, 416
    bearer vs. holder-of-key, 393
    JSON Web Token (JWT), 391
    passwords, 389
    refresh tokens, 425
    SAML (Security Assertion Markup Lan-
        guage), 391
    security tokens, 390
top-level media types, 6
topics, 283
TRACE method, 13
tracing, 199–202
transactions, 220
transforming proxies, 11
Transport Layer Security (TLS)
    goals of, 356
    in ASP.NET Web API, 357
    subprotocols of, 356
    with IIS hosting, 357
    with self-hosting, 359
Travis CI continuous integration service, 412

troubleshooting (see testability)
trust stores, 490
tunnels, 12
TypeConverterModelBinder, 323
typelessness, 170

U

unconstrained authorization, 412
unit of work, 209
unit tests
    for ASP.NET Web APIs
        ActionFilterAttribute, 457
        ApiController, 446
        HttpMessageHandler, 456
        MediaTypeFormatter, 452
    frameworks for, 438
    in Visual Studio, 438
    organization of, 438, 438
    role in test-driven development (TDD), 442
    unit testing routes, 461
    with xUnit.NET, 440
URI templates, 258
UriPathExtensionMapping, 334
URIs (uniform resource identifiers), 4
URLs (Universal Resource Locators)
    design by URL, 100
    URL reservation/access control, 272
    versioning in, 91
    vs. URNs, 4
URNs (Universal Resource Names), 4
user-client-server authorization model, 413

V

validation, 18
value providers, 323
Valuescontroller class, 56
vCards, 25
versioning
    benefits of avoiding, 91
    breaking changes and, 88
    of media type identifiers, 90
    payload-based, 89
    URL versioning, 91
    version number coordination in clients, 218
Visual Studio, unit testing in, 438

W

W3C (World Wide Web Consortium) , 16
waterfall approach, 85
WCF (Windows Communication Foundation)
    architecture of, 267
    benefits of, 46
    channel stack creation, 269
    message channel configuration, 270
    self-hosting and, 267
Web APIs
    API styles, 29–43
    basics of, 23
    core jobs of, 289
    domain-specific media types, 25
    evolution of, 24
    explosion of, 24
    guidelines for, 25
    media type profiles, 26
    multiple representations, 27
    origins of, 24
    vs. SOAP web services, 23, 46, 85, 170
web clients (see client development)
web hosting
    ASP.NET infrastructure, 254
        application element, 255
        handler element, 256
        module element, 255
    ASP.NET routing, 257
    basics of, 254
    global configuration, 261
    Web API ASP.NET handler, 263
    Web API routing, 259
Web Service Description Language (WSDL), 23, 103, 170
WebApiConfig class, 55
Windows Azure Blob Service, 395
Windows Azure Service Bus, 283
Windows Azure Service Management REST API, 371
Windows Azure Storage services, 22
Windows Identity Foundation, 364
workflow
    defining with hypermedia, 120
    in client applications, 216–224
    REST-based vs. RPC-based, 120
World Wide Web
    cool URIs, 5
    core concepts of, 2, 37
    invention of, 1

media types, 6
representations, 5
resources, 3
typelessness of, 170
URIs, 4
wrapper libraries
basic appearance of, 206
fundamental problems with, 206
individual protocol states, 209
lack of hypermedia support in, 209
lifetime scope, 208
reliability issues, 207
response types, 207

X

X.509 certificate specification, 359, 370
XBehave.NET, 158
XML serialization, 244
XmlMediaTypeFormatter, 331
xUnit.NET, unit testing with, 440

Y

Yahoo's Flickr API, 32

About the Authors

Glenn Block formerly worked on the ASP.NET team, where he drove the early vision for ASP.NET Web API. He now works at Splunk, making big data more accessible to developers. A hardcore coder professionally for almost 20 years, he cares deeply about making developers' lives easier. Glenn lives and breathes code and is rumored never to actually sleep. He's also a big supporter in the shift toward cloud development, having played a key role at Microsoft in supporting OSS stacks in Windows Azure. He is an active contributor to the Node.js and .NET OSS projects, a supporter of the community, and a frequent speaker internationally. He lives with his wife and daughter in Seattle.

Pablo Cibraro is a software architect at Tellago, Inc., and an internationally recognized expert with over 10 years of experience in architecting and implementing large distributed systems with Microsoft Technologies. He has spent the past few years working directly with the Microsoft Patterns & Practices team on sample applications, patterns, and guidance for building service-oriented applications with Web Services, Web Services Enhancements (WSE), and Windows Communication Foundation (WCF).

Pedro Félix lives in Lisbon, Portugal, where he teaches and studies programming and computer security-related subjects.

Howard Dierking is Microsoft Program Manager on the WCF Web API team, focusing on AppFabric. Prior to this position he has held several others at Microsoft, including Editor-in-Chief of *MSDN Magazine* and Product Planner within Microsoft Learning.

Darrel Miller is co-owner of Tavis Software, a software solutions and services company specializing in the manufacturing sector. He spends his days showing people how to apply the REST architectural style to business applications.

Colophon

The animals on the cover of *Designing Evolvable Web APIs with ASP.NET* are warty newts (*Triturus cristatus*). Also known as northern or great crested newts, these amphibians are found all over northern Europe, from the UK to just past the Black Sea. It is the biggest and least common of the three newts that live in the British Isles, and is protected there by the Biodiversity Action Plan, which seeks to catalog and form conservation plans for threatened animals.

Warty newts normally spend most of their lives on land, but do return to ponds and pools to breed. The larvae, or "efts," hatch after about three weeks and live underwater for a time. They undergo metamorphosis at four months old, at which point they become air-breathing juveniles who leave the ponds for land. There, they feed on worms, insects, and insect larvae. Adult newts may even hunt in ponds for other newts, tadpoles, young frogs, insects, or water snails.

Because they are relatively defenseless, warty newts prefer to live in terrestrial habitats that are covered, such as scrub, grass, and dense woodland. Females are larger than males and can measure up to 15cm long. Both genders display the same types of color patterns: dark gray to black backs and flanks, and yellow or orange undersides that are covered with black blotches. During the breeding season, males can be distinguished from females by their jagged crests, which runs along their backs.

From October to March, these newts hibernate under logs and stones in the mud at the bottom of their breeding ponds. Normally, newts return to the same breeding site each year, and generally do not stray more than half a mile from the place where they were born. Although it is possible for some warty newts to live as long as 30 years, most live for about 10 in the wild.

The cover fonts are URW Typewriter and Guardian Sans. The text font is Adobe Minion Pro; the heading font is Adobe Myriad Condensed; and the code font is Dalton Maag's Ubuntu Mono.

Get even more for your money.

Join the O'Reilly Community, and register the O'Reilly books you own. It's free, and you'll get:

- $4.99 ebook upgrade offer
- 40% upgrade offer on O'Reilly print books
- Membership discounts on books and events
- Free lifetime updates to ebooks and videos
- Multiple ebook formats, DRM FREE
- Participation in the O'Reilly community
- Newsletters
- Account management
- 100% Satisfaction Guarantee

Signing up is easy:

1. **Go to: oreilly.com/go/register**
2. **Create an O'Reilly login.**
3. **Provide your address.**
4. **Register your books.**

Note: English-language books only

To order books online:
oreilly.com/store

For questions about products or an order:
orders@oreilly.com

To sign up to get topic-specific email announcements and/or news about upcoming books, conferences, special offers, and new technologies:
elists@oreilly.com

For technical questions about book content:
booktech@oreilly.com

To submit new book proposals to our editors:
proposals@oreilly.com

O'Reilly books are available in multiple DRM-free ebook formats. For more information:
oreilly.com/ebooks

O'REILLY®

Spreading the knowledge of innovators   oreilly.com